Power of Freedom

CHINA UNDERSTANDINGS TODAY

Series Editors: Mary Gallagher and Xiaobing Tang

China Understandings Today is dedicated to the study of contemporary China and seeks to present the latest and most innovative scholarship in social sciences and the humanities to the academic community as well as the general public. The series is sponsored by the Lieberthal-Rogel Center for Chinese Studies at the University of Michigan.

Power of Freedom

HU SHIH'S POLITICAL WRITINGS

Edited by Chih-p'ing Chou and
Carlos Yu-Kai Lin

University of Michigan Press
Ann Arbor

Published in the United States of America by the
University of Michigan Press
Manufactured in the United States of America
Printed on acid-free paper
First published October 2022

A CIP catalog record for this book is available from the British Library.

Library of Congress Cataloging-in-Publication data has been applied for.
ISBN 978-0-472-07526-3 (hardcover: alk. paper)
ISBN 978-0-472-05526-5 (paper: alk. paper)
ISBN 978-0-472-90361-0 (OA)
DOI: https://doi.org/10.3998/mpub.12258711

In Memory of
Professor Yu Ying-shih
(1930–2021)

Contents

Digital materials related to this title can be found on the Fulcrum platform via the following citable URL https://doi.org/10.3998/mpub.12258711

Introduction I

A Chinese Diplomat in the Cold War: Hu Shih's View on International Politics

CARLOS YU-KAI LIN

Are we entering a new cold war era marked by competition between superpowers over primacy in technology and global political influence? This question, with all its historical and contemporary implications, has again emerged in public debates in the media over the past years. The difference this time is that instead of focusing on US-Soviet relations, much of the world's attention is now on the rivalry between China and the United States. The front line in this ideological, technological, and economic contest has moved to Asia, where China, under the leadership of the Chinese Communist Party, challenges the supremacy of the United States and the system of liberal democracy.

This transition from Europe to Asia as the new focal point of a global geopolitical struggle was foreseen almost eighty years ago by one of China's top scholars and statesmen—Dr. Hu Shih (1891–1962), who was the Republic of China's ambassador to the United States during World War II. From 1938 to 1942, he acted as the main liaison between China's Nationalist government and the United States, playing a key role in facilitating the relationship and communication between Generalissimo Chiang Kai-shek and US president Franklin D. Roosevelt. As an ambassador, Hu Shih had warned, as early as 1941, that an international-scale ideological struggle was increasingly shaping the world and would eventually divide international society into two blocs. In a speech delivered at the University of Michigan on July 8, 1941, he argued that the fundamental ideological conflict affecting the world at the time was not between the Left and the Right, or communism and fascism or Nazism, but between dictatorial totalitarianism and democratic systems.[1] He further pointed out that democratic countries, because of their complacency and unpreparedness, appeared to be rather weak and defenseless in the face of the well-coordinated and aggressive onslaught of totalitarian countries. In this speech, he supported President Roosevelt's call for American society's faith in democracy, not only as a form of government but also as a frame of life. He concluded that the ideological conflict affecting the world at the time was democracy versus tyranny, freedom versus slavery, and government by constitution versus government by blind and unconditional obedience to party and leader. Such views later became the foundation of the Cold War narrative, and more recently, have been revived in the contemporary rhetoric of US-China relations vis-à-vis their respective approaches to dealing with the COVID-19 crisis, which often leads to comparisons couched in terms of the competing values of liberal democracy and dictatorship. One could thus say that Hu Shih represents one of the earliest Chinese political theorists and intellectuals who anticipated and theorized about the rise of a second cold war.

Hu Shih was known as a leader in China's new cultural movement (ca. 1917–1921). He was an early advocate of many revolutionary sociocultural changes, including language reform, the adoption of vernacular Chinese, educational reform, and much more. Compared to his reputation as a scholar, his role as a statesman and a diplomat, however, has been relatively ignored. Many of his writings on international politics, US-China relations, and the international communist movement have been inadaquately addressed by scholars. This, of course, is partially due to his deeply held anti-authoritarian worldview. As a strident critic of the Chinese Communist Party's oligarchical practices, Hu Shih was targeted by the Party in a concerted national campaign in the 1950s to smear his reputation, cast aspersions on his works, and generally destroy any possible influence he might have in China.

For decades, and even today to a certain extent, Hu Shih's political writings are considered sensitive and even "dangerous" in China. Despite his unique place in the history of US-China relations and his considerable con-

---

1. Hu Shih, "The Conflict of Ideologies," *Annals of the American Academy of Political and Social Science* 218 (November 1941): 27. Chapter 7 in this volume.

tributions to the formation of modern Chinese culture, many of his polical writings—especially those concerning the nature of communism—remain taboo.[2] While Hu Shih was generally seen as a "Chinese liberal" who tended to prioritize the cultural aspects of social reforms, his involvement and experience in various public affairs at different stages of his life suggest that the full spectrum of his intellectual-political agenda has yet to be fully explored.

In light of Hu Shih's long-standing interest in politics, which he described as a "disinterested-interest,"[3] and his commitment to various sociocultural reforms, one may perceive his political writings as a demonstration of an interdisciplinary approach to understanding Chinese culture and history. For example, Hu Shih's reflection on the idea of a democratic China derived from his interpretation of Confucius's rational humanism and Lao-tzu's naturalistic philosophy.[4] Hu Shih's critique of Mao Zedong's totalitarian regime, for another example, was based on his understanding of a critical and self-reflexive Chinese intellectual tradition. In other words, what Hu Shih's political writings represented is his extended interpretation of Chinese civilization, and more importantly, his vision of a truly egalitarian, democratic world.

In addition to his inquiry into the cultural history of China, Hu Shih's political writings traverse a wide range of knowledge fields such as diplomatic history, comparative politics, political theory, and international relations. Through these writings, one can obtain a more comprehensive understanding of Hu Shih as one of China's most important scholars in the twentieth century. Of particular importance in his political writings are his

---

2. In *Hu Shih quanji* 胡適全集 (Complete works of Hu Shih), published by Anhui jiaoyu chubanshe in 2003, for example, most of his works on communism were omitted. In the *English Writings of Hu Shih*, published by Springer in 2013, for another example, most of Hu Shih's political writings were again not included.

3. Hu Shih, *The Personal Reminiscences of Dr. Hu Shih* (Beijing: Foreign Language Teaching and Research Press, 2012), 41. *Personal Reminiscences* is based on a series of interviews of Hu Shih by T. K. Tong as part of Columbia University's Chinese Oral History Project in 1958. Originally proposed by Clarence Martin Wilbur (1908–1997), professor in Columbia University's East Asian Institute in 1957, the project sought to provide a record of the lives and stories of eminent Chinese political figures associated with the Nationalist government after the establishment of the People's Republic of China. The interviews of Hu Shih were part of this project, in which he gave an overview of his life and work from the 1890s to the 1950s. The interview transcript was later translated by T. K. Tong into Chinese and was published under the title *Hu Shih koushu zizhuan* 胡適口述自傳 (Autobiography of Hu Shih) (Taipei: Yuanliu, 2010).

4. Chih-ping Chou's "Introduction II: Hu Shih's Anti-communist Thought" in this volume.

discussions on the political destiny of China, his inquiry into the question that whether authoritarianism or dictatorship is necessary for the prosperity of the Chinese nation, and his observation and anticipation of a Cold War that will eventually divide the international community into two distinct ideological groups.[5] Such issues are still important and relevant to the political reality of our twenty-first-century world, and Hu Shih discussed them over and over again more than eighty years ago. From this perspective, Hu Shih's political writings can and should be examined in broader historical and disciplinary contexts, and studied by scholars of both humanities and social sciences.

It is worthwhile to point out that Hu Shih's profound understanding of Chinese and American cultures derived not only from his crosscultural educational background (he was an undergraduate student at Cornell University from 1910 to 1914 and a graduate student at Columbia University from 1914 to 1917), but also from his direct involvement in the building of a modern Chinese culture, and his participation in American and Chinese discussions in international politics. His dual identity as a scholar and a statesman, a philosopher and an ambassador, a pragmaticist and an idealist, put him in a unique position to observe the changes in China and its relation to the world over the course of the twentieth century.

Aside from Hu Shih's achievement as an eminent scholar and public figure, one can also see in his writings the spiritual struggle of a leading Chinese scholar who lived, worked, and was exiled in the United States for a total of twenty-six years and seven months. As soon as he left China for America to pursue his bachelor's degree in 1910, Hu Shih embarked upon a search for a new identity and destiny as one of the first Chinese students sent to the United States for modern education under the Boxer Indemnity Scholarship Program. In 1937, Hu Shih was sent by the Nationalist government as a special envoy to Washington, DC, to seek the United States' help and support in China's "Resistance War"[6] against Japan, and a year later, in 1938, he was appointed as the Chinese ambassador to the United States, serving as the main liaison between the Chinese government and the United States. After he finished his term as ambassador, he continued to live in New York for four

---

5. Hu Shih has a specific way of defining the term "ideology." See chapter 7 in this volume for more discussion.

6. "Resistance War" is a term used by the Nationalist government to refer to the Second Sino-Japanese War (1937–1945).

years, during which time he was a Chinese delegate to the United Nations Conference on International Organization (aka the San Francisco Conference) and the Conference of the Establishment of UNESCO in 1945. During his stay in the United States, Hu Shih also lectured at many American universities and research insitutes including Harvard.

In July 1946, after living in the United States for nine years, Hu Shih returned to China and soon witnessed the drastic ascendancy of the Chinese Communist Party. He chose exile in America, where he spent the next nine years of his life, from 1949 to 1958. In April 1958, he moved to Taiwan to take up the position of president of Academia Sinica, and died in Taipei in February 1962. After he left China for America in 1949, Hu Shih did not return to his homeland ever again.

In Hu Shih's English-language political writings, which were mostly written during his exile in the United States, one can see a tormented soul concealed in rational words, and his occasional dissapointment wrapped in seemingly optimistic narrative. Readers of this book will thus gain a balanced and subtle view of Hu Shih, not only as a prominent scholar and public figure, but also as a human being with passion, anxiety, and courage, whose concern for the future of China was as strong as his love for his family and friends who were left in China during his exile in America.

A PACIFIC WAR

Before US foreign policy took a drastic turn in the 1950s with the sudden outbreak of the Korean War (1950–1953), which forced the United States to take immediate military measures to prevent a communist takeover of the Korean peninsula, Hu Shih observed that the increased military conflict and tension in both Europe and East Asia at the time signaled a breakdown of the international order established after World War I. In November 26, 1933, in an article published in *Duli Pinglun* 獨立評論, he wrote, "While we cannot be certain that a Pacific war can be completely avoided, we can predict that our international diplomatic relations in the near future will have a significant new development" (我們雖不能斷言太平洋上的戰禍可以完全避免，但我們可以預料今後的國際外交必將有重大的新發展).[7] On June 20, 1935, Hu Shih

---

7. Hu Shih, "Shijie xin xingshi lide zhongguo waijiao fangzhen" 世界新形勢裏的中

wrote to Wang Shih-chieh 王世杰 (1891–1981), China's minister of education, "There will be an atrocious war in the Pacific Ocean in the near future.
It will offer China a chance to turn the tables and eliminate the enemy's
hegemony" (在一個不很遠的將來, 太平洋上必有一度最可慘的大戰, 可以做我
們翻身的機會, 可以使我們的敵人的霸權消滅).[8] Hu Shih's accurate prediction
of a Pacific war not only demonstrates his perceptive judgement of the esca-
lating situation of East Asia, in which Japan sought to expand its economic,
political and militaristic power in the 1930s, but also reveals his conviction
that any geopolitical change in one part of the world will ultimately create
an impact on other regions of the globe, and thus a balanced world order
must be found on well-coordinated and well-communicated international
politics to be participated by all nations or at least by all nations who agreeed
to a certain set of rules and values. This logic led Hu Shih to believe that the
increasing militaristic tension in East Asia in the 1930s merits the attention
of the whole world as it might lead to a greater disaster. In fact, as early as
1915, as a graduate student at Columbia University, Hu Shih had argued in a
letter to the editor of the New York Evening Post, that if the post-WWI settlement concerning the situation of East Asia did not include the participation
of China, the growing conflicts in the Far East may ultimately lead to an
"Anglo-Japanese conflict, or a second Russo-Japanese war, or a second world
war." Hu Shih concludes in that letter:

> As the *Evening Post* has admirably said, 'Asia is part of the world.' The trouble
> with traditional statesmanship in Europe has been its inveterate failure to see
> the world as a whole, and to deal with its problems accordingly. Traditional
> diplomacy has preferred, as we Chinese express it, 'to treat the head only
> when the head aches, and treat the leg only when the leg aches.' May I now
> learn that, if China is a crater of future wars, its eruption and the concomi-
> tant disasters may yet be prevented by far-sightedness and remedial measures,
> and that the most propitious occasion for such prevention is the peace settle-
> ment after the war!"[9]

國外交方針 (China's foreign policy in a new world order), *Duli Pinglun* 獨立評論, November 26, 1933. See also Pan Kuang-che 潘光哲, ed., *Hu Shih shilun ji* 胡適時論集 (A
collection of Hu Shih's political commentary) (Taipei: Institute of Modern History,
Academia Sinica, 2018), 4: 193.
  8. Pan Kuang-che, ed., *Hu Shih zhongwen shuxin ji* 胡適中文書信集 (A collection of
Hu Shih's Chinese letters) (Taipei: Institute of Modern History, Academia Sinica,
2018), 2: 401.
  9. See Hu Shih (Suh Hu), "Asiatics Awakening to the Time O'Day," *New York Evening
Post*, November 23, 1915.

While in 1910s Hu Shih was only generally discussing the idea of a new form of statesmanship and diplomacy in case of possible future regional conflicts, by the 1930s, he was already articulating the strategic importance of China, and East Asia at large, on the world stage. In view of the volatile international order in which the possibility of a world war was looming, Hu Shih called the international community's attention to the growing threat of Japan, urging the democratic countries to form an alliance and offer assistance to one another to create a safe order for democracies.

On August 10, 1939, Hu Shih delivered an address titled "Let's Look a Little Ahead" at the Institute of Far Eastern Studies in Ann Arbor, Michigan. Hu Shih, as China's ambassador to the United States, argued that the Japanese invasion of Manchuria in 1931 was not a singular event, but a signal of the breakdown of the global order. At the end of that address, Hu Shih even quoted Franklin Roosevelt's Quarantine Speech, urging the international community to take "positive endeavors" to maintain a peaceful international order:

> [The] Sino-Japanese War, which the Japanese still call "the China incident," is no longer an isolated affair that could be confined to one corner of the globe. We now see, more clearly than ever before, that the Mukden Incident of September 18, 1931, which started the Japanese invasion into China, was in every sense the beginning of the end of the post-war order; and that all the subsequent aggressive acts of Italy, Germany and Japan, all the troubles and tribulations of Ethiopia, Spain, China, Austria, Czechoslovakia and Albania have been merely the logical steps in the rapid unfolding of the general phenomenon of international anarchy.
>
>   . . .
>
> The world problem today remains the same as President Roosevelt saw it so clearly two years ago. The problem from the very beginning has never been merely one of China vs. Japan; it has always been the problem of "positive endeavors to preserve peace" and "quarantine" international anarchy.[10]

From this address we can see that, to Hu Shih, the Japanese invasion of Manchuria in 1931 had to be perceived within the global context and a series of conflicts and tensions between countries or governments across the globe.

---

10. See Hu Shih's "Let's Look a Little Ahead," August 10, 1939. See Chih-ping Chou, ed., Hu Shih weikan yingwen yigao 胡適未刊英文遺稿 (Unpublished English manuscripts of Hu Shih), 87–101. Also see Hu Shih quanji 37: 528–543.

This view, which emphasized global and geopolitical connections, allowed Hu Shih to highlight China's significance and geopolitical connections with other parts of the world. It also enabled him to articulate the importance of Asia as a site of a global power struggle from which to observe the rapid derailing of international society. As China's wartime ambassador to the United States, whose primary mission was to seek the US government's help in resisting Japan's military invasion, Hu Shih's political writings and vision reflect precisely the type of strategic and global outlook that was needed at the time.

Although in the 1930s Hu Shih referred to the conflicts in East Asia and Europe as "international anarchy," in the 1940s he began to identify these conflicts as the inception of a second world war. In a speech titled "China and the World War" in 1940, he argued that the Japanese invasion of Manchuria in 1931 should be perceived as "the first battles of the New World War."

> It is a historical fact that the Second World War was started over eight years ago, in Mukden, China, when on September 18, 1931, Japan's armies began her invasion in China. . . . And thus has begun the Second World War which must include the Italian-Ethiopian War of 1935, the Spanish War of 1936–39, the "extinguishment" of Austria, Czechoslovakia, Albania, as well as the Wars that are now raging in Europe.[11]

Hu Shih's interpretation of World War II is thus different from the conventional one that typically regards Nazi Germany's invasion of Poland in 1939 as the beginning of the war. Yet Hu Shih's interpretation allowed him to place the Sino-Japanese conflicts of the 1930s in a broader historical and geopolitical context, thereby highlighting and assessing the significance of East Asia in an international context.

A WORLD GOVERNMENT

Hu Shih's projection of the world order was not only influenced by the historical conditions under which he lived but also conditioned by the way he

---

11. Hu Shih, "China and the World War," unpublished manuscript. Chapter 4 in this volume.

viewed the world as a closely bonded and interconnected community, in which no nation could remain completely isolated from the rest of the world. To Hu Shih, a major change in one part of the world would ultimately have effects on the rest of the world, whether in times of peace or turmoil. In "The New Disorder in East Asia and the World at Large," he argued, "The world has been made so small today that both war and peace are truly indivisible and the breaking down of the international order in one part will inevitably affect the general peace and well-being of the whole world."[12] Any country that seeks safety and prosperity therefore cannot shirk the responsibility of looking after or looking into the experiences of other countries. Hu Shih maintained that an intergovernmental support network must be organized to build a strong defensive line against any possible attack from militaristic countries or forces, and that a mutually supportive and antiaggression international society was integral to the realization of a truly sustainable world order. This view was expressed in many of Hu Shih's writings during his term as ambassador.[13]

In "What Kind of World Order Do We Want," a radio speech Hu Shih delivered in New York in 1940, he suggested that the "future world order must command a sufficient amount of organized force to support its law and order and thereby to effectively enforce peace."[14] In "Saving Democracy in China," another radio speech he delivered in 1940, Hu Shih argued that China's resistance to Japan's aggression was only part of the world's struggle to safeguard democracy as a political system and a frame of life. In other words, "saving democracy" was an international issue that all democratic countries needed to face together.[15] Hu Shih thus proposed a world government capable of addressing such an issue. In "Family of Nations," a speech delivered on

---

12. Hu Shih, "The New Disorder in East Asia and the World at Large," unpublished manuscript. Chapter 3 in this volume.

13. For example, in "China and the World War" and "Conditions in China and the Outlook," Hu Shih sought to position the Sino-Japanese War in a global context, thereby explaining the significance of establishing an international democratic alliance that could withstand and counter the onslaught of any expansionist, nondemocratic forces or countries.

14. Hu Shih, "What Kind of World Order Do We Want," November 28, 1940. See *Hu Shih quanji*, 38: 90–94.

15. Hu Shih, "Saving Democracy in China," a radio address to the New York Herald Tribune Forum on October 24, 1940. See Chih-ping Chou, ed., *Hu Shih weikan yingwen yigao* 胡適未刊英文遺稿 (Unpublished English manuscripts of Hu Shih), 199–205. Also see "China's Part in the Struggle for the Saving of Democracy," *Hu Shih quanji*, 38: 78–84.

Armistice Day (November 11) in 1939, Hu Shih reflected on the failure of the League of Nations, the first worldwide intergovernmental organization founded after World War I, arguing that a future league or union of Nations must be capable of enforcing peace, because any world government unable to enforce its policy to ensure a world order was "illusory and unreal."[16]

While endorsing the idea of a world government, Hu Shih stressed the importance of regional leadership and regional cooperation. He suggested that an effective intergovernmental effort should be made in the form of a "superfederation" with "such regional setups as the League of Europe, the Conference of American States, the British Commonwealth, the Conference of Pacific States, the Conference of Western and Southwestern Asiatic States, etc."[17] In particular, such regional federations, organized by and comprising all countries and governments in a specific region, must be built on the basis of justice and fairness. In other words, each country or government would assume a definite yet distinct amount of work or responsibility in facilitating regional affairs according to its relative ability, strength, and strategic position. Hu Shih's conception of world government thus featured the idea of graded responsibility and interregional cooperation.

IDEOLOGICAL CONFLICTS

While Hu Shih was generally celebrated as a leader of Chinese liberalism who advocated the political system of democracy, he was fundamentally neutral to any political agenda or theory. Hence, the ideological conflict he started to discuss in the 1940s referred more to a way of comprehending the development of international relations at the time than to a moral judgment on a particular governmental system. For example, in "The Conflict of Ideologies," an article published in 1941, Hu Shih defined "ideology" as a neutral concept that merely denoted "a set or system of ideas about life, society, and government" but did not necessarily imply any negative impression of a specific system:

> Since the conflict of ideologies could not be easily, and summarily dismissed as merely a conflict among the various schemes of unmitigated buncombe, it

---

16. Hu Shih, "Family of Nations," November 11, 1939. Chapter 2 in this volume.
17. Hu Shih, "Family of Nations."

seems advisable to regard the term "ideology" not as implying adverse judgment, but merely as a neutral term, meaning any set or system of ideas about
life, society, and government, originating in most cases as consciously advocated or dogmatically asserted social, political, or religious slogans or battle
cries and, through long processes of propaganda and usage, gradually becoming the characteristic beliefs or dogmas of a particular group, party, or
nationality.[18]

This sociological approach to the concept of "ideology" demonstrates
that Hu Shih used the term as an analytical tool to understand the formation
and development of a specific society or political entity. The term thus provided a cognitive framework through which the development and comparison of different political systems could be perceived. From this perspective,
liberal democracy could also be considered a type of "ideology," which, on a
conceptual level, was comparable to totalitarianism or dictatorship.

In "Do We Need or Want Dictatorship?," as another example, Hu Shih
considered whether authoritarianism or dictatorship was necessary for
China to achieve prosperity and solidarity. In this article, he engaged in a
debate with scholars and government officials who advocated a strong centralized government in China led by powerful dictators, akin to Joseph Stalin
and Benito Mussolini. Although Hu Shih maintained that it was absolutely
unnecessary for the Chinese people to embrace the idea of a dictator and an
authoritarian social system, he did not rule out the consideration of some
form of "modern dictatorship" or "enlightened despotism" as an option for
governing China. He also did not fundamentally dismiss the concept of a
"modern dictatorship," which he argued was theoretically more sophisti-
cated and advanced than an elementary-level democracy:

Great Britain and the United States are both homes of democracy; and the
very fact that government by experts (or by a "Brain Trust") has made its
appearance only in recent years is concrete proof that democracy is but an
elementary form of government, and that modern dictatorship, which calls
for highly developed technical skill in its execution, belongs really to the
politics of the most advanced seminary.[19]

---

18. Hu Shih, "The Conflict of Ideologies," 26–27.
19. Hu Shih, "Do We Need or Want Dictatorship?," *People's Tribune* 8 (February 16,
1935): 89–95. Chapter I in this volume.

It must be clarified that Hu Shih was not rooting for authoritarian rule or government. He was simply trying to figure out what the best form of government was for China and for humankind as a whole in different social and historical contexts. He rebuked any uncritical acceptance of political theories, agendas, or systems. "It must be pointed out," Hu Shih stressed, "that modern dictatorship is not dependent on the wisdom of the leader alone—although strong leadership is of primary importance—but on the numerous technical experts around him."[20] In other words, what Hu Shih sought to highlight in the concept of "modern dictatorship" was the technical aspect of modernization rather than the idea of a highly centralized government. An effective government was one that made good use of the modern techniques of science rather than relying on the judgment or power of a singular leader or oligarchical group; an ideal government should be run collectively by a group of legal representatives of the people who are equally responsible for the wealth and growth of the nation.

It is also noteworthy that the way Hu Shih defined the term "ideology" was rather scholastic. For example, the first half of "The Conflict of Ideologies" actually reads more like a lecture introducing various layers of meanings and interpretations of the term, instead of a political commentary that sought to endorse a specific political idea or agenda. For Hu Shih, the term "ideology" was more an analytical concept to assess and compare different political doctrines and systems than a political standard that seeks to produce a moral judgment on a political entity. In other words, the analytical value of the term "ideology" was more important than its denotative implication in Hu Shih's political writings.[21]

As a pragmatic philosopher, Hu Shih sought to examine all forms of political agenda that might serve the best interests of humankind. As a Darwinian historian, he believed that the value of any political system could only manifest in a specific social or historical context. Any political theory or system needed to be scientifically examined and improved in order to address the constantly changing reality during the course of historical development.

---

20. Hu Shih, "Do We Need or Want Dictatorship?"
21. It is also helpful to distinguish Hu Shih's role as an ambassador, whose mission was to endorse the policy of the government he represented, and his role as a scholar, whose aim was to assess the political situation from an objective perspective. The tension between these two roles can be observed in some of Hu Shih's writings in this period.

HU SHIH AND COMMUNISM

Although Hu Shih tolerated the idea of a "modern dictatorship" or "enlightened despotism" in the 1930s, by the 1950s he had grown disillusioned with the Chinese Communist Party. After Mao's regime was established, he realized he could no longer maintain hope that the Party would be a force to steer governmental development in China toward a multiparty system. He started to analyze the development and nature of communism, delivering a series of lectures and addresses to reveal what he called Stalin's "grand strategy" in facilitating the international communist movement. In "China in Stalin's Grand Strategy," written a year after the establishment of the People's Republic of China, Hu Shih examined the influence of Stalin on China, thereby placing the rise of the Chinese Communist Party in a global context. At the beginning of this long essay, Hu Shih wrote the following:

> I propose to use the history of the long and bitter struggle between Nationalist China and world Communism, between Chiang Kai-shek and Stalin, as source material for a new examination of that almost unbelievably successful strategy which has enabled world Communism to place under its domination immense areas of the earth and 800,000,000 of its population.[22]

According to Hu Shih, the way Stalin conquered Romania, Yugoslavia, Bulgaria, Czechoslovakia, and Hungary was similar to the way he subjugated China under the control of communism. Describing it as a "technique of cold revolution," Hu Shih pointed out that at the heart of Stalin's global strategy was the creation, preservation, and nurturing of the full strength of the equivalent of the Red Army in multiple countries and regions of the world, through which he pushed for a global expansion of the Third International.[23] In particular, Hu Shih pointed out the connection between Mao Zedong and the Clausewitz-Lenin-Stalin tactics of the "counteroffensive" and "strategy of retreat," which Mao successfully implemented in his war against the Nationalist government.

Hu Shih's analysis of the rise of Chinese communism infuriated Mao. In

---

22. Hu Shih, "China in Stalin's Grand Strategy," *Foreign Affairs* 29, no. 1 (October 1950): 11–40. Chapter 9 in this volume.
23. The Third International (1919–1943), also known as the Communist International (Comintern), was an international organization controlled by the Soviet Union that advocated world communism.

the decades to follow, the Chinese Communist Party orchestrated a long campaign to criticize and smear Hu Shih's reputation as an intellectual leader who spoke out against any form of authoritarianism. This liberal position was perceived as a threat to the newly established regime of the Chinese Communist Party. To eliminate Hu Shih's lasting influence on Chinese intellectual circles, many of his former colleagues in China at the time were forced to condemn him as a bourgeois scholar or a faithful officer of the reactionary class whose political position had betrayed the Chinese people's wish for communist rule. On May 11, 1949, Chen Yuan 陳垣 (1880–1971), Hu Shih's former colleague at Peking University, wrote an open letter to him, denouncing his incorrect and reactionary beliefs, particularly his affiliation with the Nationalist government.

In November 1951, more than a dozen scholars at Peking University were compelled to criticize Hu Shih for being feudalistic, counterrevolutionary, and pro-American (i.e., imperialistic). According to a news report by the Xinhua News Agency, Hu Shih was to be recognized as "the most representative reactionary figure of the old academic circle" (最具有代表性的, 在舊學術界集反動之大成的人物).[24] The most tragic development of this campaign occurred when Hu Shih's youngest son, Hu Sidu 胡思杜 (1921–1957), who was still living in China at the time, was forced to condemn his own father as an "enemy of the people" (人民的公敵) and "his own personal enemy" (我自己的敵人). On September 22, 1950, Hu Sidu's written confession was published in *Ta Kung Pao* 大公報, a left-wing newspaper in Hong Kong:

> After 1919, [my father] had gone astray, advocating Ibsenism as a way to support his theory on the "problem," introducing experimentalism in order to counter materialism. . . . Today, I have received the education of the Party and am no longer afraid of the historical "giant." I have the courage to recognize him and defeat him, and to evaluate his influence on the people according to the standard of historical materialism. From the perspective of class analysis, I can confirm that he is a faithful officer of the reactionary class, an enemy of the people. Politically, he is not progressive at all.

---

24. Hu Ming 胡明, "Hu Shih pipan de fansi" 胡適批判的反思 (Reflections on criticism of Hu Shih), *Ershiyi shiyji* 二十一世纪 (Twenty-first century), December 1991, 50–57. In January 1949, according to a radio station in the communist-controlled areas in China (i.e., Northern Shaanxi), the Chinese Communist Party listed Hu Shih as a "war criminal" (戰犯) and an "advocate of war" (戰爭鼓吹者). See Hu Shih's diary entry of January 27, 1949, *Hu Shih riji quanji* 胡適日記全集 (Complete collection of Hu Shih's diaries; hereafter: *HSRQ*) (Taipei: Linking, 2018), 8: 380.

一九一九年以後, 日益走入歧途, 提倡易卜生主義, 以充實他的"問題論"; 介紹實驗主義來抗唯物主義... 今天, 受了黨的教育, 我再不怕那座歷史的"大山", 敢於認識它, 也敢於推倒它, 也敢於以歷史唯物主義的天秤來衡量他對人民的作用; 從階級分析上, 我明確了他是反動階級的忠臣, 人民的敵人. 在政治上他是沒有什麼進步性.[25]

This episode in Hu Shih's life was clearly a tremendous blow to him, which he mentioned time and again in his speeches and writings during the 1950s in which he was in exile in the United States. He often wondered whether the accusations made by his son and friends in China were sincere or just a political ruse of the Communist Party to attack him. For instance, in "The Free World Needs a Free China," after sharing the story of how his own son was "indoctrinated" by the Chinese Communist Party and forced to denounce his own father in public, Hu Shih lamented, "Did my son actually say that? Was he free not to say that?" Although Hu Shih told reporters who interviewed him about these accusations that he was "not greatly disturbed,"[26] the *New York Times* recorded that he demonstrated mixed feelings about this denouncement and refused to talk about it in detail: "He [Hu Shih] observed that we were aware that there was no freedom of speech in Communist countries. We could now see, also, that there was no 'freedom of silence' either. Statements of loyalty and belief, he noted, are required of those under Communist rule."[27] "Aside from that," he said, "I would not care to comment on that matter."[28] The unwillingness of Hu Shih to comment on a "family issue," which was unfortunately also a public matter, perhaps reveals his complex feelings as China's former ambassador and a leading scholar in exile, who felt the need to share his tragic experience with the American public, informing them of the true nature of Mao's regime, of which he was a victim.

Despite Hu Shih's being fully aware that such attacks were launched by the Chinese Communist Party, these carefully orchestrated accusations by his beloved friends and family members were still too painful to talk about in public in a personal way. These experiences thus provide another window

---

25. See "Chinese Ex-Envoy Denounced by Son," New York Times, September 23, 1950. Also see *HSRQ*, 8: 522–527.

26. See "Father Not Disturbed," in *HSRQ*, 8: 519.

27. See "The Case of Dr. Hu Shih," *New York Times*, September 24, 1950.

28. See "Chinese Ex-Envoy Denounced by Son," *New York Times*, September 23, 1950. Also see "Father Not Disturbed," in *HSRQ*, 8: 519.

through which to understand Hu Shih's writings and activities during the 1950s as a scholar in exile in the United States.

HU SHIH'S POLITICAL THEORY

Given the extensive discussion of totalitarianism in many of Hu Shih's political writings, it is perhaps a bit surprising that he did not mention the work of Hannah Arendt (1906–1975), who had also been living in New York since the 1940s. One possible explanation is that Arendt did not publish her major book *The Origins of Totalitarianism* until 1951, and Hu Shih's academic interests, after leaving China for the United States in 1949, had returned to Chinese philosophy and literature.[29] He remained an acute political critic, however, who was determined to uncover the cultural roots of antiauthoritarianism and democratic ideas in China's philosophical traditions. Although Hu Shih did not appear to have read Arendt, he mentioned that he was influenced by the work of Norman Angell (1872–1967), a British political theorist who won the Nobel Peace Prize in 1933, and John Dewey (1859–1952), Hu Shih's former supervisor at Columbia University. Angell made an especially strong impression on Hu Shih, as he noted in his diary on January 9, 1950:

> Angell is the most perceptive political critic in today's world. He has been consistently warning the democracies in the West over the past forty-five years, and never got tired of doing it. I was influenced by him significantly. My shift from the philosophy of "nonresistance" to using force to suppress violence is a result of being influenced by him and John Dewey.

> Angell 是今世一個最能思想的政論家, 四十五年如一日, 為西方民主國家作先見的警告, 老而不倦. 我一生受他的影響很大. 我從[不抵抗]主義逐漸轉到用力量制裁強暴的見解, 是受了他和 John Dewey 的影響.[30]

---

29. For example, Hu Shih had focused on studying works such as *Dream of the Red Chamber* and *Commentary on the Water Classic* in his late years.

30. See *HSRQ*, 8: 467–468. In his memoir, Hu Shih also noted, "I was beginning to change in the years of 1915 and 1916. And one of the intellectual forces that influenced me was Norman Angell—one of the greatest minds of the Anglo-Saxon world and the author of the famous book *The Great Illusion*. *The Great Illusion* came out in 1909, and it was considered one of the most eleoquent appeals for a new constructive pacifism. . . . *The Great Illusion* is widely read but is often misunderstood. So let me para-

Angell was a theorist of international relations. Many of his works were concerned with the international politics of the time. For example, he published *Europe's Optical Illusion* (1909), *The Great Illusion: A Study of the Relation of Military Power in Nations to Their Economic and Social Advantage* (1910), *America and the New World State* (1912), *Peace Theories and the Balkan War* (1912), *The Foundations of International Polity* (1914), *The Dangers of Half Preparedness* (1916), *War Aims: The Need for a Parliament of the Allies* (1917), *Why Freedom Matters* (1917), *The Political Conditions of Allied Success: A Protective Union of the Democracies* (1918), and *Peace with the Dictators* (1938). A quick survey of these books reveals that many of Angell's proposals inspired Hu Shih and shaped his understanding of a new world order. For example, Hu Shih constantly referred to how "unprepared" and "defenseless" democracies were in the face of aggressive totalitarian countries. The same wording can be found in Angell's book *The Dangers of Half Preparedness*. In addition, Hu Shih constantly advocated an alliance of democracies to prepare for possible attacks from militaristic countries. Angell, too, was an early advocate for an international security system that would function like a mutual insurance corporation, in which each country contributed to the collective security of a specific region on an equal basis. The only difference was that Angell suggested each nation should contribute approximately equally to this mutual defense system, whereas Hu Shih emphasized a "graded responsibility" in which a nation's contribution was based on its ability, strength, and geopolitical position. Both Angell and Hu Shih, however, maintained that peace had to be enforced.[31]

---

phrase very briefly from Mr. Norman Angell's own autobiography to show that his philosophy doesn't mean that war is impossible. He says that war is possible because people are ignorant of the real, basic and simple facts such as the wasteful use of force. I came to know him personally during those two weeks in 1915, and was greatly impressed by his idea that the real issue was not a denial of force but the economical and efficient application of force for a mutually agreed and generally understood objective which is desired and desirable. . . . These two men, Norman Angell and John Dewey contributed to my new thinking in those years (1915–1916). I was beginning to abandon the philosophy of non-resistance; I was starting to embrace this new, more constructive conception of force, and of law as a statement of the conditions of an efficient and economical way of utilizing force." See *Personal Reminiscences*, 67, 69, 72.

31. In "The Far East and the Future Peace of the World," an address delivered at the Rollins Institute on International Relations in Winter Park, Florida in 1940, Hu Shih also discusses the work of Clarence Kirschman Streit (1896–1986), an American journalist who played a key role in the Atlanticist and world federalist movements. Streit published a book titled *Union Now: A Proposal for an Atlantic Federal Union of the Free* in 1939, in which he proposes a "Union" of fifteen countries that he considered relatively mature democracies to be organized in ways similar to the federal system of the United

There are other clear instances of Angell's influence on Hu Shih. During China's Resistance War, Hu Shih was known for his motto of "hanging on bitterly and waiting for a chance" (苦撐待變), his early suggestion for China's foreign policy. When war broke out in 1937, Hu Shih urged Chiang Kai-shek to seek a diplomatic solution to China's conflict with Japan in order to avoid a disastrous total war. After he was appointed China's ambassador to the United States in 1938, Hu Shih maintained that the best chance for China to survive this war was to wait for a change in political climate in the international community, predicting that Japan's military aggression and expansion in Asia would ultimately threaten the interests of Western countries, thereby bringing Japan to war with other powers. In 1939, however, Hu Shih started to advocate for a democratic alliance against militaristic forces, arguing that world peace must be enforced and actively maintained. This transition from "bitter waiting" to "forming an alliance" clearly reflects Angell's influence.[32]

One reason for Angell's great influence on Hu Shih was the publication of many of Angell's books in the second decade of the century, when Hu Shih was a young student in the United States and becoming interested in international politics. In his memoir, Hu Shih recalls a course he took at Cornell that introduced American politics, which he found immensely interesting, and affected him profoundly. His course professor had emphasized the importance of practical experience, asking the students to observe the presidential election that year (i.e., 1912), in which William Howard Taft, Theodore Roosevelt, and Woodrow Wilson ran for the presidency representing different political parties. That election was more competitive and difficult

---

States. While Hu Shih endorsed this book as an "expression of the sincere and earnest thinking of an idealist," he disagreed with Streit in distinguishing the concept of a union from a league. To Streit, a union is a government of the people, while a league is a government of governments, which, Streit argued, would easily lead to an "entangling alliance." Streit thus believed that the United States should not join such a league of nations. Hu Shih, however, argued that a truly functional union should have "union citizenship" and a "defense force" against all enemies, and thus "joining a league would probably involve far less entangling obligations" than Streit expected. See *Hu Shih quanji*, 37: 639–650. Also see Clarence Streit's *Union Now: A Proposal for an Atlantic Federal Union of the Free* (New York: Harper & Brothers, 1939).

32. In a 1916 essay, "Is There a Substitute for Force in International Relations?," which examined the nature of "force" in international relations, Hu Shih cited John Atkinson Hobson's (1858–1940) *Towards International Government* (New York: Macmillan, 1915), which called for the formation of a world political body to prevent wars. Hobson is thus another political theorist that may have influenced Hu Shih's view on international politics. The influence of some Euro-American political theorists on Hu Shih merits further analysis.

to predict than usual. Hu Shih's professor also encouraged him and his class-mates to participate in all election-related activities and read all newspapers to get a full picture of the political landscape of America's domestic politics. This course and the presidential election of 1912, according to Hu Shih, had a long-standing impact on him.

The 1916 presidential campaign also left an indelible impression on Hu Shih, who said that by that time he had ceased to be impressed by the politi-cal glamor of Theodore Roosevelt and instead developed an interest in the political vision of Woodrow Wilson as an international leader and states-man.[33] In his memoir he recounted the experience of joining a crowd in New York's Time Square, waiting for the result of the election throughout the eve-ning. As a supporter of Wilson, Hu Shih was worried by the prediction of several US newspapers, such as the *New York World* and the *New York Evening Post*, that Charles Evans Hughes, the two-term governor of New York, would win the election. Hu Shih thus wrote in his memoir, "My interest in Ameri-can politics, my study of American political system, my active interest in the two presidential campaigns of my student days, all this had given me a last-ing interest in government and politics."[34]

Hu Shih's interest in Wilson's political vision and rhetoric can be explained in the following ways. First, Wilson was a college professor turned president who had earned his reputation as a scholar before he became a government official. As an educator, Wilson never shied away from commu-nicating with Congress and the American public, and had worked consis-tently to apply his methods and conclusions as a political scientist to his handling of both domestic and international affairs. Wilson's career trajec-tory thus inspired Hu Shih, leading him to become a political leader himself later in life. Second, Wilson's spirit of progressive pragmatism and liberal internationalism resonated with Hu Shih's own educational experience at Columbia University, where he was mentored by the famous philosopher of

---

33. Hu Shih, *Personal Reminiscences*, 39.

34. Hu Shih, *Personal Reminiscences*, 41. In T. K. Tong's Chinese translation of the book, this passage was slightly reworked to indicate a causal relationship between Hu Shih's experience in the United States and his later interest in the development of Chi-nese politics and government: "My interest in American politics, my study of Ameri-can political system, and the two US presidential campaigns that I experienced in my student years had a decisive influence on my later interest and concern for Chinese politics and government" (我對美國政治的興趣和我對美國政制的研究，以及我學生時代所目睹的兩次美國大選，對我後來對中國政治和政府的關心，都有著決定性的影響). See *Au-tobiography of Hu Shih*, 64.

pragmatism, John Dewey, who, like Wilson, emphasized an incrmentalist approach to solving social and political problems. It is widely known that Dewey had a lifetime influence on Hu Shih's intellectual development, and Dewey's liberal stance and involvement in public affairs profoundly shaped Hu Shih's understanding of politics and the world.[35]

The international realities of the 1910s also made Hu Shih susceptive to the influence of Woodrow Wilson as a political leader. Robert Zoellick noted that the period of 1914–1917 marked Wilson's as well as America's journey to World War I, which "reveals an intellectual president making practical choices about dangerous problems that Europe's combatants forced upon his country."[36] The transition of Wilson's foreign policy from remaining neutral to declaring war on Germany thus had a significant impact not only on America's modern history, but also on Hu Shih's intellectual development. Like Wilson, Hu Shih became an intellectual political leader who sought to apply his learning to the development of his own nation. Wilson's influence on Hu Shih can also be observed in his speeches delivered in the United States during World War II. For example, when Hu Shih was sent by the Nationalist government as a special envoy to visit the United States in 1937,[37] his first public address was delivered in San Francisco through the Columbia Broadcasting System on October 1. In that radio address, Hu Shih expressed a sympathetic understanding of the American people's and government's wish to maintain neutral in international relations in the face of an entangling world war. Hu Shih, however, argued that relying on a neutral policy could not keep America out of war permanently in the ongoing international crisis, since no nation, he argued, can be entirely isolated from the

---

35. Hu Shih wrote in his memoir, "I was greatly impressed again by this example of [a] university professor's active interest in the political features of the day." *Personal Reminiscences*, 39.

36. Robert B. Zoellick, *America in the World: A History of U.S. Diplomacy and Foreign Policy* (New York: Twelve, 2020), 138. When recounting his transition from a believer in cosmopolitanism to an advocate of a new form of pacifism, Hu Shih wrote, "I want to speak especially of pacifism, my activities as a pacifist in those years of international upheaval. My student life in America lasted seven years, from 1910 to 1917. For the first four years the world was at peace, but the last three years, 1914 to 1917, comprised the first three years of the First World War before the American entry into the fighting. And it was also the most trying period in China for Chin was under constant pressure from Japan." *Personal Reminiscences*, 59.

37. From October 1937 to September 1938, Hu Shih visited the United States, Canada, and Europe on behalf of the Nationalist government but in an unofficial capacity in order to seek the international community's help in resisting the Japanese military invasion.

rest of the world. Hu Shih thus asked for the American people's and government's support of the Chinese people and government in their ongoing struggle against the Japanese agression in Asia:

> But allow me to send a word of warning. Is this mere negative pacificism really sufficient to keep you out of the war? Can you really keep out of the war by merely [remaining] peace-loving and remaining neutral? I was a student in this country when the last war broke out in 1914. I well remember—and I am sure you will all remember—President Wilson's proclamation of neutrality in which he commanded all the American people to remain neutral, neutral not only in action but also in spirit. Indeed, America succeeded in keeping out of the war for almost three years. In spite of your racial and cultural sympathy with England, in spite of your profound historic gratitude towards France, in spite of your tremendous sentimental sympathy for Belgium, in spite of all this your nation kept out of the war for three long years, and the great Woodrow Wilson was reelected in 1917 as the one man who "kept you out of war". But then the tide turned. The same great President who had kept you out of the war for three years had to go to Congress early in 1917 to ask for a mandate to sever diplomatic relations with Germany and later to declare war on Germany. Before I sailed back for China in 1917, the United States was already in the war, fighting on the side of the Allies, fighting the war that was to end war, and to make the world safe for democracy.[38]

In this speech, Hu Shih reminded the American people of President Wilson's decision to join the Allies' fight against Germany in 1917. Hu Shih suggested that Wilson's decision to go war was inevitable since it was international necessity that forced America to join the Allies. Hu Shih maintained, "In this modern world of radio and transocean clippers, there is no such thing as an isolated nation. In this world of ours, war as well as peace is truly indivisible."[39]

The political upheaval in China at that time also played a role in sparking Hu Shih's interest in international politics. The Qing dynasty that had ruled China for three hundred years was overthrown in 1912 and replaced by the new republic. This transition had a significant impact on Hu Shih, who wrote several articles discussing the meaning of the republic not only in the

---

38. Hu Shih, "What China Expects of America in the Present Crisis." See *Hu Shih weikan yingwen yigao*, 63–68. Also see Hu Shih quanji, 37: 418–423.

39. Hu Shih, "What China Expects."

history of China but also in the greater context of Asia. He published articles in several US newspapers and periodicals, such as the *New York Times*, the *New Republic*, and *The Outlook*, debating with American critics the meaning of a Chinese republic. In his late years, Hu Shih had continued to explicate the historical significance of the establishment of the Chinese republic, arguing that the abolition of the monarchical form of government was actually facilitated by an intellectual revolution that was integral to the success of any political reform.[40]

Hu Shih's political writings thus reflected his observations and experiences of the drastic changes in the world order in the first decades of the twentieth century, which in turn shaped his understanding of China and its relations with the rest of the world. One could say that Hu Shih's experiences in the United States made him particularly sensitive to the dynamics of international relations and the geopolitical connections among different countries.

HU SHIH'S POLITICAL CAREER

Hu Shih's political career started long before he was appointed ambassador to the United States. As a student at Cornell University, Hu Shih was a member and later president of the Cosmopolitan Club, an international student organization with branches in universities around the world. As president, Hu Shih, along with other student leaders from around the world, had the chance to be received by President Woodrow Wilson and Secretary of State William Jennings Bryan in Washington, DC, in 1914.

On his return from America to China in 1917, he was immediately appointed professor of Chinese literature at Peking University, where he founded and headed the Institute of Chinese Philosophy. A few years later, he was promoted to the position of acting provost and dean of the College of Liberal Arts. Later in life, in 1946, he was appointed president of Peking University. From 1928 to 1930, Hu Shih also served as president of the Chinese Public University, which was an early, modern-style university in China. Additionally, Hu Shih served as a board member for many other universities and schools, including Nankai University and the Nankai School of Economics.

---

40. Hu Shih, "The Chinese Revolution," in *Contemporary China: A Reference Digest* 5, no. 11 (October 15, 1945), 3–4. Chapter 8 in this volume.

Hu Shih's interest and involvement in various sociocultural reforms in China, however, were not limited by his work as a scholar. In fact, Hu Shih had been an active and outspoken political critic since the 1920s. As early as 1921, he and his colleagues H. C. Zen 任鴻寯 (1886–1961), Wang Zheng 王徵 (1887–?), and Ding Wenjiang 丁文江 (1887–1936) established the "Effort Society" (努力會), which sought to study and critique the sociopolitical reality of contemporary China. The society's members believed that academic study should focus on questions that reflected actual social problems. The "Manual of the Effort Society" (努力會簡章) stated that one key objective of the group was "to seek the improvement of Chinese politics and the progression of Chinese society" (謀中國政治的改善與社會的進步).[41] In 1922, Hu Shih and other like-minded scholars launched the political magazine *Nuli Zhoubao* 努力週報 (Effort Weekly), which was one of the first of its kind run by the Chinese liberals to reflect on China's social and political issues. In the second issue of the magainze, Hu Shih and fifteen other scholars, most of whom were faculty members at Peking University, published a joint statement titled "Our Political Statement" (我們的政治主張), in which three basic gudielines were proposed for future political reforms in China:

For any future political reform, we have three basic demands:

(1) We demand a "constitutional government" since this is the first step to establish a normal and sustainable political system.

(2) We demand an "open government" that includes a public system of treasury management and a fair selection process for government officials. We believe that publicity is the only weapon to destroy all political powers behind the scenes.

(3) We demand a "politics of strategic planning" since we believe that China's main problem lies in its lack of plans and its aimlessness. We believe that planning is the key to [administrative] efficiency and that a run-of-the-mill plan is better than no plan.

---

41. Hu Shih et al., "Nuli hui jianzhang," in *Hu Shih's Political Commentary*, 2:34–35. Also see Geng Yunzhi 耿雲志, ed., *Hu Shih yigao ji micang shuxin* 胡適遺稿及密藏書信 (Unpublished manuscripts and letters of Hu Shih) (Hefei: Huangshan shushe, 1994), 374–375.

我們對於今後政治的改革, 有三個基本的要求:

第一, 我們要求一個「憲政的政府」, 因為這是使政治上軌道的第一步.

第二, 我們要求一個「公開的政府」, 包括財政的公開與公開考試式的用人等等. 因為我們深信「公開」(publicity) 是打破一切黑幕的惟一武器.

第三, 我們要求一種「有計劃的政治」, 因為我們深信中國的大病在於無計劃的飄泊, 因為我們深信計劃是效率的源頭, 因為我們深信一個平庸的計劃勝於無計劃的瞎摸索.[42]

Hu Shih's view on the government was thus pragmatic and instrumentalistic. As he argued in a speech delivered on October 22, 1921, "The Principles of a Good Government" 好政府主義, the definition of a good government is an institution with an organizational structure and purposes that exercises authority only for public interests. Hu Shih thus criticized the ideas of theocracy and anarchy, arguing that a government is only a public tool created to ensure the operation of a modern society. He also mantained that the authority of the government is not based on the will and interest of a few privileged individuals, but on a legal and constitutional structure that defines the right of each social member as well as the boundary between the government and the people.[43]

In addition to elaborating the role of the government in the modern era, Hu Shih emphasized the importance of political criticism in helping steer the course of the nation. In "Political Critic and Political Party" 政論家與政黨, an article published in *Nuli Zhoubao* on June 4, 1922, Hu Shih discussed three types of political critics: those who follow the party, those who lead the party, and those who oversee the party. Among these three types of political critics, Hu Shih considered the last most important and most needed in a society. According to Hu Shih's definition, such political critics are concerned not so much with the interest of any one party as with the welfare of the entire nation, and they consider their role to be providing critical suggestions for the development of the government and the country in general, and thus are independent from the ideological control of any political party. It is precisely because of the incisiveness and independence of such political critics that they can truly mediate the tense relations between different political groups and parties in a country. Hu Shih suggested that without the

---

42. Hu Shih et al., "Women de zhengzhi zhuzhang," in *Hu Shih's Political Commentary*, 2: 112–115.

43. Hu Shih et al., "Hao Zhengfu zhuyi," in *Hu Shih's Political Commentary*, 2:55–60.

minds of independent critics, there will be endless political rivalry without coordinated efforts to advance the interest of the general public.[44]

From Hu Shih's discussions on the government and political parties, one can see that a key element in his conception of a modern soceity is the existence of active social agents who participate in its social and political development. In "Our View on Politics" 我們對於政治的主張, a document possibly written in the late 1920s or early 1930s, the author pointed out that the concept of a "party" (黨) is different from that of a "government" (政):

> We believe that overrlapping roles of the party [i.e., the Chinese Nationalist Party] and the government nowadays are unsustainable. It needs to be stipulated that the right of a party is defined by its right to participate in politics, while a government's right is defined by its obligation to govern (Here I follow Sun Yat-sen's proposed differentiation of "civil right" and "governance.") To govern is to exercise administrative power; to exercise the civil right is to oversee the government.

> 我們對於今日的「黨」和「政」的關係, 認為太不分明, 實際上行不通. 我們以為今日應該明白規定黨的權限是「政權」, 政府的權限是「治權」(這是借用孫中山分別「政權」和「治權」的主張). 治權是執行政務之權, 政權是監督行政之權.

In the 1930s, Hu Shih took on more roles in advising the governmental and many nongovernmental organizations in China. Hu Shih was an adviser to many government organs, such as the National Financial and Economic Affairs Committee, the Sino-American Joint Commission on Rural Reconstruction, the China Foundation for the Promotion of Education and Culture, and the Board of Trustees of Sino-British Gengkuan. He also played an active role in many NGOs, such as the China League for Civil Rights, the Association of Freedom of Speech, and Institute of Pacific Relations. Last but not least, he was invited to take up important positions in the government, such as minister of education, minister to Germany, and ambassador to the United States, a role he initially declined.[45]

---

44. Hu Shih, "Zhenlun jia yu zhengdang," in *Hu Shih's Political Commentary*, 2:150–152.

45. In the 1940s, when the war between the Nationalist Party and Communist Party escalated, Hu Shih was even invited by Chiang Kai-shek to serve as president of the Executive Yuan (i.e., premier of the Republic of China) and president of the Republic of China, which did not work out eventually because of complex political reasons. Even the deposed emperor of the Qing court, Puyi (1906–1967), had twice in the 1920s

Judging by the variety and abundance of Hu Shih's political experience, his appointment as China's wartime Ambassador to the United States was not sudden; he was selected for this role precisely because of his broad experience in public and international affairs. For long, Hu Shih was mostly considered and studied as a leader of China's May Fourth Movement. Yet, his role as an experienced statesman, an outspoken political critic, a wartime ambassador to the US, and a prominent public intellectual who devoted his life to various socio-political reforms, is equally important to our understanding of this historical figure. As an eminent figure in the history of modern China, Hu Shih's identity as a scholar cannot be entirely separated from his activities as a politician. His firsthand experiences as a diplomat in the Cold War and his longstanding interest and invovlement in various public and international affairs, had contributed to his profound understanding of the past and future of Sino-American relations, thereby testifying to the historical development of the international relations over the course of the twentieth century. In many ways, Hu Shih had set an example of a visionary and conscientious public intellectual, whose dedication to public affairs was necessitated by his sense of responsibility and an honest observation of the world. His action, like his intellectual work, was constantly guided by his sheer, albeit idealistic, belief in the possibility of effecting social change through genuine individual effort.

---

consulted Hu Shih about how to handle the Qing court's assets.

Introduction II

Hu Shih's Anti-communist Thought

CHIH-P'ING CHOU

In the early 1950s, the Chinese Communist Party launched a nationwide, multiyear political campaign to smear Hu Shih and his works. This campaign was implemented at every level of the Party's infrastructure and lasted for many years. For almost three decades, there were no "Hu Shih studies" in China, only criticism of him. This situation changed, however, after the sociopolitical atmosphere in China became less intense after Mao Zedong's (1893–1976) death. Not only have Hu Shih's works been republished in China in the wake of the opening up of policy, but related biographies and studies of him have increasingly appeared in the public eye. While one can say that there is a revival of Hu Shih studies since the 1980s, it does not mean that researchers have enjoyed full academic freedom in studying and discussing this prominent historical figure. In fact, many of Hu Shih's political writings still cannot to be published in China, particularly those that reflect on the nature of communism, considered too sensitive a topic by the Chinese authorities.[1] Many scholars, when introducing Hu Shih's political works, have chosen to provide only a brief overview of his works or to downplay

---

1. For example, among the nine essays collected in *Women bixu xuanze women de fangxiang* 我們必須選擇我們的方向 (We must choose our direction) published by Hong Kong's ziyou zhongguo chubanshe (Free China Press) in 1950, except for the article "Ziyou zhuyi" 自由主義 (Liberalism), which was subject to changes and included in *Hu Shih wenji* (Collected works of Hu Shih) 胡適文集 (Beijing: Beijing University Press, 1998), all other essays were excluded from the collection.

Hu's importance because of his "political incorrectness." In other words, his political works, particularly those that reflect on the nature and the spread of communism on a world scale, have never enjoyed a fair and rigorous discussion.

To a certain extent, Hu Shih's political works have also been neglected in the intellectual communities in Taiwan and the larger Sinophone world. This lack of attention to Hu Shih in these communities, however, is due not to the ideological tendency of the researchers, but to the fact that his political works were mostly written in English and published outside China. To date, only a small fraction of his English-language works have been translated into Chinese, let alone his English-language political works that discuss or criticize communism. Another reason why Hu Shih's political writings have been underresearched is that many were originally lecture notes and speech scripts that were delivered on various occasions and in different countries, and had never been formally published. This, too, makes it difficult for researchers to collect and compile these writings to delineate the full spectrum of Hu Shih's political thoughts.

The current limitation on Hu Shih studies is thus, to a certain extent, a reflection of China's political reality of the twentieth and twenty-first centuries. This collection of Hu Shih's writings on the nature and the spread of communism in the twentieth century is therefore an attempt to address that political reality by providing a richer understanding of the relation between modern Chinese history and traditional Chinese culture, a connection Hu Shih explains over and over again in his works.

Some scholars have used the term "reactionary" to describe Hu Shih's "anti-communist" works. Yet I would like to suggest that it is through these writings that Hu Shih demonstrated his independent and critical spirit as a thinker, and his courageous support of intellectual and political freedom. It is also here that Hu Shih defended the importance of a democratic China. Some scholars have said that Hu Shih tended to repeat his early work in his later writings. This is perhaps true to the extent we ignore Hu's later "anti-communist" writings, which are de facto the new works in his later years. Since Hu Shih's later works mainly concern the importance of a free and democratic international society, they still have value in illuminating the political realities in our twenty-first-century world.

THE PHILOSOPHICAL FOUNDATION OF HU SHIH'S
ANTI-COMMUNIST WRITINGS

To understand the importance of Hu Shih's anti-communist writings, we need to identify and examine those ideas and values in his works that contradict the Communist Party's doctrines. Only by doing so can we understand why Hu Shih's political writings were not simply an expression of his political views, but the philosophical manifestation of his interpretation of the humanist and liberal intellectual traditions rooted in Chinese culture.

As an advocate of John Dewey's (1859–1952) pragmatism and the concept of a "piecemeal reform," Hu Shih did not believe in any overnight revolution or any form of quick remedy for solving social problems. In fact, he had expressed such a view in his early years when he was debating with China's leftist scholars on the question whether ideological guidelines or practical issues are more important to the implementation of a social reform. This debate, which took place in 1919, was later known as the debate of "problems and -isms" and had a far-reaching impact on the intellectual development of modern China.[2] In this debate, Hu Shih constantly quoted Dewey's words, arguing that "progress is not a wholesale matter, but a retail job, to be contracted for and executed in sections."[3] This emphasis on a moderate, step-by-step reform differs from the approach taken by the leftist scholars at the time such as Li Dazhao (1889–1927) and Chen Duxiu (1879–1942), who believed that only a radical social revolution can achieve actual social changes. This debate laid the philosophical foundation for Hu Shih's later political writings.[4]

On March 10, 1930, Hu Shih wrote an article titled "Thoughts While on a Journey," in which he argued: "America will not have an [overnight] social revolution because a social revolution [of some kind] is underway every day. This kind of revolution is gradual and makes progress every day, and thus it

---

2. Hu Shih, "Wenti yu zhuyi," *Hu Shih wencun* (Taipei: Far East, 1968) (hereafter *HSW*), 1:342–379.

3. Quoted from Hu Shih, "The Conflict of Ideologies," *Annals of the American Academy of Political and Social Science* 218 (November 1941): 32. Chapter 7 in this volume.

4. This ideological difference has also led to the later division of the editorial staff of the *New Youth* 新青年 magazine with which Hu Shih, Li Dazhao, and Chen Duxiu were affiliated. After this debate, the editorial staff was divided into left and right camps. Some of them became founding or early members of the Chinese Communist Party, such as Li and Chen, while others chose the path of liberalism, such as Hu.

is a day-to-day revolution."[5] On April 13 of the same year, Hu Shih published another article expressing the same view while reflecting on China's political situation:

> What China needs now is not a revolution achieved through violent and totalitarian means, or a revolution that curbs violence with violence, or a revolution that justifies itself by creating a target out of thin air. We would rather be labeled "counterrevolutionary" than advocate those types of revolution.[6]

From this passage, we can see that Hu Shih is not a blind follower of any revolutionary cause. As he emphasizes in this article, he would rather be labeled a "counterrevolutionary" than be forced to advocate a revolution that does not have a justifiable aim, let alone resort to the use of violence in achieving social and political reform. An overnight revolution achieved through violence and authoritarian means is short-lived, counterproductive, and destructive, and would become a wasteful effort in due course. What Hu Shih advocated is thus a gradual cultural and intellectual reform that takes no shortcuts.[7]

On July 8, 1941, Hu Shih delivered a speech titled "The Conflict of Ideologies" at the University of Michigan. In this speech, he argued that one fundamental difference between dictatorship and democracy is that the former endorses a "radical revolution," the latter a "piecemeal reform." He explained, "The first basic characteristic of totalitarian regimes is that they all stand for radical and catastrophic revolution and that they all scorn and spurn specific reforms as superficial and useless."[8] It is obvious that Hu Shih held this view throughout his life. On March 5, 1954, he was invited to give a talk at an event organized by the *Free China Journal*. In this talk, Hu still emphasized the importance of a step-by-step reform, arguing that "all social radicalism

---

5. Hu Shih, "Manyou de ganxiang" 漫遊的感想 (Thoughts while on a journey), *HSW*, 3:29.

6. Hu Shih, "Women zou natiaolu" 我們走哪條路 (Which road shall we take), *HSW*, 4:14.

7. In fact, Hu Shih had been critical of the idea of an overnight revolution when he was still studying at Cornell University during 1910–1915. In his diary entry dated January 11, 1916, he wrote: "It is true that I have much sympathy with the rebels. But I do not favor a present revolution. I have come to hold that there is no shortcut to political decency and efficiency." See Hu Shih, *Hu Shih zuopin ji* 胡適作品集 (Collected works of Hu Shih) (Taipei: Yuanliu, 1986), 36:231.

8. Hu Shih, "The Conflict of Ideologies," 31.

must inevitably lead to political dictatorship."[9] To prove his point, he quoted Vladimir Lenin's (1870–1924) famous words, "Revolution is undoubtedly the most authoritarian thing in the world."[10] From this example, we can see that Hu Shih is skeptical of, and therefore maintains a critical distance from, any idea of a social revolution that promises to deliver an immediate result.

In addition to opposing to the use of violence in initiating social reform, Hu Shih highlights the importance of individualism in his political writings. In his discussion of the relation between an individual and society, he emphasized the active role that an individual can play in shaping the development of a society. And yet he also argued that an individual can reach greater achievements only by living and working within a social group.[11] This is of course not to say that Hu Shih did not believe in the power or agency of an individual.[12] Rather, he was suggesting that a society is a combination of a diverse group of individuals and thus any oppression against individuals should not be permitted. From this perspective, we can say that social equality and diversity are the two cornerstones of Hu Shih's concept of individualism. The idea that each person is unique and was born with the right to pursue his or her own way of being is integral to Hu Shih's political philosophy.

In "The Conflict of Ideologies," Hu Shih argued that another fundamental conflict between authoritarianism and liberal democracy is the difference between "uniformity" and "diversity." "The democratic way of life," he said, "is essentially individualistic,"[13] while "the desire for uniformity leads to suppression of individual initiative, to the dwarfing of personality and creative effort, to intolerance, oppression, and slavery, and, worst of all, to intellectual dishonesty and moral hypocrisy."[14]

In 1955, Hu Shih wrote "The Power of the Antiauthoritarian Movement of the Chinese Renaissance over the Past Forty Years: The Historical Implications of the CCP's Purge of Hu Shih's Thought." In this essay, Hu Shih highlights what he believes to be the true spirit of democracy, which lies in regulating the relations between an individual and society. Particularly, he emphasizes the importance of mutual respect and mutual tolerance in a

---

9. Hu Shih, "Congdao nuyi zhilu shuoqi" 從到奴役之路說起 (On the road to serfdom), *Free China Journal* 10, no. 6 (March 16, 1954): 5.
10. Hu Shih, "On the Road to Serfdom," 5.
11. Hu Shih, "Bu xiu" 不朽 (On immortality), *HSW*, 1:693–702.
12. Hu Shih, "Yi bushing zhuyi" 易卜生主義 (On Ibsenism), *HSW*, 1:629–647.
13. Hu Shih, "The Conflict of Ideologies," 34.
14. Hu Shih, "The Conflict of Ideologies," 34.

democratic society: "The way the democratic institution works as a way of life seems to be that the minority obeys the majority. In fact, the most important aspect of democracy is that the majority does not deny or disrespect the minority, and certainly does not oppress and destroy the minority."[15]

Throughout his life, Hu Shih engaged in debates on whether representative democracy could be implemented in China. While he generally endorsed the idea of democracy and fought for the realization of a democratic China, he constantly urged people to remain skeptical of any ideological statement that lacks scientific evidence. He wrote: "All ideologies and all theories deserve to be studied. Yet they cannot be regarded as unchallengeable guidelines but merely as hypothetical presuppositions, not as unalterable religious doctrines but merely as reference materials, and not as absolute truth that prevents us from thinking critically, but merely as tools that we may use to stimulate our thoughts."[16] Therefore, in his debates with leftist scholars during the 1920s and 1930s, he attacked not Marxist and socialist theories per se, but the blind obedience of Chinese socialists. He wrote in an article published in 1931, "I am very dissatisfied with today's literary and intellectual developments. There are indeed fewer people who are enslaved by [the doctrines of] Confucius and Zhu Xi, but there has emerged a new group of people enslaved [by the thoughts of] Marx and Kropotkin. The age-old classicism has been overthrown. But it is now replaced by various kinds of superficial neoclassicism."[17] In another article written in the same year, Hu Shih again expressed his disagreement with the uncritical reception of Marxist theories among Chinese leftists. He wrote, "It is indeed not wise to be controlled by Confucius and Zhu Xi. Yet it is also nothing valorous to be controlled by Marx, Lenin and Stalin."[18] From these two articles we can see that what Hu Shih criticized was not the theories of Marxist-Leninism per se, but the uncritical attitudes of their followers. After Hu Shih became the target of the Chinese Communist Party later in life, he said that it might be because

---

15. Hu Shih, "Sishi nianlai zhongguo wenyi fuxing yundong liuxia de kangbao xiaodu liliang—zhongguo gongchan dang xiaosuan hushi sixiang de lishi yiyi" 四十年來中國文藝復興運動留下的抗暴消毒力量—中國共產黨消算胡適思想的歷史意義 (The power of the antiauthoritarian movement of the Chinese renaissance over the past forty years: The historical implications of the CCP's purge of Hu Shih's thought), in *Hu Shih shougao* 胡適手稿 (Hu Shih manuscript) (Taipei: Hu Shih jinianguan, 1970), 9:548.

16. Hu Shih, "Sanlun wenti yu zhuyi" 三論問題與主義 (The third discussion on problems and -isms), *HSW*, 1:373.

17. Hu Shih, "Wode qilu" 我的歧路 (My crossroads), *HSW*, 2:333.

18. Hu Shih, "Jieshou wo ziji de sixiang" 介紹我自己的思想 (Introducing my own thoughts), *HSW*, 4:624.

his advocacy of intellectual skepticism and distrust of any political authority made him the enemy of the communist regime.[19]

Hu Shih never really accepted Marxist theories. He refused to accept the idea that the mode of production constitutes the most important factor in shaping historical development. Such an assertation is at best a "bold assumption" that has yet to be subjected to "careful scrutiny." Hu Shih's interpretation of historical development places more emphasis on the principles of contingency. He argued that history does not have a singular, final cause—an idea that he had begun developing in his early years, especially when he was reading Fan Zhen's "Shen mie lun" (On the annihilation of the soul) in Sima Guang's (1019–1086) *Zizhi tongjian*.[20] In "Shen mie lun," Fan Zhen maintains that the body and the soul are two sides of the same coin, and thus when the body is annihilated, so is the soul. This idea had a lifelong influence on Hu Shih's intellectual development, as it led him to become a scholar who would not accept any interpretation of history that implied a definite and teleological purpose.[21]

In his engagement with American economist Charles A. Beard (1874–1948), whose works were often considered the embodiment of Marxist theories, Hu Shih maintained that the making of history is by nature coincidental and is not regulated and determined by any single historical factor. In his diary entry dated January 25, 1927, Hu wrote:

> Many historical events were formed contingently. A personal hobby, a one-time mistake, or an unexpected coincidence is enough to initiate a change that may lead to a new historical phase. Such a transition may be hardly noticed at the beginning. But when you reflect on this process after a period of time, you wonder if you are looking at a different world.[22]

Hu Shih's critical response to Beard's economic theory is understandable since Beard was known for his *An Economic Interpretation of the Constitution of*

---

19. Hu Shih, "Tongqing lunxian tiemu de zhishi fenzi—dui dalu wenhua jiaoyu jie renshi guangbo" 同情淪陷鐵幕的知識分子—對大陸文化教育界人士廣播, *Collected Works of Hu Shih*, 26:209–210.

20. Sima Guang et al., *Zizhi tongjian* (Beijing: Zhonghua, 1956), 136, 9:4259. Also see Hu Shih's *Sishi zishu* 四十自述 (An autobiography at forty) (Taipei: Yuandong, 1982), 42–43.

21. Sima Guang et al., *Zizhi tongjian*, 136, 9:4259.

22. Hu Shih, *Hu Shih de riji shougao ben* 胡適的日記手稿本 (Handwritten manuscript of Hu Shih's diaries) (Taipei: Yuanliu, 1990), 6: no page numbers.

the United States, which explains historical phenomena from a materialistic perspective, a view that many Marxist scholars constantly emphasized.[23] From this perspective, we can say that Hu Shih's criticism of Beard is actually a response to the Marxist historical materialism.

In his introduction to Zhao Jiabi's (1908–1997) *Compendium of Chinese New Literature*, which was published in 1935 and the earliest collection of modern Chinese literary works, Hu Shih criticized the monistic view on the development of history:

> People who study history should seek pluralistic and individual factors from biographical materials. They should not take a lazy shortcut and hope to explain all historical events by a "final cause," whether this "final cause" is "God," "spirit," "mind," or a "mode of production," that may provide some kind of explanation of history as a whole. Yet it is precisely because each of these "final causes" can only explain history as a whole, it cannot explain any particular history at all! . . . Thus, the idea of a "final cause" that can explain all histories is particularly useless in the eyes of historians, since such an idea cannot explain any concrete and specific historical fact.[24]

In the 1920s, Marx's dialectical materialism was considered by many Chinese intellectuals the only scientific explanation of the development of human history. This rather uncritical acceptance of Marxist theories planted the seeds for the later rise of communism in China. Yet Hu Shih did not believe in dialectical materialism and rejected the idea that human history will be "completed" once the proletariat become the ruling class of the world. On the one hand, Hu Shih's philosophical training in the United States as a pragmatist prevented him from naively believing in any magical and immediate solution to social problems. On the other hand, his emphasis on taking a scientific approach in conducting all forms of research also led him to argue that "statements should always be supported by evidence." In other words, Hu Shih's philosophical training prevented him from making a premature judgment on any subject or ideological trend.

Despite his general disagreement with the leftist scholars, he had once

---

23. Charles A. Beard, *An Economic Interpretation of the Constitution of the United States* (New York: Macmillan, 1939); Max Lerner, "Charles Beard's Political Theory," in Howard K. Beale, ed., *Charles A. Beard: An Appraisal* (Lexington: University of Kentucky Press, 1954), 25–45.

24. Hu Shih, "Introduction," in Zhao Jiabi, ed., *Zhongguo xin wenyi daxi: Wenxue lunzhan yiji* 中國新文藝大系 (Compendium of China's new literature) (Shanghai: liangyou, 1935), 1:17.

endorsed the idea of socialism when he was young. In his 1926 article, "Our Attitude toward Modern Western Civilization," he wrote: "The new religious tenets of the eighteenth century were freedom, equality, and love. After the nineteenth century, the new religious tenet is socialism. It is the spiritual civilization of the modern West, a spiritual civilization that has never been seen by the oriental nations."[25] When Hu Shih was still studying in the United States, he endorsed the 1917 Russian Revolution and believed that "the future of a new Russia" has "infinite possibilities." At that time, he even wrote a few poetic lines to celebrate the success of the Russian Revolution: "Clapping and singing, long live the new Russia."[26]

Later in life, in a speech delivered at an event in 1954 hosted by the *Free China Journal*, Hu Shih expressed his regret that he had once endorsed socialism when he was young. He said he wanted to make an "open confession"[27] for having romanticized socialism as a future trend in human civilization. This "confession" marks his last comment on socialism.

To sum up, Hu Shih's moderate approach toward a social and political reform emphasizes plurality and tolerance, individualism and skepticism. It encourages a skeptical attitude toward any political authority, and highlights a pluralistic understanding of history. These ideas and perspectives are integral to his cultural-political agenda, thereby shaping the underlying logic of his political writings.

HU SHIH'S MISJUDGMENT OF THE COMMUNIST PARTY

In a diary entry dated May 18, 1928, Hu Shih recorded his conversation with Wu Zhihui (1865–1953), a Chinese scholar who endorsed anarchism. Wu worried that "when the Communist Party has its way, mayhem will inevitably befall in China." Hu Shih, at that time, disagreed with Wu.[28] Yet twenty-five years later, when Hu Shih recalled this conversation after Wu's death, he admitted that Wu was right, and was impressed by Wu's prophetic observation.[29]

In fact, during China's war with Japan in the 1930s and 1940s, there was

---

25. Hu Shih, "Women duiyu jindai xiyang wenming de taidu" 我們對於近代西洋文明的態度 (Our attitude toward Western civilization), *HSW*, 3:10.

26. Hu Shih, *Hu Shih liuxue riji* (Taipei: Commercial Press, 1963), 4:133.

27. Hu Shih, "On the Road to Serfdom," 4–5.

28. Hu Shih, *Handwritten Manuscript*, 7: no page numbers.

29. Hu Shih, "Zhuinian wu zhihui xiansheng" 追念吳稚暉先生 (In memory of Mr. Wu Zhihui), *Free China Journal* 10, no. 1 (1954): 6.

a time in which Hu Shih had hoped that Mao Zedong would renounce the use of military force and choose to work with the Nationalist Party (Kuomintang), to establish a two-party system in China. On August 24, 1945, Hu Shih sent a Chinese-language telegram from New York to Mao Zedong, who was then in Chongqing. He urged Mao to work with the leaders of the Kuomintang in order to build a better future of China:

> Mr. Runzhi [Mao's style name]: I have recently learned from Fu Sinian in the newspapers that you conveyed your regards to me. Your kind words have reminded me of our friendship in the old days, which I still cherish dearly. On the evening of the twenty-second of this month, I had a long talk with Dong Biwu, to whom I humbly suggested that the leaders of the Chinese Communist Party should reassess the current world situation for the benefit of China's future, that it should leave behind past quarrels and aim to establish itself as a second political party in China that does not rely on military force. If the Communist leaders are determined to pursue this cause, the civil war that has lasted for the past eighteen years will end immediately, and the efforts they put in the past twenty years will not be in vain. When the United States of America was first established, Thomas Jefferson worked through peaceful means for over a decade before the Democratic-Republican Party won the fourth presidential election. The Labour Party in the United Kingdom, as another example, only received forty-four thousand votes in the election fifty years ago. But after fifty years of peaceful efforts, they won twelve million votes in this year's election and became the political party that has the majority of the votes. If our Communist leaders can work toward the peaceful development of China with patience and perseverance, an infinitely bright future will lie ahead of you. Let not your intolerance of minor differences lead to a disaster![30]

Hu Shih's political naivete and "incurable optimism"[31] were evident in this telegram. In 1954, when he wrote the introduction to John Leighton Stuart's memoirs, *Fifty Years in China*, he criticized Stuart's and the US Army general George Marshall's (1880–1959) failed mission to China, which attempted to

---

30. Hu Songping 胡頌平, ed., *Hu Shizhi xiansheng nianpu changbian chugao* 胡適之先生年譜長編初稿 (First draft of an extended chronological biography of Hu Shih) (Taipei: Linking, 1984), 1894–1895.

31. Hu Shih was hailed as an "incurable optimist" by his close friend Elmer Eugene Barker.

negotiate between the communists and the Nationalists. He described Stuart's and Marshall's plan for KMT-CCP peace talks as a pipe dream. "The Marshall Mission," he maintained, "failed because of its inherently impossible objectives." While criticizing the unrealistic goals of the mission, Hu Shih confessed that he too was too naive in hoping for cooperation between the communist and the Nationalist leaders:

> In fact I, too, was just as naive a tyro in national and international politics in those days of expansive idealism. So naive, indeed, was I that shortly after V-J Day I sent a lengthy radiogram to Chungking to be forwarded to my former student Mao Tse-tung, solemnly and earnestly pleading with him that, now that Japan had surrendered, there was no more justification for the Chinese Communists to continue to maintain a huge private army. . . . Of course, to this day I have never received a reply.[32]

In fact, it was not until 1947 that Hu Shih started to realize that the communist regime would pose a threat to the democratic world. In an article titled "Two Fundamentally Different Political Parties," he considered the Communist Party of Russia, the Fascist Party of Italy, and the National Socialist Party of Germany as the same type of political party, since they were all by nature a top-down hierarchical organization whose members had little freedom, and they had to rely on secret service agencies to monitor people's speeches, ideas, and actions. Such political parties seek to obtain their political interests at all costs and would "never recognize any opposition, or allow for its existence. All opposition forces are considered reactionary that need to be completely annihilated." While Hu Shih did not refer to the Chinese Communist Party explicitly in this article, two years after its publication, Mao's revolutionary army had swept over China and imposed authoritarian rule on the entire country.[33] Perhaps when Hu Shih was writing this article, he had already anticipated the inevitable success of communism in China.

On August 1, 1947, twelve days after the publication of "Two Fundamentally Different Political Parties," Hu Shih delivered a speech titled "The Cur-

---

32. Hu Shih, "Introduction" to John Leighton Stuart's *Fifty Years in China* (New York: Random House, 1954), xix. Chapter 23 in this volume.

33. Hu Shih, *Liangzong genben butong de zhengdang* 兩種根本不同的政黨 (Two fundamentally different political parties) and *We Must Choose Our Direction* (Hong Kong: Free China Press, 1950), 3.

rent Trend of the World's Culture" from Peking's Central Radio Station, in which he said:

> From a historical perspective, the trend of the world's cultures is developing toward the realization of freedom and democracy. This is an important goal and obvious direction of the world trend over the past three hundred years. In my opinion, the recent movement of antifreedom and antidemocratic collectivism and authoritarianism over the past thirty years is just an insignificant setback and temporary regression. We don't need to overlook this three-hundred-year democratic movement just because of a temporary thirty-year regression.[34]

When Hu Shih delivered this speech in 1947, he had probably sensed the looming presence of an antifreedom and antidemocratic force that was about to take over China. What he could do at the time was try to convince his country fellows retain faith in the values of freedom and democracy. It probably never occurred to Hu Shih that this "temporary regression" would grow into a tidal wave that would engulf all of China in two years.

Twenty-three days after the publication of "The Current Trend of the World's Culture," Hu wrote another article, "We Must Choose Our Direction," in which he argued:

> We Chinese must recognize the trend of the world cultures nowadays. We must choose for ourselves which direction we need to take. Only freedom can liberate our national spirit. Only a democratic government can unite the power of all people to solve a nation's problem. Only freedom and democracy can cultivate a humane and civilized society.[35]

On March 21, 1948, Hu Shih wrote a long letter to Zhou Gengsheng (1889–1971), a Chinese scholar of international law, in which he expressed his disillusionment with the Soviet Union: "The postwar Soviet Union is a frightening aggressive force . . . possibly more terrifying than Germany and Japan." After Stalin managed to secure Soviet interests in northeast China without the agreement of the government of the Republic of China at the

---

34. Hu Shih, "Yanqian shijie wenhua de qvxiang" 眼前世界文化的趨向 (The current trend of the world's culture), in *We Must Choose Our Direction*, 11.

35. *We Must Choose Our Direction*, 17.

Yalta Conference in 1945, "I was forced to recognize a lot of terrifying truths, and had to abandon my fantasy of a new Russia that I had some twenty years ago."[36]

From these examples, we can see that during 1947–1948, Hu Shih became more and more anxious about the expansion of communism on the world scale. It is interesting to see that while Hu Shih sought to reveal the aggressive and totalitarian nature of communism, his criticism was mainly directed at the international Communist Party and the Communist Party of Russia. In this period, he did not really criticize or mention the Chinese Communist Party in his works. This is not to say that Hu Shih was unaware of the political schemes of the CCP. It is just that he chose to maintain a neutral position in the political struggles between the CCP and the KMT. As a liberal scholar who hoped for the establishment of a two-party system in China, Hu Shih still had hope for both the communists and the Nationalists. At least this is the case before 1949.

ANTI-COMMUNISM IN CLASSICAL CHINESE PHILOSOPHY

Anti-communism is a main theme in Hu Shih's later political writings. It is also his new mission. In an unfinished, handwritten manuscript dated around 1955, Hu Shih changed the title of the essay from "Hu Shih Should Be Purged" to "I Fundamentally Reject Communism."[37] While this is only an unfinished article, the change of title merits our attention. It is obvious that in the 1950s, Hu Shih had come to realize that his political philosophy was

---

36. Hu Shih, "Guoji xingshi lide liangge wenti—gei zhou gengsheng xiansheng de yifeng xin" 國際形勢裡的兩個問題—給周鯁生先生的一封信 (Two questions about the international situation—a letter to Mr. Zhou Gengsheng), in *We Must Choose Our Direction*, 19–23.

37. In this short and unfinished manuscript, which is currently preserved in the Hu Shih Memorial Hall of Academia Sinica in Taiwan, Hu Shih wrote:

Since last November, the CCP's newspapers in mainland China have published many articles criticizing Hu Shih's thoughts. Many of them were written by my old friends and students. I have argued a long time ago that under the rule of the Communist Party, there is no freedom of speech and no freedom of silence. Therefore, when I read these articles written by my old friends who were forced to condemn and criticize me, I do not bear any grudge against them. I read their words with sympathy and understanding.

fundamentally anti-communist. Not only did he not shy away from expressing his position, but he wrote a series of essays criticizing the communist
regime in China.

In 1955, when the CCP's smear campaign against Hu Shih was at its peak,
he wrote in a long article titled "The Power of the Antiauthoritarian Movement of the Chinese Renaissance over the Past Forty Years: The Historical
Implications of the CCP's Purge of Hu Shih Thought." In it he asserted that
"over the past thirty years, I have never published anything that criticizes
Marxism." And yet he was still labeled by the communist propagandists as
"the mortal enemy of Marxism," "the primary and most cunning enemy of
the Marxism front alliance," and an enemy who "plotted to fundamentally
destroy the foundation of Marxism." Zhou Yang, a communist literary theorist, called Hu Shih "the earliest, most persistent and most irreconcilable
enemy of Chinese Marxism and socialism."[38]

This militant language revealed the CCP's fear of Hu Shih's power in dis-
seminating the ideas and ideals of liberalism. It also demonstrates that Hu
Shih was a true public intellectual in China whose works had, and will likely
continue to have, a profound impact on the Chinese people.

One can thus say that Hu Shih's "anti-communist" writings made a special contribution to the intellectual development of modern China, since it
is in these writings that Hu Shih articulated the modern, universal values of
free speech and intellectual freedom in traditional Chinese philosophy. Specifically, there are two philosophical traditions in ancient China that he
made references to in his political writings: Lao-tzu's naturalistic philosophy
and Confucius's rational humanism. These two intellectual traditions
formed the basis of Chinese culture for thousands of years, and they are by
nature antitotalitarian and antiviolence. Any form of violence, religious
fanaticism, and dictatorship therefore could not easily win the hearts of the
Chinese intellectuals. For Hu Shih, Confucian rational humanism and Dao-
ist naturalist tradition had been the greatest obstacles to the spread of Buddhism and Christianity in China, and they would surely be a formidable
force that resisted the control of the Communist Party.

In the 1950s, Hu Shih wrote an article in English titled "Communism,
Democracy, and Culture Pattern." A main question that he discussed in this
article is this: Is there any component in Chinese culture that cannot be
destroyed by the authoritarian rule of a communist regime and might even-

---

38. Hu Shih, "Power of the Antiauthoritarian Movement," 9:493–495.

tually become a force that could overthrow the regime's tyranny? As a scholar who was well versed in traditional Chinese culture and literature, Hu Shih was convinced that there were at least three components in China's cultural tradition that might enable a long-term and effective resistance against any totalitarian rule:

1. An almost anarchistic aversion for all government interference.
2. A long tradition of love for freedom and fight for freedom—especially for intellectual freedom and religious freedom, but also for the freedom of political criticism.
3. A traditional exaltation of the individual's right to doubt and question things—even the most sacred things.[39]

The implication of individual freedom in Lao-tzu's philosophy and the tradition of "noninterference" in the Han dynasty's governmental policy was obviously referenced to in Hu Shih's elaboration of China's intellectual tradition of antiauthoritarianism. For him, this tradition is completely opposite to the authoritarianism of the CCP, which in the 1950s had penetrated almost every household in rural China, seeking to control the lives of the people, from what to eat to what to speak, with the ultimate aim being to dictate their minds and behaviors. Hu Shih thus wrote: "I cannot believe this inveterate individualistic and anarchistic mentality inculcated by conscious philosophy and especially by twenty centuries of unconscious living could be liquidated by a few months or even a few years of all-pervading totalitarian rule."[40]

To further illustrate the Chinese cultural tradition of love of freedom, Hu Shih quoted a famous saying of Confucius: "The scholar must be stout-hearted and courageous, for his burden is heavy and his journey is long. Humanity is the burden he imposes upon his own shoulders: is that not a heavy burden? And only death ends his toils: is that not a long journey?" He also cited Mencius's words—"the individual [should be] shouldering the grave burden of the world"—to demonstrate the Chinese literati's time-honored tradition in developing a sense of duty in intervening in political reality for nearly two thousand years. Hu Shih argued that the ethical-political responsibility that can be demonstrated through the saying "The

---

39. Hu Shih, "Communism, Democracy and Culture Pattern." Unpublished manuscript. Chapter 17 in this volume.
40. Hu Shih, "Communism, Democracy, and Culture Pattern."

rise and fall of the nation is the concern of every citizen" makes Chinese intellectuals unable to accept any rule of tyranny that deviated from morality and reason.

In this article, Hu Shih also mentioned examples of courageous officials in different dynasties who had risked their lives by speaking up for truth and justice instead of for personal gain and interest. Hu Shih thus considered this time-honored tradition a sustaining historical force that would ultimately prevail in all stages of political struggles in the history of China.[41]

From today's perspective, Hu Shih's description of the power of China's liberal intellectual tradition may seem overoptimistic. One may also say that he underestimated the Communist Party's ability, in using modern technology, to control the behaviors and the thoughts of the people. Take the Anti-Rightist Movement in 1957 and the Cultural Revolution during 1966–1977, for example, during which hundreds and thousands of Chinese intellectuals were imprisoned and persecuted. We saw little evidence in these periods that the liberal tradition of Chinese culture played any positive role in resisting the rule of the Communist regime.

While we can question Hu Shih's political optimism, we need to understand that it derived from his perspective as a historian and philosopher. As a perceptive historian, Hu Shih was able to observe and identify the pattern of historical development, elaborating how different social, cultural, and historical factors were at work in shaping the course of human history, thereby envisioning the future. As a visionary philosopher, what Hu Shih sought to achieve was not simply to reflect on a few separate historical incidents, but outline the overall, grand trend of human civilization, in which Chinese culture must take part. What Hu Shih criticizes thus is not a single totalitarian regime, but all forms of social and political oppression that limit a modern individual's right to freedom and self-expression. From this perspective, the seventy years of the authoritarian rule of the Chinese Communist Party is a blink of an eye in comparison to the three thousand years of Chinese history and civilization. Hu Shih tried to convince his readers that we should not dismiss too quickly the continual influence of traditional Chinese philosophy on contemporary Chinese people.

Hu Shih also often discusses the Chinese traditions of freedom, democracy and science in his English writings. In 1941, when China was fighting against Japan's military aggression, Hu Shih published "Historical Founda-

41. Hu Shih, "Communism, Democracy, and Culture Pattern."

tions for a Democratic China," in which he argued that the concept of democracy was not entirely new to the Chinese because there were a few historical factors in the development of Chinese culture that enabled China to become the first country in Asia to abolish monarchy:

> These historical factors have been at work for tens of centuries and have given to the Chinese people the tradition and the preparation for the development of modern democratic institutions.
>
> Of these historical foundations I shall mention only three: first, a thoroughly democratized social structure; secondly, 2,000 years of an objective and competitive system of examinations for civil service; and thirdly, the historic institution of the government creating its own "opposition" and censorial control.[42]

The question whether these factors really constituted the democratic foundations of China can be subject to further discussions and debates. But we should at least appreciate Hu Shih's efforts to articulate and elaborate the "Chinese roots" of the modern concept of democracy, thereby explaining from the historical and cultural perspective why dictatorship and violent rule are not suitable for the Chinese.

In 1954, Hu Shih presented a paper titled "The Right to Doubt in Ancient Chinese Thought" at the Sixth Annual Conference of the Far Eastern Association. In this paper he highlighted Confucius's humanist skepticism by drawing attention to Confucius's famous saying "While you are not able to serve men, how can you serve their spirits?" Elsewhere in the paper Hu Shih discusses the Han dynasty philosopher Wang Chong's (27–100) concept of "hating the false," which advocated a scientific spirit in seeking the truth. Hu regarded these examples as the early manifestation of the idea of science in China. By contrast, he described the post-1949 authoritarian rule of the Communist Party as a "temporary barbarization brought by military conquest." As he wrote at the end of this paper: "It will be this Chinese spirit of doubt—this Chinese intellectual birthright to doubt and criticize—that may yet ultimately save China from her present state of temporary barbarization."[43]

---

42. Hu Shih, "Historical Foundations for a Democratic China," in *Edmund J. James Lectures on Government: Second Series* (Urbana: University of Illinois Press, 1941), 1–12. Chapter 5 in this volume.

43. Hu Shih, "The Right to Doubt in Ancient Chinese Thought," *Philosophy East and West* 12, no. 4 (January 1963): 295–299.

In this paper, Hu Shih again saw the humanist and naturalist intellectual traditions, separately espoused by Confucius and Lao-tzu, as the most effective
cultural forces in Chinese history that might resist any form of political
oppression.

In 1960, two years before he passed away, Hu Shih wrote another important English essay, "The Chinese Tradition and the Future," in which he
wrote:

> I am inclined to believe that what I had glorified as "the humanistic and
> rationalistic China" still survives on the Chinese mainland, and that the
> same spirit of courageous doubt and independent thinking and questioning
> which played important roles in the Chinese revolt against the great medi-
> eval religions and in their final overthrow may yet live long and spread even
> under the most impossible conditions of totalitarian control and suppres-
> sion. In short, I believe the tradition of "the humanistic and rationalistic
> China" has not been destroyed and in all probability cannot be destroyed.[44]

Hu Shih's philosophical approach in his political writings can be inter-
preted as an expression of cultural nationalism. The idea of nationalism is
often discussed in terms of its political nature rather than its cultural implications. Yet the foundation of nationalism lies in the formation of a cultural
identity and awareness. It is perhaps for this reason that Hu Shih would criticize the Communist Party as an "'un-Chinese' dictatorship."[45] The expression of "un-Chinese" is interesting because it means that Hu Shih did not
recognize the Chinese Communist Party and its totalitarian rule in China
after 1949 as having any Chinese characteristics. On the contrary, the May
Fourth intellectuals' advocacy of science and democracy, if viewed from Hu
Shih's historical perspective, is more firmly and deeply rooted in the Chinese
cultural tradition.

Although Hu Shih, like many other May Fourth intellectuals in the New
Culture Movement, had once forcefully criticized the Chinese cultural tradition, he remained an enthusiastic and dedicated researcher on traditional
Chinese culture, from which he drew resources to counter the Chinese communists' propaganda. In his writings, particularly his political discussions,

---

44. Hu Shih, "The Chinese Tradition and the Future," in *Sino-American Conference
on Intellectual Cooperation: Reports and Proceedings* (Seattle: University of Washington,
Department of Publications and Printing, 1962), 22. Chapter 34 in this volume.
45. Hu Shih, "Communism, Democracy and Culture Pattern."

Hu Shih time and again expressed his respect for and faith in traditional Chinese culture in regulating and refining Chinese society and Chinese civilization. From this perspective, the study of Hu Shih cannot be separated from the study of "China." If we ignore the question of "China" in our inquiry into Hu Shih, our understanding of him as one of the most prominent intellectuals in twentieth-century China will be severely limited. Whether we choose to recognize or criticize him, our evaluation of Hu Shih and his works will be more accurate if we put him in the broader context of twentieth-century China, which is characterized by drastic political changes both domestically and internationally. While Hu Shih does not fit into the typical image of a nationalist, his role in and contribution to the formation of a modern China and his advocacy of freedom and democracy in the Chinese context are far more important than the works of any "typical" nationalist.

In short, one of the key messages that Hu Shih wanted to repeatedly convey in his political writings is that the Chinese philosophical traditions of naturalism and humanism are essentially antiauthoritarian and antiviolence. From this view, the authoritarian rule of the Communist Party in post-1949 China is by nature incompatible with the nation's intellectual tradition. The ultimate solution to this political anomaly is therefore inherent in the Chinese cultural tradition itself.

HU SHIH'S CRITICISM OF THE COMMUNIST PARTY

In addition to pointing out that authoritarianism is incompatible with the Chinese intellectual tradition, Hu Shih also explained why Marxist-Leninism appealed to many Chinese intellectuals. After 1949, Hu Shih was disillusioned with the Communist regime. He knew that once the CCP assumed power, there would be little freedom in China. In an English-language speech delivered in November 1950, "The Free World Needs a Free China," Hu Shih argued that after 1949, it was not just the Chinese people who lost their freedom. The Chinese Communist Party itself had also lost its freedom:

> But it is not the Chinese people alone who are not free. It is more important for the free world to understand that the Chinese communist regime itself is not free. Mao Tse-tung, the Chinese Communist Party, and the entire Chinese communist government are not free: they are all under the bondage

which the USSR imposes on her satellite countries. They have always taken orders from the Kremlin, and they must continue to take such orders because they are fully conscious that Communist China has been and will long continue to be dependent on the military and industrial power of the Soviet Union.[46]

In this speech, Hu Shih provided a new explanation of the idea of "free China." He argued that the term "free China" does not simply refer to Taiwan, but also to all those who suffer from the oppression of the communist regime. It is thus a "peace-loving and freedom-loving force" that firmly stands in alliance with the democracies in the whole world. Hu Shih thus defines the term in the following way: "By 'Free China,' I mean the vast majority of the Chinese people who are mentally and emotionally anti-Communist even though they are physically living and suffering under the iron yoke and behind the Iron Curtain."[47] At the end of the speech, he resolutely argued:

> Free China exists as a reality because, of all the peoples conquered by world communism so far, my people are the most civilized and have lived under a civilization noted for its individualism and its centuries-long fights for intellectual, religious and political freedom. My people cannot long remain captive.
>
> This is no wishful thinking on the part of a Chinese philosopher who has been called the incurable optimist of China. No, this conclusion is the studied, sober judgment of a lifelong student of Chinese thought and history. If history and civilization mean anything at all, there shall always be a free China.[48]

The idea of "free China" that Hu Shih describes in this speech is not a political entity, but a historical force that had developed over centuries and had cultivated among the Chinese a willingness to fight for freedom. The development of human history tells us that no tyranny can suppress the will of the people and exist forever. Hu Shih was adamant about this fundamental rule of history.

---

46. Hu Shih, "The Free World Needs a Free China." Unpublished manuscript. Chapter 10 in this volume.

47. Hu Shih, "Free World Needs a Free China."

48. Hu Shih, "Free World Needs a Free China."

After the 1949 revolution, many overseas Chinese were enamored with Mao's famous statement, "The Chinese people have stood up." Many returned to China to build what they imagined to be a new and promising socialist China. Nevertheless, many of these Chinese intellectuals who returned to China ended up being purged and persecuted in the power struggle within the communist regime in the years to follow. These intellectuals' nationalist sentiment was admirable. Yet their romanticization of the Chinese Communist Party was deplorable.

Such a romanticized and idealized understanding of the communist regime was not specific to Chinese intellectuals. It was shared by many American cultural elites during the 1940s and 1950s. One example is John King Fairbank (1907–1991), a leading sinologist who shaped the direction of postwar China studies in the United States. In his personal history *Chinabound: A Fifty-Year Memoir*, published in 1982, he described Yan'an, the communists' stronghold during the civil war, as a city that "glowed in the distance."[49] Fairbank's admiration for the Communist Party was similar to Edgar Snow's (1905–1972), whose famous *Red Star over China* is one of the earliest journalistic accounts of Chinese communism in the Western world.

Having visited China during World War II, Fairbank recorded his observations on the communist revolution: "The primary conviction that I took back to Washington in 1944 was that the revolutionary movement in China was inherent in the conditions of life there and that it could not be suppressed by the provocative coercion of the CC clique and Tai Li police. The ideals of liberation for the peasantry and of science and democracy inherited from the May Fourth era twenty years before were patriotic and kinetic."[50] What Fairbank failed to see is that after the Communist Party assumed power, it would quickly become a totalitarian regime that would exert even tighter control over the Chinese people.

In the face of the international community's optimistic attitude toward the rise of the Chinese Communist Party, Hu Shih felt compelled in 1947 to emphasize that it would culminate in a totalitarian dictatorship. In 1950, he again argued that 1949, when the People's Republic of China was estab-

---

49. John King Fairbank, *Chinabound: A Fifty-Year Memoir* (New York: Harper & Row, 1982), 266.

50. Fairbank, *Chinabound*, 286. Tai Li (or, in pinyin, Dai Li) was head of the KMT government's secret service. The CC Clique was a political fraction within the KMT. It was led the brothers Chen Guofu and Chen Lifu who were close advisers to Chiang Kai-shek.

lished, was not a year of liberation, but a year when the Chinese people lost their freedom and power to control their own fate.[51]

After 1949, many Chinese failed to "stand up" as Mao had once promised. Instead, many Chinese intellectuals were forced to kneel before the new political authority and were subjected to persecution. This page of modern Chinese history is still being denied by many PRC scholars. What's more, no scholars in mainland China ever mentioned the fact that Hu Shih had once called for the solidarity of China's intellectuals to support those who were persecuted by the Communist Party after it came to power.

On April 29, 1952, Hu Shih gave a talk at a meeting of the association Aid Refugee Chinese Intellectuals. In this speech, titled "The Suffering Chinese Intellectuals behind the Iron Curtain," he gave a passionate account of the ordeals that the Chinese intellectuals had undergone under the new regime. At the beginning of his speech, Hu Shih thanked the association's chairman, Dr. Walter Judd (1898–1994), and his colleagues for rescuing Chinese intellectuals who had fled from China. His words were strong and full of emotion:

> It is an undeniable fact—and an understatement—that in the long history of my people, there has never been a period in which the intellectuals are subjected to so great moral and spiritual torture as they are today in Communist China.
>
> Not even in the long centuries of the unified empire under the unlimited powers of the absolute monarchy, was there such universal and inescapable oppression of intellectuals as is daily and everywhere practiced in the Red-controlled mainland today.[52]

Later in the speech, Hu Shih argued that in the ancient times there was a much smaller army in China. There were no secret police or undercover agents who were constantly monitoring its people. People at that time at least enjoyed the freedom to remain silent, whereas in modern times they were forced to speak out loud for the interest of the Party. The communist regime encouraged parents and children, teachers and students to keep each

---

51. In early 1950, Hu Shih once tried to dissuade Chinese historian Wang Yuquan 王毓銓 from returning to China. See Hu Shih's diary entry of January 4, 1950, *Handwritten Manuscript*, 16: no page numbers.

52. Hu Shih, "The Suffering Chinese Intellectuals behind the Iron Curtain." Chapter 19 in this volume.

other under surveillance, inviting them to report to the Party anyone's "misconduct." Under such a tightly controlled society, there was no personal freedom or dignity.

In this talk, Hu Shih also told the story of how his own son, Hu Sidu (1921–1957), was forced to condemn his father as an "enemy of the people" in the press.[53] This lack of "freedom to remain silent" was one of the most inhuman situations under the totalitarian rule of the communist regime. Only two and a half years after the establishment of the PRC, many Chinese intellectuals were already forced to become a "slogan-mouthing automation,"[54] a human machine of propaganda.

The idea of the freedom to remain silent that Hu Shih proposed is perhaps more important than the freedom of speech. The freedom to remain silent allows a person to remain neutral on certain issues, but without such a right, one has no choice but to tell lies. At the time, the American understanding of the Chinese communist regime was limited and meager. Perhaps this is why Hu Shih produced so many English-language articles and delivered numerous talks in the 1950s to expose the Communist Party's nature and its persecution of the Chinese people. In this sense, Hu Shih's English articles bore witness to this dark period of Chinese history.

In his diary entry written on September 24, 1950, Hu Shih enclosed an English-language newspaper article describing his son's public condemnation of him. The author of the article showed sympathy for Hu Shih, criticizing the Communist Party's unscrupulous and inhumane practices. In the margin of the newspaper clipping, Hu Shih wrote: "My son, Sidu, who stayed in Peking, suddenly became a news figure yesterday! This means that the Communist Party had read my long article and thus reacted to it."[55] If Hu Shih's judgment is correct, the long article that irritated the Party is his essay "China in Stalin's Grand Strategy," which he published in *Foreign Affairs* in October 1950.

---

53. In "Dui wo fuqin—Hu Shih de pipan" 對我父親—胡適的批判 (A criticism of my father—Hu Shih), published in *Dagongbao* on September 22, 1950, Hu Sidu wrote: "He [Hu Shih] is a servant to the reactionary class, an enemy of the people" (他是反動階級的忠臣, 人民的敵人). This article drew the attention of many critics outside China. *Time* magazine conducted an interview with Hu Shih in New York about his son's statements. That interview was later published under the title "Danger Zones: No Freedom of Silence" in *Time* on October 2, 1950. See Hu Shih's diary entry of September 23, 24, 26, 1950, *Handwritten Manuscript*, 16: no page numbers.

54. This is a press release issued by Aid Refugee Chinese Intellectuals, Inc. See manuscript 4–2 6, America I.

55. Hu Shih, *Handwritten Manuscript*, 16: no page numbers.

The main argument of this article is that the success of the Communist Party was not achieved by policies that allegedly won the approval of the Chinese people. Rather, it was made possible through the rapid expansion of military power, which was enabled and aided by the Soviet Union and the international communist movement during 1937–1945, when the Nationalist government was putting all its resources into resisting Japan's aggression. In addition, the Xi'an Incident and the secret treaty signed at the Yalta Conference also contributed to the defeat of the Kuomintang.[56] In a letter to Fu Sinian (1896–1950), dated September 6, 1950, Hu Shih maintained that his "intention was to let people know that the loss of China was not as Dean Acheson and others had described, that Chiang Kai-shek's army had fallen apart immediately after Mao came out of the cave. The defeat was achieved only after a long twenty-five years of bitter struggle."[57]

The culturalist approach that Hu Shih took in his political writings is similar to his strategy in the New Culture Movement. He highlighted the importance of reevaluating traditional Chinese culture and of refraining from making broad statements. In these political writings, Hu Shih explained not only why the totalitarian regime of the Communist Party should be criticized, but also why socialism had attracted so many Chinese intellectuals.

In another speech delivered in the 1950s—"China's Lesson for Freedom," he provided a detailed explanation of why Marxist-Leninism had appealed to Chinese intellectuals:

> (1) The idealistic appeal of a hitherto unrealized Utopia, (2) The emotional appeal of the power of a radical revolution to right all wrongs and redress all injustices, and (3) last, but not least, the magic power of big and undefined words.[58]

"Dictatorship of the proletariat," "people's democratic dictatorship," "people's republic," and "people's government" are among the terms Hu Shih identifies among this class of nouns.

In the speech Hu Shih lists three lessons China had learned from the struggles of the international communist movement in the past few decades:

---

56. Hu Shih, "China in Stalin's Grand Strategy," *Foreign Affairs* 29, no. 1 (October 1950): 11–40. Chapter 9 in this volume.

57. Hu Shih, "Hu Shih to Mr. and Ms. Fu" 胡適致傅斯年夫婦, in Geng Yunzhi 耿雲志 and Ouyang Zhesheng 歐陽哲生, eds., *Hu Shih shuxin ji* 胡適書信集 (Collected letters of Hu Shih) (Beijing: Beijing University Press, 1996), 3:1197.

58. Hu Shih, "China's Lesson for Freedom," unpublished manuscript. Chapter 32 in this volume.

1. That blind worship of an untried or unchallenged "end" or "ideal" without due consideration of the necessary means of achieving it inevitably leads to the immoral philosophy of the end justifying the means.

2. Impatience in social and political thinking invariably leads to theoretical or ideological justification of violence and violent revolution, which tends necessarily toward dictatorship, despotism, and destruction of freedom.

3. Do not belittle the magic power of big words, which are the most important stock-in-trade in the hands of modern tyrants and despots. The only antitoxin is a little measure of doubt, a few ounces of incredulity, and a little rigid, merited discipline to make ideas clear.

In the conclusion of this speech, Hu Shih painfully observes: "So millions and tens of millions have been murdered, and hundreds of millions have been enslaved and a 'living hell' has been created in my beloved China—all in the name of an unknown god—the blindly worshipped ideal of a utopia society!"[59]

On April 1, 1953, Hu Shih delivered a paper titled "The Three Stages of the Campaign for Thought Reform in Communist China" at the Fifth Annual Conference of the Far Eastern Association.[60] In this paper, he criticized the implementation of "thought reform" and "brainwashing." The so-called "confessions," "self-criticism" and "criticism and self-criticism," under a dictatorial rule, were all made under "force and intimidation," which destroyed human dignity and independent thinking. To illustrate the wide-ranging, deplorable scope of self-criticism, Hu Shih cited the cases of renowned professors from the Peking University and Tsinghua University such as Feng Youlan, Zhou Peiyuan, Jin Yuelin, and Liang Sicheng.

On December 7, 1952, at a reception hosted by the alumni of National Peking University, Hu Shih talked of the CCP's ongoing smear campaign against him. Yet, instead of reproaching his old friends and students who publicly condemned him, he responded to these criticisms with great tolerance and sympathetic understanding:

These friends of mine were forced to publicly reject and criticize Cai Yuanpei's and my thoughts under inhumane conditions. We should offer them

---

59. Hu Shih, "China's Lesson for Freedom."
60. Chapter 21 in this volume.

our deepest sympathy, knowing that they did not have the freedom to speak freely, nor did they have the freedom to remain silent. We need to understand that what they said did not come from their heart.[61]

Hu also pointed out that the CCP's purge of his works actually encouraged others to read them. Thus he commented, "They are actually doing me a favor by promoting my works, and this makes me happy."[62]

Hu Shih's tolerance of and sympathy for those who were forced to criticize him can also be found in other articles. For example, on January 9, 1950, he published an article titled "There Is Absolutely No Freedom under the Communist Rule."[63] The subtitle of this article is "A Postscript to the So-Called Open Letter from Chen Yuan to Hu Shih," which is a response to his former colleague's open denunciation of him after the Communist Party's takeover of China.

Chen Yuan's letter was written on April 29, 1949, and published in *People's Daily* on May 11 of the same year. In his letter, Chen Yuan eulogized how successful the Communist Party's thought reform was and how much he had benefited from it. In response, instead of simply accusing Chen of lacking the courage to stand up to the communist authorities, Hu Shih analyzed the grammar and the wording in the letter and concluded that it could not have been written by his friend.[64] Hu Shih knew that under a totalitarian regime, Chen Yuan did not have a chance to speak for himself. Therefore, Hu Shih reckoned that if he simply accused his friend of lacking the courage to stand up to the communist regime, he was ignoring the greater tragedy that the communist regime had brought to his friend.

Hu Shih wrote at the end of this article, "Three months after the Communist troops entered Peking, [Chen Yuan] had to declare that while his pre-

---

61. Hu Shih, "Beida tongxuehui huanyinghui shang jianghua" 北大同學會歡迎會上講話 (Talk at the Beida alumni reunion), *Hu Shhi yanlun ji* 胡適言論集 (Collected speeches of Hu Shih) (Hong Kong: Ziyou zhongguo, 1950), 2:61–62. Cai Yuanpei (1868-1940) is the president of Peking University and a leading scholar in China's new culture movement who played a key role in the history of modern Chinese education.

62. Hu Shih, "Talk at the Beida Alumni Reunion," 2:61–62.

63. Chen Zhichao 陳智超, ed., *Chen Yuan laiwang shuxin ji* 陳垣來往書信集 (The correspondence of Chen Yuan) (Shanghai: Guji, 1990), 191–195. Also see Hu Shih's reply to Chen Yuan, "Gongchandang tongzhi xiajue meiyou ziyou" 共產黨統治下絕沒有自由 (There is no freedom under the rule of the Communist Party), *Free China Journal* 2, no. 3 (1950): 57–61.

64. Chen Yuan, *Correspondence of Chen Yuan*, 191–195.

vious academic approach was scientific, it was fundamentally incorrect! He was forced to declare that he had begun to study dialectical materialism and historical materialism, which would be his academic approach in the future!" This example again demonstrates that "under the Communist rule, there is absolutely no academic freedom," a truth that Hu Shih had long ago revealed for us.[65]

CONCLUSION

Over the past forty years, there has been a revived interest in Hu Shih's works in Chinese intellectual communities. New editions of Hu Shih's works have been published every year, and new research about him had also been conducted. In many bookstores in Beijing, one can find a display section that features his works. This demonstrates that Hu Shih's works are still being read nowadays and have a great appeal to the general readers. He has not been forgotten in today's China and has instead made the successful comeback that has been long anticipated.

Many scholars have argued that Hu Shih criticized the Communist Party only to win the favor of the Nationalist government. This is a great misunderstanding and misinterpretation of his works. For Hu Shih, the survival of a nation is more important than the survival of a political party, and the concept of a nation also outlives any regime. The same scholar who was once denounced as a "running dog of imperialism" and the "sworn enemy of Marxism" has become a best-selling author, now widely considered one of the foremost scholars in the history of modern China. His uneven fate in modern Chinese history not only reveals the historical rise and fall of "Hu Shih studies," but also demonstrates, as Hu Shih himself repeatedly pointed out, that the deeply rooted humanist and liberal tradition in Chinese thought and culture since the pre-Qin era cannot be eliminated.

On January 14, 1953, Hu Shih spoke on a radio broadcast to mainland China. The interviewer, Zeng Xubai, asked him, "Will the Communist Party's efforts to eliminate your thoughts be successful?" Hu Shih replied: "I believe their efforts to eliminate my thoughts will ultimately fail. There is an ancient saying that goes, 'A wild fire cannot deplete the land; when the

---

65. Chen Yuan, Correspondence of Chen Yuan, 191–195.

spring winds blow, grass will sprout again.' The Communist Party simply cannot understand this common sense." More than seventy years have passed since the Party sought to eliminate any idea or practice that might jeopardize its ruling position. Yet the idea of a democratic China that Hu Shih has hoped for and fought for still persists in China. Perhaps the spring winds of the twenty-first century will germinate the seeds of freedom and democracy that Hu Shih planted in China in the twentieth century.

CHAPTER I

Do We Need or Want Dictatorship?[1]

On November 27 last President Wang Ching-Wei and General Chiang Kai-Shek issued a joint circular telegram to the nation, the concluding part of which read as follows:

> The state of affairs and the trend of events in China today do not point to any necessity and possibility for her to institute the kind of political systems now in vogue in Soviet Russia and Italy.

On the same day, in the course of an interview given to a representative of the *Osaka Mainichi*, General Chiang made a similar statement:—

> As China's position differs from that of Germany, Turkey, and Italy, so there is no need for a dictator.

In an atmosphere clouded by politicians and scholars publicly advocating dictatorship for China, these two statements deserve the careful attention of the whole nation.

That the actual state of affairs and general trend of events in China today, as explicitly stated in the Wang-Chiang manifesto, do not point to any necessity for, or possibility of, the institution of a dictatorship, is no doubt very unpleasant to the ears of those who speak so enthusiastically in favour

---

1. This article was originally published under the title of "Zhongguo wu ducai de biyao yu keneng" (中國無獨裁的必要與可能) in *Duli pinglun* 獨立評論 (Independent critic) in 1934. It was later translated into English and published in the *People's Tribune* in 1935. The translation was presumably done by Hu Shih himself, as the English article was published under his name. See *People's Tribune* 8 (February 16, 1935): 89–95. Also see *Duli pinglun* 130 (December 9, 1934): 2–6.

of having a dictator, but we must admit that the conclusions arrived at are quite correct.

First, let us take the point that there is, today, no necessity for China having a dictator.

Among the scholars who have recently advocated the contrary opinion Dr. Tsiang Ting-Fu (蔣廷黻) and Dr. Chien Tuan-Sen (錢端升) are outstanding. In an article contributed to *Eastern Miscellany* (東方雜誌) (Vol. 31, No. 1) entitled "Democracy or Totalitarianism?," Dr. Chien said:—

> I am of opinion that what China needs today is a powerful and ideal dictator. It is of imperative necessity that China become, within the shortest time possible, a powerful nation with great strength behind it. . . . In the course of ten or twenty years the coastal provinces must be made to undergo a high degree of industrialization, so that agriculture in the interior provinces can become mutually dependent with the industries along the coast. . . . In order to achieve this industrialization of the coastal provinces, it is absolutely necessary that the Government possess all the powers of a totalitarian State, and in order that the Government may enjoy possession of such powers, it is also necessary to have a dictatorship that commands the whole confidence of the people.

The end which Dr. Chien seeks—industrialization of the coastal provinces—is in itself questionable, because few of these provinces possess the essential requirements of an industrial district, such as coal and iron. Moreover, in view of the world situation today, a country which does not possess an adequate navy simply cannot protect its coast-line, and this is why people of foresight have urged the establishment of economic centres in the interior. Furthermore, the industrialization of China is by no means dependent on Government authority alone, for the essential conditions are most complex. However great may be its powers, the Government cannot, to speak metaphorically, produce congee without rice, make horses out of paper, nor create an army out of a handful of beans. Can the Government secure capital, technical experts, or raw materials merely by the possession of wide administrative powers? Let us dwell on the question of technical experts alone. The Five-Year Plan of Soviet Russia requires the participation of 1,500,000 technical experts. Manifestly, these cannot be well turned out merely by the establishment of a dictatorial totalitarianism. Therefore, if the need of a dictator is only for the purpose of industrializing the coastal provinces, we cannot agree that such a step is necessary.

The reason Dr. Tsiang advocates the establishment of a dictator is for the sake of political solidarity. His views are set forth in the *Independent Critic* (獨立評論) Nos. 80 and 83, and the essential ideas expressed therein are as follows:—

We must have a strong centralized Government. The present condition of China is an autocracy of scores of individual autocrats. What I am proposing is to have a stronger hand to take over the power from all the weaker ones. The men who stand in the way of national unification today are really the minor militarists, hence the problem of national unification becomes a problem of how to dispose of these men. . . . who can only be eliminated by a stronger military force. Since personal fidelity among Chinese as a rule outweighs public spirit, it is comparatively easy to institute a strong military authority by having an outstanding personality as the central dynamic force.

This briefly explains why Dr. Tsiang advocates military unification of the country by some powerful personality, and such proposals have been dealt with at greater length in an earlier number (85) of the *Independent Critic*.

Generally speaking, however, the problem is not so simple as Dr. Tsiang believes it to be. He has himself admitted that "the whole trouble does not rest with the militarists, but in the mentality and material conditions of the Chinese people." If, then, the trouble does not rest wholly with the militarists, we cannot say that the problem of national unification is simply a matter of eliminating the minor militarists. It is true that in the brief space of two months the Kwangsi faction was suppressed, and it is also true that within six months the powerful Feng-Yen combination was overthrown, but has the experience of the past five years taught us nothing? The true reason for the disunity which existed lies precisely where Dr. Tsiang himself has stated—"in the mentality and material conditions of the Chinese people." Paradoxical though it may seem, what resort to military force fails to achieve can be sometimes brought about by the creation of a certain "mentality." For example, the overthrow of the Manchu regime was certainly not the result of military success, but the sequel to the irresistible tendency of the times. The collapse of Yuan Shih-Kai's dreams of Imperial power also was not an achievement of military force, but of the irresistible power of a new "mentality." The withdrawal of Marshal Chang Tso-Lin beyond the Great Wall in 1928 was not due so much to military necessity as to the prevalence of a certain "mentality" which made it necessary for him to retreat. The obstacles to national unification today are not to be found solely in the armed resistance of the minor militarists; the disruptive influence of certain "mentalities" is just as

58 POWER OF FREEDOM

powerful, to say nothing of the influence of the Communists. A feeling of opposition to any dictator "on principle," so to speak, is one of the important factors accounting for national disunity today.

Dr. Tsiang has also said:—"Whenever there looms a possibility of national unification, the minor militarists immediately join hands and proceed to defeat it under the pretext of fighting autocracy." Now, the fact that the slogan "down with autocracy" is powerful enough to render national unification impossible indicates the irresistible nature of the new mentality of a new age, which cannot be imposed upon by the same old trick practiced by Liu P'ang and Chu Yuan-Chang, founder and first emperor of the Han and Ming Dynasties respectively. Professor Wu Ching-Chao, after completing an analytical study of the civil wars in Chinese history, established what he calls "the eight stages of Chinese civil wars," and also holds the view that only military force can accomplish the task of national unification (see *Independent Critic* No. 84). But he forgets that in his analysis of the eight stages of civil war there was never any such thing as a stage of "Down with the dictator!" New ideas cannot forever be subjugated by military force. In the present age, when new ideas have become irresistible, the resort to a dictatorship cannot be countenanced as a proper means of attaining political solidarity. Therefore, from the standpoint of political consolidation, we cannot believe that a dictatorship is necessary.

Next let us discuss whether there is any possibility of having a dictator in China. In the *Independent Critic* No. 82, I advanced three points to show why a dictatorship is impossible in China today. First, I do not believe that there is in China any outstanding personality capable of becoming a dictator, nor is there any political party or any class of people capable of shouldering the responsibility of a dictatorship. Secondly, I do not believe there is in China today any vital problem of such a nature as to call for the sentimental and reasoned support of the whole of the Chinese people, which would enable the whole nation to accept the leadership of any one single individual, or of a certain political party, or of a certain social class, in order to re-establish the regime of a new order of autocracy. Thirdly, I do not believe that either the intelligence or experience of the Chinese people today is capable of carrying successfully into operation a modern dictatorship, which requires superior intelligence and highly specialized technique for its execution. I have not up to now received a single satisfactory answer to any one of the three points I raised, and of which I think the third ranks as most important. I have said, "Looking over the political systems of the world during the past several decades, I feel that Republican Constitutionalism is a form of elementary politics best suited to training a people lacking in political experience. The essence of democracy lies in the facts that it does not call for exceptional talent; that political rights can expand gradually with a great degree of flexibility; that it promotes the welfare of all by seeking the advice of many, so that the multitudes of O Tou[2] can also put up a good showing with an assemblage of their mediocrity; and in that it affords the mass of mediocre men the opportunity to participate in administrative affairs, so that they may be taught to protect and to further their own interests and rights."

Generally speaking, democracy is a political system of common intelligence, while enlightened despotism is a system of special talents. Exceptional ability is not always easy to get; on the other hand, common intelligence is comparatively easy to train. In a country like ours, which is remarkably lacking in really great talent, the best political expedient is one of Republican Constitutionalism in which the political rights of the people can be gradually expanded. I have also said, "Few of those who are dreaming of an enlightened despotism (modern dictatorship) realize that a despotic political experiment is really the most complicated and most difficult of human enterprises. . . . To assume that a vast country like China, with 400 million O Tou can be made into a new nation, is no small task, and its accomplishment cannot even be dreamed of by a group of militarists or politicians who have never had any rigorous training for the work."

In other words, the way I look at it is that democracy is government of the kindergarten, while a modern dictatorship may be said to be the politics of graduates. For a whole year this view has not seemed to attract the attention of political experts in this country, perhaps due to the fact that it is out of harmony with the views commonly expressed in books of political science. My contention, terrible though it may sound, is derived nevertheless from patient observation of actualities. Take, for instance, the democracy of Great Britain, which is, as has always been the case, government based upon common intelligence, yet the British people have always regarded their method of government as one of "muddling through." Not until the last few decades did a group of keen observers begin to emphasize the importance of expert knowledge and special technique in government. The activities of the Fabian Society may be taken as best representing such a new realization.

---

2. The term (阿斗) is used to indicate the mass of ignorant and incapable people. O Tou was the dull son of a brilliant father, Liu Pei, Emperor during the Three Kingdoms, and the term is frequently applied to persons notoriously stupid.

During the latter part of the World War, and during the recent economic crisis, when there was an unusual extension of administrative powers, the principle of government by experts had for the first time an opportunity to be experimentally tested on a large scale. Again, look at the American Commonwealth. In what respect is this not a government of an elementary nature? Only since a year and a half ago have we seen in operation what is known as government by a "Brain Trust." This is due simply to the fact that in normal times democracy does not call for special expert knowledge and technique, and it was not until the recent threat of economic collapse that Congress was compelled to confer upon the President such extensive powers as to make possible an experiment in modern dictatorship. Not until the economic crisis did the people feel the necessity of a "Brain Trust." Great Britain and the United States are both homes of democracy; and the very fact that government by experts (or by a "Brain Trust") has made its appearance only in recent years is concrete proof that democracy is but an elementary form of government, and that modern dictatorship, which calls for highly developed technical skill in its execution, belongs really to the politics of the most advanced seminary.

This is why I say that a people such as ours, with poor knowledge and very little training, will not be capable in the near future of experimenting with modern dictatorship. It must be pointed out, however, that modern dictatorship is not dependent on the wisdom of the leader alone—although strong leadership is of primary importance—but on the numerous technical experts around him. Some time ago we heard Dr. V. K. Ting, one of China's foremost geologists, say that the Bureau of Geological Survey and Mining Investigation of Soviet Russia had in its service 3,000 active geologists, and in actual field-work there were 2,000 corps. We cannot help feeling amazed at such figures. In the last number of the *Independent Critic* Professor Chen Si-Ying declared that since the inauguration of the Five-Year Plan in Soviet Russia, there had been need for 1,500,000 technical experts, of whom 440,000 were engineers and technicians functioning in industrial projects, 90,000 high-grade and 36,000 medium-grade agriculturists; 11,000 high-grade and 27,000 second-grade specialists engaged in forestation, and 30,000 high-grade and 120,000 medium-grade technical experts functioning in transportation work. Such formidable figures should not be lost sight of by those who clamour so loudly for a modern dictatorship in China. Democracy only asks of those who are eligible to vote that they exercise their right of suffrage without fear or abuse. Such political training is not at all difficult. I have witnessed two national elections and a great number of local elections in the United States, and have noticed that citizens of poor intelligence and low general standards are quite capable of exercising their voting power. Modern dictatorship not only calls for a vast "Brain Trust" to function as its brain, but for hundreds of thousands of technical experts to serve as its limbs and senses. Such a demand cannot be easily met.

Neither Soviet Russia nor Italy is easy of imitation. In Italy there are two universities each having a history of 1,000 years, and universities of 500 years standing and more are found practically everywhere. In Soviet Russia universities 200 years old can also be found. Besides, these two countries enjoy the advantage of having the whole continent of Europe as their training-ground of learning. How about China? We claim that our country has a civilization 5,000 years old, yet there is not a single university in China which has a history of over 40 years! Where can we get the training for specialists? Where are we going to obtain training for leadership? Obviously the capable and ideal dictator of whom Dr. Chien dreams, and the enlightened despotism which Dr. Tsiang speaks of, are alike unattainable in China today.

CHAPTER 2

Family of Nations[1]

To all lovers of peace and international order, the twenty-first anniversary of Armistice Day must be sad occasion indeed. A great war has been going on in East Asia for twenty-eight months; a greater war has been developing in Europe for seventy days, while the League of Nations, the great symbol of the postwar world order, has practically ceased to function. The dreams of the years of Wilsonian idealism seem now to have been completely shattered.

It profits us little to lament the failures and errors of the past. The bygone is beyond recall.

It may be more useful for us to reflect on the lessons which we should learn from these past failures so that the dreamers and builders of a future world order may be benefited by them.

In a remarkable address of two weeks ago, the new British Ambassador to the United States, the Marquess of Lothian, said:

> One of the mistakes the democracies made after the last war was to think that the peace would come in the main through disarmament. Disarmament on a large scale, of course, is necessary. But peace comes from there being overwhelming power behind law, as you found when you had to deal with gangsters within your boundaries.

I think Lord Lothian has drawn the most important lesson that can be drawn from the recent history of international relationship and govern-

---

1. This address was originally broadcast through the Columbia Broadcasting System in New York on Armistice Day, November 11, 1939. In this address, Hu Shih envisions a future world government, to be structured in the form of regional federations in which each country or government will take responsibility according to its ability, strength, and strategic position.

ment. The future League or Union of Nations must be a "League to Enforce Peace." An international government that cannot enforce its law and order is illusory and unreal.

In order to make this fundamental idea workable, a few guiding principles seem to be quite necessary:

First, the future world order must be built up on the basis, not of vague generalistics and abstractions, but of definite and precise commitments by the states. The Kellogg-Briand Pact of Paris is an example of vague generalization. The British and French pledges to Poland, Rumania, and Greece in 1939, on the other hand, are definite commitments. The Earl of Lytton once said, "It is broadly true, however paradoxical it may sound, that the greater and the more precise are the commitments of a country, the less is its liability to be drawn into war." He cited the Monroe Doctrine as a case of a definite commitment.

Second, the old idea of formal equality among the nations must be greatly qualified and supplemented by the principle of Graded Responsibility according to the ability, strength, and geographical or strategic position of the states. It is absurd, for instance, to expect Denmark to undertake the same responsibility as Great Britain in a given international situation. Why not therefore frankly recognize the fact and apportion the responsibilities according to their respective abilities?

Third, a necessary corollary from the idea of graded responsibility is the principle of Regional Leadership and Cooperation. The fatal mistake of the League of Nations is that it could not effectively function even as a League of Europe. Its pretensions as a world government were largely responsible for the failure to set up regional machineries to deal effectively with important local conflicts. The historic part played by the United States in the Western Hemisphere best illustrates what I mean by the idea of Regional Leadership and Cooperation. The future world government should be a superfederation of some such regional setups as the League of Europe, the Conference of American States, the British Commonwealth, the Conference of Pacific States, the Conference of Western and Southwestern Asiatic States, etc.

A world state of regional federations and confederacies with definite and precise commitments according to the graded responsibilities of the states or groups of states—this is the formula which I wish to recommend to the serious reflection of all dreamers of a better and more workable world order.

CHAPTER 3

The New Disorder in East Asia and the World at Large[1]

On the 3rd of November, 1938, the Japanese Government announced to the world that "what Japan seeks is the establishment of a new order that will insure the permanent stability of East Asia." Two weeks later, on November 18, in a note to the US Government, the Japanese Foreign Minister said, among other things, that "Japan at present is devoting her energy to the establishment of a new order based on genuine international justice throughout East Asia, the attainment of which is not only an indispensable condition of the very existence of Japan, but also constitutes the very foundation of enduring peace and stability in East Asia."

To this ambitious declaration, the American Government, in a note dated December 31, replied, "This Government is well aware that the situation has changed. This Government is also well aware that many of the changes have been brought about by action of Japan. This Government does not admit, however, that there is need or warrant for any one Power to take upon itself to prescribe what shall be the terms and conditions of 'a new order' in areas not under its sovereignty and to constitute itself the repository of authority and the agent of destiny in regard thereto." The undeniable fact is that there ain't no such animal as "a new order in East Asia." Instead there is only anarchy, war, wanton slaughter, and indescribable misery—all brought about by the acts of aggression on the part of Japan, which have completely destroyed some semblance of international order that had been

---

1. A speech in which Hu Shih discusses how Japan's invasion of China led to the breakdown of the international order in East Asia. He mentions that he was in Switzerland "last summer." Since Hu Shih visited Switzerland in 1938, this speech must have been delivered in 1939.

evolving in the Western Pacific during the last four decades. The historic mission which the Japanese military has accomplished during these last eight years is therefore the replacement of a long-existing international order by the present new disorder in East Asia.

In order to better understand this historic transition from some form of international order to disorder, I must invite you to go back with me a few decades in history to a time when the Colonial Empires of the West were seeking concessions, leased territories, and colonies on the continent of Asia. This struggle for colonies and concessions became most acute during the last decade of the last century. Russia, Germany, France, and Great Britain all succeeded in obtaining footholds on the coast of China. Japan, the rising militaristic Power of Asia, fought the Sino-Japanese War and won territorial annexations and a huge indemnity from China. By the last few years of the last century, the international situation was so grave that farsighted observers could see that a world war might break out at any time on the soils of China.

And a miniature world war actually broke out in the year 1900, when the armed forces of eight Powers marched on Tientsin and Peking and Russian armies were pouring into Northern Manchuria. There were serious talks about the partitioning of China.

But, by the turn of the century, a new idealism in international relations had been dawning on the world. And there were idealists in England and America who were trying to influence the American and British Governments for some constructive policy that might save China from the aggressors and the world from an imminent conflagration. In the year 1899 and again in 1900, the American Government, under the leadership of John Hay, proclaimed to the world this policy of the "Open Door" in China.

The "Open Door Policy" has been usually understood as a merely economic doctrine, meaning the equality of opportunities for all nations trading in China. But the Open Door Policy is in reality more important as a political doctrine. It emphasizes the preservation of the independence and territorial integrity of China as a necessary condition for the maintenance of the equality of trading opportunities to all nations.

It is this political aspect of the Open Door Policy which has been of the greatest importance to China during the last four decades. Its implications were more explicitly and unmistakably restated in the "Nine-Power Treaty" of the Washington Conference, under which, as we all know, the eight Signatory Powers solemnly pledged themselves to respect the independence, the sovereignty, and the territorial and administrative integrity of China, and to give to China the freest and most unembarrassed opportunity to develop for herself a stable and effective government. And they further pledged not to take advantage of conditions in China to further their own economic or territorial aims.

It is these political aspects of the Open Door Policy, reinforced by the Nine-Power Treaty, that has not only saved China from the fate of being partitioned among the imperialistic Powers, but has also given the Chinese people thirty years to work out their own problems of political and social reorganization. I have no hesitation to recognize the historical fact that China has survived largely as a result of a semblance of international order brought about first by the Open Door Policy as proclaimed by John Hay in 1899 and 1900, and later more explicitly in the Nine-Power Treaty of 1922.

And since the last world war, there has grown up a more general world order, not only in the form of the League of Nations, but more generally supported by a host of idealistic international treaties and agreements, such as the treaties of the Washington Conference, the "Treaty of Locarno," and the "Kellogg-Briand Pact of Paris." To this general world order, the international order of the Far East, as above described, was intimately linked as one of its integral parts.

For a period of twelve years, the war-weary world thrived under this new world order, under which, not only the small and weak nations prospered in peace, but even the great Powers were the greatest beneficiaries. The naval powers, under the Washington Treaties, actually stopped their mad rivalries in naval armaments and fortifications. France never felt more secure than in those years; even Japan enjoyed the highest prestige as one of the "Big Four" at Geneva and as the acknowledged leader in the Western Pacific.

China, undoubtedly, was one of the nations that profited most under this new world order. During these years, China succeeded in bringing about a Nationalist Revolution and in establishing for the first time "a stable and effective government," which in the course of a few years was able to unify the major portions of the country, to increase by a hundred times the modern means of transportation and communication, and to modernize the country in education, national defense, and social reconstruction. The dreams of the founders of the Open Door Policy for an independent and modern China were at last being realized, and a modern national state of China was emerging as an indisputable reality.

Unfortunately, the rise of a modern national state of China was not to the liking of our nearest neighbor, Japan, which always regarded a unified and strong China as a menace and a formidable check to her continental imperialistic ambitions. She did everything to hamper the growth of this nationalistic China. In 1928, Japan sent an army to Tsinan in Shantung to stop the march of the Nationalist armies northward. But even that did not prevent the union of the whole of China under the Nationalist flag. And when the Chinese leaders in Manchuria declared their allegiance to the National Government at Nanking, that was regarded by Japan as a signal for aggressive action. Therefore, two years after the whole of Manchuria returned to the unified control of Nationalist China, Japan's military started the famous "Mukden Incident" on the eve of September 18, 1931. In the course of a few weeks, Japanese troops occupied almost the whole of the Three Eastern Provinces.

That marked the beginning of the new disorder in Eastern Asia. For, as I have stated before, the independence, the sovereignty, and the territorial and administrative integrity of China had been explicitly guaranteed by the Powers interested in the Far East, and these guarantees have become a part of the new world order. In order to crush Nationalistic China and to violate the sovereignty and territorial integrity of China, Japan had first to destroy that international framework which included the Nine-Power Treaty, the Covenant of the League of Nations, and the Kellogg-Briand Pact. China naturally appealed to the League of Nations and to the signatories of the Nine-Power Treaty for help. Unfortunately, the world was not prepared for such a severe test. The League appointed a Commission of Inquiry to study the situation on the spot and report. The Lytton Commission report was accepted by the League and by the Chinese Government. But when Japan refused to accept the recommendations of the League Commission of Inquiry and resigned from the membership of the League, the supporters of the new world order were incapable of invoking and unprepared to invoke those sections of the Covenant which provided sanctions against the breaker of the peace in violation of the Covenant. Thereupon the whole structure of postwar world order broke down under the blow of the Japanese mailed fist.

But the evil effect of the breakdown of this international order in Eastern Asia is easily seen by all observers on the scene. Hallet Abend, the special correspondent of the *New York Times*, who certainly cannot be accused of being particularly anti-Japanese, cabled from Shanghai on February 1, 1939, these words, with which he opened his series of ten articles on conditions in China under Japanese domination: "An anonymous British wag, writing to one of the Shanghai newspapers, satirically praises Japan for her outstanding success in creating the new disorder in East Asia. That actually is what has been happening in China during the last nineteen months of hostilities—the creation of a new disorder—the steadily blasting away of the foundations of law, order and social and economic security, upon which the Chinese Government had been laboring with considerable success. There has been in China a progressive spreading of the gravest disorders—economic, financial, social, military and political." These disorders are the natural outcome of Japan's war of aggression, which has been going on for twenty-three months and which in all probability will go on for another two or three years. All competent observers point to the undeniable fact that Chinese morale continues to be good and the Japanese invaders are being dragged further and further into a sea of ever-deepening mire. And the so-called "new order in Eastern Asia" is not visible even under microscopic examination. There are a few pessimistic critics who predict that the present disorders in the East will someday culminate in a gigantic international conflagration in Eastern Asia, which may eventually reduce Japan to a third- or fourth-rate Power with her naval power destroyed and her colonial possessions made into independent states.

But it is not in Eastern Asia alone that this new disorder has prevailed. The world has been made so small today that both war and peace are truly indivisible and the breaking down of the international order in one part will inevitably affect the general peace and well-being of the whole world. It has been reported that, when Japan withdrew from the League of Nations, one German Cabinet Minister said to the Japanese representative, "We do not think that Japan is right, but we thank you for the good example." This was in 1932, a year before Hitler came into full power in Germany, and three years before Italy embarked on the Ethiopian campaign. The Japanese "example" has been faithfully followed by other aggressor nations in other parts of the world, and the result is a world living in the constant fear of an imminent outbreak of a general conflagration of unprecedented magnitude and cruelty. You, the blessed citizens of a peaceful continent, have not escaped the terrible anxiety and anguish which the radio and the cable have brought to you every day from a war-scared Europe. This is what I call "the new disorder in East Asia and the world at large." The question that is uppermost in the mind of all peace-loving people is—what can be done about it? Shall mankind declare itself as intellectually and politically bankrupt in coping with the situation and preventing the great calamity so evident to all? Or is there is still left some farsighted, constructive statesmanship which may yet save mankind and its civilization from catastrophic destruction and make the world once again safer for humanity to live in?

I do not propose to answer these questions tonight, but I do see encouraging signs, not only in the revival of a new wave of international idealism as best expressed in Mr. Streit's new book, *Union Now*, but also in the numerous concrete evidences of farsighted positive statesmanship best exemplified in the published statements of policy by the leaders of the American Government.

Naturally, there are still many who wish to comfort themselves by the thought that these disorders do not affect them in their immediate environments. They wish to wash their hands of all responsibilities for the disorders in the world and therefore for the restoration of order. But can we wash our hands of all responsibilities for our sins of omission as well as of commission? Last summer when I was in Switzerland, I went up Mount Pilatus, named after the famous Roman Governor, Pilate. Local legends in that region still tell us that on cloudy days and on moonlit nights, the spirit of Pilate is often seen on the top of the mountain washing his hands incessantly in the clouds. Nineteen centuries ago there was brought before Pilate a prisoner whose life was demanded by the mob. When he saw that he could prevail nothing and that a riot was forthcoming, Pilate took water and washed his hands before the multitude, saying, "I am innocent of the blood of this just man. See ye to it." Nineteen centuries have passed. Has mankind ever acquitted Pilate of the responsibility for the blood of that just man?

CHAPTER 4

China and the World War[1]

The topic—"China and the World War"—has been assigned to me by the Institute. I have accepted it on the ground that, when my old friend James Grover McDonald uses the term "the World War," I am sure he knows what he is talking about. So we are having a "World War," and I am here to present my view of China's relation to it.

I

It is a historical fact that the Second World War was started over eight years ago, in Mukden, China, when on September 18, 1931, Japan's armies began her invasion in China. On that memorable evening, a section of a railway was destroyed and the Japanese army shelled the Chinese city of Mukden and occupied it. Thus began the Sino-Japanese Conflict which has lasted eight years and four months. And thus has begun the Second World War, which must include the Italian-Ethiopian War of 1935, the Spanish War of 1936–39, the "extinguishment" of Austria, Czechoslovakia, Albania, as well as the wars that are now raging in Europe.

For on that memorable evening, it was not only a section of a railway that was destroyed, nor merely a city that was shelled. It was the New World Order that was attacked and destroyed—the New World Order which we in those days of Wilsonian idealism had dreamed of and which had cost $200 billion and eight and a half million human lives to bring into being.

That New World Order did not consist of the League of Nations alone,

---

1. In this speech delivered in January 1940, Hu Shih considers the Mukden Incident (aka the Manchurian Incident), which took place on September 18, 1931, to be the first battle of World War II.

but stood on the basis of a host of more or less idealistic international agreements and understandings, including the Covenant of the League of Nations, the Statute of the Permanent Court of International Justice, the Nine-Power Treaty and other treaties of the Washington Conference, the Locarno Pacts, and the Kellogg-Briand Pact of Paris. By means of these overlapping and interlocking agreements, the postwar World Order was able to embrace almost the whole civilized world, including the United States, which, though not a member of the League of Nations, is a signatory to the Nine-Power Treaty, the Naval Disarmament Treaties, and the Kellogg-Briand Pact of Paris.

It was this New World Order that was attacked on the night of September 18, 1931. For the Japanese invasion in Manchuria was the most severe and important test of the strength and stability of this international order. Article 10 of the League Covenant, for example, stipulates, "The Members of the League undertake to respect and preserve as against aggression the territorial integrity and existing political independence of all Members of the League." Article I of the Nine-Power Treaty says, "The contracting Powers . . . agree to respect the sovereignty, the independence, and the territorial and administrative integrity of China, and to provide to the fullest and most unembarrassed opportunity to China to develop and maintain for herself an effective and stable government." And the Pact of Paris says, "The High Contracting Parties solemnly declare, in the name of their respective peoples, that they condemn recourse to war for the solution of international controversies and renounce it as an instrument of national policy in their relations with one another"; and they further "agree that the settlement or solution of all disputes or conflicts, of whatever nature or of whatever origin they may be, which may arise among them, shall never be sought except by pacific means." All these and many other chief supporters of the New World Order were now subjected to the test of a real, unprovoked, and undisguised aggression by Japan in China.

China naturally appealed to the League of Nations and to the signatories and adherents of the Nine-Power Treaty. What happened during those memorable years of 1931 and 1932, when the League of Nations attempted to mediate for a peaceful settlement of the Sino-Japanese dispute, need not be retold here. Suffice it to say that the world at that time was not prepared to support that international order by curbing the aggressions of Japan. The League pronounced judgment and proposed a settlement which was tantamount to surrender to Japan's wishes. Yet Japan still refused to accept the settlement and withdrew from the League in March 1933. Nothing was done by the supporters of Collective Security.

When Japan left the League, a German Cabinet Minister said to the Japanese representative at Geneva, "We don't think you are right, but we thank you for your good example." The good example of Japan has since been successfully followed by other aggressor states in East Africa and Europe.

The whole structure of postwar World Order under which the nations, the great and strong as well as the small and weak, lived in comparative peace for more than a decade rapidly broke down, and is now almost completely scrapped. The failure of this New World Order to support its own principles during this early stage of the Sino-Japanese dispute not only doomed it to ultimate downfall, but also greatly encouraged and tempted the other discontented and militaristically prepared countries to go on with more daring and more far-reaching aggressions until the whole world is plunged into a stupendous conflagration.

It is, therefore, historically accurate to say that the Second World War was started eight years ago in Mukden, China. The first shots of September 18, 1931, now known to have been planned and executed by two young officers of the Japanese army—Ishihara and Itagaki—will surely be acknowledged by history as the first shots of the world conflagration.

II

Thus China has been the first victim of the breakdown of the World Order, and has been fighting the first battles of the New World War—intermittently for over eight years, and continuously for the last two years and a half.

Two years ago, or even half a year ago, if I should have told the world that China was fighting the first battles of a world war, very few people would have believed it. But the recent developments in Europe have brought into prominence that striking similarity between China's War of Resistance and the war being fought by the European democracies against aggression.

Such a similarity should make the outside world better understand that the thirty months of China's heroic resistance to Japanese aggression are truly an integral part of the World War, the end of which no one can yet envisage.

The New World War, whether in its China phase or in its European phase, has one thing in common—namely, that everywhere the war has been forced on a peace-loving state by a militaristic aggressor-state.

In March 1935, the British Government, in a White Paper, confessed that, during the years past, "there has been a steady decline in the effective strength of our armament by sea and land," and "in the air, we visually disarmed ourselves in 1919, and subsequently, from time to time postponed attainment of the minimum air strength regarded as necessary to our security in the face of air developments on the Continent." In the same document, the British Government admitted, "We . . . are approaching a point when we are not possessed of the necessary means of defending ourselves against an aggressor."

This state of unpreparedness on the part of Great Britain explains the British policy of appeasement from 1931 to 1938. The British Government, in describing this unilateral disarmament, said, "We have taken risks for peace." But, a year later, the British Government had to admit, "Taking 'risks for peace' has not removed the dangers of war."

If Great Britain, one of the few most powerful countries in the world, had to confess that she was "not possessed of the necessary means of defending ourselves against an aggressor," it should not be difficult for the world to understand that China, where the whole cultural tradition of at least twenty centuries had condemned military conquest and despised the profession of the soldier, was caught in 1931 entirely unprepared to defend herself against premeditated aggression of Japan. China had no navy, no air force worth speaking of, and no modern war equipment for her army. Naturally she wanted to avoid a war against an invader who happened to be one of the greatest military and naval powers in the world. Naturally and quite sincerely, she, for six long years, adopted a policy of appeasement toward Japan in the face of the most unbearable insults, indignities, and humiliations.

But after six years of patient but unsuccessful appeasement, she was forced at last to take up the fight in July 1937, just as Great Britain, after eight long years of consistent policy to appease the aggressor, was forced to take up the challenge on September 3, 1939. Indeed, we were forced to fight this war of resistance just as Abyssinia, and Poland, and Finland were forced to fight their wars of resistance.

These bitter and tragic happenings in Europe should be sufficient to make China's friends better understand and more fully appreciate the desperate but heroic fight we have been making during these terrible years. We are fighting the same war as Poland, and Great Britain and France, and Finland have been fighting. We are fighting and will continue to fight simply because we are determined not to suffer the fate of Abyssinia, Austria, Albania, and Czechoslovakia. We are fighting because we want to be free and independent.

My Government and my people have repeatedly declared that we are fighting to resist aggression, to preserve our sovereignty and our territorial and administrative integrity, and to uphold the sanctity of international treaties, especially the Nine-Power Treaty, the League Covenant, and the Pact of Paris. These are our war aims, and these are our peace aims.

These are not mere high-sounding words from a suffering nation appealing for the sympathy of the larger world. No, they are real and concrete issues. And all of you who have followed the stirring events in Europe during the past fifteen months can easily understand that they are real and concrete issues.

On the night of September 27, 1938—the night before Hitler's invitation to Munich—I was in London, and heard Prime Minister Chamberlain's broadcast to the British Empire and to the world, in which he said:

> However much we may sympathize with a small nation confronted by a big powerful nation, we cannot in all circumstances undertake to involve the British Empire in a war simply on her account.
>
> If we have to fight, it must be on larger issues than that.
>
> I am myself a man of peace to the depth of my soul. Armed conflict between nations is a nightmare to me. But if I were convinced that any nation had made up its mind to dominate the world by fear of its force, I should feel it must be resisted.

On that evening, and in subsequent weeks, Mr. Chamberlain was still trying to separate the fate of a small nation from the "larger issues." And the Peace of Munich seems to have made on the assumption that violation of the territorial integrity of a small nation did not involve the "larger issues."

What has happened since Munich clearly demonstrates that the fate of a small nation in the claws of a powerful and aggressive neighbor is simply a concrete embodiment of the "larger issues." Indeed, there are no "larger issues" apart from these concrete cases.

Great Britain and France are now fighting—technically because they have given a pledge to Poland to the effect that, in case of Poland's national independence being violated, if Poland should resist such violation with her armed forces, Britain and France would come to her assistance. When Poland was invaded and she chose to fight, Great Britain and France were forced to declare war on Germany.

In this case, it was clearly also "a small nation confronted by a big powerful nation." Yet, when Great Britain and France declared war, they all proclaimed to the world that they were all fighting for the "larger issues" of which the invasion of Poland was merely a concrete illustration. Thus Premier Daladier said on September 3:

> We are fighting to defend our land, our homes, our liberty. . . . The cause of France is the cause of justice. It is the cause of all peaceful and free nations.

Thus King George VI said on the same day:

> We have been [unclear] into a conflict, for we are called, with our allies, to meet the challenge of a principle which, if it were to prevail, would be fatal to any civilized order in the world.
>
> It is a principle which permits a state in the selfish pursuit of power to disregard its treaties and its solemn pledges, which sanctions the use of force or threat of force against the sovereignty and independence of other states.
>
> If this principle were established through the world, the freedom of our own country and of the whole British Commonwealth of Nations would be in danger.
>
> But far more than this, the peoples of the world would be kept in bondage of fear, and all hopes of settled peace and of security, of justice and liberty, among nations would be ended.
>
> This is the ultimate issue which confronts us. For the sake of all that we ourselves hold dear, and of the world order and peace, it is unthinkable that we should refuse to meet the challenge.

And Prime Minister Chamberlain said on November 26, 1939:

> Our war aim can be stated very shortly. It is to defeat our enemy: and by that I mean not merely the defeat of the enemy's military forces. I mean the defeat of that aggressive, bullying mentality which seeks continually to dominate other peoples by force, which finds brutal satisfaction in the persecution and torture of inoffensive citizens, and which, in the name of the state, justifies the repudiation of its own pledged word whenever it finds it convenient.

Why should I trouble you with all these high-sounding generalities expressed by the heads of the governments of the warring nations? I want to tell my friends that, when I read them, they are no mere high-sounding generalities, but concrete descriptions of real issues which are so real and so compelling that millions of men are actually fighting and dying for them. I can feel their reality because millions of my own people have for thirty months been fighting and dying "to defend our land, our homes, and our liberty," and to resist the establishment of the principle which permits a state to disregard its treaties, and which "sanctions the use of force or threat of force against the sovereignty and independence of other states."

Such, then, are the common features which characterize China's War of Resistance and the wars now raging in Europe as different aspects of the New World War. They are all the results of the breakdown of the postwar World Order. They are all forced on the peaceful and militarily unprepared peoples by the aggressor-states whose appetite for aggression grows with every new success. China and the warring democracies of Europe have the same war aims, which include the defeat of aggression and the defeat of the philosophy of aggression. And they probably have the same peace aims, which at least include the reestablishment, reorganizing, and reinforcement of the World Order that shall make the recurrence of such a world conflagration impossible.

III

As China's friends and sympathizers, you are naturally interested in what effects the European wars have had or will have on our War of Resistance.

During the weeks just before and shortly after the outbreak of war in Europe, there were grave apprehensions on the part of the Chinese leaders and the Chinese people. There was the danger of Great Britain and France being forced to make important concessions to Japan at the expense of China; there was even the danger of the Indo-China and the Burma routes being closed by the French and British at the point of the Japanese bayonet; and there was the danger of Soviet Russia abandoning her policy of assistance to China, or even of Soviet Russia forming a bloc with Germany and Japan.

So far the situation has turned out to be very much better than it had first appeared. The Soviet-German Pact, apparently negotiated and concluded without the knowledge of Japan, was considered by Japan as a betrayal by her supposed friend and ally, Germany. In her strong resentment against Germany, the Japanese Government declared the Anti-Comintern Pact dead. She now feels herself more isolated than ever. She does not know where to turn next. She will probably remain in that state of bewildered isolation for some time to come.

Japan's sympathies are naturally with the aggressors of Europe. And she naturally wishes to seize this opportunity to oust Britain and France from Eastern and Southeastern Asia, and from the Western and Southern Pacific. In the last days of last August, the British colony of Hong Kong was actually daily expecting a Japanese attack by land, sea, and air.

But Japan was apparently bewildered and perplexed. She had had eight years of continental warfare. She had been greatly weakened as a military power, and is probably not fully prepared to start another major war with any of the great powers. Her armed forces were on the border of Hong Kong for months, but they were all withdrawn last week. No doubt, she has been threatening French Indo-China. But Japanese bombing of the French railway in Yunnan last week seems to indicate that the Japanese military still believe the French colonial authorities there are allowing Chinese goods and materials to go through into China.

Japan has recently captured the city of Nanning in Kwangsi, thereby cutting one of our highway routes leading from Indo-China. But there are other routes from this French colony. We are completing new ones. And, of course, there is the Burma route, which cannot be closed by force without a war between Great Britain and Japan.

It is quite possible that the European situation may force the British and the French to make some minor concessions to Japan in the mainland of Asia. But we are reasonably confident that these democratic powers, which have undertaken to fight a terrific war for the purpose of defeating the continual threat to dominate the world by force, surely will not betray or desert China. Indeed such a betrayal of China would emphatically belie all their professed war aims and peace aims.

The real stabilizing force in the Pacific is the economic and naval power of the United States. Therefore, Great Britain and France are likely to do nothing in China that will displease or offend the American Government and people. The British and French are relying on American supplies.

Japan too has been importing from the United States to the extent of 56 percent of her war materials. With the European war on, she may be more dependent on American supplies and materials. And she is most anxious to secure a new treaty of commerce after the old one expires on January 26. Therefore, Japan too probably will hesitate a great deal before she does anything in China or in the Pacific which may help rally American sympathy and support for the British and French, or which may justify America to undertake economic measures against herself.

It is probably this stabilizing force of the American commonwealth which has so far prevented any radical change of the situation in the Far East during these four months since the outbreak of the European war.

As to what Soviet Russia will do in the Far East, no one can tell. I can only faithfully report a few facts.

When China began to resist Japanese aggression with armed forces, Soviet Russia was at the height of her international idealism. For over two years, therefore, China has been receiving much assistance from the Soviet Union in the form of arms, munitions, materials, warplanes, and volunteer technicians and pilots.

And, in 1938 and again in 1939, Soviet troops had been fighting two wars with Japanese troops on the Manchurian-Mongolian borders. The border war of last summer lasted almost four months, and Japanese casualties were reported to be enormous.

Then, on September 15, Russia and Japan signed an agreement which brought about a cessation of hostilities on the Mongolian-Manchurian border and established a joint commission to examine and determine the disputed boundaries.

On October 31, Premier Molotov of the Soviet Union, in the course of his report on foreign affairs to the Supreme Soviet, said that "the possibility has been established of starting Soviet-Japanese trade negotiations" and that they (the Soviets) "look with favor on Japanese overtures of this kind." A few days later (November 4), however, the Executive Committee of the Communist International in Moscow issued a manifesto, in which we read that "for more than two years now . . . Japanese imperialists have been tearing at the flesh of China, which is fighting for its independence"; and that "the Communist International call on you (Proletarians and Working People throughout the World) to defend the Chinese people against the imperialist bandits."

On December 31, 1939, Soviet Russia signed with Japan a one-year renewal of the Kamchatka fisheries arrangement; and Japan, in return, promised to pay to Russia the remaining 5,809,000 yen still due on the Chinese Eastern Railway.

On January 4, 1940, Moscow announced the receipt of a check for 5,809,565 yen. But on January 5, Moscow also announced that the Presidium of the Supreme Soviet had ratified the Russo-Chinese trade treaty, concluded at Moscow last June 16, and containing provisions governing the material assistance which the Soviet Union has been giving to China in her war with Japan.

In short, there have been "beginnings of improvement of relations" between the USSR and Japan, and there have been "Japanese overtures" for trade negotiations; but Soviet Russia apparently is still continuing to give help to China in her war against the Japanese "imperialist bandits."

Whatever effects the European war may produce on the Sino-Japanese conflict, and whatever changes may come in the international lineup in the Far East, one thing is certain: namely, that the Chinese people are determined to fight on, for many more months and possibly for many more years to come, until our enemy is economically so exhausted and militarily so bogged down that it will be willing to accept a just and endurable peace. This is not impossible. You will remember that in November 1918, when the Armistice came to the last world war, Germany was still occupying almost the whole of Belgium and a large position of France, but the war had been lost for the Germans.

And this breakdown of Japan can be greatly accelerated by an effective boycott of Japanese goods and an effective embargo of essential war materials to Japan by the peace-loving and democratic peoples who have been supplying Japan with foreign exchange and with scrap iron, oil, copper, cotton and metalworking machinery. When Japan's unfavorable trade balance is becoming unbearable, when her domestic loan issues can no longer be absorbed by the native banks and investors, when her gold holding is completely exhausted and when she has nowhere to go to replenish her exhausted war supplies, then a little pressure from without will tell effectively just as the proverbial last straw breaks the back of the camel.

CHAPTER 5[1]

Historical Foundations for a Democratic China[2]

I

In these days when China is being regarded as a partner and ally fighting on the side of the democracies, it is natural that political scientists and students of comparative government should ask some such questions: Is China a democracy? Has Chinese republicanism or Chinese democracy any historical basis?

There have been different answers to such questions. Some say that there is not an iota of democracy in China. Others want us to believe that the only hope for Chinese democracy is found in the Communist-controlled districts of Northern Shensi, and that a Communist triumph will make China democratic.

. . . My paper purports to describe a few historical factors which have made China inevitably the first country in Asia to abolish the monarchy once and for all and seriously to work out a democratic form of government; and which, in my opinion, furnish the solid foundation on which a democratic China can be successfully built up. These historical factors have been at work for tens of centuries and have given to the Chinese people the tradition and the preparation for the development of modern democratic institutions.

Of these historical foundations I shall mention only three: first, a thoroughly democratized social structure; secondly, 2,000 years of an objective

---

1. This article was published in *Edmund J. James Lectures on Government* (Urbana: University of Illinois Press, 1941), 1–12. It was also included in the *Proceedings of the Institute of World Affairs*, vol. 21, *Problems of the Peace* (Los Angeles: Published for the Institute of World Affairs by the University of Southern California, 1944–45), 54–63.

2. Delivered March 12, 1941. [This note was included in the original document.]

and competitive system of examinations for civil service; and thirdly, the historic institution of the government creating its own "opposition" and censorial control.

You will notice I have singled out only the institutional foundations and have not included the theoretical or philosophical basis for a democratic China. I believe that the best way of showing the influence of a philosophical tradition is through the historic institutions which are both the product and the embodiment of those intellectual forces.

But before taking up these historical institutions, I would like to say a word about a few powerful philosophical ideas which have had a great influence in molding the social and political development of the Chinese people. The first of these is the Confucianist conception of human nature as essentially good. In a rhymed primer which was written in the Sung Dynasty, and was still used in all village schools during my childhood, the opening lines read:

In the beginning
Man's nature is good.
Near to one another by nature,
Men are set apart by practice.
Without teaching,
Nature degenerates.

These ideas which go back to Confucius, and particularly to Mencius, have been the basis of Chinese education and have inculcated into the people the sense of human equality. Confucius laid down the philosophy in four words: "*Yu chiao wu lei*" (With education there is no class). This conception of the essential goodness of human nature and of the infinite possibility of education is the most important philosophical idea which has produced an almost classless society in China. Centuries before China came into contact with the democratic ideas of Western countries, Chinese children in all village schools were humming such popular rhymes as the following:

Prime Ministers and Generals do not belong to any class:
Youths should exert themselves.

That is a popular paraphrase of the Confucian doctrine that with education there is no class.

The second important democratic doctrine is the scriptural justification of rebellion against tyrannical government. The story is told of Confucius who passed by the foot of Mount Taishan and heard a woman crying plaintively. He asked her what was the cause of her deep sorrow. She said, "My father was carried away by a tiger; recently my husband was killed by a tiger and now my son was devoured by a tiger." "Why don't you run away from this place infested by such ferocious tigers?" And the woman said, "There is no tyrannical government here." Confucius thereupon turned to his disciples and said, "Remember this! Tyrannical government is more oppressive than ferocious tigers!"

Mencius in particular was the most out-spoken advocate of the right of rebellion against tyrannical government. He said, "When a ruler treats his subject like grass and dirt, then the subject should treat him as a bandit and an enemy." And he characterized some of the historical rebellions, not as revolts of subjects against rulers, but as justified revolutions against despots whose misrule had alienated them from the people. This doctrine of justifiable rebellion against tyranny and misrule was easily and naturally revived with the coming of revolutionary and democratic ideas from the Western world.

The third important political doctrine is that the subordinate has a sacred duty to criticize and oppose the wrong-doing of his superior. A little classic, the *Book of Filial Piety*, has this saying of Confucius: "If an Emperor has seven out-spoken ministers [chêng ch'ên: literally, "ministers who fight or oppose him"], he could not lose his empire in spite of his misdeeds. If a feudal lord has five out-spoken ministers, he could not lose his state in spite of his misdeeds. If a minister has three out-spoken servants, he could not lose his family fortune in spite of his misdeeds. . . . Therefore, in the face of a wrong or unrighteousness it is the duty of the son to oppose his father and it is the duty of the servant to oppose his sovereign."

This idea of encouraging out-spoken advice and even opposition from one's subordinates has been a most important political tradition which has made possible the development, not only of the institution of the government's own censors, but also of the hundreds of great personalities who made history by fighting fearlessly against the misdeeds of despotic rulers and powerful ministers.

It is from these basic seeds of Chinese political thinking that there have been developed social and political institutions which have played, and will continue to play, an important role in shaping the political development of my people.

II

China was unified for the first time in 221 B.C. The First Empire, founded on military conquest of the contending states, did not last more than a dozen years, and was overthrown by a revolution of the people. The Second Empire, the Empire of Han, lasted 400 years (202 B.C.–219 A.D.).

Even before the first unification under the First Empire, the numerous small states which flourished at the time of Confucius were gradually being absorbed and consolidated into seven great powers. The old feudal society was rapidly disappearing in an age of conquest, migration of races, and political concentration. Practically all the seven states of the fourth and third centuries B.C. had highly centralized government and administration. That tendency of centralized political control was made uniform under the First Empire, which divided the whole country into 36 administrative districts or provinces governed by officials appointed by the central government.

During the 400 years of the Han Empire, this tendency of political consolidation was continued and perfected. In their first reaction against the despotic consolidation of power under the First Empire, the founders of the Han Dynasty created new feudal states and gave them to the princes of the blood of the new royal family. But the statesmen of the second century B.C. soon realized the mistake of this political anachronism which had led to armed revolts by some of these powerful princes against the central government. In order to avoid an abrupt departure of policy, the political wisdom of these statesmen devised a peaceful method for abolishing the new feudalism. This new procedure consisted of abolishing the law of primogeniture and of dividing the hereditary fief equally among the sons of a deceased or banished prince. After a few generations of equal division of feudal estates among the male heirs, all the newly created principalities were reduced to political nonentity and were peacefully subject to the civil administration of the governors and prefects appointed by the central imperial government. Feudalism has never been revived during the last twenty-one centuries.

This tradition of equal division of hereditary property among the sons of a family was adopted by all classes of people and has worked for the equalization of wealth and landed property. Primogeniture seemed to have been swept overboard with the disappearance of ancient feudal society, and this new procedure came to be recognized as just and equitable. Because of this, no great estate could stand three generations of successive equal division among the sons. The result has been the total absence of large holdings of land by wealthy and powerful families for any great length of time. This economic equalization has tended greatly to bring about a social structure in which there are practically no class divisions and not even any enduring differences between the rich and the poor.

The founders of the Han Empire came from the lowly strata of society, including butchers, sellers of dog meat, undertakers, peddlers, and farmers. Many of their women were of poor and lowly origin. This was the first and probably the greatest dynasty and empire founded by the people. That fact alone was an important asset in the democratic tradition of China. The 400 years of political and social development under the Han Empire practically shaped and conditioned the main lines of historical evolution of Chinese national life and institutions throughout the later ages.

In addition to the institution of equal division of hereditary estates, the Han statesmen were responsible for initiating as early as the second century B.C. the system of selecting men for public office from among those persons either recommended by public opinion of the localities for their special achievements, or chosen through a competitive examination on their knowledge of the classical literature of ancient China. Throughout the Empire men of poverty and lowly origin often arose to highest positions of honor and power. One of the greatest generals, who fought the Huns and drove them far beyond the Great Wall and the desert, arose from slavery. And hundreds of cabinet ministers came from families of destitution.

The earlier statesmen of the Empire consciously practiced the policy of laissez-faire and strict economy in order to allow the people to recuperate from the devastations of the terrible wars of the third century and to grow accustomed to the peace and order of a unified Empire. It was a conscious effort to put into practice the political philosophy of *wu-wei* (nonactivity) taught by the school of philosophic Taoism. Under this laissez-faire policy commerce and industry flourished and the Empire prospered. There grew up a class of wealthy merchants and "capitalists" who lived in comfort and luxury.

The new political leaders after 140 B.C. were largely Confucianist scholars who were trained on books that exalted a static and essentially agricultural society and who viewed with suspicion and disapproval the rising commercial class, whom they considered as social parasites that toiled not nor spun but lived on the sweat and blood of the toilers. There were several serious attempts to limit the amount of land owned by any single individual and to undertake governmental action for the amelioration of the conditions of the poor. These reform movements culminated in the socialistic policies of Wang Mang, who, in the first years of the Christian era, acquired political power and proclaimed himself Emperor of the New Dynasty, which lasted 16 years (8–23 A.D.). Wang Mang nationalized all land, emancipated all slaves, and instituted government regulations and monopolies of salt, wine, coinage, credit, mining and natural resources. He was the first "New Dealer."

Wang Mang's many socialistic reforms were swept away and he was killed in the revolution which overthrew his dynasty and restored the Han regime. But anti-mercantile, agrarian, and equalitarian thought had become a part of orthodox social and political thinking of Chinese intelligentsia and accounts for the low position which the merchant occupies in the social scale. The conventional ranking of the professions (not classes) into the scholar, the farmer, the artisan, and the merchant is a product of this anti-mercantile tradition.

All these factors—the abolishing of primogeniture, the custom of equal division of inherited property among the sons, the recognition of the justice of people arising to power from lowliness, the selection of men for office-holding by means of competitive examination, the conscious curbing of the men of wealth—all these factors continued to influence the social structure of China, making it more and more democratic. There was no aristocracy as a class except that of learning, and learning was always accessible to all who had the intelligence and the will to acquire it. The social structure was so thoroughly democratized and the process of leveling had gone so far that when the Manchu Dynasty was overthrown in the Revolution of 1911–1912, no one could think of a Chinese family sufficiently prominent to be qualified as a possible candidate for the throne left vacant by the downfall of an alien dynasty. Some thought of the family of Confucius; but it happened that at the time the direct lineal descendant of Confucius, and the inheritor of the ducal title reserved to the Kung family, was a little child hardly one year old. So he was passed over, and even the so-called "constitutional monarchists" had to agree with the republican revolutionaries that the monarchy must be abolished and that a republic was the only thing feasible.

III

All important schools of Chinese thought of the classical period agreed that government should be in the hands of the wisest and best-informed people. They were unconsciously undermining the feudal society by this advocacy of government by those best qualified to govern. With the passing away of feudalism, and especially with the establishment of a unified empire founded and governed by people who arose from the masses, there was felt a great need for securing men of knowledge and wisdom for the ordering of the state.

The founder of the Han Dynasty, who was an unlettered political genius, once rebuked a scholar in these words: "I conquered the Empire on horseback; what use have I for your classical books?" The scholar retorted: "Sire, it is true you have conquered the Empire on horseback; but can you govern it on horseback?" The early years of the Second Empire witnessed the gradual rise of the scholarly class who tamed the conquerors on horseback and helped them to write the laws and institutes, to work out the details of administration, to remedy the grotesque mistakes of the uncouth rulers, and to pacify and stabilize the Empire.

The task of empire-building was truly tremendous. The Han Empire in its great days was almost as large as the China of today. Without modern means of transportation and communication, the work of administering such a vast empire from a central government at Chang-an, maintaining unity and peace for 400 years, and thereby setting up a permanent framework of a unified national life for 2,000 years, was the greatest achievement of the political genius of the Chinese people.

The civil service system originated in the realization of the need for men who knew the language of the classical literature of ancient China. The Empire was composed of vast areas which spoke different dialects, and the only common medium of empire communication was the classical language, which had been at one time a living dialect of fairly wide currency in eastern and northern China, but had become dead by the time of the Second Empire. The first step was to establish a government university with separate faculties or "doctoral colleges," each specializing in one of the ancient classics. But the revival of learning through university education took time and the Empire needed men for government offices. About the year 120 B.C., the Prime Minister, Kung-Sun Hung, in a memorial to the throne, said that the edicts and the laws which were written in elegant classical style were often not understood even by the petty officers whose duty it was to explain and interpret them to the people. Therefore, he recommended that examinations be held for the selection of men who could read and understand the classical language and literature and that those who had shown the best knowledge should have the first preference in appointments to offices requiring the use of the written language. His recommendation was adopted and marked the beginning of the civil service examination system.

Throughout the 400 years of the Han Empire, however, there was not worked out any systematized procedure for the selection of men for public offices. Broadly speaking, there were three methods in use. In the first place, there were the examinations, which had not yet commanded much respect and were apparently limited to clerical and secretarial offices. Secondly, there was the university, which in the second century A.D. was said to have 30,000 students and was becoming a political power much feared by the politicians. The university education naturally gave the youths a fairly reliable chance of civic advancement. Thirdly, from time to time the government would ask the provincial authorities to recommend men of various kinds of attainment. Men were recommended for their "filial piety and purity of character" (*hsiao lien*), for "marked talent" (*mou ts'ai*), for "specially distinguished attainments" (*tso i*), etc. Such recommendations were often, but not regularly, requested by the central government, and those persons thus recommended were usually given offices.

Ts'ao Ts'ao (d. 219 A.D.), one of the greatest statesmen of the age, worked out a system of classifying men into nine grades according to their ability, knowledge, experience, and character. When his son became Emperor in 220 A.D., this system of nine-grade classification was officially adopted for the selection of men for government service. Under this system, the government appointed a special official for each administrative area, who was called "Chung Cheng" (the Impartial Judge) and whose duty it was to list all possible candidates for office and all men of good family, and, on the basis of public opinion and personal knowledge, grade them into nine grades according to their deserts. These gradings, which were to be revised periodically, were to serve as the basis for appointment of these men to offices in the local, provincial, or central government.

This system, known in history as that of "Nine-grade Impartial Judgment," naturally involved much subjective opinion, family influence, and political pressure. It was humanly impossible to find an objective standard for the nine degrees of grading. After being tried out for fully four centuries, it was finally abolished under the Sui Dynasty, which re-unified the country in 589, after a long period of division, and instituted the Government Examination for civil service in 606.

From the beginning of the seventh century to the beginning of the twentieth century, for 1,300 years, the main system of selection of men for office was by open and competitive examination. Roughly speaking, this system has undergone three stages of evolution. The first period, approximately from 600 to 1070, was the age of purely literary and poetic examination. There were other subjects, such as history, law, the Confucian classics and others, in which examinations were regularly held. But somehow the purely literary examinations came to be the only highly prized and universally coveted channel of entrance into public life. The best minds of the country were attracted to this class of examinations. The winners of the highest honors in these poetic and literary examinations became idolized by the whole country and especially by the women; and the successful candidates in these literary examinations usually attained the heights of governmental power more rapidly than those who took the other more prosaic examinations. In the eyes of the nation only these literary and poetic examinations commanded the interest and the admiration of the people, and the other examinations seemed not to count at all.

The reasons for this peculiar pre-eminence of the literary and poetic examinations are not far to seek. While the other examinations required book knowledge and memory work, this class of *ching shih* (advanced scholars) was expected to offer creative poetic composition. The difficult themes assigned and the strict rules prescribed only made the successful winners shine more glamorously. And it is not true that poets are always born and not made. Fashion and training can always make a poet of some sort out of a man of native intelligence. Besides, these original compositions required wide reading, wealth of knowledge, and independence of judgment. For these reasons the *ching shih* came practically to monopolize the civil service for almost four centuries, and great statesmen and empire builders came out of a system which, though fair, seemed completely devoid of practical training.

The second period of the civil service system may be called an age of transition. The purely literary examination had been severely criticized on the ground of its failure to encourage the youths of the nation to prepare themselves in the practical and useful knowledge of morals and government. In the year 1071, the reformer-statesman Wang An-shih succeeded in persuading his Emperor to adopt and proclaim a new system of examinations, in which the poetic compositions were entirely abolished and the scholars were required to specialize in one of the major classics as well as to master the minor classics. Under the new system the scholars were also asked to write an essay on some historic subject and to answer in detail three questions of current and practical importance. This new system was naturally severely attacked by the sponsors of the old poetic examinations. For 200 years the government wavered between the two policies. The prose classical examination was several times discarded and again re-established. Finally the government compromised by offering a dual system placing the poetic composition and the prose classical exposition as two alternate systems for the candidates to choose.

Then came the third period during which the prose classical examination finally became the only legitimate form of civil service examination. The Mongol conquest of North China, and later of the whole of China, had brought about much interruption and dislocation of Chinese political life, including the abolition of the civil service examination system for many decades. When the civil service examinations were revived in 1314, the classical scholars had their way in triumphantly working out an examination system entirely centering around the Confucian classics. In order to make it more attractive to the creative minds, a special form of prose composition was gradually evolved which, though not rhymed, was highly rhythmic, often running in balanced sentences, and so rich in cadence that it could be often sing-songed aloud. All candidates were also required to write a poem on an assigned theme as a supplement to every examination paper. These new developments seemed to have satisfied both the desire for original poetic expression and the more utilitarian demand for a mastery of the Confucian classics, which were supposed to be the foundation of the moral and political life of the Chinese nation. So this new examination system lasted from 1314 to 1905 with comparatively few radical changes in the general scheme.

In a broad sense, therefore, the statesmen of China have seriously attempted to work out and put into practice a system of civil service examination open to all people, irrespective of family, wealth, religion, or race. The subject-matter of the examinations, whether it be original poetic composition or rhythmic prose exposition of the classics, has been severely and probably justly criticized, as useless literary gymnastics. But the main idea behind these examinations is a desire to work out some objective and impartial standard for the selection of men for public offices. The sincerity of that desire was attested throughout history by the development and improvement of the safe-guards against favoritism and fraud in the examinations. One of the safe-guards was the method of sealing the name of the examinee so that no name should appear on the examination paper. Another safe-guard was to have every examination paper copied by the government copyists and to submit to the examiners only the copy and not the original, so that the examiner could not recognize the hand-writing of his own students, friends, or relatives. These techniques were invented about the year 1000 and have been in use in all the later centuries. Fraud in the examinations was punished by the heaviest penalties.

IV

Indeed, the system was so objective and fair that scholars who repeatedly failed to pass the examinations rarely complained of the injustice of the system itself but often comforted themselves with the proverb, "In the examination hall literary merit does not always count," meaning that luck may be against you. As the subject-matter was always taken from the few classics and in later centuries always from the "Four Books" for the lower examinations, it was possible for the poorest family to give a talented child the necessary education, which cost practically nothing in books or in tuition. In the popular theatres, one often sees well-known plays portraying a poor young man or a poor son-in-law of a beggar-chief successfully taking high honors in the examinations. It was a just system which enabled the sons of the poorest and lowliest families to rise through a regular process of competition to the highest positions of honor and power in the Empire.

Throughout the centuries of training under this system, there has grown up a deep-rooted tradition in the minds of the Chinese people that government should be in the hands of those who are best fitted to govern; and that officers and officials of the state are not born of any special class but should be selected through some system of competitive examination open to all who are prepared to take it.

V

The office of the Imperial Censor, or literally the "Imperial Historian," probably derived its extraordinary censorial authority from the very ancient days when the historian was a religious priest and represented the will of the gods. At the time of Confucius stories were told of historians who defied despotic rulers and powerful prime ministers in insisting upon telling and recording the truth as they saw it. They preferred death to changing their recordings.

Confucius himself tried to write a kind of history where every word would imply a moral judgment of approval or disapproval, so that rulers and leaders of states might be encouraged to do good and refrain from evil-doing by their natural regard for the judgment of posterity.

In later ages the historians rarely kept up this rigoristic tradition of truth-telling, but there grew up a new tradition of out-spoken advice and admonition on the part of the Imperial Censors. The duty of out-spoken interrogation and censure of the misdeeds of all government officials from the highest to the lowest was not confined to the Imperial Censors alone or to any particular censorial office. It was in fact a right and a moral duty of all officials of rank to speak freely and frankly to the Imperial Government on all matters concerning the misery and suffering of the people, or astrological signs or warnings pointing to bad government in any particular direction, or policies which should be promoted or abolished. In short, Chinese moral and political tradition required of every government official this sacred duty of serving as the out-spoken adviser of his sovereign.

All political thinking of ancient China taught the importance of out-spoken censure as the only means for the ruler to know his own faults, the disastrous policies of his government, and the grievances of the people. An ancient statesman of the eighth century B.C. is recorded to have said: "To stop the voice of the people is more dangerous than to dam the flow of a river. The wise manager of the river deepens its basin and facilitates its flow. The wise ruler of men encourages them to speak up freely." Free expression and out-spoken opposition are, therefore, safety-valves through which the complaints, protests, and grievances of the people are expressed and heard. They are also mirrors in which the rulers can see their own shortcomings. It is, therefore, the duty of the ruler to tolerate all forms of out-spoken advice and opposition, however offensive they may be.

Throughout the long history of China, there are numberless cases of statesmen who incurred the displeasure of their rulers by courageously opposing what they considered as ruinous policies of the government. Not a few of these out-spoken advisers were put to death or subjected to bodily torture. But, in general, even the most notorious despots usually had an almost religious regard for the tradition which exalted tolerance of frank censure as one of the highest virtues of the ruler. With the exception of the few dark periods of the Ming Dynasty, most of the dynasties treated the out-spoken censors with tolerance and leniency. Some of the great rulers, such as the second Emperor of the Tang Dynasty, were famous for their eagerness to seek frank advice from their ministers. The intimate memorials to the throne by such famous statesmen as Wei Cheng of the seventh century and Lu Chih of the eighth century read like heart-to-heart advice of one faithful friend to another. They cover all kinds of topics from private conduct to military campaigns of great importance. Such works have been an inspiration to statesmen throughout the ages.

Even in those periods when out-spoken censors were punished brutally by the despotic rulers, those martyrs in the cause of free political criticism were usually vindicated, sometimes after a few years and sometimes after one or two generations. In such cases the vindication came in the form of conferring posthumous honors on the martyred censors, some of whom were given seats in the Temple of Confucius. The policies they had sponsored were now adopted and the persons against whom they had fought were now disgraced. As a philosopher of the seventeenth century put it: "There are only two things that are supreme in this world: one is reason, the other, authority. Of the two, reason is the more supreme. For in the history of the struggle of the righteous statesmen against the powerful prime ministers and eunuchs, reason always triumphed over authority in the end." This best expresses the spirit of the Chinese censors: they represented the Chinese historic struggle for liberty.

In a sense, the censorial system may be called the Chinese counterpart for a parliament. Indeed, the censors were called "The Officials Who Speak" (*yen kwan*), which is an etymological reminder of the modern democratic parliaments. The Censorial Office, or Tribunal, was not a law-making organ but undertook almost every other political and semi-judicial function of a modern parliament, including interrogation, impeachment of government officials, passing on the accounts of the governmental departments, and receiving complaints and grievances of the people. Tradition gave it the right "to speak out even on hearsay." There was naturally the danger of malicious libel and political attack without sufficient evidence. But the main idea was to encourage free speech and to initiate investigation in cases where evidence could not be easily obtained without the effort of special investigators.

VI

As I have pointed out, the right and duty to advise the government were not confined to the censors alone. All central and provincial officials above a certain rank had the right and the duty to petition the throne on all matters affecting the policy of the government or the interest of the people. In the light of history, much of the advice offered was ridiculous, and many of the issues bitterly fought were trivial. But this tradition of encouragement to out-spoken opposition has, on the whole, played an important and beneficial part in the molding of Chinese political life. It has not only trained the nation to regard out-spoken and fighting officials as national heroes and protectors of the interests of the people, but it has also taught the people to think that government needs censorial check and control and that outspoken opposition to the misdeeds of government officials and even of emperors and empresses is a necessary part of a political constitution.

These three historical factors—a democratized and classless social structure, a traditional belief in the selection of office-holders through an objective competitive examination, and a long history of encouragement of outspoken censorial control of the government—these are the heritages of my people from the political development throughout the long centuries. They are the historical factors which alone can explain the Chinese Revolution, the overthrow of the monarchy, the establishment of a republican form of government, and the constitutional development of the last 30 years and of the years to come.

The best evidence of the great importance of these historical heritages is the fact that Dr. Sun Yat-sen, the Father of the Chinese Revolution and of the Republic, deliberately adopted the power of examination for civil service and the power of censorial control of the government as two of the five divisions of governmental power, the other three being the traditional executive, legislative, and judicial powers. In these three decades of revolutionary wars and foreign invasion, China has not yet worked out a permanent constitution. But it is safe to predict that the future constitution of China will be a workable democratic constitution made possible by these historical factors without which no importation or imitation of foreign political institutions can function and take root.

CHAPTER 6

Ambassador Hu Shih Describes China's Ten-Year Fight for Freedom, Struggle against Aggression[1]

"Five main factors—space, numbers, historical unity, internal reconstruction and external aid—have made the miracle of China's sustaining power possible and enabled her to fight on against such a formidable foe."[2]

DR. HU SHIH

Today, September 19, 1941, marks the beginning of the eleventh year of Japan's latest aggression in China and of China's fight for freedom.

The general public outside China only remember that Japan's war of aggression in China was started on July 7, 1937, and that China has been fighting for her national freedom and independence for over four years and two months. But students of history and our people in China always remember that the Japanese war in China was begun ten years ago last night, September 18, 1931, when the Japanese army carried out a well conceived plot to attack the Chinese city of Mukden on that night and to place the whole of Manchuria under Japanese military conquest.

The plot was successful. All the three provinces of Manchuria were occupied by the Japanese army in a few months. By January 1932, the war was extended to Shanghai, where the first Shanghai War lasted forty days and resulted in tens of thousands of casualties and hundreds of millions of dollars in destruction of Chinese property. In the same year, Japan, in open defiance of the opinion of the civilized world, set up "Manchukuo" as a puppet

---

1. *Life Association News* 36, no. 2 (October 1941): 136–138, 213–215. Reprinted with permission from the National Association of Insurance and Financial Advisors.
2. This callout was inserted in the original document.

kingdom under the military and economic control of Japan. By the spring of 1933 the Japanese army carried the war beyond Manchuria, beyond the Great Wall into North China. Throughout the years 1933 to 1937, Japan tried every conceivable form of political intrigue and armed threat to nip off North China from the jurisdiction of the National Government of China.

At the first stage of Japan's aggression in China, the New International Order, as represented by the League of Nations and the Signatories of the Kellogg-Briand Pact, did what it could to mediate for a peaceful settlement of the Sino-Japanese conflict. But all its efforts could not bring Japan's military caste to its senses. It pronounced a judgment and proposed a settlement which was tantamount to almost complete surrender to Japan's wishes in Manchuria. Even that was refused by Japan. She withdrew from the League of Nations in March, 1933.

The civilized world at that time was not prepared to support the World Order by curbing Japanese aggression with effective economic and political power. Nothing effective, therefore, was done by the supporters of the so-called Collective Security.

China, therefore, was left to work out her own salvation by herself. For six long years, from 1931 to 1937, China tried every possible means patiently to appease Japan in order that a large-scale war might be postponed as long as possible, and in order that China might have more time to better prepare herself for the war which every competent observer knew was inevitable and imminent.

But no amount of appeasement could stop or even postpone the unlimited and insatiable aggression of Japan. On July 7, 1937, Japan started her full-fledged war of aggression in the North. On August 13, her army, navy and air force began their Central China campaign with the second Shanghai War.

Peking and Tientsin fell on July 28, 1937. After almost three months of most heroic resistance, the Chinese armies were forced to withdraw from Shanghai in November, 1937. Nanking, the national capital, fell in December of the same year.

In October, 1938, Canton was captured by the Japanese invaders. Hankow, the First Provisional capital of China, was lost in the same month.

With the loss of Canton, China was cut off from her important accesses to the sea, having lost most of the other coastal cities during the first year of the war. Since then China has had to rely upon back-doors for exports and for war supplies from the outside world.

At one time there were three such back-doors. The first was the French

Railroad through Indo-China to the province of Yunnan; the second, the "Burma Road" which includes the Burma Railroad from Yangon to Lashio and the highway from Lashio to Kunming: and the third, the trans-continental highway to Soviet Russia.

Since the collapse of France last summer and since the Japanese invasion into French Indo-China last September, the French Railroad has been closed to all Chinese traffic. We are now relying only on the two-thousand-mile highway to Russia and the famous Burma Road for all our war supplies from abroad and for all our exports with which to pay for these supplies.

NO ACCESS TO SEA

Thus, a great population of hundreds of millions has been fighting hard and terrible war against a first class military and naval power for all these four years without direct access to the sea. Our enemy is in complete control of the sea, the air, and most of the important types of railroads and waterways. We have lost practically all the cities shown to you as centers of population, of trade and manufacture and of education and culture—all the centers of modern commerce and industry, from Harbin to Canton, from Peking to Hankow, from Shanghai to Ichang, have been either devastated or occupied by the invaders.

At least over a million lives have been lost, and millions have lost their homes, their farms, their shops, their livelihood.

Practically all the important universities and colleges have been in exile in the vast interior provinces, often one thousand or even two thousand miles from their original sites, and mostly operating without the minimum library and laboratory equipment, and in constant danger of air raids.

PRICES HAVE SOARED

Prices of commodities have soared sky-high, in some places the food price has risen 1,100 percent of the pre-war level. Clothing material, piece goods and leather goods are exceedingly difficult to obtain. A package of shaving blades is regarded as a great luxury.

The inhuman bombings of cities and towns without the slightest military importance have been going on for all these four years. The city of

Chungking, the present capital of China, has been subjected to most cruel bombings for over two years. In May 1939, when the city was unprepared for air raids, over ten thousand people were killed in one devastating raid. During the last two years Chungking has developed into a most perfectly sheltered city against air raids, and the loss of lives has been comparatively small. But that city has been almost completely destroyed three times during the last three summers. An American newspaper correspondent, Mr. A. T. Steele, who was witness during several raids, reported: "Japanese planes laid a mile-long row of two hundred fifty pound bombs along what was left of Chungking's Main Street in as senseless and cruel a piece of bombing as I had ever seen."

I have cited these few facts in order to give you, however inadequately, some idea of the great hardship and terrible suffering under which my people have been fighting during these years. I want all friends of China to understand that, in spite of this hardship and suffering, the Government and the people of China are determined to fight on, unflinchingly, possibly for many more months to come, possibly for many years to come. Your Founding Fathers of the Republic fought almost eight long years before American independence was finally achieved. In the same way and with the same determination, China's resistance to the aggressor will go on until she has achieved her objective of national freedom and independence.

THE FIVE FACTORS

You will probably ask me how it is possible for China to fight on so long under such great handicaps against such a formidable foe. China's four years' fight against Japanese aggression has been called a modern miracle, and I shall devote the remainder of my time to an explanation of the factors which have made this miracle possible.

In brief there are five main factors which have made up China's sustaining power:

1. Space
2. Number
3. Historical unity
4. Internal reconstruction
5. External aid

First—Space. China has the rich inheritance of vast space to move about in. After ten years of intermittent war, and especially after four years of large scale hostilities, our enemy can barely claim effectively to have occupied more than 10 percent of China's territory. Mr. Hallett Abend of the *New York Times* estimates the area under Japanese military occupation as 12 percent of Chinese territory. But others would place this area far below 10 percent. Generalissimo Chiang Kai-shek has told the world that the principle of his strategy in the war against Japan is "to trade space for time." The spatial factor has been most important in China's ability to bog down the Japanese invader and gain four years' time. This factor of space was not fully understood until Hitler's blitzkrieg succeeded in conquering more than a dozen European countries in the brief space of a few months. Those countries in western and northern Europe and in the Balkans have fallen one after another because they were lacking sufficient space with which to trade for time. The recent success of Soviet Russia in withholding the onslaught of the German Panzer Divisions on all fronts has furnished fresh proof that the most effective weapon against a blitzkrieg is time which can only be gained by means of vast space and large man power.

THE VAST POPULATION

The second factor is number, that is, vast population as actual and potential supply of man power. In all these four years, China has suffered great military reverses in the face of superior mechanized armies of the invader, but, because of our numerical superiority, the enemy has never been able to encircle or trap any large Chinese army. And we have been able to utilize the time gained in training more and more new divisions and new officers so that even the Japanese military High Command states that Generalissimo Chiang Kai-shek still has at least three million trained soldiers under his command. That is to say, even our enemy admits that the size of the Chinese army, not counting the vast guerilla forces, is greater today than it was four years ago when the war started. And we are confident that a nation of seventy million Japanese can never conquer a nation of four hundred fifty million.

NATIONAL UNITY

The third factor is our historical national unity. It is not true, as you have been frequently told, that China has been unified by the Japanese invasion and by four years of war. Such a miracle can not happen in so short a time. Let it be said once and for all that the Chinese national unity has been of twenty-one centuries' making. China was unified into an Empire about 200 B.C. During these last twenty-one centuries and a half, there have been short periods of separation and of foreign invasion. But broadly speaking, the Chinese people have been living continuously for over twenty-one centuries under one Empire, one government, one system of law, one written language, one form of education and one historical culture. This continuity of unified national life has no parallel in the history of any race, nation or continent, so that it is rarely fully appreciated by the foreign observer, who often writes about Chinese disunity during the first two decades of the Republic, and fails to grasp the fundamental feeling of national unity, behind, and in spite of the internal political strife. It is this age-long sense of historical unity that is now holding the whole country together, inspiring the people to fight on most heroically for the deliverance of their country from the invader, comforting them in their adversity and misery and making it possible for millions of them patiently to bear great humiliation and agony in enemy-occupied territory, never despairing that final victory would be with their long-lived Fatherland.

INTERNAL RECONSTRUCTION

The fourth factor in China's sustaining power has been a whole decade of internal reconstruction. China was caught ten years ago totally unprepared to fight an enemy who happened to be a first rate military and naval power. Our leaders fully realized that as soon as a large scale war began, China would have to lose all the modern cities on the eastern and south-eastern coast and possibly all along the lower half of the Yangtze River, and to face defenselessly a rigid blockade by the powerful navy of the enemy. Therefore during those years of apparel appeasement, our leaders were not only drilling, training, equipping and, as far as possible, modernizing our army units, but were also taking important steps in mapping out a long-term economic and industrial reconstruction in the vast hinterland of China's west and south-west in anticipation of the imminent war and naval blockade.

THE BURMA ROAD

The first step in this direction was to build railroads and highways towards the west, north-west and south-west. A great network of motor roads has been built up during these ten years which includes the trans-continental highway to Russia and the famous Burma Road. Only last week, Mr. F. Tillman Durdin of the *New York Times* reported from Burma on the wonderful feat of the Burma Road. I quote a few sentences from his despatch to give you a picture of China's achievement in the field of interest transportation. "The Burma Road," says Mr. Durdin, "has never been adequately described. Built almost entirely by hand labor, the road is a staggering achievement and without doubt the greatest highway construction feat of modern times. It twists over seemingly impassable 18,000-foot mountains and finds its way through 3,000-foot gorges. At places the road has been chiseled into the face of sheer mountainside with thousands of feet of canyon below. The southern section runs through the worst malarial jungles in the world."

INDUSTRIAL PLANTS

Equally important was the step to establish modern industrial plants in the interior. Shortly before the outbreak of the war, the Government took the decisive step in dismantling more than four hundred factories and transporting their mechanical equipment to the interior, including the equipment of machine works, metallurgical plants, chemical works, cotton mills, flour mills and paper factories. The total weight of the machinery thus transported with Government help amounted to over seventy thousand tons. In addition, blast furnaces, iron and steel furnaces and other related materials necessary for the steel industry were also sent into the interior. In order to feed the planned industries in the interior, mining equipments including hoisting, pumping and other equipment were transported from the mines of Honan into the south-western provinces in order that coal mines may be operated with more up to date equipment. The total weight of these materials from the mines and the furnaces thus transported was about fifty thousand tons. To supplement these transported plants, the Government also started a number of new factories including electrolytic copper plants, electrical apparatus factories and machine works. This new equipment totaled over ten thousand tons in weight.

It took from one year to two years to transport, set up and operate these factories in the hitherto unindustrialized interior. They are widely distributed in the vast interior in localities unknown even to myself and are now in full operation. It is these almost miraculously transported and transplanted factories which have been making arms for our defensive warfare, feeding the mechanical needs of our vast war machine, mining our old and new mines and producing chemicals, textiles, flour and paper for the military and civilian needs of Free China.

These measures for building up a vast system of communication and transportation and for the industrialization of the interior provinces constitute the fourth factor of China's power of resistance—the reconstruction of the great west.

The last, but not the least, factor is external assistance to China. It is no exaggeration to say that China has been able to fight on all these years because we have been able to receive important assistance from our friends abroad. Throughout these years, we have been receiving aid in one form or another from Soviet Russia, Great Britain, the United States and France before her collapse. This assistance has taken various forms—sometimes in the form of loans or commercial credits, sometimes in the form of military supplies purchased under barter, sometimes in the direction of maintaining our air routes and trade routes for our communication with the outside world and for transportation of our exports and imports, and sometimes in the form of economic embargo of important military and industrial supplies and materials against our enemy.

POLICY OF ASSISTANCE

Of these four friendly powers aiding China, the United States has been most consistent and generous in her policy of giving assistance to countries resisting aggression. Even in those early days of isolation sentiment and neutrality legislation, the American Government took great pains in searching for ways and means to help China in her distress. The first American aid came in the form of purchasing Chinese silver, which gave my people the first source of foreign exchange with which to buy our war supplies in America. The second aid was the commercial credit of twenty-five million dollars given to China at a time when China had just lost Canton and Hankow and was probably at the lowest ebb in her national morale. This loan, announced on

December 15, 1938, therefore served as a kind of miraculous injection to a sinking heart. Since that first loan, there have followed the twenty million dollar commercial credit of April 1940; the twenty-five million dollar commercial credit of September 1940 and the one hundred million dollar loan of December 1940. In addition to these forms of financial aid, the United States Government has taken other steps which have proven as effective as these loans in helping China and curbing her enemy. One of these steps was the abrogation, in July 1939, of the Treaty of Commerce with Japan. Another was the various forms of limited embargo of essential materials against Japan.

THE LEASE-LEND ACT

A very important step was taka in March 1941, when Congress passed the Lease-Lend Act and appropriated seven billion dollars to carry out the national policy of giving material assistance to the countries resisting aggression. In one of his historic speeches, President Roosevelt said: "China shall have our help." During these several months, China has been receiving important material assistance under the Lease-Lend Act. A special mission of military and technical experts under the leadership of Brigadier General John Magruder is going to Chungking to take charge of the Lease-Lend materials at the China end.

Another and probably the most important step in this direction was undertaken by the American Government in the last days of July when Japanese assets in this country were ordered frozen, all aviation gasoline and motor fuel and all oil products from which these could be derived were placed under embargo, and Japanese commerce and shipping with this country were virtually entirely stopped.

This last economic pressure on Japan has been made more effective by the support and "parallel" action of the entire British Empire and the Netherlands East Indies.

ECONOMIC PRESSURE

This most effective economic weapon against Japanese aggression, which American public opinion had been advocating all these years, has now been in full operation for about six weeks. It is already beginning to show important effects on the national life and militaristic tempo of Japan. For Japan is a nation most vulnerable to this economic embargo. While she can manufacture most of the weapons of war, she is extremely lacking in the raw materials with which to manufacture these weapons. She is also lacking in oil and motor fuel. Seventy-five percent of the oil has been coming from the United States. More than half of the imported iron ore and scrap iron and steel also came from America. From this country came also over 80 percent of her imported raw cotton. As recently as 1939, 57 percent of her imported machines and machine-tools came from the United States, the remaining 43 percent coming from Germany, Britain and other counties.

An American embargo, supported by the British and the Dutch East indies Governments, on all these coal materials, is therefore the most powerful weapon to curb the aggressive and destructive power of Japan. I am quite confident that the American people, once fully realizing the wonderful efficacy of this economic weapon, will not lightly relax or abandon it until its enforcement has succeeded in driving home to the Japanese military and the Japanese people the plain lesson that aggression does not pay and war is suicide.

TOWARD YORKTOWN

These, then, are the five factors which go to make up China's power of resistance. We still have the vast space. We still have the unlimited man power. Our historical sense of national unity has gone through a few baptisms of fire and blood and has come out of it more solid and more unshakable than ever. Our internal economic and industrial reconstruction in the interior is showing more and better results every month: we are making more arms and producing more goods for export and home consumption. And, on top of all these, the whole international situation has turned more and more in our favor and against the enemy. The political isolation and moral ostracizing of Japan has long been completed by her own action. And the economic encirclement and strangling of Japan is now being completed—again by her own action.

China has long left her Valley Forge and is now confidently marching on to her final victory at her Yorktown!

For October, 1941

Dr. Hu Shih was born in Shanghai and came to study in America in 1910 on a Chinese government scholarship. Four years later he was graduated Phi Beta Kappa from Cornell University, and then took up graduate studies at Cornell and Columbia, where he took his Ph.D. degree. It was at this time that he conceived the idea of a common written language for the Chinese, took a dialect known to 90 percent of his people as its basis, and formed what is now the accepted literary language of China. From 1917 to 1932 he spent most of his time in China as a member of the faculty of some of his country's leading universities, lecturing, writing, and working for greater understanding of China and its people among Occidentals. He lectured at the University of Chicago in 1933, and was one of the moving forces in the Institute of Pacific Relations. He edited and published a weekly review of liberal opinion from 1932 to 1937, and spent the following year lecturing and traveling in the United States. He was appointed Chinese Ambassador to the United States in September, 1938.[3]

---

3. This author bio was included in the original document.

CHAPTER 7

The Conflict of Ideologies[1]

In the 1940 edition of *Webster's New International Dictionary* the fashionable word "ideology," as it is currently used, is defined as follows:

> 4. *a* A subjective interpretation of observed phenomena, esp., of social phenomena. *b* A systematic scheme of ideas about life. *c* Manner or content of thinking characteristic of an individual or class; as, bourgeois *ideology*.

USE OF THE WORD "IDEOLOGY"

In what sense do we use the term "ideology" when we talk about "the conflict of ideologies"?

In a column dated July 2, 1941, Miss Dorothy Thompson made frequent use of this term. She says:

> The Soviet-German war has ideological consequences, the first being that the Red Army chooses to rally the people around the battle cry of homeland and Russian soil, rather than world Communism. . . . What the ideology of the Red Army may be, time will tell. We suspect that it is nationalist and Russian. . . . In fact we suspect that three ideologies will be liquidated by this war—Communism, Nazi-ism, and Toryism.

---

1. This paper was first presented at the University of Michigan on July 8, 1941, and later published in the *Annals of the American Academy of Political and Social Science*, an issue titled "Public Policy in a World at War," 218 (November 1941): 26–35. It was also translated into Chinese under the title "Minzhu yu jiquan de chongtu" (民主與極權的 衝突), which was published in the first issue of the *Free China Journal* 自由中國 in November 1949. See *Free China Journal* *1* (November 1949): 5–8.

In the latter part of her column, Miss Thompson advocates that the United States spend "the cost of one battleship" to finance a "gargantuan propaganda campaign" to present the broad outlines of an American peace to the world—"openly on the air waves of the planet, and twenty-four hours a day." But she says:

> Such a campaign should not be ideological—it should be addressed to the reason, realism, common sense, and heart-broken yearnings of the people of the whole world. . . . Precisely, because the ideologies have all proved themselves to be unmitigated buncombe, the voice of reason—reason combined with power—has an audience.

In these passages, one of the masters of journalistic prose seems to have used the term "ideology" as meaning some system of ideas which has come to be the accepted scheme of thinking of a group, e.g., of the Communist Party, the Nazi Party, or the English Tories, or, as Miss Thompson suggests, possibly of the Red Army of Soviet Russia as a result of the new phase of the war. It is significant to note that Miss Thompson seems to have regarded "ideologies" as having "all proved themselves to be unmitigated buncombe" and as opposed to "the voice of reason." When a set of ideas, such as "the broad outlines of an American peace," is addressed to the reason, realism, and common sense of the people, then it is *not* ideological, even though it be aggressively preached by means of a "gargantuan propaganda campaign," in all languages "and twenty-four hours a day."

Here the question arises: Must the term "ideology" be limited to "unmitigated buncombe"? If, according to Miss Thompson, Toryism is an ideology, how about Whiggism and Liberalism? And if the Red Army of Soviet Russia should actually abandon the ideology of world revolution and adopt an ideology which is nationalist and Russian, would it necessarily be another "unmitigated buncombe"?

Since the conflict of ideologies could not be easily and summarily dismissed as merely a conflict among the various schemes of unmitigated buncombe, it seems advisable to regard the term "ideology" not as implying adverse judgment, but merely as a neutral term, meaning any set or system of ideas about life, society, and government, originating in most cases as consciously advocated or dogmatically asserted social, political, or religious slogans or battle cries and, through long processes of propaganda and usage, gradually becoming the characteristic beliefs or dogmas of a particular group, party, or nationality.

In this sense we may better understand the conflict of ideologies of our own times. This conflict is a real conflict among the several contradicting and opposing systems of ideas about life, society, economic organization, and political institutions. It is not merely a conflict between the ideologies of the Left and the Right—between the ideology of the communism of Marx, Lenin, and Stalin and the ideologies of fascist Italy and Nazi Germany. No. A more real and more fundamental conflict has come about because each of these totalitarian systems has undertaken to condemn, combat, and destroy what all of them regard as their common antithesis, their common enemy, namely, the system of democratic ideas, ideals, practices, and institutions.

DEMOCRACIES WERE UNPREPARED

The conflict of ideologies is therefore in reality an aggressive onslaught of the totalitarian systems against the ideologically defenseless and unprepared democracies.

The liberal and democratic peoples were unprepared for such an offensive assault because, ever since the great democratic revolutions of the seventeenth, eighteenth, and nineteenth centuries, the movement of political democracy had carried the day and was triumphantly and confidently beginning to convert the whole civilized world to its several slightly divergent but essentially similar systems of constitutional, parliamentary, democratic forms of government. The age of heated debate and pamphleteering on the pros and cons of republicanism and democracy, of human equality and liberty, had long passed, and the democracies had settled down to consolidate and enjoy their historic gains and had contented themselves with merely making minor modifications or reforms here and there to perfect their social and political institutions. They had least expected, on the eve of winning a stupendous world war waged to make the world safe for democracy, to find themselves suddenly caught in a world revolution which sought to establish the dictatorship of the proletariat and to "smash" all bourgeois parliamentarianism and bourgeois democracy—a world revolution which openly justified the dictatorial rule of the proletariat over the bourgeoisie, "a rule unrestricted by law, based on force," and which set up the new totalitar-

ian form of government that recognized only the leadership and dictatorship of one party "which does not share and cannot share their leadership
with other parties."

The self-complacent democracies were not prepared to deal with this
new movement. Indeed they did not know what to do with it. They were
horrified by its ruthless excesses. At first they sought to fight it with armed
force. Later they tried to isolate it.

But neither armed force nor diplomacy nor isolation could stop the
spread of this antidemocratic movement throughout the world. And the
world had not been made safe for democracy. Wherever there was confusion,
disorder, and discontent, there was fertile soil for the rise and growth of dictatorship. Autocratic rule seemed to point the way to Order, Strength,
Employment, Prosperity, and Glory. Indeed it promised Utopia.

Thus in the course of two decades, antidemocratic movements have
taken possession of many lands and large populations. By 1922 Mussolini's
fascism captured Italy. By 1933 Hitler's national socialism conquered Germany. International communism and nationalistic fascism and Nazism,
while they differ in numerous details, agree in their attack on the democratic
ideas and ideals and in their totalitarian dictatorial political systems.

ROLE OF PROPAGANDA

This new despotism was forceful, unscrupulous, ruthless, and self-righteous.
It had vigor, freshness, and glamour. It was, above all, aggressive in its attacks
on the democracies. The democracies were dazzled and puzzled by this
aggressive and destructive criticism. They were not ready to answer back.
They were vaguely conscious of the historical value of their own institutions;
they vaguely talked about their own "way of life" as being worth preserving;
but they were backward and inefficient in organizing propaganda and in
working out a simplified and unified scheme of ideological defense. They are
too proud and too self-complacent to defend themselves against what they
consider unmitigated bunk. And they are too individualistic ever to undertake organized propaganda effectively. For it is propaganda which has been
chiefly responsible for the great success in the spread of antidemocratic
movements and in the attack on and discrediting of democratic ideas and
institutions. In the words of Adolf Hitler, the greatest master of the science
and art of propaganda, the task of propaganda

has not to search into truth as far as this is favorable to others, in order to present it to the masses with doctrinary honesty, but it has rather to serve its own truth uninterruptedly . . . it has to confine itself to little and repeat this eternally. . . . The purpose of propaganda is not continually to produce interesting changes for a few *blasé* little masters, but to convince; that means, to convince the masses. The masses, however, with their inertia, always need a certain time before they are ready even to notice a thing, and they will lend their memories only to the thousandfold repetition of the most simple ideas.[2]

It is this "thousandfold repetition of the most simple ideas" which has gradually undermined the faith of thousands and hundreds of thousands of people in the ideas and ideals of the democratic movement which had become fairly generally accepted by the intelligentsia and the people of the modern world. "Representative democratic government is the political concomitant of economic capitalism." "Democracy is the decadent form of government." "The goddess of Liberty is dead and her body is already putrescent."[3] "Down with bourgeois parliamentarism and bourgeois democracy." Against the powerful propaganda of such simple ideas, the democratic peoples, in their traditional disdain and self-complacency, have made no attempt to defend their own institutions and the philosophies behind them.

DEMOCRACIES ARE AROUSED

It is only during these last years of the second World War that a few great leaders of the democracies have begun to fight back the organized attack of the totalitarian nations. It has taken an unprecedented war and the rapid conquest of a dozen free and democratic nations to make these leaders realize the seriousness of the antidemocratic campaign. The great tragedy of Europe and the great threat to the Anglo-Saxon world have now begun to force upon the surviving democracies the real gravity of the conflict of ideologies—a conflict which, in the last analysis, is no more and no less than a well-planned and powerfully directed ideological propaganda against the very foundations of democratic institutions and democratic civilization.

2. *Mein Kampf* (New York: Reynal & Hitchcock, 1941), 236, 238, 239.
3. Mussolini in March 1923, quoted by George Catlin in *The Story of the Political Philosophers* (New York: McGraw-Hill, 1939), 720.

Of the few great leaders who are fully aware of the dangers of this anti-democratic attack stands pre-eminently President Franklin D. Roosevelt. In his Dayton speech of October 12, 1940, President Roosevelt said:

> We are determined to use our energies and our resources to counteract and repel the foreign plots, the propaganda, the whole technique of underground warfare originating in Europe and now clearly directed against all of the republics on this side of the ocean.
>
> That propaganda repeats and repeats that democracy is a decadent form of government. They tell us that our old democratic ideal, our old traditions of civil liberties are things of the past.
>
> We reject that thought. We say that we are the future. We say that the direction in which they would lead us is backward to the bondage of the Pharaohs, backward to the slavery of the Middle Ages.

In his Third Inaugural Address of January 20, 1941, he sounded the same battle cry:

> There are men who believe that democracy, as a form of government and a frame of life, is limited or measured by a kind of mystical and artificial fate— that, for some unexplained reason, tyranny and slavery have become the surging wave of the future, and that freedom is an ebbing tide. But we Americans know that this is not true. . . .
>
> Most vital to our present and to our future is this experience (of the last eight years) of a democracy which successfully survived crises at home; put away many evil things; built new structures on enduring lines; and, through it all, maintained the fact of its democracy.
>
> For action has been taken within the three-way framework of the Constitution of the United States. The co-ordinate branches of the government continue freely to function. The Bill of Rights remains inviolate. The freedom of elections is wholly maintained. Prophets of the downfall of American democracy have their dire predictions come to naught.
>
> No, democracy is not dying.
>
> We know it because we have seen it revive and grow.
>
> We know it cannot die because it is built on the unhampered initiative of individual men and women joined together in a common enterprise—an enterprise undertaken and carried through by the free expression of a free majority.

We know it because democracy alone, of all forms of government, enlists the full force of men's enlightened will.

We know it because democracy alone has constructed an unlimited civilization capable of infinite progress in the improvement of human life.

In these utterances the conflict is defined, the challenge accepted, and the battle joined. It is a conflict of democracy versus tyranny, of freedom versus slavery, of government by constitution and law versus absolute dictatorial power, of free expression of men's enlightened will versus blind and unconditional obedience to party and "leader."

In a remarkable communication published in *The New York Times* on May 11, 1941, Mr. Max Eastman (who was twice tried and barely escaped a jail sentence for having too vigorously opposed American entrance into the last World War) strongly advocates that "vicarious belligerence" in the form of all-out aid to Britain is not enough and that the American Nation

> ought to be ready, in case of certain need, to fight by England's side . . . this war is not merely a struggle for national power, but a struggle between democracy and tyranny. This war is, if any war in history ever was, a war between two ways of life. . . . The conflict between Babylon and Judea, Egypt and Assyria, Athens and Sparta, Greece and Persia even, showed no cultural contrast to compare with that between modern democracy and totalitarianism.

CHARACTERISTICS OF TOTALITARIANISM

To prove this emphatic statement of the gigantic struggle Mr. Eastman enumerates twenty-one major traits of totalitarianism, "every one of them to be found in Germany, Italy, and Russia, not one in England or the United States." As his "condensed list" represents a concrete method of describing the two opposing ways of life lying behind the conflict of ideologies, I reproduce it here in further condensed form. The twenty-one major traits of totalitarianism are:

1. Nationalistic emotion is exalted to the point of religious frenzy.
2. A single party, disciplined like an army, takes over the power of the state.

3. Dissenting opinion is ruthlessly stamped out.

4. Supernatural religion is subordinated to the religion of nationalism.

5. The "leader" forms the focus of devotion and becomes to all intents and purposes a god.

6. Anti-intellectualism in the form of flattery to the ignorant and severe penalty to honest thinking.

7. Anti-intellectualism in the form of destruction of books and distortion of historical and scientific truth.

8. Anti-intellectualism in the form of abolishing disinterested science and honest scholarship.

9. Dogma replaces debate and the press is controlled by the party and the state.

10. Cultural isolation of the population in order to prevent it from knowing the real condition of the outside world.

11. Party control of creative art.

12. Immoralism in all forms of political lying and governmental hypocrisy.

13. Immoralism in the form of state-planned crimes.

14. Encouragement of the people to bait and torture the so-called public enemies.

15. Revival of the barbaric principle of family and tribal guilt for the crime of such public enemies.

16. Preparations for perpetual war and complete militarization of the population.

17. Reckless encouragement of increase in population.

18. Subordination of women.

19. Liberal use of the phraseology of working-class revolution against capitalism.

20. Prohibition of strikes and protests from labor, and the destruction of labor movements.

21. Industry, commerce, and agriculture are controlled by the party and the leader.

President Roosevelt refutes the charge that democracy is the decadent and dying form of government by showing that the democratic system has the vitality to revive and grow. Mr. Max Eastman dramatizes the sharpness of the fundamental struggle by enumerating the evil and barbaric features peculiar to totalitarianism and absent in the democracies. These represent two distinct and valuable ways to meet the antidemocratic challenge and attack. They present two approaches to the study of the "conflict of ideologies."

But there seems to be room for a third and possibly other approaches to the problem. In the remaining portion of this article, I propose to resolve the conflict of democratic and antidemocratic ideologies into a few deeper and more basic philosophical conflicts.

What, then, are the basic concepts which differentiate the democratic way of life from the antidemocratic way of life?

Going beyond the old and familiar slogans and ideas (such is "liberty, equality, fraternity," and "natural and inalienable rights," etc.) I should like to suggest that the real conflict between the democratic and antidemocratic way of life is centered around two basic contradictions or antithesis: (1) It is the technique of radical and cataclysmic revolution versus the technique of progressive and piecemeal reform. (2) It is the principle of uniformity versus the principle of diversified individual development.

RADICAL REVOLUTION VERSUS PIECEMEAL REFORM

The first basic characteristic of totalitarian regimes is that they all stand for radical and catastrophic revolution and that they all scorn and spurn specific reforms as superficial and useless. Not only have they achieved absolute political power through revolution and violence, but they have all invariably sought to perpetuate the technique of violent revolution and to universalize that technique in order to bring about similar cataclysmal revolution throughout the whole world. They are the self-appointed apostles and champions of "total revolution," of "world revolution," of "permanent revolution," of "eternal war."

The *Communist Manifesto* of 1848 calls for a world-wide communist revolution:

> Communists scorn to hide their views and aims. They openly declare that their purpose can only be achieved by the forcible overthrow of the whole extant social order.

All the totalitarian systems that have arisen since 1917 have been revolutions of the radical and cataclysmal kind in the sense that they all seek, in the words of Adolf Hitler, "to pull down a world and build up a new one."

Moreover, their leaders were all obsessed by the idea that it was not possible to overthrow the whole extant social order in any one country without at the same time overthrowing the same social order in the neighboring countries. Hence the necessity of world revolution, of "total" revolution. And the technique of revolution must be violent and catastrophic: it must destroy everything of the old order. "There is nothing," says Hermann Rauschning in his *Revolution of Nihilism*, "that this destruction would spare. And nothing will be taken over from the old order into the new, neither army nor church, neither the institutions of property nor the elements of culture."[4]

It is this eternal stress on the necessity of radical and violent revolution, both as an internal political technique and as world policy, which constitutes the first basic concept differentiating these totalitarian systems from the *modern* democracies. I say "modern democracies" advisedly, for, as we can recall, one hundred and fifty years ago there were apostles of republicanism, like Robespierre, Saint-Just, and Babeuf, who believed in and practiced the technique of violent revolution. Even Thomas Paine gloried in the prospect of a general revolution in the system of governments of Europe. He wrote to Lafayette in February 1792: "When France shall be surrounded by Revolutions she will be in peace and safety."

PROGRESS AS VIEWED BY THE DEMOCRACIES

But the modern democracies have in general abandoned the idea of radical revolution and are content with piecemeal processes of social, economic, and political reform. Vaguely and unconsciously, but unmistakably, the basic philosophy of modern democratic political procedure is that progress is not made by violent and destructive upheavals, but by the steady accumulation of specific improvements and reforms.

American philosophers have tried to make this unconscious tendency into a conscious and articulate philosophy. William James used the word "meliorism" to denote an ethical philosophy which teaches that the world is imperfect and incomplete but that man has the power to aid its betterment. John Dewey has developed a theory of progress: "Progress is not a wholesale matter, but a retail job, to be contracted for and executed in sections."[5] This

---

4. Hermann Rauschning, *Revolution of Nihilism: Warning to the West* (New York: Alliance Book Corporation; Longmans, Green, 1939), 87.

5. John Dewey, "Progress," *International Journal of Ethics*, April 1916; reprinted in his

conception of progress calls for neither radical revolution nor fatalistic laissez faire, but for individual effort, devotion, intelligence, and patience. In
the words of President Roosevelt: "Democracy alone has constructed an
unlimited civilization capable of infinite progress in the improvement of
human life." As the history of the centuries has shown, that progress in the
improvement of human life has been in the main brought about through
what Dewey calls "a retail job."

This difference between radical catastrophic revolution and piecemeal
improvement I consider the most fundamental antithesis between the democratic and the totalitarian ways of life. This basic difference explains almost
everything else in the conflicting systems.

It explains, for instance, why antidemocratic regimes must be dictatorial
and totalitarian. All social radicalism must inevitably lead to political dictatorship, because only absolute power can achieve the task of radical revolution; only violence and unlimited terroristic despotism can accomplish the
complete overthrow of the extant order and prevent its return or revival. As
Lenin put it:

> Revolution is undoubtedly the most authoritarian thing in the world. Revo-
> lution is an act in which one section of the population imposes its will upon
> the other by rifles, bayonets, and other such exceedingly authoritarian
> means.[6]

For such a revolution, it was thought absolutely necessary to have dictatorship, which Lenin himself defined as "an authority relying directly upon
force, and not bound by any laws." Marx had said that a revolutionary dictatorship of the proletariat was probably necessary for the period of transition
from capitalist to communist society. But the task of cataclysmic revolution
can never be completed; and there is always the danger of the return to power
of the dispossessed and overthrown opposition. The much-heralded world
revolution seems so slow in coming. And there have arisen counterrevolu-
tions in those countries where revolutions had been expected. So the dictatorships must continue indefinitely!

---

collected essays entitled *Characters and Events: Popular Essays in Social and Political Philosophy* (New York: H. Holt, 1929), 2:824.
    6. Nikolai Lenin, *The Proletarian Revolution and Kautsky the Renegade* (London: Mod-
ern Books, 1929), 24.

DICTATORIAL POWER RARELY NEEDED

On the other hand, the democratic regimes which have been accustomed to the method of piecemeal legislative remedies and reforms have rarely felt the need for absolute dictatorial power. In time of war or grave internal crisis, they can always delegate special powers to their executive leaders. But in time of peace, they are content with their "retail job" of meting out specific measures to meet the particular needs of the nation. It may take twenty years to make a Federal income tax possible. It may take a decade to repeal national prohibition. In the life of a nation the apparent wastage of a few days of debate or even a few years of discussion is nothing compared with the loss of basic liberties under an absolute totalitarian rule.

The same fundamental difference also explains why so many idealistic spirits are much attracted to antidemocratic systems. The democratic procedure of specific remedial reforms is often so slow and so superficial and inadequate that impatient souls are naturally attracted to the so-called "revolutionary" systems in which dictatorial power seems to promise more thorough, more radical, and more rapid realization of their idealistic dreams. It often requires long years of hard experience and sad disillusionment before these idealistic dreamers can realize that there is no short cut to progress, and that the peaceful and piecemeal process of reform and amelioration is after all the truly democratic way of life.

UNIFORMITY VERSUS DIVERSITY

The second basic characteristic of totalitarian civilization is that it cannot tolerate diversity or individual variation, but always seeks to bring a whole people to conform to a uniform pattern. This is true of political belief, religious faith, intellectual life, as well as economic organization. Political activity is directed and controlled by a minority clique which is regimented like a military machine and which pledges its absolute obedience to the leader. All opposition and dissent are proscribed and stamped out. In religious life, the leaders of these totalitarian regimes claim to have been emancipated from the shackles of the traditional supernatural religion; but they seek to impose their antireligionism upon the entire population and to suppress all freedom and independence in religious groups. In intellectual life, no freedom of thought and expression is permitted. Science and education must be subor-

dinated to the interest of the party and the state, and thought must not deviate from the "party line." In economic life, the state seeks to impose a uniform system on the whole society in accordance with the determined
economic policy of the time. Whether it be communism, state socialism, or
collectivization of agriculture, it is always a uniform system enforced by the
ruthless power of the state. Labor movement is nonexistent in all totalitarian
regimes, because industry and production are carried on by the state. There
is no strike, no protest of labor; and sabotage, the only method of passive
protest, is a crime punishable by the most severe penalties.

In every one of these various phases of life, it is always the leader, the
party, or the state—which are one and the same thing—that decides upon
the "norm" to be accepted by all. No individual is allowed to differ, deviate,
or dissent from the official policy or party line. "There is no freedom of the
individual," says Dr. Goebbels, "there is only freedom of peoples, nations, or
races." Dr. Goebbels defends the right of the party to be intolerant to nonconformity in these words: "As we are convinced that we are right, we cannot
tolerate any other in our neighborhood who claims also to be right."

It is this extreme desire for uniformity and suppression of diversity in all
phases of life that clearly characterizes the antidemocratic civilization as distinct from the democratic way of life.

The democratic way of life is essentially individualistic. Historically it
began with religious nonconformity. It was this primary religious individualism which inspired the first ideas of freedom. The defenders of religious
freedom were willing to sacrifice their lives and property in their struggle
against oppression and interference. The freedom of the individual to worship his God in his own way was at the root of all the historic beginnings of
the modern democratic spirit and institutions.

The same spirit of nonconformity is responsible for the other liberties:
freedom of thought, of the expression and publication of thought, freedom
of assembly, and so forth. The fundamental thing is the desire of the individual to secure free development and expression of his personal and private
feeling, thought, and belief. It is a fight for the right to differ—the right not
to conform to an established or dictated pattern.

Democratic institutions have been the products of this spirit of nonconformity in religious belief, in intellectual conviction, in social and political
opinion, and in life in general. Democratic civilization is the creation by
those individualistic and freedom-loving persons who valued their liberty
above their bread, and truth above their life. The political systems which

have come to be called democratic are no more and no less than the political safeguards which these nonconformist free spirits have devised or evolved for the protection of their liberties.

Even the economic aspect of democratic civilization is not uniformly capitalistic as it has often been thought to be. If private ownership and free enterprise have been long maintained and at a time even elevated as a natural and inalienable right, it was because historically they were efficient and conducive to the development of individual initiative, and because they were thought to have made possible a standard of economic well-being higher than any other economic system had ever attained.

DIVERSITY OF ECONOMIC DEVELOPMENT

But the distinctive feature of the economic aspect of modern democratic civilization is best shown in the rich diversity of economic development. As has been pointed out by a contemporary economist,[7] modern American economic life, for example, can be analyzed into at least five divergent systems, flourishing simultaneously side by side. There is (1) the traditional capitalist system of small individual owners of stores, farms, laundries, teashops, and so on. There is (2) the economic system of Big Ownership—the great corporations. There is (3) the economic system of the public utilities. There is (4) the economic system of public corporations such as the Post Office and the T.V.A. And there are (5) the various types of "private collectivisms"—the universities, the churches, and the consumer and producer co-operatives. All these and possibly other various "systems" are functioning simultaneously to satisfy the economic needs of the people. And the same picture is more or less true of the other democratic countries. The important thing to note is the absence of any serious attempt to bring these various systems under a single scheme.

Thus we can say that the second basic concept which differentiates the democratic from the totalitarian civilization is the rigid uniformity in the one and the rich diversity and individuality in the other. This contrast cuts through all phases of life. The desire for uniformity leads to suppression of individual initiative, to the dwarfing of personality and creative effort, to intolerance, oppression, and slavery, and, worst of all, to intellectual dishon-

---

7. John Chamberlain, in *Fortune*, October 1940.

esty and moral hypocrisy. On the other hand, the traditional respect for and encouragement of diversity and nonconformity leads to enrichment of personality and associated life, to the development of free institutions, to the free flowering of disinterested and creative scholarship and thought, and, above all, to the spirit of tolerance and the love of freedom and truth.

CONCLUSION

In conclusion, therefore, I should like to suggest that the real conflict of ideologies can be resolved into a conflict between these basic concepts: It is, on the one hand, a conflict between the technique of radical and catastrophic revolution and the technique of patient, piecemeal, and specific amelioration; and, on the other hand, it is a conflict between the desire to enforce uniformity in all phases of life and the respect for free and diversified individual development. The defense of the democratic way of life and democratic institutions can only be based on a clear understanding of the value of a wholesome individualism of free and nonconformist personalities and a deep appreciation of the importance of patient forbearance for the slow but truly democratic technique of piecemeal reforms. Progress is always a retail job, and civilization is barren without individual diversity and initiative.

Hu Shih, Ph.D., Litt.D., LL.D., D.C.L., is Chinese Ambassador to the United States. He has been professor of Chinese philosophy, professor of history of Chinese literature, and dean of the College of Letters at the National Peking University, Peiping, China. He is author of numerous works in Chinese, including a History of Chinese Philosophy and fourteen volumes of Collected Essays. His writings in English include "The Development of Logical Method in Ancient China" (1922) and "The Chinese Renaissance" (1934).[8]

---

8. This author bio was included in the original document.

CHAPTER 8

The Chinese Revolution[1]

We are here to commemorate the 34th anniversary of the Chinese Revolution—the 34th birthday of the Republic of China.

My duty tonight is not to make a fiery "4th of July" oration, but to give you a historical report on what the Chinese Revolution and the Chinese Republic have achieved in these 34 years.

The founders of the Revolution, under the leadership of Dr. Sun Yat-sen, set out with three main objectives: 1. To liberate China from 270 years of alien rule under the Manchus. 2. To overthrow the monarchy which had been the prevailing form of government for thousands of years. 3. To build up a democratic, modern, and prosperous national state.

The first of these objectives was apparently achieved with the easy overthrow of the Manchu Dynasty. The second objective—the abolition of the monarchical form of government—was also apparently accomplished with only very slight opposition. China became the first non-European nation to overthrow the monarchy once and for all.

But the third and the chief constructive objective of the Revolution—namely, the building of a new China—was not so easy to achieve. It has taken us all these 34 years to work for this great objective. We have made some progress, but the progress has been slow and many times cruelly thwarted by external forces beyond our control.

As I look back upon these 34 years, three items stand out pre-eminently as the achievements of the Republican era: 1. an intellectual revolution; 2. a social revolution; and 3. a political reconstruction.

---

1. Originally delivered as a speech at the Carnegie Hall of New York on October 10, 1945, this text was later published in *Contemporary China: A Reference Digest* 5, no. 11 (October 15, 1945): 3–4. In the original document, Hu Shih was introduced as "President of Peking University, former Chinese Ambassador to the United States."

What I call an intellectual revolution is in reality the growth of the spirit of free criticism in the Chinese intellectual world.

The slogan of the age was "the revaluation of all values." Doubt and criticism were the new intellectual tools of reform. Nothing is too sacred to be subjected to the process of doubting and questioning. Confucius and Confucianism, Buddha and Buddhism, Taoism, God, the gods and spirits, religion and philosophy, the family, filial piety, marriage, funeral, mourning, widowhood—each one of these time-honored institutions has been freely discussed in the periodical literature of the time.

This spirit of criticism has done much in undermining the traditional values and in bringing about significant changes in the ideas, beliefs, and institutions of the country. It breaks down blind conservatism and prepares the mind for change and reform.

An example of Chinese reform through constructive criticism may be seen in the fundamental change in the Chinese language and literature.

Entirely through public criticism and discussion, the classical language of China has been now discarded as a medium of literature and education; a living language of the people has been adopted in the schools for the last 24 years; and a new literature, both poetry and prose, entirely written in the living tongue, has grown up.

And it is this intellectual revolution which will furnish you the best guaranty that China will be a free and democratic country.

The second great achievement in republican China during the last 34 years has been our social revolution. Its far-reaching effects are seen in every phase of Chinese society; the family, the position of women, the changes in the law and the courts, the rise of the new professions, etc.

A most striking example of the Chinese social revolution is the emergence of the new Chinese woman. Just try to recall the picture of a Chinese woman of 40 years ago—with her small feet, her awkward gait, her helplessness, her social and economic disabilities, her state of segregation and exclusion from social life. Then compare her with the Chinese woman of today. The contrast is most astonishing even to us in China. Once the Chinese woman is freed from her physical disabilities and is given the benefits of modern schooling and exercises, she bursts forth in full blossom as one of the most beautiful and graceful species of womanhood.

Ever since 1919 she has enjoyed the benefits of co-education. Ever since the promulgation of the new Civil Code of 1928 she has gained full rights of inheritance of family property. And in the last 20 years, she has been an active participant in almost every kind of social, political, and business life.

The third great achievement has been our political reconstruction in the last 18 years.

Throughout the early years of the Republic (1912–1927), China was not successful in the re-establishment of national unity and political stability and continuity.

The father of the Revolution, Dr. Sun Yat-sen, after a whole decade of futile effort to achieve national unity and democratic government, finally decided to reorganize his party on a new foundation. The party was to enlist the sympathy and active support of the youth of the nation on the revived principle of nationalism. This revived nationalism was to be founded on the issue of liberating China from the shackles of foreign domination and encroachment. Two years after Dr. Sun's death the National Government was established in Nanking, which in the course of the next few years became the acknowledged new national authority of the whole of China.

For the first time in many years, China was establishing a stable, unified, national political authority. The National Government was building up a political center of modernized power so great that it could not be challenged by any local group or combination of groups.

Bur this new national unity did not rest on military strength alone. It was building up a physical unity by the rapid development of railways, highways, motor roads, airlines, and the rapid increase of telegraphic and radio communication throughout the country. And after 1935 the National Government was achieving national financial unity by the absorption of the provincial currencies into the national currency. China for the first time in history was feeling and pulsating as one unified nation.

Moreover, the Government was undertaking a gigantic program of national reconstruction in many other fields. Universities and colleges increased ten times in the course of a few years. Secondary and primary schools increased four times.

To sum up, China has not wasted her 34 years. In these brief years, she was bringing about a fundamental revolution in her intellectual life and in her cultural and social institutions and was actually achieving a political unity and stability which even 14 years of Japanese aggression and eight years of most terrible war, devastation, and deprivation have failed to destroy.

But alas! All these developments and achievements in China were not to the liking of our next-door neighbor—Japan!

Our overthrow of the monarchy was regarded as dangerous to the stability of the Mikado tradition in Japan. Our intellectual and social movements were viewed with grave suspicion by the reactionaries in Japan. And, in particular, the new Nationalist Revolution of 1925–1927 and the successful establishment of political unity and stability under the National Government were most feared by Japan as the greatest obstacle to her dreams of continental aggression and world conquest.

So the militaristic leaders of Dai Nippon resolved to nip the new China in the bud. Thus was started the first invasion of Manchuria on September 18, 1931, an invasion which history now records as the real beginning of World War II.

There was nothing left for China to do except to work for more time in order to prepare for the day when she would be forced to take up the fight for our national existence and survival. That day came in July, 1937. For eight long years China fought on. The rest of the story is common history which need not be told here.

The Chinese Revolution of 34 years ago would have ended in complete failure if China had not fought the eight-year war and ultimately won it. Our overthrow of an alien rule in 1912 could have been in vain, because Japan, if she had won the war, could have placed the Manchus back on the Chinese throne as she actually did in Manchuria. Our abolition of the monarchy could also have been in vain, because Japan could have restored the monarchy in China or even imposed the rule of the Mikado over the whole of Eastern Asia. And all our intellectual and social reforms, and all our efforts in nation-building, could have been brought to naught if our enemy had carried the day.

Therefore, on this 34th anniversary of the Revolution, we give thanks to the millions of Chinese soldiers and civilians who gave their lives in order that the Revolution might not be in vain and that the Republic might not fail. We give thanks to China's great leader, President Chiang Kai-shek, who in all these years never wavered in his determination to fight on and never erred in his choice of friends and allies. And we give thanks to our allies and their fighting forces and their people, without whose powerful and effective assistance my people could not have won the war and thereby saved the Revolution which we are here to commemorate.

CHAPTER 9

China in Stalin's Grand Strategy[1]

In the following pages I propose to study Stalin's grand strategy of world conquest as it can be discerned in China—its stages of experimentation and modification, of successes and failures, and its victories after long failures. The story covers 25 years, from 1924 to 1949, and culminates in the recent and, I trust, temporary conquest of continental China by the overwhelming military power of world Communism. I propose to use the history of the long and bitter struggle between Nationalist China and world Communism, between Chiang Kai-shek and Stalin, as source material for a new examination of that almost unbelievably successful strategy which has enabled world Communism to place under its domination immense areas of the earth and 800,000,000 of its population.

Nearly two years ago, there was published in *Foreign Affairs* a learned and very remarkable essay entitled "Stalin on Revolution," by an author who signed himself "Historicus."[2] It is a study of Stalin's theory, program, strategy and tactics of "world revolution," and is evidently based on careful research and documentation.

The author's method is literary and documentary, relying mainly on the published works of Stalin. This method has serious limitations which the author himself fully admits:

> As generals are not accustomed to publish their operational directives, so it is unreasonable to expect Stalin to publish his. From his writings it is possible to reconstruct certain main lines of strategy and tactics, but the writings also contain definite acknowledgment that "illegal" or underground activities

---

1. Originally published in *Foreign Affairs* 29, no. 1 (October 1950): 11–40.
2. *Foreign Affairs*, January 1949.

play a major role in Communist operations. . . . Therefore it must remain a question to what extent Stalin's published view on Communist strategy and tactics are supplemented or modified by doctrine reserved for the Communist high command.

I believe, therefore, that the documentary method needs to be supplemented by the historical approach. Although "generals are not accustomed to publish their operational directives," an historian can reconstruct their strategy and tactics by following the details of their field operations and studying how these succeeded or failed.

How did Stalin annex the Baltic States? How did he twice conquer Poland? How did Vyshinsky take over Rumania in February 1945? How did Communism take over Jugoslavia, Bulgaria and Hungary? What were the steps leading to the coup d'état in Czechoslovakia in February 1948? What was Stalin's strategy in his conquest of Manchuria? And how did Stalin direct the campaign for the conquest of China and how did he finally succeed after 25 years of stubborn resistance by Nationalist China? Can we discern some similarity in the pattern of conquest? Can we reconstruct the strategical lines of the great Stalin from the fruits of these successful campaigns of conquest?

Towards the end of his essay, "Historicus" makes reference to "the technique of 'cold revolution' . . . illustrated recently in Eastern Europe." He seems to regard Stalin's conquest of Eastern Europe as "an exception to the general rule that revolutionary violence is necessary . . . in that it also dispenses with the need of overt violence." Does he really believe that "the technique of 'cold revolution' illustrated recently in Eastern Europe" is an "exception" to the Stalin strategy of conquest? I believe that from the historical standpoint, what has happened in Eastern Europe from 1945 to this day, just as what has happened in China from 1924 to this day, gives us the authentic subject matter for studying the real strategy and tactics of Stalinist Communism for the conquest of the world. "The technique of cold revolution" in Eastern Europe is no exception to the rule: it is the rule itself; it is the strategy in its more finished form.

All the strategical elements mentioned in the "Historicus" study are present in the Eastern European conquests just as they are present in the Asiatic conquests. There is always the Communist Party in full strength; there is always the maximum aid including armed force from the "base of Socialist revolution"; and there is, above all, the objective condition of revolution, namely, the greatest war in human history.

But there seem to be other equally important elements not revealed in a documentary research which can be clearly seen in a comparative study of the many Communist conquests extending from the Baltic Sea to China and Korea. First, it is not enough to have the conscious leadership of the Communist Party. To be an effective instrumentality of conquest, the Party must be fully armed: it must have a strong army of its own. Second, it is not enough to use Soviet Russia as a base for revolution. It is necessary first to make Soviet Russia the greatest military Power in the entire world, and then to achieve "revolutionary" conquests of adjacent and contiguous territories by sheer overwhelming superiority of military strength. Third, to avoid the appearance of "overt violence" or "revolutionary violence," it is necessary to bring about a "coalition government" with all the "democratic" and "anti-Fascist" parties or groups in a country. And lastly—and above all—there is the strategy of deceit which has been best expressed by the great Lenin, "We must be ready to employ trickery, deceit, lawbreaking, withholding and concealing truth."[3]

But there are also negative results that may be just as valuable as the positive findings. Such an historical study will show *what is not present* in this strategy. For instance, such a study will show that this strategy has nothing to do with such Marxist-Leninist-Stalinist economic theories as that of "Productive Forces vs. Productive Relations" which, according to "Historicus," is "an integral part of the bedrock of Marxist 'scientific' certainty about the future course of history on which Stalin evidently bases his entire life work."

Let us read such authentic historical records as the secret documents from the archives of the German Foreign Office, captured by the American and British armies in 1945, and published by the U.S. Department of State in 1948 under the title, "Nazi-Soviet Relations, 1939–1941." Let us note, for example, how in a nine-day secret negotiation, August 14–23, 1939, the whole relationship between Germany and Soviet Russia was reversed, they became allies, and the western democracies became enemies of both Germany and the U.S.S.R. As a result of these rapid negotiations, Soviet Russia acquired a free hand to annex the Baltic States and got the lion's share in the new partitioning of Poland. The record of the secret negotiations covers scores of pages, but there is no reference whatever to such economic theories as the contradictions of international capitalism or the interplay of Productive Forces vs. Productive Relations!

---

3. Lenin, "The Infantile Disease of Leftism." The translation here used is from Sir Norman Angell, *The Steep Places* (New York: Harper, 1948), 73.

The same is true of that portion of the secret documents which deal with the German attempt to induce the Soviet Union to join the Three Power Pact of September 1940. Stalin and Molotov were tempted. They frankly indicated Soviet Russia's interest in Turkey, Bulgaria, Romania and Hungary, and her willingness to participate in the division of spoils in the imminent breakup of the British Empire, and in particular her desire to designate "the area south of Batum and Baku in the general direction of the Persian Gulf . . . as the center of the aspirations of the Soviet Union." Neither Stalin, nor Molotov, in these protracted secret negotiations, ever makes reference to any of the "fundamental" economic causes such as the Productive Forces vs. Productive Relations.

In short, the whole strategy is no more and no less than a strategy of naked militarism aided from time to time by the most unscrupulous use of all possible forms of trickery and deceit. Such a strategy could never have succeeded in a world of peace and orderly international life. Its success has depended upon "the objective condition" of an unprecedented world war—a condition which the author of the strategy has sought by all available means to prolong and perpetuate.

II

There is one historical fact which differentiates the Chinese Communist Party from the Communist movements in any other country outside of Soviet Russia—a fact which is essential to a clear understanding of what has been happening in China during the last quarter of a century. It is that the Chinese Communist Party, partly by design and partly by extraordinary historical circumstances, has possessed a formidable army of its own almost from the very early years of its founding. Mr. Edgar Snow, sizing up the Chinese Communist Party at the end of 1937, said, "It is the strongest Communist Party in the world, outside Russia, and the only one, with the same exception, that can boast a mighty army of its own."[4] This unique feature of the Chinese Communist Party has been the most important source of its strength, which Stalin, the masterful strategist of world Communism, has been able to nurture, support, and in the course of 25 years develop into a most powerful instrumentality for subjugating China and thereby dominating the whole Asiatic continent.

---

4. Edgar Snow, *Red Star over China* (New York: Random House, 1938), 140.

Last year, on August 1, a special commemorative postage stamp was issued to mark the 22nd anniversary of the Red Army. Chinese Communist leaders proudly announced to the world that the Red Army, now renamed the "People's Liberation Army," had a regular strength of 4,000,000 men. A year later, August 1, 1950, the newspapers report that Communist China is celebrating the 23rd anniversary of the founding of the Red Army in China. A New York Times dispatch from Hong Kong says, "Preparing to mark their Red Army Day tomorrow, the Chinese Communists today described their 5,000,000-men force as 'one yet destined to play a significant role in defending the peace of East Asia and the world." This Red Army of 5,000,000 men, supported by a Russian-trained and Russian-supplied Air Force, is the ever-growing Asiatic arm of the militaristic power of world Communism today.

There seems no doubt that the organization of a Communist armed force in every country occupies a very important place in the grand strategy of Stalin and the Comintern for the ultimate success of the world proletarian dictatorship. In the program of the Communist International adopted by the Sixth World Congress on September 1, 1928, one of the eight most important special tasks that the Communist Party in every country must seek to accomplish is specified as "the organization of revolutionary workers' and peasants' armies."[5] In the same program, there is a section devoted to "The Fundamental Tasks of Communist Strategy and Tactics." One of these "fundamental tasks" is for the Communist Party to lead the masses to a direct attack upon the bourgeois state whenever the time is considered ripe for this final step of revolution. "This it does by organizing mass action. . . . This mass action includes: a combination of strikes and demonstrations, a combination of strikes and armed demonstrations, and finally the general strike conjointly with armed insurrection against the State power of the bourgeoisie. The latter form of struggle, which is the supreme form . . . presupposes a plan of campaign, offensive fighting operations and unbounded devotion and heroism on the part of the proletariat. An absolutely essential condition precedent for this form of action is the organization of the broad masses into military units . . . and intensified revolutionary work in the army and the navy."

Among the 21 "Conditions of Admission to the Communist International," adopted at the Second World Congress of the Comintern, July–August 1920, the fourth condition reads, "Persistent and systematic propa-

---

5. Communist International, *Blueprint for World Conquest* (Chicago: Human Events, 1946), 121.

ganda and agitation must be carried on in the army, where Communist groups should be formed in every military organization. Wherever, owing to repressive legislation, agitation becomes impossible, it is necessary to carry on such agitation illegally. But *refusal to carry on or participate in such work should be considered equal to treason to the revolutionary cause*, and incompatible with affiliation to the Third International."[6]

Since no country under normal conditions will permit either revolutionary propaganda and agitation in its army or the organization of an armed force by a revolutionary party, it was a most extraordinary opportunity for the Third International to be requested in 1923–1924 by Dr. Sun Yat-sen, leader of a revolutionary party and many times head of an independent regional government, to send political and military experts to China, not only to help reorganize his own party, but actually to organize a new army for a new revolution. It was equally extraordinary for Dr. Sun Yat-sen, in his sincere desire to "bolster the strength of revolutionary elements in the country," to admit Communists as regular members of his own Nationalist Party, thereby making it possible for Communists to influence the policy of the Nationalist Party and even to carry on revolutionary propaganda and agitation in the new army.

The Chinese Communist Party, founded in 1921, had already affiliated itself with the Communist International. The three years of collaboration between the Kuomintang and the Chinese Communist Party (1924–1927) formed the period when the Comintern was making full use of a most unusual opportunity to try out its strategy of world revolution on a large scale in one of the most important strategical areas of the world—China.

This was the time when Stalin was formulating his thesis of the consolidation of Soviet Russia as the base for world revolution, a thesis which never meant abandonment of the cause of world revolution in favor of "Socialism in one country" but only emphasized the importance of effective aid that could come from a strong base. A political struggle for power was then going on in Russia between Stalin and Trotsky, but Stalin was already in full control of the policies of the Comintern. There is little doubt that Stalin was directing the Comintern's China adventure throughout those years of Nationalist-Communist collaboration.

The basis of this collaboration had been clearly defined in a joint state-

---

6. Communist International, *Blueprint for World Conquest*, 67. Italics inserted.

ment issued by Dr. Sun Yat-sen and A. Joffe, a representative of Soviet Russia and the Comintern:

> Dr. Sun Yat-sen holds that the Communist order or even the Soviet system cannot actually be introduced into China because there do not exist here the conditions for the successful establishment of either Communism or Soviet-ism. This view is entirely shared by Mr. Joffe, who is further of the opinion that China's paramount and most pressing problem is to achieve national unification and attain full national independence, and regarding this task, he has assured Dr. Sun Yat-sen that China has the warmest sympathy of the Russian people and can count on the support of Russia.

Dr. Sun, the father of the Chinese Revolution which in 1911–1912 over-threw the Manchu Dynasty, abolished the monarchy and established the first republic in Asia, had long advocated a threefold platform: nationalism, political democracy and the people's livelihood. He was here, however, reminded by his Russian adviser that nationalism—especially the struggle "to achieve national unification and attain full national independence"—was still the most pressing issue. This joint statement practically defined the issue of the Nationalist Revolution: it was to achieve national unification by destroying the military power of the separatist war lords, and to attain "full national independence" by abolishing the special privileges enjoyed by the foreigner in China, by abolishing the "unequal treaties" which the foreign Powers had imposed upon the Chinese people. It was clear from the very beginning that this latter phase of the Nationalist movement had to be essentially an anti-foreign movement, a revolution against the imperialist Powers. Unwittingly, Dr. Sun's Party was being thus guided toward a possible international war.

The Communist International went all-out in giving aid to the Nationalist-Communist collaboration. Aid came largely in the form of maté-riel and expert advisers. The Comintern was able to send to China a remark-able group of political and military advisers, headed by Mikhail Borodin, one of the most brilliant and astute revolutionary organizers, and General Galen, who years later came to be better known as Marshal Blucher. Borodin soon became the dictator of the Chinese Communist Party and at the same time the most influential man in the new government, directing the policy and the strategy of the Revolution. The Whampoa Military Academy was established in Canton in June 1924, with General Chiang Kai-shek as its

Director. The Russian military mission under Blucher was helping Chiang to train large numbers of new officers who were to be the nucleus of a new revolutionary army.

Chiang Kai-shek's future Army of Nationalist Revolution was organized on the model of the Russian Red Army and was under the political discipline and indoctrination of the political commissars, many of whom were trained Communists. In that way, Communists and Communism were able to exert much influence over the officers and men of the Nationalist Army. Important Communist leaders of the future, such as Mao Tse-tung, Chou En-lai, Lin Tsu-han (Lin Po-ch'u), etc., played important roles in the government and in the army. These Communists helped to organize the masses, conduct propaganda and indoctrinate the officers and men of the army. The training centers in Moscow—the Lenin University, the University of the Toilers of the East, and, later, the Sun Yat-sen University—were sending back well-trained young men for work in the Party and in the Army.

Dr. Sun Yat-sen died in March 1925. In June 1926, the Army of National Revolution, led by Chiang Kai-shek as Commander-in-Chief, launched the Northward Expedition from Canton. The progress of the revolutionary armies was almost an uninterrupted series of victories. The northern armies were incapable of effectively resisting an inspired army supported by powerful propaganda and organized masses. Changsha was taken in July, Hankow in October, Kiukiang and Nanchang in November. Early in 1927, the Revolutionary forces had reached the Yangtze Delta. The Chinese city of Shanghai was taken in March, and only strong forces of foreign marines protected the foreign settlement from the Nationalists.

Then came the great crisis of the revolution. On March 24, 1927, Nationalist troops entered the city of Nanking after the flight of the northern forces, savagely attacked foreigners in the city, looted and defiled foreign dwellings and consulates, and killed a few of the foreign residents, including the vice-president of the American missionary University of Nanking. Foreign gunboats stationed in the river were forced to fire a barrage to warn against further violence and to guide the fleeing foreigners to escape to the boats.

"The (Nanking) incident," says Professor Latourette, "so aroused the ire of foreigners that for a time extensive intervention seemed imminent."[7]

On the day of the Nanking incident, I was travelling from New York to

---

7. Kenneth S. Latourette, *The Development of China*, 6th ed. (Boston: Houghton, 1946), 260.

Chicago, and I could sense that American public opinion which had up to that time been sympathetic toward the Nationalist Revolution had changed overnight and turned against the revolutionary cause. But I never fully realized how dangerously close this "extensive (foreign) intervention" was until nearly a month later, when I was in Tokyo and a Japanese friend in the Foreign Office was guiding me on a sightseeing tour. The *Tokyo Asahi* was holding an "Exhibition of Modern Journalism" in its new building. My Japanese friend said to me, "Dr. Hu Shih, I just want you to see one little room." The three walls of this small room were covered by the original cablegrams sent from Nanking and Shanghai to the *Tokyo Asahi* office on the looting of the Japanese Consulate in Nanking, the defiling of the portrait of the Japanese Emperor, the attempt of the Japanese captain of the Consulate Guards to commit hara-kiri because he was ordered not to resist, etc. There were over 400 urgent cablegrams in a single day, March 24, 1927. "You can even now feel how Japan must have felt on that fateful day," said my friend. He then told me that the Powers held serious consultations on the question of intervention in China, and that Japan, according to his information, was among those governments opposing intervention.

As we now look back, the Nanking incident seems to be the last of a series of deliberate anti-foreign moves designed to force the foreign Powers to resort to armed intervention and thereby to create a situation of a real "imperialist war"—which, we must remember, Stalin and the Comintern regard as the necessary "objective condition" for the victory of the revolution. The commanding general of the offending army in the Nanking incident was General Ch'en Ch'ien, who is now with the Chinese Communist regime. And the man who was considered by the United States Government as being responsible for the whole affair was Mr. Lin Tsu-han, the chief political commissar of the Army. Mr. Lin is one of the most prominent Communist leaders today.

During this period of collaboration, the Chinese Communist Party was functioning efficiently, and the work of infiltration into the Government and especially into the Army was going on smoothly and successfully. What was lacking was a real war, a great imperialist war, without which, according to the Stalinist line of thinking, it was difficult to capture the whole of the Russian-influenced Nationalist Army and convert the Nationalist Revolution into another glorious "October Revolution." All the gigantic anti-British strikes and boycotts throughout 1925–1926 had been directed toward breaking British power in China and forcing Britain to armed intervention. But

Britain chose not to fight back. Even after the British Concession at Hankow had been seized by force on January 4, 1927, the British Government persisted in its policy, and ordered its Peking Legation to send a mission to Hankow to negotiate a settlement with the Hankow regime which was under the domination of the Communists. The British Concessions at Hankow and Kiukiang were officially returned to China as a result of these negotiations. But this nonresistant attitude of the British defeated the Communist strategy, which was to start an international conflagration in China by pushing the British to the wall. It is quite probable that the Nanking affair of March 24 was a deliberate strategical move to involve many foreign Powers in armed intervention, which, as I have shown, almost became a reality.

This danger of foreign intervention and a Communist Revolution was averted by the decision of Chiang Kai-shek and the moderate leaders of the Kuomintang to "split" with the Communists, end the collaboration, and "purge" the Nationalist Party of the Communists and their sympathizers. The "purge" began on April 12, 1927, in Shanghai and later in Canton. On April 18, Chiang, with the support of the Elder Statesmen of the Party, set up the National Government in Nanking.

III

Mr. Edgar Snow reports that as early as 1926 Trotsky began urging the formation of Chinese soviets and an independent Chinese Red Army.[8] Such advice from Stalin's opposition at least indicated a line of thought fairly current in Communist circles at that time.

After the moderate wing of the Kuomintang had brought about the "split" and the "purge" in the lower Yangtze Valley, and had set up the National Government at Nanking, the Kremlin sent a secret message to Borodin in Hankow ordering the Chinese Communists to demand majority control of the Kuomintang, confiscation of land of the landowners and the formation of a separate Workers' and Peasants' Army. Borodin did not want to present these demands, but Roy, the Indian representative of the Comintern, gave the message to Wang Ching-wei, chairman of the Left Wing Kuomintang Government at Hankow. Even the Left Wing Kuomintang could not tolerate such open violation of the terms of the collaboration.

---

8. Snow, *Red Star over China*, 377.

Borodin and the other Russian advisers were expelled from the Party and ordered to leave China. Eventually the Hankow regime collapsed and was merged with the Government at Nanking.

It is significant that the organization of a Chinese Workers' and Peasants' Red Army was actually ordered by the Kremlin and therefore constituted a part of the strategy of Stalin. And the order was carried out by those Communist leaders and army commanders—Chu Teh, Ho Lung, Yeh T'ing, Mao Tse-tung, Li Li-san and others—who wanted to carry on the Chinese Communist Party but who realized that, after the 1927 coup d'état, the Party must have an armed force of its own. It was these men who started the Nanchang Uprising on August 1, 1927, and the Autumn Crop Uprising in Hunan in September, and who after their defeat and retreat into the mountains, pooled their remnant forces to form the first Red Army.

The Red Army probably began with less than 10,000 men. In the course of a few years, it grew in numerical strength and in fighting experience. Its mobile units carried on insurrections mainly in the provinces of Hunan, Hupeh, Kiangsi, Kwangtung, and the border areas of Fukien. By 1930, the Red Army was said to number about 60,000 men.

Toward the end of 1927, the first "soviet" was set up in Chaling, in Hunan. The soviet form was extended to larger areas and early in 1930 a Provisional Soviet Government of Southern Kiangsi was proclaimed. In August 1931, the Executive Committee of the Communist International advised the Chinese Communist Party to establish in some secure region a full-fledged "central Soviet Government" and to carry out a "Bolshevik national policy."[9] Such a "Central Soviet Government of the Soviet Republic of China" was set up in December 1931, with its capital at Juichin, Kiangsi, near the border of Fukien. Mao Tse-tung was elected Chairman of the Central Soviet Government, and Chu Teh, Commander of the Red Army.

There is no authentic record regarding the highest numerical strength attained by the Red Army in those years of the Kiangsi Soviets. At the 13th Plenary Session of the Executive Committee of the Comintern held in December 1933, Wang Ming (Ch'en Shao-yu), the Chinese delegate, reported that in the territory of the Chinese Soviet Republic, "the regular formations of the Red Army numbered 350,000 men; the irregular forces, 600,000."[10]

---

9. David J. Dallin, *Soviet Russia and the Far East* (New Haven: Yale University Press, 1948), 109.

10. Dallin, *Soviet Russia and the Far East*, 111. Cf. Snow, *Red Star over China*, 290, quoting a Red squad leader: "In our Kiangsi Soviets we had a population of only 3,000,000, yet we recruited volunteer partisan armies of 500,000 men!"

At the Seventeenth Congress of the Communist Party of the Soviet Union, held in Moscow in 1934, Dmitri Manuilsky, reporting on the progress of Communism in China, paid this tribute to the Chinese Party and its Army: "The young Communist Party of China is becoming one of the best sections of the Communist International, also because both they and the Red Army have passed through the years-long school of civil war."[11]

This Red Army was essentially a guerrilla force, having terroristic control of the rural area which is the source of food supply and manpower. It was a fighting force of great mobility. Snow[12] has made famous these slogans of Red Army tactics:

1. When the enemy advances, we retreat!
2. When the enemy halts and encamps, we trouble them!
3. When the enemy seeks to avoid a battle, we attack!
4. When the enemy retreats, we pursue!

The declared object of the Army at that time was "to overthrow the Kuomintang regime and destroy its military power." Even the outbreak of Japanese aggression in Manchuria in September 1931 and its rapid expansion into North China and Shanghai did not stop or even diminish this fierce antinationalist insurrection. The National Government issued an appeal for unity against Japan. But the Communists responded with the manifesto of September 30, 1931, in which they vehemently condemned the talk about "a united front against the external enemy" as "ridiculous, absurd, and lying inventions." They declared, "The Communist Party of China is and remains the irreconcilable enemy of the imperialists and the Kuomintang."[13] And in Moscow the Executive Committee of the Comintern adopted a resolution in September 1932, emphasizing that "the Communist Party of China must fight for the overthrow of the Kuomintang, the agent of imperialism."[14]

The Communists in the Red areas of Kiangsi did in February 1932 send out a circular telegram "declaring war" against Japan in the name of the Provisional Central Government of the Soviet Republic of China. Yet in the same month, when a part of the Fifth Army of the Nationalist Government was ordered from Kiangsi to fight the Japanese in the "First War of Shang-

---

11. Dallin, *Soviet Russia and the Far East*, 111–112.

12. Dallin, *Soviet Russia and the Far East*, 159.

13. Dallin, *Soviet Russia and the Far East*, 126, quoting Mif et al., "Okkupatsiya Man-chzhurii," 153.

14. Dallin, *Soviet Russia and the Far East*, 126.

hai," the withdrawing troops were attacked at Kan Hsien, Kiangsi, by the Communist armies from the rear and suffered heavy losses.

In 1933, the Communists issued a proclamation which, while still attacking Chiang Kai-shek and the imperialist Powers, announced that the Chinese Communists were ready to "cooperate with any White army on three conditions: (1) cessation of civil war and of attacks on the Chinese Soviet area, (2) guarantee of civil liberties and democratic rights to the people, and (3) arming the masses for an anti-Japanese war." Note that the offer was made only to any White army—that is, any government army that was blockading or attacking the Red area.[15]

From 1930 to 1934, the National Government forces under Generalissimo Chiang Kai-shek carried out a number of military expeditions against the Communist armies. By the fall of 1933 the Red districts were being narrowed down to a relatively small area in the border regions between Kiangsi and Fukien. To counteract the mobility of the partisan warfare, the 1933–1934 campaign (which is often termed the Fifth or Last Campaign) relied mainly on a combination of military encirclement and economic blockade. This campaign lasted over a year and is said to have involved the mobilization of nearly 1,000,000 men. By means of a network of military roads and thousands of small fortifications, Generalissimo Chiang Kai-shek's strategy was designed to build around the Soviet districts a kind of Great Wall "which gradually moved inward. Its ultimate aim was to encompass and crush the Red Army in a stone vise."[16]

The encirclement and the economic blockade proved so effective that the Red Army and Government were forced to adopt the bold strategy of retreat—to escape annihilation by retreating westward, then southwestward, then northward, and then northeastward, finally reaching their destination in northern Shensi. This retreat has been called "the Long March," which lasted for a whole year and covered about 6,000 miles.

The Long March, in Mao Tse-tung's own words, "was begun in October 1934. . . . By January 1935, the main force of the Red Army reached Tsunyi in Kweichow. For the next four months the army was almost constantly moving and the most energetic combat and fighting took place. Through many, many difficulties, across the longest and deepest and most dangerous rivers of China, across some of its highest and most hazardous mountain passes,

---

15. Mao Tse-tung, "On Coalition Government," April 1945, 23; Snow, *Red Star over China*, 166; Dallin, *Soviet Russia and the Far East*, 127.

16. Snow, *Red Star over China*, 173.

through the country of fierce aborigines, through the empty grasslands, through cold and through intense heat, through wind and snow and rain-storm, pursued by half the White armies of China, through all these natural barriers, and fighting its way past the local troops of Kwangtung, Hunan, Kwangsi, Kweichow, Yunnan, Sikong, Szechuan, Kansu and Shensi, the Red Army at last reached northern Shensi in October 1935, and enlarged the present base in China's great Northwest."[17]

How great were the casualties suffered by the Red Army in the battles and in the Long March? Mr. Snow tells us that Chou En-lai admits that "the Red Army itself suffered over 60,000 casualties in this one siege" (i.e., the long blockade of 1933–1934). Mr. Snow also records that "the main forces of the Red Army" at the start of the retreat from Kiangsi, October 1934, were "esti-mated at about 90,000 men," and that in October 1935, at the end of the trek, they numbered "less than 20,000 survivors."[18]

But the most significant fact is that the Red Army had survived the great extermination campaign of 1933–1934, had survived the one-year-long heroic march, and was now joined by the Communist forces that had already established a small Soviet base in Shensi in 1933. Here, in northern Shensi, just below the Great Wall, the survivors of the Red Army and the leaders of the Chinese Communist Party now settled down to build up their new base as close as possible to the borders of Soviet Russia—the base of revolution.

No record is preserved of the discussions at the Red Army Conferences at Juichin in 1934, which finally made the decision to withdraw from the Kiangsi-Fukien border-region and to transfer the nucleus of the living forces of the Red Army to some new base in the west or the northwest. But in later years when Chinese Communists could freely associate and converse with their non-Communist friends it was reliably reported that leading Commu-nists attributed the success of the Long March to what Stalin had taught as "the strategy of retreat." For it was Stalin who, in his best known work, "Prob-lems of Leninism," had laid down the strategical line of "a maneuvering of reserves designed for a correct retreat when the enemy is strong and when retreat is inevitable, when we are beforehand aware of the disadvantages of engaging in battle which the enemy imposes on us, when, given the ratio of forces, retreat is the only means of preventing a blow on the vanguard and of

---

17. Snow, *Red Star over China*, 167.

18. Snow, *Red Star over China*, 174, 175, 194. Cf. Dallin, *Soviet Russia and the Far East*, 112: "Of the approximately 100,000 men who left the former Soviet area, less than half reached the final destination; the rest were killed or left behind."

maintaining the reserves behind it." Here Stalin quoted Lenin for support: "The revolutionary parties must complete their education. They have learned how to attack. Now they must understand that it is necessary to supplement this by a knowledge of how best to retreat. They must understand (and the revolutionary class learns to understand by its bitter experience) that victory is impossible without learning both how to attack and how to retreat properly." "The object of this strategy," concludes Stalin, "is to gain time, to decompose the enemy, and to assemble forces so as to take the offensive later."[19]

So, according to my source of information, it was this Lenin-Stalin doctrine of "correct retreat" that had influenced the military thinking at Juichin in 1934 and had resulted in the Long March and the survival of the Red Amy.

IV

But the remnant Red Army settling in northern Shensi—one of the poorest areas in the whole of China—was still facing the danger of being once more surrounded and destroyed by the superior military power of the National Government, which had become increasingly strong in the years 1934–1936. One of the unexpected results of the Long March of the Communists was the fact that the National Government, in following the trail of the Red Army, was able to consolidate its political control over such southwestern provinces as Kweichow, Yunnan and Szechuan, which had previously succeeded in maintaining a degree of regional autonomy. The rich and economically self-sufficient inland province of Szechuan, for example, when it was invaded by the Red Army in 1935, sent a representative delegation to Nanking to request the Government for adequate military aid to help the provincial armies combat the Red forces. It was, therefore, the Red Army's Long March which enabled Chiang Kai-shek to consolidate the great southwest as the future base in the long war against Japan. And the Generalissimo was determined to exterminate the military power of Chinese Communism before he had to face the greater war of resistance to Japan.

Stalin and the Communist International were then to play another and

---

19. Stalin, "Problems of Leninism." This translation is taken from William C. Bullitt, *The Great Globe Itself* (New York, Scribners, 1946), Appendix III, 299. This passage was quoted *in toto* in Chang Hao (Lin Yü-ying), "The Tactical Line of the Chinese Communist Party," 28.

even more important role in protecting and preserving the Red Army strength and providing it with ample opportunities for growth and expansion. The new strategical line was to be the "united front."

Even when the Red Army was fighting its way to the northwest, the policy of the Communist International underwent an important change. The Seventh World Congress, held in Moscow from July to August 1935, officially proclaimed the policy of a "united front" against the rising dangers of aggression by the "Fascist" Powers. The Congress called upon Communist Parties in all countries to cooperate or seek coalition with bourgeois governments and political parties willing to fight Fascism. Special attention was paid to China and the Chinese Communist Party. It elected Mao Tse-tung, Chou En-lai, Chang Kuo-t'ao and Wang Ming to the Executive Committee of the Comintern; and Wang Ming, who was stationed in Moscow as the Party's resident delegate, was also made a member of the International Presidium. The Party was, however, censured for having "not yet succeeded in carrying out these tactics [of the united front] really consistently and without mistakes."[20] One of the great mistakes specifically singled out was the failure of the Chinese Communists to unite with the leaders of the Nineteenth Route Army who had rebelled against the Nationalist Government and set up a People's Government in Fukien in 1933. The quick collapse of the Fukien rebellion enabled the Nationalist Government to enforce a more effective blockade against the Communist area in the following year.

The Comintern policy of the "United Front in China" was intended as a scheme to protect the greatly weakened Red Army from renewed attacks by Nationalist forces. But the Chinese Communist Party which had fiercely fought Chiang Kai-shek over eight long years could not yet bring itself to a public retraction of its avowed objective of "overthrowing the Kuomintang and destroying its military power." It was proclaiming such slogans as "Chinese don't fight Chinese!" "Stop all civil war!" "Unite all parties, all groups, all armies, in our common fight against Japan!" and "Down with all Traitors!" Nevertheless it was still demanding the downfall of the "arch-traitor," Chiang Kai-shek, and his regime. In Communist literature of the time, the

---

20. Department of State, *United States Relations with China: With Special Reference to the Period 1944–1949* (Washington, DC: Government Printing Office, 1949), 46, quoting Wang Ming, *The Revolutionary Movement in the Colonial Countries, Report to the VII World Congress of the Communist International, August 7, 1935* (New York, 1935); Dallin, *Soviet Russia and the Far East*, 128–129.

"United Front" was described as one of "resistance to Japan and opposition to Chiang."

Under this new party line, the Chinese Communist Party was organizing all kinds of front organizations such as "The Association for National Salvation and Resistance to Japan," "The People's United Association against Japan," and so on. These associations were carrying on antigovernmental agitation under the cloak of anti-Japanism. They demanded immediate war against Japan and immediate cessation of the civil war against the Communists. In the summer and autumn of 1936, seven well-known leaders of the National Salvation Societies were arrested, and that, of course, gave cause for more agitation against the Government. Throughout the winter of 1935–1936, student strikes and student demonstrations broke out in Peiping and other metropolitan centers of education. Hundreds and even thousands of young students, boys and girls, would often block railway transportation by lying down on railroad tracks and demanding free passage to Nanking to petition the Government to fight Japan.[21]

These anti-Japanese demonstrations and the popular demands for a united front against Japan could not fail to affect the psychology of the Government troops who were sent to Shensi to fight the remnant Red Army. This was particularly true of the Tungpei (Northeast) Armies, which had retreated from Manchuria after the Japanese invasion and were now under the command of their former leader, the "Young Marshal" Chang Hsueh-liang, Deputy Commander-in-Chief of the campaign against the Red Army in Shensi, with his headquarters at Sian, the capital of Shensi Province. The propaganda slogans against these armies were especially effective, "Go back to Your Old Home and Fight the Japanese Devils!"

Before long, the "Bandit-Suppression Army Officers" were beginning to fraternize with the "bandits." By the summer of 1936, some kind of secret understanding was reached between the Communist leaders in Northern Shensi and Chang Hsueh-liang and his Sian colleague, General Yang Hu-ch'eng, Pacification Commissioner of Shensi Province. The war against the Reds was slowing down, thereby giving the Red Army a much-needed opportunity to rest and recuperate.

Chang Hsueh-liang, the Young Marshal, then in his middle thirties, was a

---

21. Years later, Communist leaders like Mao Tse-tung openly claimed that the Chinese Communist Party was responsible for organizing this mass action of the students. December 9, the date of the first big demonstration in Peiping in 1935, is now named "Students' Day" in Communist China.

spoiled child who never matured intellectually. Born to wealth and power, he was ambitious and vainglorious. Being patriotic and intensely anti-Japanese, he was easily persuaded to lend his support to the work of anti-Japanese agitation and demonstration by the National Salvation Societies and student bodies. The Nanking Government began to hear reports that the Deputy Commander-in-Chief of the Bandit-Suppression Campaign, second only to Chiang Kai-shek in command, was financing the antigovernment front organizations. He was drifting into a position where he could imagine himself at the head of the anti-Japan and anti-Chiang "United Front."

It was against such a background that the "arrest" of Chiang Kai-shek by Chang Hsueh-liang took place in Sian on the morning of December 12, 1936. Because of the almost complete absence of authentic records, the story of the Sian affair has never been, and may never be, fully told. But the following facts seem to be of importance.

First, Chiang Kai-shek went to Sian with the full knowledge that he was going into the territory of the conspirators. Dr. Wong Wen-hao, my geologist friend who was serving as Secretary-General of the Executive Yuan, told me in Nanking at least five days before the coup that the Generalissimo was fully aware that the Young Marshal was plotting a revolt against the Government. Then why did Chiang go? The answer has to be a conjecture. Chiang was a prodigal son turned Puritan Christian at a mature age, and the world must try to understand him in that light. He probably wanted to win back his wayward "younger brother," Chang Hsueh-liang, by convincing him that he still had complete trust in him. He not only went to Sian practically unguarded; he actually called a military conference to meet at Sian to which all his highest ranking generals were summoned. The conference began on December 7. So what actually happened on the morning of December 12 was the arrest of Chiang Kai-shek and of practically all the best-known generals of Nationalist China, the only notable exceptions being Ho Ying-ch'in and Ku Chu-t'ung.

Why did he call the military conference? Chiang probably wanted to convince the conspirators how futile it would be for them to attempt any revolt in face of the overwhelmingly strong position of Government forces in Loyang and along the Lunghai railway. He probably also wanted them to see how the Government could carry on the anti-Red campaign even without their help. In short, it was possible that the military conference was called at Sian for the purpose of convincing the conspirators that the Government had nothing to hide from them.

Second, Chang Hsueh-liang must have planned the whole affair by himself. He was fully capable of quick decision and coldblooded murder, as he
had shown in his killing of two of his father's ablest and most trusted
generals—Generals Yang Yu t'ing and Ch'ang Yin-huai, when the victims
were dinner guests in his own home. And he must have planned it as a part
of a rebellion under the banner of "the Anti-Japan and Anti-Chiang United
Front." This is shown by the announcement on December 14 of the formation of the United Anti-Japanese Army, to consist of the armed forces of the
Red Army, the Northwest Army of Yang Hu-ch'eng and the Northeast Army
of Chang Hsueh-liang. And the Young Marshall was "elected" chairman of
the United Anti-Japanese Military Council.

Third, for a time, Chiang Kai-shek's life was in real danger. He could have
been killed in his residence when Chang's troops opened fire before day-
break and 30 of his bodyguard were killed. During the fortnight of his captivity, there were persistent demands for his execution or for his public trial. All
the finely mimeographed news-sheets of Communist or "National Salvation" underground that I could obtain in Peiping during those days were
unanimous in demanding Chiang's death.

Fourth, the many reports about the "intrigue for capture of the hegemony of power" in Nanking are not true. The Kuomintang, the National
Government and the Military Commission held an all-day conference on
December 12. Every Elder Statesman who knew his history pointed to the
historical parallel of the Sixth Emperor of the Ming Dynasty who was captured in battle by a Mongol tribe in the year 1449. The statesman Yu Ch'ien
proposed that, in order to forestall the Emperor's being held as hostage for
impossible terms of peace, the Heir Apparent should be proclaimed Emperor
and the Government should carry on as before. His proposal was adopted
and the captive Emperor was returned in a year. So on December 12, 1936,
Nanking decided that the manifold duties of the Generalissimo should be
temporarily taken over by his colleagues in the Government, the Party and
the Military Commission, so that all these organs could go on in the absence
of the Generalissimo.

Fifth, the Government's decision to move a number of divisions of troops
to the Honan-Shensi border quickly and to send squadrons of airplanes daily
over Sian was the result of careful consideration and was clearly motivated
by the desire to hasten Chiang's safe return and to make the conspirators
realize the gravity of their own situation. Chiang Kai-shek fully understood

this: he wrote in his diary that he was very glad when he heard the airplanes over the city.

And, lastly, the all-important question: Why was Chiang Kai-shek able to fly back to Nanking on Christmas Day? What had happened to make that possible? Miss Agnes Smedley, who was in Sian at the time, reported that after Chiang's party had left Sian a group of young Northeast officers and National Salvation leaders said to her, "We have been betrayed! The Red Army induced the Young Marshal to release Chiang."[22] Edgar Snow believes that the Communist delegates (Chou En-lai, Yeh Chien-ying and Po Ku) whom Marshal Chang summoned to Sian were "most effective" in bringing about Chiang's release.[23]

The United States Department of State and David J. Dallin seem to agree that the release of the Generalissimo was apparently ordered by Moscow. "The Chinese Communist Party . . ." says the Department of State, "at first favored the execution of the Generalissimo, but, apparently on orders from Moscow, shifted to a policy of saving his life. The Chinese Communist concept, inspired from Moscow, became one of promoting a 'united front' with the Generalissimo and the National Government against the Japanese; this concept seems to have played a considerable role in saving the life of the Generalissimo."[24]

Mr. Dallin, however, points out that, before the Sian incident, Moscow and Nanking had already made progress in negotiating "a new nonaggression pact of momentous importance." This new pact (not signed until August 1937) was to serve as the basis for future Russian aid to China in the early years of the Sino-Japanese war. So Dallin believes that "Moscow . . . valued a pact with Chiang more highly than one with the irregular forces of the insurrectionists," and that this probably explains why Moscow "adopted an unequivocally hostile attitude toward the Sian rebellion."[25] As evidence of this "hostile attitude," Dallin quotes the editorial from *Izvestia* of December 14, the very first day that the news of the Sian rebellion was published in Moscow. "Under whatever slogans and program the Sian insurrection be conducted," says the *Izvestia* editorial, "this move . . . represents a danger not only to the Nanking government, but to all of China. It is clear that despite

---

22. Agnes Smedley, *Battle Hymn of China* (New York: Knopf, 1943), 149.
23. Snow, *Red Star over China*, 420.
24. Department of State, *United States Relations with China*, 47.
25. Dallin, *Soviet Russia and the Far East*, 67–69.

Chang Hsueh-liang's anti-Japanese banner, his move can benefit only Japanese imperialism. *So long as the Nanking government conducts a policy of resistance to the Japanese aggressors, the united popular front against Japan is understood by all its participants to mean not a front against Nanking, but a front together with Nanking.*[26] Mr. Dallin's conclusion, therefore, is that "there is no doubt that the position taken in Moscow had a decisive influence on the course of events in Sian and perhaps did save Chiang's life." But, Dallin adds, "in the last analysis Chiang owed his rescue to Japan's vigorous offensive on the Asiatic continent, and to the reality of the Japanese menace to both Russia and China." In other words, the Kremlin was worried about the Japanese menace and was convinced that Chiang Kai-shek was capable of offering greater resistance to Japan than any of the insurrectionist groups who talked loudly about "immediate armed resistance to Japan." For reasons of her own security, Russia wanted China to be in a position to fight Japan. Hence the secret negotiations for a nonaggression pact between China and Soviet Russia. Hence the hostile attitude of Moscow toward the Sian rebellion.

While the above conclusions may be correct in general, I am inclined to think that, in the light of the future trend of events, Stalin's strategy was probably greatly influenced by his solicitude for the future of the Chinese Red Army, which, we must remember, was one of his own creations. My friend, the late Agnes Smedley, may be more revealing than she meant to be when she quotes a young Army officer as saying, one hour after Chiang Kai-shek and Chang Hsueh-liang had left Sian by air, "The Red Army induced the young Marshal to release Chiang." The Reds knew that the newly-formed "United Anti-Japanese Army" could not stand the furious attacks of the advancing Nationalist armies that were already surrounding Shensi on all sides. And they knew what opportunities for expansion there would be if their Army were to become a part of the National Army.

From one of the secret pamphlets issued by the Chinese Communist Party after the Sian affair we can learn that there was so much criticism and dissatisfaction after December 1936 that explanation "lectures" had to be prepared in order that the Party and the Army might fully understand the action at Sian. In these secret explanations, it is interesting to note that the central argument was that the Party must obey the directives of the Comintern which were motivated by considerations for the "larger benefits" and

---

26. *Izvestia*, Moscow, December 14, 1946. Quoted by Dallin, *Soviet Russia and the Far East*, 69. Italics inserted.

"greater victories" in store for the Communist Party. The following passage is most revealing:

> When the December [1935] Resolution was issued, the policy was "Fight Chiang and Resist Japan." Now it is "Ally with Chiang, and Resist Japan." If we want to resist Japan, we must unite with Chiang. If the Communist Party wants to secure greater victories, it must fight Japan.
>
> In the Sian Affair, Chang Hsueh-liang and Yang Hu-ch'eng and the other militarists were really more interested in opposition to Chiang than in resistance to Japan. The Communist Party saw this clearly and used all its power to advocate a peaceful settlement, for internal fighting would only benefit Japan, and would injure our Party. Moreover, if the Sian Affair should arouse the wrath and dissatisfaction of the other militarists against the Communist Party, a war would be disastrous [for us]. Therefore our tactical lines were: "Peaceful settlement of the Sian Affair!" and "End all civil wars!"
>
> *Because the Chinese Communist Party is an International Party and the directives we received from the Third International also said that a peaceful settlement would be right and profitable, it was decided that for the greater benefits of the future, we must have peace.*[27]

So once more it was Stalin's strategy which brought about a peaceful settlement of the Sian Affair and saved the lives of Chiang Kai-shek and practically all his highest-ranking generals.

The Generalissimo returned to Nanking amidst the really spontaneous rejoicings of the Chinese people. He left Sian without having to sign any terms. But this Puritan Christian was won over, probably for the first time in his life, by a masterful stroke of strategy. Of all the things Stalin has ever done, that act came closest to statesmanship. The Generalissimo felt reassured that he could take in the Chinese Communists as partners in the common fight against the Japanese aggressor. The war for the extermination of the Red Army was ended. The Red Army was saved.

Seven months later, in July and August 1937, China took up the fight against Japan. The Second World War, which had actually started on September 18, 1931, in Manchuria, and which Chiang Kai-shek had for six years tried to avoid, often under most humiliating circumstances, was now in full swing.

---

27. Chang Han (Lin Yü-ying), "The Tactical Line of the Chinese Communist Party" (probably 1937), 48. Italics inserted.

Another month later, in September 1937, the Red Army was incorporated as the Eighth Route Army of the National Army. It was now sent to the war front in Shansi, where it looked forward to a future of unlimited growth and expansion.

V

When the Red Army was first incorporated in the National Army in September 1937, its numerical strength was officially estimated at 25,000 men. Seven years later, in September 1944, Lin Tsu-han, a member of the Central Committee of the Chinese Communist Party, reported to the People's Political Council that "in the course of more than seven years of war, the Communist military force has developed along the right tracks and consists now of an army of 475,000 men and a people's militia force of 2,200,000 men."[28] And a few months later, in April 1945, Mao Tse-tung presented a 50,000-word report to the Seventh Congress of the Communist Party, held at Yenan, in which he said, "As I am preparing this report, our regular army has already expanded to 910,000 men and our people's militia force has increased beyond 2,200,000 men."

So, in the course of eight years' war against Japan, the Communist armies, instead of suffering heavy losses, were able to achieve a 3,540 percent increase! And should we include the 2,200,000 "people's militia force," the increase would be 12,340 percent. That, said Mr. Lin Tsu-han, is because "the Communist military force has developed along the right track."

From 1935 to 1937, the Communists on the Shensi-Kansu border area occupied only 21 or 22 counties. According to their own estimate, the population was about 1,500,000. But in April 1945, Mao Tse-tung claimed that "the Liberated Area now extends from Inner Mongolia in the north to the Hainan Island in the south, extending into 19 provinces and containing 95,500,000 people." "In most of the territories occupied by the Japanese enemy," said Mao, "there will be found the Eighth Route Army, or the New Fourth Army, or some other people's armies carrying on partisan activities." The 19 provinces mentioned by Mao include Liaoning, Jehol, Chahar, Suiyuan, Shensi, Kansu, Ninghsia, Shansi, Hopei, Honan, Shantung, Kiangsu, Chekiang, Anhui, Kiangsi, Hubei, Hunan, Kwangtung and Fukien.

---

28. Department of State, *United States Relations with China*, 545.

The Chinese Government has expressed doubts about the figures of Red Army strength. According to its estimate, Communist forces of 25,000 in 1937 were increased at the end of the war to 310,000.[29] Mr. Dallin also considers Mao Tse-tung's figure of 910,000 men as much exaggerated. Dallin thinks that the real strength of the Chinese Communist armies in 1945 probably amounted to from 300,000 to 350,000.[30]

That was a small army scattered over 19 provinces. And it was poorly armed and poorly supplied. After 1941 it had practically ceased to receive monetary subsidy or allotment of ammunition from the National Government. Soviet Russia tried to act properly during the years of the war: the military supplies under the Sino-Soviet barter arrangement were delivered to the Central Government. The amount of ammunition that could come through from Soviet territory to the Communist area in the northwest must have been very small.

American aid and arms for the Communists in China never materialized. Even President Roosevelt's attempt in 1944 to place General Joseph W. Stilwell in command, under Chiang Kai-shek, of all Chinese forces, "including the Communist forces," did not succeed. The President had said to Chiang Kai-shek, "When the enemy is pressing us toward possible disaster, it appears unsound to reject the aid of anyone who will kill Japanese." But Chiang Kai-shek was opposed to it. His position was supported by the American Ambassador, Patrick J. Hurley. So General Stilwell was recalled. The Chinese Red Army remained poorly armed and ill-equipped. It remained a guerrilla force of great mobility and skill, but as late as the last year of the war, it had not attained the stature of an established army that could face the Japanese enemy or the Government forces in open battles.

Then came the sudden end of the Pacific war in August 1945. On August 9, Soviet Russia declared war on Japan. On the same day, the Soviet Army began to move into Manchuria. On August 14, Japan surrendered. Air landings of Soviet troops were made at Mukden, at Kirin, and at Changchun. Before the end of August, Soviet Russian troops were in complete control of Manchuria—of its railroads, of the great naval base of Port Arthur, of the great port of Dairen, and of all the other ports and cities.

On August 11, General Chu Teh, Commander-in-Chief of all Communist forces, issued an order to four Communist Army Groups to march on to the northeast into the provinces of Chahar, Jehol, Liaoning and Kirin.

---

29. *China Handbook: 1950* (New York: Rockport Press, 1950), 262.
30. Dallin, *Soviet Russia and the Far East*, 223.

Within two or three months large numbers of Chinese Communist troops were in control of many important sections of Manchuria. Many of these Communist soldiers came into Manchuria camouflaged as unarmed "civilians" and uniformed "Nationalists," who upon their arrival inside Manchuria, were quickly and fully armed and equipped from the huge military stocks left over by the surrendered Japanese Kwantung army.

With the invading Soviet armies there also came the Chinese Army that had been organized on Soviet soil out of different Chinese detachments which had left Manchuria in the 1930's. "A considerable number of Chinese Communists who had spent years in Russia came with them. This force . . . brought with it technical and administrative skill, discipline, and loyalty to Russia; it was to play a primary role in the future of Manchuria."[31]

The Soviet Army did not withdraw until the end of April 1946. During the nine months of occupation in Manchuria, every facility was given to the Chinese Communists, while serious obstacles were placed in the way of Nationalist troops that were being slowly transported into Manchuria with the logistical support of the United States Government.

In October 1945, Vice-Admiral Daniel E. Barbey's fleet was ordered to escort Chinese Government troops to Manchuria. But all the seaports on the Manchuria coast were closed to them. At Hulutao, Communists on shore fired upon a launch from Admiral Barney's flagship. The American task force and transports turned away. On October 29, Marshal Malinovsky, the Commander-in-Chief of Soviet forces in Manchuria, agreed that Chinese Nationalist troops could land at the port of Yingkow, and that Soviet troops would leave the port by November 10. But on November 6, Admiral Barbey learned that the Russians had deliberately evacuated five days ahead of schedule and left the port in the hands of the Chinese Communists who threatened to open fire on the American convoy. Once more Admiral Barbey's flotilla turned away. The Chinese Government troops were eventually landed at the port of Chinwangtao, inside the Great Wall—from which point they commenced the long march overland into Manchuria, which the outside world considered already lost to world Communism.[32]

In June 1946, the Chinese Communist broadcast announced to the world that the People's Liberation Army now numbered 1,200,000 in its regular

---

31. Dallin, *Soviet Russia and the Far East*, 250.

32. George Mooard, *Lost Peace in China* (New York: Dutton, 1949), 91–92; Dallin, *Soviet Russia and the Far East*, 252.

formations. In a speech broadcast on December 25, 1947, Mao Tse-tung said that "from 1937 to 1947, in 11 years, the Chinese Communist Party has developed a Party membership of 2,700,000 and a People's Liberation Army of 2,000,000 men." A Communist broadcast dated October 14, 1948, placed the Red Army's strength at 3,000,000. On August 1, 1949, it was 4,000,000. On August 1, 1950, it was 5,000,000.

In December 1947, Mao Tse-tung presented a report to the Central Committee of the Party under the title, "The Present Situation and Our Duties." In this lengthy report, he painted a glowing picture of the military successes of the Red Army:

> The Chinese People's Revolutionary War has now come to a turning point. The People's Liberation Army has smashed the offensive war of Chiang Kai shek's reactionary armies, and has now started its own offensives. In the first year (July 1946–June 1947), our Armies defeated Chiang's offensive attacks on several fronts, and forced him to take a defensive position. In the first quarter of the second year (July-September 1947) our Armies have turned to offensive attacks on a nation-wide scale.

Out of Manchuria, Communist armies, newly equipped and reconditioned, were pouring into Shantung across the sea, and into North China by land. By September 1948 Shantung was lost. By November, Manchuria was lost. By early 1949, North China was lost. Through a most astute and wicked stroke of strategy, Stalin had taken Manchuria and made it the contiguous base for the new military strength of Chinese Communism, behind which lay the unlimited support of Soviet Russia, now the mightiest military Power in the whole world.

A conference of the Big Three had been held at Yalta in February 1945. The conference lasted seven days. At one of the very last sessions, Prime Minister Churchill was not present, and President Roosevelt, according to Harry Hopkins' record, "was tired and anxious to avoid further argument." At this meeting, Stalin proposed the conditions for Soviet Russia's entry into the Pacific war. The resulting agreement was kept secret from China until June 14 when Ambassador Hurley informed Generalissimo Chiang Kai-shek in Chungking that on February 11, 1945, Roosevelt, Churchill and Stalin, on behalf of their Governments, signed at Yalta a secret agreement. The following is the text:

The leaders of the three Great Powers—the Soviet Union, the United States of America and Great Britain—have agreed that in two or three months after Germany has surrendered and the war in Europe has terminated, the Soviet Union shall enter into the war against Japan on the side of the Allies on condition that:

(1) The status quo in Outer-Mongolia (the Mongolian People's Republic) shall be preserved.
(2) The former rights of Russia violated by the treacherous attack of Japan in 1904 shall be restored, *viz.*:
    (a) The southern part of Sakhalin as well as all the islands adjacent to it shall be returned to the Soviet Union.
    (b) The commercial port of Dairen shall be internationalized, the preeminent interests of the Soviet Union in the port being safeguarded and the lease of Port Arthur as a naval base of the U.S.S.R. restored.
    (c) The Chinese Eastern Railroad and the South-Manchurian Railroad which provides an outlet to Dairen shall be jointly operated by the establishment of a joint Soviet-Chinese Company, it being understood that the preeminent interests of the Soviet Union shall be safeguarded and that China shall retain full sovereignty in Manchuria.
(3) The Kuril Islands shall be handed over to the Soviet Union.

It is understood that the agreement concerning Outer-Mongolia and the ports and railroads referred to above will require concurrence of Generalissimo Chiang Kai-shek. The President will take measures in order to obtain this concurrence on advice from Marshal Stalin.

The Heads of the three Great Powers have agreed that these claims of the Soviet Union shall be unquestionably fulfilled after Japan has been defeated.

For its part the Soviet Union expresses its readiness to conclude with the National Government of China a pact of friendship and alliance between the U.S.S.R. and China in order to render assistance to China with its armed forces for the purpose of liberating China from the Japanese yoke.

By these very loosely worded articles, the fate of Manchuria, and of China as a whole, and of Korea (although she is not mentioned here) and very possibly of the whole continent of Asia, was sealed and history was set back 40 years. Of the three signatories, apparently Stalin alone had remembered his history well. For on Japan's surrender, Stalin issued a proclamation in which he depicted his four-day war with Japan as Russia's revenge for her defeat in 1904–1905 at the hands of Japan. "The defeat of Russian troops in 1904, . . ." said the proclamation, "left bitter memories in the minds of the people. It lay like a black spot on our country. Our people believed and hoped that a day would come when Japan would be smashed and that blot effaced. Forty years have we, the people of the old generation, waited for this day."[33]

That is the historical meaning of the principal clause in the secret agreement that "the former rights of Russia violated by the treacherous attack of Japan in 1904 shall be restored." It was in this historical light of Russia's revenge that Stalin appealed for the support of Roosevelt. According to Hopkins' record, "Stalin said to Roosevelt that if his conditions were not met, it would be very difficult to explain to the Russian people why they must go to war against Japan. . . . However, Stalin said, if the required political conditions were met, then it would not be difficult for him to explain to the Supreme Soviet and the people just what was their stake in the Far Eastern war."[34]

The whole affair was a strategy of deceit. China was not a participant, but the President was to take measures in order to obtain China's concurrence. Even this undertaking by the President was not enough. Stalin insisted that this agreement must be put in writing and must contain the statement, "The Heads of the three Great Powers have agreed that these claims of the Soviet Union shall be unquestionably fulfilled after Japan has been defeated."[35] That is to say, Soviet Russia must have these claims fulfilled even if China refuses to give the concurrence!

That Stalin was deliberately deceiving and blackmailing Roosevelt, I have not the slightest doubt. For years past, Stalin and Molotov had taken every occasion to impress on the American leaders that Soviet Russia had no interest in supporting Chinese Communists, because they were not Communists at all. The Soviet leaders had insisted that Chiang Kai-shek was a great man and deserved support, and that the United States must take a leading part in giving aid to China. Molotov in August 1944 even told Ambassador Hurley and Mr. Donald Nelson the "inside" story about the Generalissimo's imprisonment at Sian in December 1936, and assured them that it was "the politi-

33. Bolshevik, No. 16, Moscow, August 1945, quoted in Isaac Deutscher, *Stalin: A Political Biography* (New York: Oxford, 1949), 528.
34. Robert E. Sherwood, *Roosevelt and Hopkins* (New York: Harper, 1948), 867.
35. Sherwood, *Roosevelt and Hopkins*, 867.

cal and moral support of the Soviet Government" that saved Chiang's life and returned him to the seat of his government.[36]

Henry Wallace, Hurley and Hopkins had all told President Roosevelt of this friendly concern and political and moral support which Soviet Russia and Stalin had for Chiang Kai-shek. In the Department of State version of the Yalta Agreement on the Far East, there is a very revealing footnote which quotes Ambassador Harriman's comment on the clause relating to the "lease of Port Arthur as a naval base of the U.S.S.R." Mr. Harriman says, "I believe President Roosevelt looked upon the lease of Port Arthur for a naval base *as an arrangement similar to privileges which the United States has negotiated with other countries for the mutual security of two friendly nations.*"[37]

Mr. Harriman's comment brings my memory back to a September day in 1939, when I was calling on President Roosevelt in my official capacity as Chinese Ambassador. The war had broken out in Europe, and the President was worried. He said to me, "I have been thinking about mediating for a peace between China and Japan. The most difficult question, of course, is Manchuria. I have a new formula: I can settle this question of Manchuria on the same basis as the new agreement we have just signed with Britain regarding the joint interest and control over the two islands in the Pacific: the Canton and Enderbury Islands. Some such arrangement can be made with regard to Manchuria for the benefit and security of both China and Japan."

When I left him, I tried to find out more about these two coral islands. I subsequently found that Canton Island was nine miles long and 500 yards at the widest. Its population was 40. Enderbury Island was three miles long and one mile wide, and had a population of four persons! Manchuria, of course, has a population of 33,000,000 and an area of about 413,000 square miles.

I am sure that at Yalta in 1945 President Roosevelt had in mind his favorite case of the Canton and Enderbury Islands which were placed under a United States–British condominium for a period of 50 years by an agreement between the two Governments concluded on April 6, 1939.

History will not forgive the man who played such deliberate tricks on the generous idealism of a great humanitarian.

---

36. Department of State, *United States Relations with China*, 71–72.
37. Department of State, *United States Relations with China*, 114. Italics inserted.

VI

Such, in brief, is the story of the unfolding of Stalin's strategy of conquest in China. The heart of this strategy has been the creation, preservation and nurturing to full strength of the Chinese Red Army. It has taken nearly a quarter of a century for the Red Army to achieve sufficient power for the conquest of continental China. This Red Army was many times defeated, broken up and nearly annihilated by Chiang Kai-shek's armies; and Stalin and world Communism might never have succeeded in China if the greatest war in human history had not intervened.

Stalin himself has summed up the China situation in one sentence, "The special characteristic of the Chinese revolution lies in the fact that it is an armed people fighting an armed counter-revolution."[38] In plain language, this formulation meant that the Communist conquest of China by armed force had up to then been successfully resisted by the armed force of Nationalist China. Because of this successful resistance by the Government, the whole Chinese Communist movement came to be conceived by Mao Tse-tung and his fellow militarists as essentially an armed struggle for power. "In China," said Mao in a 1939 speech, "there is no place for the proletariat without armed struggle; there is no place for the people without armed struggle; there is no place for the Communist Party without armed struggle; and there is no victory of the revolution without armed struggle."

---

38. Quoted with enthusiastic approval by Mao Tse-tung in his article "The Chinese Revolution and the Chinese Communist Party," November 1939, 19.

CHAPTER 10

The Free World Needs a Free China[1]

Nineteen months ago, I arrived at San Francisco from China on the sad morning of April 21, 1949. On that day, the papers reported that the Chinese Government at Nanking had rejected the Communist terms of peace, or more correctly the Communist terms of unconditional surrender, and that Civil War had again broken out after nearly one hundred days of so-called "peace talks."

Two days later, Nanking fell. A month later, Shanghai fell. And before the end of the year 1949, nearly the whole of continental China, with the exception of the guerrilla areas, came under the conquest and control of World Communism.

In September 1949, the Chinese Communist Party put up a great show in Peiping. A new "People's Political Consultative Conference" was held there and was attended by 635 delegates designated by the Communist Party. The Conference, on September 29, passed three documents: (1) the Common Program of the PPCC, which was hailed as the Constitution of the Communist regime; (2) the Organization Law of the Central Government of the People's Republic; and (3) the Organization Law of the PPCC itself.

On September 30, before it adjourned, the Conference elected Mao Tse-tung to be the Chairman of the Government Committee of the People's Central Government of the People's Republic. It also elected six Deputy Chairmen and fifty-six other members of the People's Central Government Committee. It is this Government that is ruling over most of China's mainland today.

The first article of the "Common Program" gives this definition of the Communist State and Government in China: "The People's Republic of

---

1. Unpublished manuscript written around November 1950.

China is a state of the New Democracy, that is, a state of the People's Democracy. It carries out the People's Democratic Dictatorship which is led by the working class and based on the alliance of workers and peasants and which unifies all democratic classes and all races in the country." Translated into plain language, it means that "the People's Republic of China" is a dictatorship of the Chinese Communist Party in the name of the "People."

It is called "a state of the New Democracy" because in 1940 Mao Tse-tung published a pamphlet entitled "The New Democracy" which was an attempt to present the political policy of the Chinese Communist Party under the disguise of liberalism. The New Democracy was the high-sounding name for the "united front" or "coalition" of all democratic groups against fascist and imperialist aggression. It was to be "a state of the combined dictatorship of several revolutionary classes."

My former student Mao Tse-tung, being an orthodox Communist, could conceive of all states and governments only as class dictatorships. Therefore he tells us in his pamphlet that in the whole world, there are only three forms of state:

1. Republics of bourgeois dictatorship, which prevail in all old democratic countries.
2. Republics of proletarian dictatorship, which is the form of state of the Soviet Union.
3. Republics of joint dictatorship of several classes, which Mao calls "the New Democracy."

This slogan of "the New Democratic State" as a joint dictatorship of all democratic or revolutionary classes was offered about ten years ago as a kind of political bid for the sympathy and support of non-Communist liberals or progressives. In that pamphlet, Mao Tse-tung actually talked about "an election based on a real popular and equal suffrage irrespective of differences of sex, belief, property and education," which alone could secure the spirit of the "New Democracy."

But of course no Communist Party could ever tolerate the sharing of political power with non-Communist groups or parties. So today when the victorious Communist Party is in complete control of political power, all pre-victory slogans and promises are conveniently forgotten, and the "People's Government" is indisputably a dictatorship of the one and only Party, with a number of non-Communist "democratic personages" holding nominal and honorary posts.

And the first sentence in the Communist "Constitution" proclaims to the world that the Chinese Communist regime is to be "the People's Democratic Dictatorship!"

Two months before the PPCC—on July 1, 1949, the twenty-eighth anniversary of the founding of the Chinese Communist Party, the official Communist News Agency broadcast a lengthy article by Mao Tse-tung on "The People's Democratic Dictatorship." A complete English translation of it is included in the Department of State's "white paper" on "U.S. Relations with China, 1944–49" (pp. 720–729). This article has formed the guiding principle of the Communist "Constitution" and has become the required reading of all "Political Science" courses which all teachers and students of all grades must take. A few sentences from this famous essay by Mao will best describe the dictatorial and absolutistic character of this regime:

> Our experiences (of 28 years) may be summarized into one single point—the People's Democratic Dictatorship based on the workers and peasants' alliance led by the working class (through the Communist Party).
>
> "You are dictatorial." Yes, dear gentlemen, you are right and we are dictatorial. The experience of several decades amassed by the Chinese people tell us to carry out the people's democratic dictatorship, that is, the reactionaries must be deprived of the right to voice their opinion, and only the People are allowed to have the right to voice their opinion.
>
> Who are "the people"? At the present stage in China, they are the working class, the peasants, the petty bourgeoisie, and the national bourgeoisie. Under the leadership of the working class and the Communist Party, these classes unite together to form their own state and elect their own government to carry out dictatorship over the "running dogs" of imperialism—the landlords, the bureaucratic class, the Kuomintang reactionaries and their henchmen—these classes shall oppress them and only allow them to behave properly, and not allow them to talk and act wildly. If they talk and act wildly, they shall be curbed and punished immediately.
>
> The democratic system is to be carried out within the ranks of the people only, giving them freedom of speech, assembly and association. The right to vote is given only to the People, and not to the reactionaries.
>
> These two aspects, namely, democracy among the People, and dictatorship over the reactionaries, combine to form the People's Democratic Dictatorship.

Why should it be done this way? It is obvious that if this is not done, the revolution will fail, the people will suffer, and the state will perish.

"Do you not want to do away with the State authority?" Yes, but not at the present. Why? Because imperialism still exists, the internal reactionaries still exist, and classes in the country still exist.

Our present task is to strengthen the People's state apparatus, which refers mainly to the People's Army, the People's Police, and the People's Court. . . .

The Army, the Police, the Court—these machineries of the state are instruments for classes to oppress classes. To the hostile classes, the state apparatus is an instrument of oppression. It is violent, and not benevolent.

I cite these arrogant and insolent words of Mao Tse-tung in some detail, because they give the reader a very vivid picture of the dictatorial and oppressive rules under which about four hundred million of the Chinese people are now living and suffering.

Article 5 of the "Common Program" stipulates that the people of the Chinese People's Republic shall have eleven kinds of freedom, namely, the freedom of thought, speech, publication, assembly, association, correspondence, the person, residence, migration, religious belief, and demonstration parade. But article 7 says:

The People's Republic must suppress all counter-revolutionary activities, must severely punish all Kuomintang, counter-revolutionary, war-criminal, and other unrepentant reactionary leaders who collaborate with imperialism, betray the fatherland, and oppose the people's democratic activities. With regard to all reactionaries, feudalistic landlords, bureaucratic capitalism, after they are disarmed and their special influences are liquidated, they must be deprived of their political rights, but at the same time given some means of livelihood and forced to reconstruct themselves to become "new men" by means of hard labor. If they persist in counter-revolutionary activities, then they should be severely punished.

Here we find the institution of forced slave labor for the national opposition already dignified into a "constitutional" provision!

Under such a regime, there is absolutely no freedom for the nonconformist of any kind. There is no freedom of the press, no freedom of information—all information, all news, and of course all editorial opinion, strictly controlled. There is no freedom of speaking out, and there is no freedom of silence. At any moment, a man may be called upon to make positive statements of his own belief and disbelief.

A year ago last May, the Chancellor of the Catholic University in Peiping, an old historical scholar of very high standing, was made to publish an open letter addressed to me, in which my old friend and fellow academician said emphatically that there was no real freedom anywhere except in the areas liberated by the Communists. Did he really say that? Did he have the freedom not to say that?

A few weeks ago, all newspapers in Communist China and a few in Hong Kong published what purported to be a written confession of my younger son, in which he denounced me as "an enemy of the people" and also his own enemy. Did my son actually say that? Was he free not to say that?

II

But it is not the Chinese people alone who are not free. It is more important for the free world to understand that the Chinese Communist regime itself is not free. Mao Tse-tung, the Chinese Communist Party, and the entire Chinese Communist Government are not free: they are all under the bondage which the USSR imposes on her satellite countries. They have always taken orders from the Kremlin, and they must continue to take such orders because they are fully conscious that Communist China has been and will long continue to be dependent on the military and industrial power of the Soviet Union.

In a recent article published in the October issue of *Foreign Affairs*, I have tried to tell the story of the unfolding, in twenty-five years, of Stalin's grand strategy of conquest of China. It was Stalin who conceived and ordered the creation of the Chinese Red Army. It was Stalin who throughout two decades carefully protected and nurtured this Red Army to full strength. It was Stalin who wrested from President Roosevelt and Prime Minister Churchill the secret Yalta Agreement which made it possible for Stalin to convert both Manchuria and North Korea into contiguous bases for the USSR to effectively aid the Chinese and Korean Communist armies in their military conquest of China.

All this indebtedness to the USSR has been openly acknowledged by the leaders of Chinese Communism. Mao Tse-tung in his article "The People's Democratic Dictatorship" made this historical observation:

> Let us think it over. If the Soviet Union did not exist, if there were no victories of the anti-Fascist Second World War, and especially, for us, no defeat of Japanese imperialism, if there were no rising struggles of the oppressed nations in the east, if there were no struggles of the masses of peoples in the United States, Britain, France, Germany, Italy, Japan and other capitalist countries against the reactionary clique ruling over them, and if there were no sum total of these things . . . could we have won victory under such circumstances? Obviously not. It would be impossible to consolidate the victory when it was won.

In the same article, Mao declared that Communist-led China must "lean to one side," must "ally with the Soviet Union, with the new People's Democracies, and with the proletariat and masses of the people (that is, the Communists) in the other countries, to form an international united front."

This allegiance has been actually formally stipulated into the "Common Program" which is the Constitution of the Communist State in China. Article 11 of the Common Program says:

> The People's Republic of China allies itself with all those states and peoples who love peace and freedom. First of all, it allies itself with the Soviet Union, and with the People's Democracies and with all oppressed nations, standing together on the international battlefront of peace and democracy and jointly fighting against all imperialist aggression, in order to defend the lasting peace of the world.

This "Constitutional" provision was made before Mao Tse-tung and Chou En-lai visited Moscow and signed the Moscow Treaty of Friendship and Alliance with Russia. That Treaty, of course, made Communist China and Soviet Russia partners in a defensive and offensive alliance.

Communist China must lean to one side and must consider itself bound to ally with the USSR and her satellites. There is no freedom of choice. "Internationally," says Mao, "we belong to the anti-imperialist front headed by the USSR, and we can only look for genuine friendly aid from that front, and not from the imperialist front."

What has been happening in Tibet and Korea, and what is now happening in Korea on a stupendous scale, are best evidences that Communist China has no choice but to march on wherever it is ordered to move.

What could be more foolish than for the Chinese Communists to send an army to invade Tibet, thereby alienating the undoubted sympathy and support of a most friendly and accommodating India? The only possible explanation is that Communist China was under orders to do so.

And what could be more insane and suicidal than for the new state of Communist China to embark on the certain path of war with the forces of one of the two greatest powers in the world? The only possible and logical explanation is that the great prestige of World Communism is at stake if the Communist state of North Korea is allowed to be wiped out by the United States and United Nations forces and that therefore Communist China has been ordered to come to the rescue of North Korea regardless of all possible consequences:

> Theirs not to make reply,
> Theirs not to reason why,
> Theirs but to do and die.

III

My subject for this talk was announced weeks ago: "The free world needs a free China." But the events of the world have moved with such terrific speed in the last few weeks that today I find it almost unnecessary to develop this thesis.

It becomes self-evident now that all the trouble in Korea and in the Far East today stems from the fact that China is no longer free and that it has become a Captive Nation of World Communism. The free world is at war with Captive China.

If China had remained free, all this would have been absolutely impossible. Indeed it would have been absolutely impossible even to imagine a free China fighting the United States!

The other day, Mr. Dean Acheson uttered these words of warning and challenge to the Chinese Communists:

> This is their hour of decision. The authorities of Communist China stand
> before the bar of the judgment of mankind. The world will watch their

actions in Korea and at Lake Success. Will they represent their own interests, or will they let themselves be the dupes of others?

Of course, Mr. Acheson knows the answer to his own question: Communist China is Captive China, which has no free choice but to fight the free world which World Communism considers as an enemy that must be destroyed.

It is very important for the free world constantly to keep in mind this distinction between Free China and Captive China. Captive China is attacking you, but Free China is still your friend, ever ready to help you and fight shoulder to shoulder with you.

By "Free China," I do not mean merely the six hundred thousand well-trained soldiers and the seven million population in the island bastion of Formosa. Nor do I mean merely the vast numbers of Chinese guerrilla units now fighting in various parts of the Chinese mainland against the Communists.

By "Free China" I mean the vast majority of the Chinese people who are mentally and emotionally anti-Communist even though they are physically living and suffering under the iron yoke and behind the Iron Curtain.

My friends, let me assure you that a Free China still exists and [is] growing in number and in strength every day. Let me assure you that a Free China exists as a peace-loving, freedom-loving, pro-American, and pro-Western force, which has not been and cannot be destroyed by the short period of Communist conquest and control.

Free China exists as a reality because, of all the peoples conquered by World Communism so far, my people are the most civilized and have lived under a civilization noted for its individualism and its centuries-long fights for intellectual, religious, and political freedom. My people cannot long remain captive.

This is no wishful thinking on the part of a Chinese philosopher who has been called the incurable optimist of China. No, this conclusion is the studied, sober judgment of a lifelong student of Chinese thought and history. If history and civilization mean anything at all, there shall always be a Free China.

And I can assure you that this Free China is pro-democracy, pro-American and pro-West—because, as a historian, I am firmly convinced that the one hundred years of China's contact with modern Western ideas and institutions has not been in vain; because the over one hundred years of Christian missionary work in China has not been in vain; because the seventy-five years of intensive education and training of thousands of Chinese youths in the American universities and colleges has not been and cannot be in vain. No, as the Buddhists used to say, "No effort is ever in vain." A Free China exists, as real as day and night.

And my people have had the sad experience living and suffering for the last few years under the Communist rule. That is a blessing in disguise. This experience has enabled my people to understand clearly what Communism and Communist rule are.

Let the free world make it absolutely clear to the people of China that it is fighting the Communist dictatorship in China and not the vast majority of the people of China; that any movement on the part of the people of China to sabotage the Communist conquerors or to rid themselves of their Stalinist puppet dictators will have the moral support and, whenever possible, the material support of democratic and peace-loving peoples of the world.

When the free world gives the word, Free China will surely respond.

[Handwritten note attached to the end of the essay:]

1. Healthy individualism
2. Anarchist mentality against gov't interference
3. Love of freedom and fight for freedom
4. Doubt everything

All these are powerful forces which make China resistant to Communism. These are the forces that make a Free China.

CHAPTER 11

Address to the Commonwealth Club of San Francisco, CA[1]

Before the end of 1949, nearly the whole of continental China, except for the guerilla areas, came under the conquest of World Communism.

In September, 1949, the Chinese Communist Party put up a great show in Peiping. A new People's Political Consultative Conference attended by 635 delegates designated by the Communist Party passed three documents: 1) the Common Program of the P.P.C.C. hailed as the Constitution of the Communist regime; 2) the Organization Law of the central Government; and 3) the Organization Law of the P.P.C.C. itself.

DICTATORSHIP BY PARTY

The first article of the "Common Program" gives this definition: "The People's Republic of China is a state of the New Democracy, that is, a state of the People's Democracy. It carries out the People's Democratic Dictatorship which is led by the working class. . . ."

Translated into plain language, it means that "the People's Republic of China" is a dictatorship of the Chinese Communist Party in the name of the "People."

It is called "a state of the New Democracy," because in 1940 Mao Tse-tung published a pamphlet "The New Democracy" which was an attempt to present the Chinese Communist Party under the disguise of liberalism.

---

1. This address was delivered on December 1, 1950, and was later published in *The Commonwealth: The Official Journal of the Commonwealth Club of California* 26, no. 50 (December 11, 1950): 229–231. Reprinted with permission from the Commonwealth Club of California.

The "New Democracy"—high sounding name for the "united front"—was to be "the combined dictatorship of several revolutionary classes."

PRE-VICTORY SLOGANS FORGOTTEN

My former student Mao Tse-tung, being an orthodox Communist, could conceive of all states and governments only as class dictatorships. Therefore he tells us in his pamphlet that in the whole world, there are only three forms of state: 1) Republic of *bourgeois dictatorship*, which prevails in all old democratic countries. 2) Republic of *proletarian dictatorship*, which is the form of state of the Soviet Union. 3) Republic of *joint dictatorship* of several classes, which Mao calls "the new democracy."

Mao Tse-tung actually talked about "an election based on a real popular and equal suffrage irrespective of differences of sex, belief, property and education."

But of course no Communist Party could ever tolerate sharing political power with non-Communist groups or parties. So today all pre-victory slogans and promises are conveniently forgotten, and the "People's Government" is indisputably a dictatorship of the one and only Party, with a number of non-Communist "democratic personages" holding nominal and honorary posts.

MAO ADMITS DICTATORSHIP

On July 1, 1949, the official Communist News Agency broadcast a lengthy article by Mao Tse-tung which has become required reading for all teachers and students. A few sentences:

> "You are dictatorial." Yes, dear gentlemen, you are right and we are dictatorial. . . . the reactionaries must be deprived of the right to voice their opinion, and only the People are allowed to have the right to voice their opinion.
>
> Who are "the people?" At the present stage in China, they are the working class, the peasants, the petty bourgeoisie, and the national bourgeoisie. Under the leadership of the working class and the Communist Party, these

classes unite together to form their own state and elect their own government to carry out dictatorship over the "running dogs" of the imperialism—the landlords, the bureaucratic class, the Kuomintang reactionaries and their henchmen—these classes shall oppress them and only allow them to behave properly, and not allow them to talk and act wildly. If they talk and act wildly, they shall be curbed and punished immediately. . . .

INSTRUMENTS OF OPPRESSION

These two aspects, namely, democracy among the People, and dictatorship over the reactionaries, combine to form the People's Democratic Dictatorship. . . .

"Do you not want to do away with the State authority?" Yes, but not at the present. Why? Because imperialism still exists, the internal reactionaries still exist, and classes in the country still exist. . . .

The Army, the Police, the Court—these machineries of the state are instruments for classes to oppress classes. To the hostile classes, the state apparatus is an instrument of oppression. It is violent, and not benevolent.

These arrogant and insolent words of Mao Tse-tung give a vivid picture of the dictatorial and oppressive rule under which about 400,000,000 Chinese are now suffering.

Article 5 of the 'Common Program' stipulates that the people of the Chinese People's Republic shall have eleven kinds of freedom.

But Article 7 says:

. . . With regard to all reactionaries, feudalistic landlords, bureaucratic capitalists, after they are disarmed and their special influences are liquidated, they must be deprived of their political rights, but at the same time given some means of livelihood and forced to reconstruct themselves to become "new men" by means of hard labor. . . .

Here we find forced slave labor already dignified into a "constitutional" provision!

NO FREEDOM OF SILENCE

Under such a regime, there is no freedom to be a nonconformist. There is no freedom of speaking out, and *no freedom of silence*. At any moment, a man may be called upon to make positive statements of his own belief and disbelief.

A year ago last May the Chancellor of the Catholic University in Peiping was made to publish an open letter in which my old friend and fellow-academician said emphatically that there was no real freedom anywhere except in the areas liberated by the Communists. Did he really say that? Did he have the freedom not to say that?

A few weeks ago, all newspapers in Communist China published what purported to be a written confession of my younger son, in which he denounced me as "an enemy of the people" and also his own enemy. Did my son actually say that? Was he free not to say that?

I cite this to show how oppressive the Communist regime is!

But it is not the Chinese people alone who are not free. The Chinese Communist regime itself is not free.

CHINA'S GOVERNMENT IN BONDAGE

Mao Tse-tung, the Chinese Communist Party, and the entire Chinese Communist Government are not free: they are all under the bondage which the U.S.S.R. imposes on her satellite countries.

They have always taken orders from the Kremlin, and they must continue to take such orders because Communist China is dependent on the military and industrial power of the Soviet Union.

It was Stalin who conceived and ordered creation of the Chinese Red Army. It was Stalin who throughout two decades nurtured this Red Amy to full strength. It was Stalin who wrested from President Roosevelt and Prime Minister Churchill the secret Yalta Agreement which made it possible for Stalin to convert both Manchuria and North Korea into contiguous bases for the U.S.S.R. to aid effectively the Chinese and Korean Communist armies in their military conquest of China.

All this indebtedness to the U.S.S.R. has been openly acknowledged by the leaders of Chinese Communism.

Mao has declared that Communist-led China must "lean to one side," must "ally with the Soviet Union, with the new People's Democracies, and with the proletariat and masses of the people [that is, the Communists] in other countries, to form an international united front."

ALLEGIANCE TO STALIN

This allegiance has been formally stipulated into the Constitution of the Communist State in China. Article 11 says:

> The People's Republic of China allies itself with all those states and peoples who love peace and freedom. First of all, it allies itself with the Soviet Union. . . .

The Moscow Treaty made Communist China and Soviet Russia partners in a defensive and offensive alliance.

What has been happening in Tibet, what is now happening in Korea, are best evidences that Communist China has no choice but to march wherever it is ordered to move.

What could be more foolish than for the Chinese Communists to invade Tibet, thereby alienating the undoubted sympathy and support of India? The only possible explanation is that Communist China was under orders to do so.

AT WAR WITH CAPTIVE CHINA

And what could be more insane than for the new state of Communist China to embark on war with one of the two greatest powers in the world? The only possible explanation is that the great prestige of world Communism is at stake and that therefore Communist China has been ordered to come to the rescue of North Korea regardless of all possible consequences.

It becomes self-evident now that all the trouble in Korea and in the Far East today stems from the fact that China is no longer free, has become a captive nation of World Communism. *The free world is at war with Captive China.*

It would have been absolutely impossible even to imagine a free China fighting the United States!

Captive China is attacking you, but Free China is still your friend, ever-ready to help you and fight shoulder to shoulder with you.

By "Free China," I do not mean merely the 600,000 well-trained soldiers and the seven million population in the island bastion of Formosa. Nor do I mean merely the vast numbers of Chinese guerrilla units now fighting on the Chinese mainland against the Communists.

By "Free China" I mean the vast majority of the Chinese people who are mentally and emotionally anti-Communist even though they are physically living and suffering under the iron yoke.

ALWAYS BE FREE CHINA

Free China exists as a reality because, of all the peoples conquered by World Communism, my people are the most civilized and have lived under a civilization noted for its individualism and its century-long fights for intellectual, religious and political freedom.

If history and civilization mean anything at all, there shall always be a Free China.

And this Free China is pro-democracy, pro-America and pro-West. The one hundred years of China's contact with modern Western ideas and institutions has not been in vain; the over one hundred years of Christian missionary work in China has not been in vain; the 75 years of intensive education and training of thousands of Chinese youths in the American universities and colleges has not been and cannot be in vain.

KNOW WHAT COMMUNISM IS

The sad experience of living and suffering under Communist rule has enabled my people to understand clearly what Communism and Communist rule is.

Let the free world make it clear to the people of China that it is fighting the Communist dictatorship in China and not the vast majority of the people of China; that any movement on the part of the people of China to sabotage the Communist conquerors or to rid themselves of their Stalinist puppet dictators will have the moral support and, whenever possible, the material support of democratic and peace-loving peoples of the world.

When the free world gives the word, Free China will surely respond.

CHAPTER 12

Why the Main War Will Be Fought in Asia— Not Europe

An Interview with Hu Shih

FORMER CHINESE AMBASSADOR TO U.S.—CHINA'S LEADING
PHILOSOPHER[1]

Editor's Note: How strong is the Communist hold on China and the rest of Asia? Can the armies of Generalissimo Chiang Kai-shek win back the country he lost to Communist Mao Tse-tung? Will the Russia-China partnership hold together, and where will it strike next?

Answers to these questions are an answer to the bigger question of World War III. To get the views of one of China's outstanding scholars and statesmen, the editors of *U. S. News & World Report* invited Dr. Hu Shih to their conference rooms for an interview on the present plight of his native land, and what the U. S. can do about it. That interview follows.

Dr. Hu Shih is a political independent and belongs to none of China's political parties, though he is a friend of Chiang Kai-shek.

Dr. Hu was China's Ambassador to the U. S. during much of World War II. He was connected with Peiping University many years, beginning in 1917, and became its president after the war. In 1947 he was given credit for averting student riots through his prestige with the student body. He later defended campus demonstrators against charges of Communism. In 1948 he declined appointment as Foreign Minister. He left China in April, 1949, before the Communist victory, and now is at Princeton University.

---

1. This interview was published by *U. S. News and World Report* on January 19, 1951. An editor's note was provided in the magazine before the main text of the interview.

Q: *How much popular support is there for the Communists in China, Dr. Hu?*
A: As far as I know, there is very little popular support today.

Q: *On what do they rest their power, then?*
A: Force. The story of the conquest of China by the strategy of Stalin covers 25 years, from 1924 to 1949. China is the best place to see this strategy slowly unfolding in detail. Nowhere else do you have this chance of watching the unfolding of a continuous, persistent, wicked conspiracy.

Q: *What is that strategy?*
A: Stalin's strategy consists of three main conditions. The first is what is called "the subjective condition of the success of the Revolution": You must have a strong Communist Party, preferably a Red Army supporting the party.

Secondly, there must be an objective condition for the success of the Revolution—that is war: You must have a big war—the bigger, the better—a world war. It was a world war that made the Bolshevik Revolution possible. And it was the Second World War that made Russia the greatest military power in the world. So you must have war—a condition which Stalin and the Kremlin have sought to perpetuate ever since 1945.

And the third condition, which is equally important, is the consolidation of Soviet Russia as the base from which to support the revolutions in other parts of the world. But the Second World War made it possible for Russia to conquer North Korea and Manchuria, and made Korea and Manchuria contiguous bases to Russia—strong bases from which to give effective military aid to the Chinese Communist Army.

Q: *What is the relation between the Communist Party and the Army?*
A: In China we had the unique experience of being the first country where the Communist Party had, almost from the early years of its founding, a formidable Red Army. No country will permit the Communist Party to have an army, or to carry on conspiracy in the army and in the navy, which is one of the 21 conditions for admission into the Third International, the Comintern.

China had an extraordinary experience. Dr. Sun Yat-sen, founder of the Republic, father of the Chinese Revolution, in his desire to have a successful second revolution, voluntarily asked the Third International in 1924 to send experts to help reorganize his party and to send military experts to train a revolutionary army for him. The head of the Russian military mission to China was General Galen, whose real name was General Blucher, one of the greatest generals in the Soviet Union.

So, 25 or 26 years ago, there was a Russian-sent military mission of considerable size to train an army intended, no doubt, by the Comintern to be a Red Army. During the 25 years Stalin's policy was to preserve that Army and nurture it to full strength. During the first 20 years this Army was defeated many times, smashed to pieces, by the Government armies, and Stalin had to resort to what is known as the Lenin-Stalin doctrine of the strategy of retreat. The object of this strategy of retreat, says Stalin, "is to gain time, to decompose the enemy, and to assemble forces to take the offensive later." And the better opportunity came with the Second World War, especially with the Yalta Conference.

Q: *You think, then, that the whole Red Army marching into the interior of China was part of Moscow's strategy?*
A: There is no doubt.

Q: *Then Russian support of Chiang Kai-shek during the war was a form of hypocrisy?*
A: Surely—there is no doubt of it.

Q: *What is Stalin's strategy now—having conquered China? Where does it lead from this point?*
A: The next thing is to prevent any possibility of a Chinese Tito. What is happening today in Manchuria and Korea is the most conclusive evidence that Mao Tse-tung can never become a Chinese Tito. Soviet Russia has made Communist China go to the extreme of fighting the Americans. That is to make Mao Tse-tung burn bridges with the West—that's the way to prevent a Tito. Mao has been saying that Communist China must "lean to one side"—that is, lean to the side of Soviet Russia. To make war on the U. S. and the U. N. is the best way for Mao Tse-tung to demonstrate that he really leans to one side and will never waver.

CHINA'S DEPENDENCE ON RUSSIA

Q: *Do you think there will be any Tito in China?*

A: No, impossible—because Stalin wouldn't permit a second Tito to come up.

Q: *How would he avoid it?*

A: It's very easy. It's now being done effectively. Stalin is making Communist China burn all bridges—all approaches to the West. But the important thing is to make Communist China completely dependent upon the military and industrial strength of Soviet Russia.

For instance, this Red Army celebrated its 23rd anniversary on the 1st of August, 1950—the independent Red Army, apart from the earlier army that had been part of the National Revolution Army under Chiang Kai-shek. A year earlier they claimed that this Army had 1 million men. And on Aug. 1, 1950, they claimed to have 5 million. Who is going to supply and equip, and continue to supply and equip an Army of 5 million? Certainly the United States is not going to supply this huge Chinese Red Army. Certainly the British Commonwealth isn't going to do that.

Q: *Who will do it—the Chinese?*

A: To do it, the Chinese have had to rely on the industry of Manchuria. But Russia is absolutely in control of Manchuria, which is the most highly industrialized area in the whole of Asia.

Q: *Why?*

A: The Russian Army is on the border, and in Manchuria, too, and on the Korean border. And, if you look at a map, the control of Port Arthur, the best naval base, is in their hands. Now, in addition to Port Arthur, the Russians control Chefoo [in Shantung], the other naval base. Russia controls the two best naval ports in North China. So, in any war, Peiping and Tientsin will be at the mercy of the Russian Navy and Air Force.

Q: *Will the Chinese Communists like that?*

A: They may not like it, but the Chinese Communists today are entirely
dependent upon Russia's military and industrial strength for existence, and cannot do otherwise.

Q: *What about the Yugoslav theory that the Chinese Communists really are*
going ahead in Korea contrary to Soviet wishes?

A: That's nonsense. Months ago I predicted that Communist China
would come into the war. I was asked "Why?" I said: For two main
reasons. In the first place, the Korean Communists and Chinese Communists, the Korean Red Army and the Chinese Red Army, are more
than blood relations—they have for years fought together as brothers
in distress. As you know, the Russians had five years of complete control of North Korea. In the first part of those five years, Russians didn't
have a free hand in Manchuria because they still had some regard for
world opinion—for American opinion. They didn't have a free hand
in training the Red Army in Manchuria, but they had a completely
free hand in training this effectively trained and equipped Army in
Korea. That Korean Army fought more successfully in Manchuria
than the Chinese Communist Army and they helped the Communists to conquer Manchuria and to conquer North China and to conquer Central China and this Korean Army went as far as Hainan
Island.

But now the process is reversed. The Chinese Communist armies
went back to help Communist Korea. They had to. Because the Korean Red Army and the Chinese Red Army are blood brothers in need.

But there is a second and more important reason: If the Communist state in North Korea should be permitted to be conquered by the
U. N. Army, MacArthur's Army, while Soviet Russia on the northeastern border stands by without helping, and the Chinese Communists
on the northwestern border stand by without helping—if that were
to happen, the prestige of world Communism would fall to pieces,
and this would affect the Communist movement in Japan, in China,
in Korea, in India and in Eastern and Western Europe. So Soviet Russia cannot permit it. Hence Communist China must come in.

FORCED SERVICE IN ARMY

Q: *You say there is not much public support or good will for the Communists.
How can they maintain an Army of 5 million, then? Is that a conscript
Army?*

A: It's a conscript Army. The Communists go into every village—and villages are the source of food supply and man-power supply. Now,
when the Communist agents come to a village, first they requisition
all the grain and foodstuffs and then they take a census of the able-
bodied men and women for the Army. By controlling all food supply,
they control all man-power. It's really forced conscription—much
more effective than any other form.

Q: *Wasn't that true under Chiang Kai-shek too?*

A: No. Under the Nationalists, conscription was never effective. That's
the trouble with a constituted government—there are many things
you can't do. They asked the villages to deliver men and the villages
delivered their most undesirable people—the invalids, the people
that they wanted to get rid of.

On the other hand, when the Communists went into the villages
they controlled the source of food supply, and, by controlling the
food supply, they controlled the life and death of the people they
wanted for the Army.

Q: *Do you think we should undertake a war on the mainland of China in order to rectify the situation?*

A: All those things are beyond anybody's planning or wishes. Events
may force you to do it. Seven months ago nobody would have dared
to say that in less than six months the President of the United States
would declare a state of national emergency.

Nobody in America or in Europe wants to fight a war on the Asiatic
continent. Everybody is afraid that military involvement in Asia
might greatly weaken the Western powers on the European front. But
let me say that Europe is safe—the war is going to be fought in Asia,
and Stalin being a shrewd strategist will not lightly open a second
front in Europe.

WHY EUROPE IS "SAFE"

Europe is relatively safe for four reasons: First, Europe is protected by the North Atlantic Pact, which is not really appreciated by your own people. But, to outsiders, this North Atlantic Pact is really the most radical departure from your 160 years of foreign policy. For the first time you have signed an offensive and defensive alliance with 11 countries—and some of the countries are the weakest, for example, Luxembourg and Iceland. Article 5 of the Treaty says that an armed attack against any one of the signatories shall be regarded as attack against all of them, and they will undertake necessary measures, including the use of armed forces, to assist the attacked party to restore peace and maintain the security of the Atlantic area. The gangsters understand the significance of this Treaty and will not lightly subject it to a test.

And, secondly, Stalin has said that Hitler destroyed himself by opening up a second front. Stalin is not going to destroy himself by opening up a second front in Europe.

And, thirdly, if there should be a second front, it will not be in Europe, because Stalin doesn't feel he has a sufficient hold over his satellites. Poland would be the first to revolt, Czechoslovakia, the second. Bulgaria, Hungary and Rumania would be the next. Stalin doesn't want these satellites to take advantage of a European war.

And fourthly, and most important of all, is this question of equipment and supply—the industrial ability of the U.S.S.R. to maintain the huge armies in Asia and in Europe. MacArthur has said there are over 1 million Chinese and North Korean Communist troops in Korea. And it has been said that there are over 175 divisions ready to be mobilized in Europe, if Stalin wants it. But who is going to equip and keep on supplying these 175 divisions plus the 1 million or 2 million of Chinese troops? The industrial power of Soviet Russia is backward compared with the democratic countries. That should be an important determining factor in this problem.

So I maintain this war is going to be fought in Asia. Don't call it a Third World War. It is just the unfinished business of World War II.

Q: *How strong is Mao in his hold on the people? I mean, could we chisel in there in any way?*

A: Of all the peoples conquered by world Communism up to date, China is the most civilized. It has the highest civilization of all these Communist-dominated countries—including the fatherland of world Communism. If civilization means anything, I would predict that China, the last to be conquered, may be the first to revolt.

Q: *Do you expect a palace revolt, or a mass, guerrilla revolt?*

A: You can never expect the unarmed masses to succeed in any revolt. There are still many armed Nationalist forces scattered in various parts of the mainland that make hundreds of thousands of guerrillas. I read the papers of Hong Kong—it is still a British colony where the British tradition of permitting all kinds of newspapers to be published prevails—and I see that not only in the Canton area there are every-day reports of guerrilla activity, but also in Southeastern China, West China and Northwestern China. I read these reports, which somehow get through to be printed in Hong Kong.

So as to what you can do really—

Q: *Somebody has to decide whether to give the Chinese people arms or not—*

A: That's right—but, being a democracy, you do not often "decide" until you are forced by events.

Q: *How much influence has Chiang with the Chinese people?*

A: He still has a great deal. One of the things to remember is that conti-nental China has been living and suffering under Communist rule for a year, two years, or longer—and the people who have had a real taste of Communist rule are beginning to have a much better opinion of Chiang Kai-shek and his Government of more than 20 years.

MAO'S STUDENT DAYS

Q: *What about the use of Mao? Wasn't he a student of yours?*

A: He was an "auditor," a special student at the National University of Peiping. He couldn't take the entrance examinations, which are usu-ally quite stiff, but he was allowed to attend classes without credit.

In those days, 1918 and 1919, our University was regarded as the center of new intellectual life. So these students, like Mao, came long distances to be under the inspiration of these new professors. He was poor, so we gave him a job in the library to give him some financial support. He was an eager student, and in those days idealistic. The Communist Party was founded in China in 1921 by 12 men, mostly from the University, on whose faculty I was.

Q: *Is this Communist Army a good army, a loyal army?*
A: It is hard to say. This army that is fighting MacArthur is mostly from the Fourth Field Army.

Q: *Is that the best one?*
A: It is the best equipped. It contains from 20 to 30 per cent Korean troops from North Korea. That's really the strongest army.
   In the East there is a great poverty due to inflation. And food is always a problem. People in the Army live better, have better food and therefore they can supply some form of fighting spirit.

Q: *Do you expect they will move into Indo-China?*
A: There is no doubt of it. There is a fairly large Communist army on the Chinese border of Indo-China.

GOOD FORTUNE OF JAPAN

Q: What about Japan?
A: Japan is different, because Japan, after all, is better protected and has the good fortune of being occupied by one occupying power and that means that Japan has had five years of recuperation, compared with Germany, Austria and Korea.

Q: *China would oppose any army in Japan, though, probably?*
A: I don't think so. That problem is one of detail. The real problem is not a question of the arming of Japan or the arming of Germany.

Q: *What if we should bomb Manchuria?*

A: Your Ambassador to China, Dr. [J. Leighton] Stuart, said to me that when Nationalist planes were bombing Nanking, he thought the people would be hating these Nationalists, but to his great surprise when he talked to the people in Nanking, he found them rejoicing that the Nationalists were able to come back at all.

Q: *You think the goal of the Communists is to embrace all the rest of Asia—India, for example, as well?*

A: Oh, surely—the revolution never stops.

Q: *That is Mao's idea?*

A: That is Stalin's idea.

Q: *Don't you think, though, that lines have been drawn as to where Chinese interests end and Moscow's begin? For instance, would India fall into China's sphere or Russia's sphere?*

A: Russia's, of course.

Q: *Does Russia always expect to be dominant?*

A: Oh, yes.

Q: *How do you think this war is going to end?*

A: Nobody knows. I have a feeling that collapse of the Communist gangsters may come sooner than you and I would dare to expect.

Q: *You think it would come within China?*

A: Within China, within Eastern Europe, and even within Russia.

CHAPTER 13

Communism in China[1]

THE ANNUAL MEETING OF THE NATIONAL INSTITUTE OF SOCIAL
SCIENCES WAS HELD AT THE UNION CLUB, NEW YORK CITY, ON
THE EVENING OF APRIL 12, 1951, AT EIGHT FORTY-FIVE
O'CLOCK. THE PRESIDENT OF THE INSTITUTE, MR. HUGH
BULLOCK, PRESIDED.

INTRODUCTORY REMARKS BY MR. HUGH BULLOCK

Our distinguished speaker was Chinese Ambassador to the United States
from 1942 to 1944. He is going to talk to us on "Communism in China." But
he is no Communist. Rather, he is a great scholar, one of the greatest that
China has today or has ever had.

He was born in Shanghai in 1891. He graduated from Cornell in 1914. He
holds honorary degrees from Yale, Harvard, Princeton, Columbia, I think a
total of something over thirty American universities. He has taught at outstanding Chinese universities. He has been President of the University of
Peking. One of his pupils was Mao Tse-tung. But our speaker is a much wiser
and a much finer man than his pupil.

It gives me great pleasure to present to you one of the really great Chinese
living today, His Excellency, Dr. Hu-Shih.

---

1. An address delivered at the Annual Meeting of the National Institute of Social
Sciences held at the Union Club of the City of New York on April 12, 1951.

COMMUNISM IN CHINA

BY THE HONORABLE HU SHIH

Former Chinese Ambassador to the United States; Chinese Delegate to United Nations Convention, San Francisco; recent Chancellor National Peking University.

Mr. President, Members and Friends of the National Institute of Social Sciences: When some months ago I received the courteous invitation to speak at the Annual Meeting of the Institute, I was thinking of preparing a lecture on the social sciences, on social thinking. I have always had a feeling that much of the evil and the suffering of the world today stems from the irresponsible thinking of the social scientists, social-political scientists.

It has been my lifelong preaching that social thinking, social-political thinking, is always thinking for a generation, sometimes for many generations. Social thinking, political thinking, is always thinking for the world, for society as a whole, for mankind, and should be undertaken with a sense of reverence, a sense of responsibility. So I actually thought of preparing a rather preaching lecture on the responsibility of social thinking. But when I received the announcement of the Institute I saw that I was asked to speak on a much lesser but more timely subject: "Communism in China." Of course, it is much easier and probably more popular.

When the time, April 12 approached, I felt the subject was too timely. But I have never dreamed that the delivery of the speech should occur on the day after a great event: the dismissal of General of the Army MacArthur from all his posts. In the last thirty-six hours, wherever I went, I was asked, "Dr. Hu-Shih, tell me, what do you think of this thing?" So my very "timely" subject, "Communism in China," seems a bit too remote today!

I don't know what you will think of me if I begin my talk by quoting, in the premises of the Union Club, President Truman's talk last night. I would like to quote a few sentences which interested me very much. Last night President Truman said, "We are trying to prevent a third World War." "It is right for us to be in Korea now. It was right last June and it is right today."

Then, President Truman said, "The Communists in the Kremlin are engaged in a monstrous conspiracy to stamp out freedom all over the world. If they were to succeed, the United States would be numbered among their principal victims. It must be clear to everyone that the United States cannot and will not sit idly by and await foreign conquest. The only question is, 'When is the best time to meet the threat and how?'"

The President further said, "The best time to meet the threat is in the beginning." Then he went on to tell us where "the beginning" was. He mentioned the first beginning was the threat to Greece, the second was the Berlin Blockade, and the third was Korea.

I agree entirely with the President of the United States in his sizing up of the real threat of aggression, but I would like very much to suggest very humbly that the real beginning of Communist aggression was not Greece, nor the Berlin Blockade, nor Korea, but China.

China's trouble began long ago. But nothing effective was done in time to save her, because the Western world at that time was war-weary and anxious to avoid trouble with Soviet Russia and World Communism. Everybody saw that China was being threatened and that China and the Eastern European countries from the Baltic to the Balkans were earmarked for immediate conquest by World Communism, but nobody seemed to be able or willing to do anything to stop the new aggressor from his easy picking of these ripe fruits, made ripe by the Second World War.

The democratic countries of the West were weary and were in an isolationist mood. They pretended to tell themselves that the Second World War had ended in August 1945. So the United States and her Western allies went on demobilizing and disarming themselves. The disarming of the United States—the mainstay of the Western, democratic, peace-loving world—went so far that General George C. Marshall said in a speech a few months ago that in 1947—when he was Secretary of State, when people were shouting to give the Russians "the works"—he knew that at that time there was only one division and a third of a division in the whole United States ready for military service. That was the extent of the demobilization and disarming of the West.

In all these last six years, World Communism has been arming and arming, arming not only the USSR but arming all satellite countries; not only arming but conquering one country after another. First, Roumania. Mr. Vishinsky went there in February 1945, and the Communists took over the government of the country only two weeks after the termination of the Yalta Conference. The same with Bulgaria, the whole of the Balkans, Poland, Hungary and later, the last of them all, Czechoslovakia, exactly three years after Mr. Vishinsky had taken over the control of Roumania.

What about China? Last year I published in the October issue of *Foreign Affairs Quarterly* an article on "China in Stalin's Grand Strategy." In that article, I tried to tell the story of the twenty-five years' struggle between Nationalist China and World Communism. What I am going to say this evening is a brief and popular summary of that story.

The Communist conquest of China did not come about, as some American statesmen imagined, when Mao Tse-tung, a former student of mine, came out of the caves and then the Nationalist armies just collapsed, melted away. That is not true. The fight between Chinese nationalism and Communism has been going on longer than any other Communist and anti-Communist struggle in any other part of the world. It began some twenty-six years ago, in 1924, and has been going on ever since.

World Communism's design to conquer China is an integral part of the grand strategy of world conquest which is sometimes misnamed "World Revolution." This grand strategy consists in the creation and full manipulation of three essential conditions necessary for the success of world conquest:

First, you must have the "subjective condition," namely, you must have a strong Communist Party in every country to be conquered, preferably to have a Communist Party with an armed force—a Red Army. That is the subjective condition of success for world revolution.

Second, you must have an "objective condition." You must have a war situation. The bigger the war, the greater the success. Preferably a world war. It was the First World War which gave the Bolsheviks the opportunity of capturing one of the biggest contiguous territories in world history—Russia. Without the First World War, the success of the Bolshevik Revolution would have been impossible; and without the Second World War, Communist Russia could not have become the strongest military power and the conqueror of so many states from the Balkans to the Baltic Sea and from Central Europe to Korea and China.

The second condition, the objective condition, is therefore a world war.

The third condition of success, to use an Aristotelian terminology, we may call the "efficient condition." That is, you must "consolidate" Soviet Russia as the base, as the efficient and effective base for the support and assistance of revolution in any other country in the world.

You will remember that after the success of the Bolshevik Revolution in Russia, Lenin was very anxious to see revolution started in other countries. The first country to start such a revolution was Hungary, where the Bolshevik agent, Bela Kun, brought about a revolution in March 1919. Lenin was most anxious to help this Communist revolution in Hungary, and he did send money and czarist jewelry to help Bela Kun's revolution. But the Bolsheviks in Hungary were not strong enough, and at that time it was not easy for Russia to reach Hungary with effective aid. Nor was Soviet Russia strong enough to give powerful aid to Bela Kun. And there was no longer the general war in Europe. So the Bela Kun Revolution collapsed after a few months.

But Russia was learning a lesson. In order to have a successful revolution, you must have a combination of these conditions. First, you must have a strong Communist Party, preferably one that is armed with a Red Army, and second, you must have a general war situation so that you might fish more profitably in muddied waters. And, third, you must first make Russia a strong and effective base for the support of revolution in other countries.

By extraordinary, unprecedented circumstances, China was the next country to be selected for experimentation of the grand strategy of world conquest by World Communism. This was in 1923 and 1924. Dr. Sun Yat-sen, the father of the Chinese revolution of 1911–1912 and founder of the Chinese Republic, was dissatisfied with the results of the revolution. Somehow, the fruit of the revolution had been appropriated by the reactionaries, the conservatives, and the militarists. Dr. Sun, the unsuccessful revolutionary leader, wanted to have a second revolution more successful and more thorough than the first. He was attracted by the success of the Bolshevik Revolution and in particular by the success of the Bolsheviks in suppressing the civil war and reunifying that vast country. So Dr. Sun was willing to accept Soviet Russia's offer to help.

It was therefore a most extraordinary circumstance that Dr. Sun Yat-sen, the Chinese revolutionary leader, invited the Third Internationale, the "Comintern," to send to China a political commission to help him reorganize his revolutionary party and a military mission to organize and train a revolutionary army. That was 1923—only two years after the founding of the Chinese Communist Party in 1921.

Soviet Russia, through the Comintern, sent to China a military mission headed by a man who came under the assumed name of General Galen, but who turned out to be no other than the future Marshal Vasilie Konstantinovich Blucher, one of the greatest soldiers of the Soviet Union. Also from Russia came the political mission headed by the famous Communist organizer Michael Borodin.

So in those three years (1924–1927) of "collaboration" between the Chinese Communist Party and the Nationalist Party, there was every deliberate effort to fulfill all the conditions for the success of the "Great Revolution" in China. That Communist Party began with fifty members in 1921 and rose to sixty thousand in 1927. This Chinese Communist Party was early affiliated with the Communist International and had the strong support of the USSR. And there was the Army of National Revolution reorganized on the model of the Red Army, every unit of which was to have a political commissar to do the indoctrination on a revolutionary basis. That is, the army was to be so trained that it could be taken over at least partially as a future Red Army.

Then there was deliberate inciting of antiforeign sentiments. At first it was anti-British. In the years 1925–1927, Chinese sentiments were anti-British. There were anti-British boycotts and gigantic strikes against the British interests. Hong Kong, you will remember, was practically ruined as a great center of commerce in those years, particularly in 1926. The idea was to force the British to fight back. Military intervention in China by the British would be the beginning of an international war.

But, somehow, Great Britain was not in the mood to fight back. In 1925 Britain took the attitude of nonresistance. Again, in 1926—the year of the General Strike and the coal strike in England—Great Britain was determined not to fight back, thereby unwittingly defeating the plot of World Communism to start an international war in China.

Then, after Britain had practically capitulated, the Communists started international trouble on March 24, 1927. On that day, a Revolutionary Army entered the city of Nanking. There was no fight, but suddenly this army, which had been admired by the people as a well-disciplined army, suddenly turned loose on the foreign population and violated the foreign consulates, missionary centers, and missionary schools. That was known as the "Nanking Incident" of March 24, 1927. A few foreigners were killed, including the Vice President of the American Missionary University of Nanking, Dr. J. E. Williams. Many were wounded, including the British and Japanese Consuls. The defiling of the Japanese Consulate was such that the captain of the Japanese guards, because of orders from higher up not to fight, attempted to commit hari-kari after leaving Nanking.

The offending army was under the command of such men as Lin Tsu-han, who was then serving as the chief political commissar of the army and who is now the number-four ranking leader in the Chinese Communist Party. There was no doubt that the Nanking Incident of March 1927, made foreign intervention almost a reality. (See *The China Year Book: 1928*, pp. 723–736.)

It was at this time that the leader of the Nationalist Army, Chiang Kai-shek, turned against the Communists, and on April 12 brought about the purge of the Communists. On April 18, Chiang founded the Nationalist government in Nanking. That brought about the first failure of World Communism to capture China. If you follow the Communist literature, you will find that the Chinese revolution of 1925–1927 was called the "Great Revolution." The failure of that revolution was due to Chiang Kai-shek's revolt against Communism and his purging of Communists from the Nationalist Party. After all, Russia was still weak and too far away to be of effective assistance.

What happened after that first failure? To make a long story short, what happened after that was that the Russian missions were sent back and the Communist movement failed temporarily. One part of the National Revolutionary Army broke away from the Nationalist ranks and, apparently on instructions from Stalin and the Comintern, formed the beginning of the independent Chinese Red Army. And my former student, Mao Tse-tung, has since been a sort of master strategist and leader of that movement.

The Red Army was many times defeated by Chiang Kai-shek's Nationalist troops. If you follow the Communist accounts, you will read about the "five annihilation campaigns" carried on by Chiang Kai-shek's armies against the Communists. You will see that it was almost a hopeless fight for the Communists during those years from 1927 to 1935, eight years of terrific struggle, in which Stalin and Mao were always defeated and Chiang Kai-shek came out victorious. That was the historic fact.

Throughout the years 1934–1937, when the Red Army was weak, Stalin and the Chinese Communists adopted what was called "the strategy of retreat." When Lenin died in 1924, they found among his books one volume of lectures on war by the great Prussian strategist Clausewitz. Lenin had read and reread the book and made many marginal notes. Lenin and Stalin picked from Clausewitz three very important elements of strategy. First, that war is not different from politics; that war is merely the "continuation of politics by violent means." Second, the strategy of retreat. Both Lenin and Stalin have emphasized the importance of strategic retreat. The object of the strategy of retreat, to quote Stalin's words, "is to gain time, to decompose the enemy, and to assemble forces so as to take the offensive later." And third, the doctrine of the counteroffensive—the decisive counteroffensive after the enemy's offensive has failed to achieve decisive results of war. (See Byron Dexter: "Clausewitz and Soviet Strategy" in *Foreign Affairs*, October 1950.)

It seems certain that the Chinese Communist leaders have diligently practiced all these elements of the Clausewitz-Lenin-Stalin strategy. The famous "Long March" of the Communists from southeastern China was an example of the strategy of retreat. When they were facing almost certain annihilation by Chiang Kai-shek's armies, the Red Army suddenly broke through and marched westward and then northwestward and then eastward and again northward and finally ended in the northwest part of China. It took a whole year (October 1934–October 1935) to complete that flight of about six thousand miles.

Another and even more important example of the strategy of retreat came in December 1936, just two weeks before Christmas, when Generalissimo Chiang Kai-shek was kidnapped in Sian by the pro-Communist "Young Marshal," Chang Hsueh-liang. Do you remember the sensation of December 12 and 13, 1936, throughout the world when the news of the kidnapping of Generalissimo Chiang Kai-shek was published?

On that occasion the Communists practiced a master stroke of strategy, a strategy of retreat which came nearest to statesmanship. The first day when Moscow published the news, both the two leading Communist papers in Moscow came out with an editorial condemning the kidnapping of the Generalissimo. Your Department of State's "White Paper" on China (pp. 71–72) tells us that, eight years later, when General Hurley, your Ambassador to China, and Mr. Donald Nelson visited Moscow in August 1944, on their way to China, Molotov told them the "inside story" of the kidnapping and assured them that it was "the political and moral support of the Soviet Government" that saved Chiang Kai-shek's life and allowed him to return to Nanking.

To understand the full significance of this strategy of retreat, it is necessary to recall that the time of the kidnapping of Chiang Kai-shek (December 1936) was only one year after the "Long March" and the Red Army was numerically very small and could not possibly survive a concerted attack of the enraged government armies that were closing in on Sian and the Communist areas. By releasing Chiang and restoring him to Nanking, the Red Army was not only saved from probable destruction, but was practically assured an opportunity for unlimited growth and expansion when it was incorporated as a part of the National Army shortly after the National Government took up the fight against Japan (July 1937).

Thus the Communist Army once more became a part of the Nationalist Army. It was financed and equipped on the quota of 25,000 men in 1937, and later, of 45,000 men. This army of 45,000 men in 1938 became an army of 475,000 in 1944; and by April 1945, Mao Tse-tung claimed that his army had expanded to "910,000 men plus 2,200,000 in the people's militia." And on August 1, 1950, Mao announced to the world that the Red Army in China now numbered five million men under arms.

The first condition of Communist success was complete; a strong Communist army that grew from 25,000 in 1937 to five million in 1950. And there was the Second World War, the greatest war in human history, the best fulfillment of the second condition.

The third condition was to make Russia so strong as to be able to give effective aid and support to all Communist revolutions in all countries. That condition was amply fulfilled by the two greatest statesmen in the world, Winston Churchill and Franklin D. Roosevelt.

Read that third volume of Mr. Churchill's memoirs, *The Grand Alliance*. On June 21, 1941, Hitler's Panzer Divisions invaded Russia. Churchill gave a broadcast on the twenty-second. In the broadcast, he said: "No one has been a more consistent opponent of Communist than I have for the last 25 years. But all this fades away before the spectacle which is now unfolding . . . We have but one aim and one single irrevocable purpose. We are resolved to destroy Hitler and every vestige of the Nazi regime . . . Any man or state who fights on against Nazidom will have our aid . . . We shall give whatever help we can to Russia and the Russian people. We shall appeal to all our friends and allies in every part of the world to take the same course, and pursue . . . to the end."

From that time on, Russia has been steadfastly built up into the greatest military power in the world.

But geographically, Communist China was still not in direct contact with Soviet Russia. It remained for the secret Yalta Agreement of February 1945, to bring the Soviet Union into the Pacific War and thereby to make her the contiguous base to aid and support the Communist armies in China.

The great leaders of the Western world, Roosevelt and Churchill through the Yalta secret agreement, gave Russia a position in the Far East one thousand times stronger than she had ever held prior to the Russo-Japanese War of 1904–1905. In that capacity she entered the Pacific War for four days and took possession of Manchuria, half of Korea, and made herself adjacent to the Chinese Communist armies which were racing to reach Manchuria. You know the outcome. The Japanese-surrendered arms and the Japanese-developed war industry in Manchuria were now ready to arm, equip, and supply the Chinese Communists.

And as soon as Russia went into North Korea the Iron Curtain came down. Behind that Iron Curtain, Russia trained a wonderfully efficient and effective army, the North Korean Communist Army. That army came into Manchuria to help the Chinese Communists to fight in Manchuria, in North China and Central China, and after 1949 even as far south as the Hainan Island. The North Korean Red Army and the Chinese Red Army form the Asiatic arm of World Communism's powerful instrumentality of conquest.

This, Mr. President, is the story of the conquest of China by World Communism in the course of twenty-five years. It is a story of the successful establishment and manipulation of the essential conditions for the success of the grand strategy of conquest. Few people realize that the Chinese Communist Party differs from any other Communist Party in any other country on one score, namely, that the Chinese Communist Party has almost from its founding years had a formidable armed force, the Red Army. This army forms the central point in the unfolding of the grand design of the conquest of China. It is this army which Stalin and Mao Tse-tung have throughout the twenty-five years tried to preserve and nurture to the present strength of five million. And it was the Second World War which furnished the leaders of the Kremlin with the most extraordinary opportunities for the fullest development of the potentialities of this wicked strategy. The war has been so beneficial and so profitable to the arch-conspirators of World Communism that they have tried their best to prolong and to perpetuate it to this day!

So when you talk about the Third World War, ladies and gentlemen, believe me as a historian, there is no Third World War. What we are seeing is a world war, but it is a continuation of the Second World War, which has never been finished anywhere. Tell me any corner of the world where you can say that the Second World War has ended. It is certainly not in Japan, which is under occupation by the victors. It is not finished in Germany; Germany is under the occupation of the victors. Nor in Austria. Certainly not in Eastern and Central Europe from the Balkan States to the Baltic. Certainly not in Korea. And certainly the Second World War has never ended in China. And now you in this wonderful country, too, are having a wartime economy, wartime productions, and wartime military draft. Why? Because you are finding that the Second World War has never been finished.

Mr. President, I have given you my prepared speech on "Communism in

China" and have tried to paint for your members and guests a larger and bolder picture of China on a world canvas as a part of the grand strategy of World Communism. In doing this, I drew inspiration from President Truman's speech of last night. China is the best illustration of the President's grave accusation that "the Communists in the Kremlin are engaged in a monstrous conspiracy to stamp out freedom all over the world."

And the twenty-five-year story of China's struggle with World Communism, I believe, may be helpful to our understanding that the threat of Communist aggression did not begin with the border troubles in Greece, or with the Berlin Blockade, or with the invasion of the Republic of Korea by the North Korean Communist forces last June. What happened in Greece in 1946–1949, for instance, cannot be fully understood except as a part of the Communist conquest of Eastern Europe and the Balkans. And the conquest of Eastern and Southeastern Europe cannot be fully understood except as a part of the grand strategy of world conquest which failed in Hungary as early as 1919, which almost succeeded in China in 1925–1927, and which took a quarter of a century to achieve final fruition in China and Eastern Europe.

The pattern of conquest is the same in China and Korea as in Roumania, Bulgaria, Hungary, Poland, and Czechoslovakia. It is the pattern of conquest by force and violence projected from the contiguous Russian base.

The most important lesson for all of us to learn is that the gangsters of World Communism have always had a "world strategy" which may from time to time have undergone minor modifications and alterations, but of which the main outlines have never wavered. Sometimes they may have to resort to the strategy of retreat. Sometimes they may have to wait for years or even decades before striking a decisive blow and achieving their main objective of conquest. But they seem never to lose sight of the main objectives of their "world strategy." And so far that strategy has succeeded.

Can the great leaders of the free world learn this lesson and try to get together and work out their own "global strategy" for the salvation of man and his freedom?

• • •

PRESIDENT BULLOCK: I am glad you gave up your prepared speech, Mr. Ambassador. This was much better than the other could have been. I suggest we have a brief question period and then that we follow through with something else. Would you care to ask Dr. Hu-Shih a few questions?

QUESTION: May I ask whether our guest has any suggestions as to what may be done to combat Communism in this era?

DR. HU-SHIH: Mr. President, that question cannot have any adequate answer. I have been asked the same question in other places. My answer is always the same, that the important lesson for the free world is that for thirty-three years World Communism has always had a plan, a world strategy, a plan of world conquest. For thirty-three years, these gangsters have been using their best information, their best spy system and propaganda, their best minds, to plan and execute their great conspiracy of world conquest.

On the other hand, the democratic world of the West has been sleeping, and just living from hand to mouth with no plan. The Chinese have a proverb: "When you have a headache, take a headache pill. When you have foot trouble, put a plaster on your foot." The important thing is for the leaders of the Western world to get together and forget the past errors. We are human beings and we all make mistakes. Chiang Kai-shek made mistakes. China made mistakes. Mr. Roosevelt made mistakes. Mr. Churchill made mistakes. I must say that Stalin, too, has made some mistakes; otherwise he would have been much more successful.

Let us not cry over spilled milk. Let the past be buried, including this MacArthur tragedy. Let us put our best heads together and work out a world strategy concerning what shall be done on a world scale to get rid of this monster Leviathan, this monstrous thing in the history of mankind.

There has never been so great, so strong and so sinister an evil as this World Communist Empire, all contiguous from the Baltic States to Bulgaria, from Poland to China and Korea. You see this octopus stretching its tentacles out to Persia, to Greece and Turkey, to India, to all the Near East and the Mideast. Don't treat this problem as a China problem or as a Democratic or Republican problem. This is one of the greatest problems of mankind—the survival of mankind. We must have a world strategy, in which Korea is a part, China is a part, Formosa is a part, Europe is a part, in which England, France, Italy, Germany, the Baltics, and the Balkans are all parts.

Let us take China, take Korea, take all similar problems out of party politics and put them on world scale, on a world canvas. Let us use our best minds, including experienced soldiers like General MacArthur; and let us forget the past and work toward the future.

PRESIDENT BULLOCK: I suggest we have one more question and then we will have other questions in the adjoining room.

QUESTION: Can it be that our difficulties arise because we tolerate politicians in high places instead of statesmen?

DR. HU-SHIH: That is universal. Don't be too hard on your own country. It is a universal trait.

PRESIDENT BULLOCK: Thank you very much, Your Excellency, for giving us a very interesting evening, a wonderful evening. Thank you all for coming. I suggest we call the meeting adjourned for refreshments.

CHAPTER 14

My Former Student, Mao Tse-Tung[1]

There is a real dearth of biographical information about my former student Mao Tse-tung, the present ruler and dictator of Communist China. For many years the only available material on his life story has been the six chapters entitled "Genesis of a Communist" which form Part Four of Edgar Snow's "Red Star Over China." For the last eight years a Chinese translation by Fang Lin of Snow's report of Mao's "Autobiography" has been in circulation in Communist China and in Hong Kong. This Chinese version seems to have had the benefit of some slight correction and revision either by the Chinese Communist Party or by someone who had semi-official authorization to make the revision. For instance, Mr. Snow named only eight members of the First Central Committee of the Chinese Communist Party founded in 1921. The Chinese translation has added four more, including T'an P'ing-shan. Of Snow's original eight, one name was transcribed as "Sun Yuan-lu," which is almost unidentifiable: the Chinese version has the correct name, Shen Hsuan-lu.

In August 1949 there was published in Shanghai a small book by Hsiao San on "Comrade Mao Tse-tung's Childhood and Youth," which tells of Mao's early life, in particular his student days at Changsha (1911–1918), with more detail than Snow's account, but which ends the story in 1920—a year before the founding of the Party—when Mao was only twenty-seven years old. In 1945, Hsiao San had published a magazine article on "Comrade Mao Tse-tung's First Period of Revolutionary Activity," which covered Mao's life in the years 1920–1923. That article has had many unauthorized reprints in many parts of Communist China. But that "first draft" is said to require so much revision that it has never been allowed to appear in book form.

---

1. A review of Robert Payne's *Mao Tse-Tung* published in *Freeman*, July 2, 1951, 636–639.

The above list practically exhausts all the available biographical data concerning Mao Tse-tung. "Comrade Mao," says Hsiao San in his preface, "ever since he once yielded to the persistent persuasion of the American journalist, Snow, has never indulged in talking about his own life, nor does he want other people to write his biography." Hsiao San admits that his informants were mostly Mao Tse-tung's old comrades in the Party and in the revolutionary wars, and that his writings about Mao's life had never been read or authorized by Mao himself prior to their publication. Apart from some interesting details of the local geography of Hsiangt'an and Ch'angsha, Hsiao's new book adds little new material to the autobiography as told to Snow and as corrected in Chinese translation.

All this points to the undeniable fact that it is very difficult today to attempt a full-size biography of Mao Tse-tung. The scarcity of narrative biographical material might be partly overcome by some linguistically competent researchers if they would only study systematically Mao's numerous published speeches and writings, and chronologically arrange and present the important ideas and policies contained therein.

Any writer who tries to produce a full-length biography of Mao, but has not the patience or the training to study Mao's numerous speeches and articles, is doomed to miserable failure. He will be forced to appropriate Mr. Snow's record with its numerous small errors. He will be forced to supplement Snow by Hsiao San—and add to the composite, not the results of patient research, but often the labored inventions of an audacious imagination.

PAYNE'S MEAGER RESOURCES

That seems to be what Mr. Robert Payne has done in his biography, "Mao Tse-tung: Ruler of Red China."[2] The core of his book is of necessity taken from Mr. Snow's account of Mao's autobiography. But Mr. Payne has not made use of the Chinese version, which could have corrected many of his mistakes. Although Mr. Payne acknowledges in the introduction that he has been "helped by long talks with Hsiao San in Kalgan," the latter's book and article on Comrade Mao Tse-tung are not listed in Payne's bibliography.

The remainder of the book is Mr. Payne's laborious padding. It is really

---

2. Robert Payne, *Mao Tse-Tung: Ruler of Red China* (New York: Schuman, 1950).

painful to watch the young author straining his pitifully meager store of knowledge of things Chinese merely to fill the pages of an impossible book.

For instance, Mr. Snow (p. 152) quoted Mao as saying that en route from Tientsin to Nanking, "I stopped at Ch'u Fou and visited Confucius' grave . . . I also stopped by the river where Yen Hui, one of Confucius famous disciples, had once lived . . . On this trip climbed T'ai Shan, the sacred mountain of Shantung." These sentences are expanded by the imaginative Mr. Payne into two pages of elementary geographical and historical discourse (pp. 61–62) to prove that Mao Tse-tung "had never wholly departed from Confucianism." And what ridiculous information he gives us in those pages! He identifies the river where Yen Hui lived as the Huai River, which is absurd. And he says that Liu Pang, founder of the Han dynasty, raised the standard of revolt "when he was still a shepherd" and created his capital in Sian, "a few miles south of Yenan," all of which is crazy.

Mao Tse-tung had told Snow that when he was in the Hunan Normal School, he was obliged to study the writings of Han Yu and master the old classical phraseology (p. 143). This one sentence of one line and a half is expanded into a sophomoric dissertation on Han Yu, covering fully fifty-nine lines (pp. 31–33) and placing Mao's study of Han Yu in his village school days even before he went to the Senior Primary School in Hsianghsiang.

In recalling the winter scenery of the North Lake in Peking, Mao quoted to Snow (p. 151) one line of verse by the T'ang dynasty poet Ts'en Ts'an (Chen Chang in Snow's transcription) which most school children of Mao's generation used to read and memorize from the popular anthology "Three Hundred Poems of the T'ang Dynasty." That casual reference to Ts'en Ts'an leads Mr. Payne to write another sophomoric dissertation of two pages and a half (pp. 223–225) on that poet, who, Mr. Payne tells us, has "deeply influenced" Mao Tse-tung's poetry. But all Mr. Payne's diligent searches for Mao's poetry have netted him only three short poems totaling twenty-eight lines in free translation; and one of these, "The Snow," is a *tz'u* (written originally to the tune of a popular melody, but in recent centuries written slavishly to the strict metric pattern of a long-forgotten tune) which is a form of Chinese versification unknown to the age of Tu Fu and Ts'en Ts'an. (Had Mr. Payne seen Hsiao San's "Comrade Mao's Childhood and Youth," he could have found a fourth poem of Mao's, also a *tz'u* written to the same forgotten tune.) It is beyond my comprehension that any critic in his senses should be able to judge from three mediocre poems that their author had been "deeply influenced" by a certain poet of the eighth century A.D.

Indeed, Mr. Payne's whole dissertation, thirty-odd pages long, on Mao Tse-tung as a great poet and art critic (pp. 208–240) is the best illustration of the author's great art of filling space with nothingness. From these pages I select this most delicious specimen of sheer nonsense:

> Even his [Mao's] signature dances, the characters having a wild, curving ebullience, and perhaps it is no accident that part of his signature closely resembles the serpentine curve shown in the map of the Third Annihilation Campaign. His signature, based on T'ang dynasty models, flows like water; Chiang Kai-shek's signature, based on the classic Han dynasty script, is squat and square like a toad. A Chinese, comparing their signatures, would know which would conquer the other. (p. 236)

Such instances of empty padding, though highly insulting to the intelligence of the reader, are relatively harmless compared with the hundreds of items of fabricated or falsified history with which this supposed "biography" is filled. One group of glaring examples of falsified history is found in Mr. Payne's account of the May Fourth Incident (pp. 64–71). Mao Tse-tung was not in Peking at the time of the Peking students' demonstration on May 4, 1919; so there was only one passing reference to it in his autobiography (p. 153). Mr. Payne has undertaken to supply an account of this historic event. And a wonderful imaginative account it is, for it contains at least forty instances of false history! Out of this large number, I offer these five major examples of absolutely untruthful reporting:

1. Ch'en Tu-hsiu had for some time been awaiting an explosion of this kind. His plans were prepared, and he carried them out with a masterly sense of order.
2. He [Ch'en Tu-hsiu] addressed the 5000 students of Peking University, told them to elect committees to tour the neighboring colleges, and urged them to elect by ballot a supreme committee to be devoted to direct action.
3. There was to be a student cabinet and a council of wardens to carry out the decisions of the supreme committee.
4. There was to be nothing casual: everything must be done quietly and systematically. The purpose of the new political movement was to overthrow the government . . .
5. They [the students] were more than 10,000 strong, and they were

armed with wooden clubs, iron bars, and cans of gasoline removed
from the laboratories.

All five of these statements (taken from the brief space of twenty lines on
pp. 64–5) are without the slightest basis in fact. My friend and colleague,
Ch'en Tu-hsiu, having already resigned from the Peking University early in
1919, never addressed the students either on that day or before or after. May
4 (Sunday) being his editorial day, he spent the whole day at his home writing editorials for his six-month-old *Weekly Review*. And he actually knew
nothing of the student demonstrations until late in the evening. If there was
conscious effort involved in that historic incident, it came from some patriotic elder statesmen who served as members of President Hsu Shih-ch'ang's
Special Commission on Foreign Affairs, and who had deliberately passed on
to the educational circles the then still secret news that the Paris Peace Conference had decided to yield to Japan all the former German concessions and
interests in Shantung.

The spread of this alarming news led to the hasty calling of the students'
mass meeting. The purpose of the meeting was not "to overthrow the government," but to discuss the ways and means of voicing the students' protest
against the decision of the Paris Conference. It is a matter of public record
that the students were not armed in any manner. And it is a well-known fact
that at that time the Peking students had no inter-school organization, and
it was not until the month of June that there was some semblance of a
national student organization. The whole May Fourth affair was spontaneous and unorganized; and it was the crowd psychology of the moment that
led a part of the parade to the house of Ts'ao Ju-lin, then Minister of Foreign
Affairs.

SOME WHOPPING MISTAKES

Of the hundreds of instances of false history in Payne's volume, I shall select
only the more outrageous:

> In all he [Yen Fu] translated more than 112 books from five languages, even
> from languages of which he was entirely ignorant. . . . He was not a good
> translator. He was often inaccurate. (p. 17)

This is criminal calumny against the good reputation of a most conscientious scholar and translator. So conscientious was he as a translator that he will always be remembered for his famous remark, "The final decision on the translation of a single new term often cost me ten days or even a month of careful consideration." In a lifetime he translated only eight works, seven from English, one from French. Here is another example (p. 17):

> Yen Fu returned from the Naval College at Greenwich with a rough draft of a translation of Darwin's "Origin of Species" in his pocket, completed the translation in Peking, and had it published. The Empress Dowager read the book, admired the classical perfection of his prose, and shook her head uncomprehendingly.

This makes a good story but it is absolutely untrue. Yen Fu never translated any work of Darwin. "Origin of Species" was translated by my teacher and friend, Mr. Ma Chun-wu.

In Mr. Payne's account of the "Long March," there occurs this jewel of truly marvelous literary inventiveness:

> The strain of the Long March was beginning to tell. Mao was very lean, with dark hollows under his eyes, and often ill. . . . He wore a faded blue uniform, carried no caps, and there were usually books in his pocket—a copy of the monkey tale, "Journey to the West," and the old dog-eared copy of "All Men Are Brothers." The book, "Journey to the West," described a pilgrimage of a learned monkey through China, Tibet and India, *and what was surprising was the accuracy of a medieval fairy tale when it came to describing the borderlands of China and Tibet.* (p. 154, italics mine)

Is it possible that Mr. Payne has never read Mr. Arthur Waley's delightful translation of "Monkey," which has both English and American editions! Where did he get such absurd information about this Chinese fairy tale which has absolutely nothing in the way of "accurate" geographical information about "the borderlands between China and Tibet"?

ABSURD FABRICATION

All this elaborate padding and absurd fabrication is unnecessary when there are so many published speeches and pamphlets by Mao Tse-tung which are accessible to anyone who reads Chinese. Not a few of Mao's writings are available in English translations. Almost every one of his speeches and articles is clearly dated. All these dated writings constitute a large collection of important and truly biographical data for the writing of any life story of Mao Tse-tung.

Unfortunately, Mr. Payne has neither the linguistic training nor the research technique to make full use of this mass of useful material. He does have a chapter entitled "Five Books," which attempts to summarize five of Mao's "books" or pamphlets. But that chapter is most disappointing in many ways. In the first place, the five works are not presented in their chronological order. Secondly, Mr. Payne fails to give us a comprehensive and intelligible summary of any of these five works. A possible exception is "The Chinese Revolution and the Communist Party of China," from which Mr. Payne has quoted fairly full passages of some importance. But the reader will not be able to understand the content of any of the other writings from Mr. Payne's scanty quotations and unmethodical discussions. Mao's booklet on "Coalition Government" has 50,000 words in Chinese, and Mr. Payne quotes only twenty-five lines: the reader is never told what kind of "coalition government" was demanded by Mao for the period of the War against Japan and for the postwar period. Mr. Payne, in another chapter entitled "Five Battles," makes use of Mao's summary of the five Annihilation campaigns of the Nationalist forces, which Mao had used as illustrations in his five lectures on "The Strategic Problems of China's Revolutionary Wars." But neither in that chapter, nor in the chapter on "Five Books," has Mr. Payne shown any understanding of the importance of this work, in which Mao Tse-tung, without ever mentioning the names of Clausewitz, Lenin and Stalin, devotes forty-eight of his seventy pages to a detailed and eloquent exposition of the Clausewitz-Lenin-Stalin strategy of the "counter-offensive" and of the great value of the "strategy of retreat." Nowhere else is Mao better shown as a master strategist and as (in the words of the Communist Ch'en Pai-ta) "the gifted disciple of Stalin."

In the third place, Mr. Payne has left out a number of Mao's important writings which must be included in any biographical study of this ruler and dictator of Communist China. Of these, I may mention the following:

1. His speech on "The Three Purges" (February 1942), demanding "purification" in thought, in the party leadership, and in the literature produced by the Party.
2. His speech on "Oppose All Party-line pa'ku" (the eight-legged essay) of February 8, 1942, which represents Mao Tse-tung at his best in both destructive and constructive criticism of Communist literature, and in particular of the prose style.
3. His speeches at the opening and conclusion of the Round Table Meeting of Writers and Artists at Yenan, May 2 and 23, 1942, which Payne barely touches in his book. (pp. 238-9)
4. The "Present Situation and Our Duties" (December 25, 1947) which contains his famous ten principles of the Communist strategy and tactics. The English translation of this bears the title, "Turning Point in China."
5. "The People's Democratic Dictatorship" (June 30, 1949) which best describes the dictatorial and despotic nature of the present regime in China, and which has been made required reading for all teachers and students in all grades of schools from primary school to university.

This last mentioned article, "The People's Democratic Dictatorship," has been translated in full, and the whole English text was included in the Department of State's "United States Relations With China" (popularly known as the "White Paper on China," pp. 720-729). From this version Mr. Payne apparently took one sentence about Hung Hsu-chuan (please note where Payne derived this wrong spelling of the name of the leader of the Taiping Rebellion), Yen Fu, Kang Yu-wei and Sun Yat-sen as "the four men who sought the truth from the West." On the strength of this casual sentence, Mr. Payne wrote his first chapter of twenty-one pages on "the Forerunners." But he has completely ignored the main body of this very important document. Why is he so unwilling to present to his readers this most eloquent and most outspoken exposition of the despotic nature of the state and government under which four hundred million human beings are now living and suffering?

How can the world understand the real Mao Tse-tung if his biographer deliberately, or unwittingly, leaves out such interesting revelations as this passage from his speech on the sixtieth birthday of Stalin (1939):

Stalin is the leader of world revolution. Stalin's emergence in the history of mankind was a momentous event; thanks to Stalin, the cause of the revolution has progressed successfully. You know that Marx is dead, that Engels is dead, and Lenin is dead, and who could have given orders and issued commands if it had not been for Stalin? The fact that Stalin has come into the world is . . . fortunate. Today, when we have the Soviet Union, the Communist Party and Stalin—all's right with the world.

In short, Mr. Payne's "Mao Tse-tung" is an ignorant and irresponsible book. Mr. Payne's ignorance of the Chinese language and Chinese history is truly appalling; but his pretense to knowledge is even worse than his ignorance. To praise Mao's poems, for example, is ignorance; but to say that "from that moment [of the publication of Mao's airplane poem, 'The Snow'] hundreds of Chinese, particularly in the Universities, came to feel a real respect for Mao as a poet," and to describe that poem as one "which would embrace the whole of Chinese legend and Chinese history in a moment of time," is unpardonable pretense of knowledge of things of which he is deplorably ignorant. Mr. Payne does not know that Chinese critics have publicly pointed out that it was sheer ignorance for Mao Tse-tung to say that Wu Ti of Han or T'ai Tsung of T'ang was "hardly lettered" and that Genghis Khan "knew only how to bend his bow at the eagles." Any Chinese can tell Mr. Payne that Mao mentioned the eagles in describing Genghis Khan merely because the word *tiao* (eagle) happened to rhyme with the other lines which all have the end-rhyme of *-ao* or *-iao*.

And very often Mr. Payne's ignorance of Chinese language and history furnishes ample evidence to prove the doubtful character of some of his sources of information. One such source of information was supposed to be Mao Tse-tung himself, whom Mr. Payne claims to have interviewed in Yenan and whose conversation fills pages (215–221) of his book. Here is a part of that conversation:

> I asked when there would be peace. . . . "When the people rule," he [Mao] answered. He had a way of saying *ming-sheng*, the people's rule, which was like the sudden, startling pealing of a bell. (p. 218)

Mathews's *Chinese-English Dictionary* (1950) lists fourteen Chinese words pronounced *ming*, but none meaning "the people"; and eighteen words pronounced *sheng*, but none meaning "to rule" or "government." What could possibly be the language or dialect that Mr. Payne has put into the mouth of Mao Tse-tung? Or was it some "foreign devil" posing as the future "Ruler of Red China?"

What is most offensive in Mr. Payne's book is his complete unawareness of a sense of intellectual and historical responsibility in undertaking to write a work of biography, which should be a part of authentic history.

CHAPTER 15

Review of John De Francis's Nationalism and Language Reform in China[1]

Mr. De Francis' book attempts to study the problem of the alphabetizing of Chinese, not as a simple linguistic problem but "as an instrument of political change," "as part of the nationalist movement in China" (pp. vii–viii). Therefore, he claims to have made use of a "dual approach," "an interdisciplinary approach, counting on political science to illuminate the political aspect and linguistic science to solve the linguistic problems."

The book therefore is a discussion of a linguistic problem with a special political slant. His "political science" has led him to accept unquestioningly most of the special pleadings of the Chinese Communists and their fellow travelers, including absurd assertions, such as: "If the ideographs are not destroyed, China is sure to die"—a statement which some irresponsible propagandist attributed to the famous Lu Hsün in a sickbed interview (p. 117).

In his linguistic chapters (pp. 139–208), however, he comes to the fair conclusion that the National Language Romanization (Gwoyeu Romatzyh, or G.R.), the Latinxua (Latinization, also called Sin Wenz or S.W., meaning New Writing) and other schemes (such as the Yale Romanization) are all "eminently workable" (pp. 206–207). The important difference between the G.R. and the S.W., the author points out, lies in the fact that the former system indicates tones by changes in the spelling of the syllable itself, while the latter system dispenses with tone-indication altogether (p. 207). These are the two latest systems for the phonetic writing of Chinese speech.

It is a well-known fact that the Latinxua or Sin Wenz system was worked out by the Chinese Communist scholar Ch'ü Ch'iu-pai (1899–1935) and the

---

1. A review of John De Francis's *Nationalism and Language Reform in China* (Princeton: Princeton University Press, 1950). It was published in the *American Historical Review* 56, no. 4 (July 1951): 897–899.

Soviet Russian sinologists, Kolokolov, Dragunov, B. M. Alexeiev, and others (pp. 92–104) and was used in the Soviet Union for the education of the Chinese minority who at one time numbered about 100,000. Mr. De Francis gives us the interesting information that the 1939 census shows "only 29,620 registered as having Chinese nationality," and that Latinxua, the script which had been especially created for the Chinese in the Soviet Union, was discontinued after 1937 (pp. 105–108).

Mr. De Francis also tells us how energetically the Chinese Communists and their friends tried for a few years to promote the New Script (Sin Wenz) in China and in Hong Kong, and especially in the Communist-controlled areas. Then, following the Japanese attack on Pearl Harbor in December, 1941, "at one stroke, the flourishing activities in behalf of Sin Wenz in Shanghai, Hong Kong, and other foreign-controlled areas taken over by the Japanese were brought to an end" (p. 131). Strangely enough, even in the Communist-controlled areas, the movement for a phonetic script was also brought to an end in the years 1940–44 (p. 133). Even after the surrender of Japan, only "discussion" of the problem was resumed, and that "on a more modest scale" (p. 134). Our author has offered to explain this "halting" of the New Script movement in Communist regions (pp. 133–134). But his "political science" will not allow him to accept the real explanation, which is neither linguistic nor political but psychological and cultural.

In the very last chapter, De Francis quotes Gunther Stein, who reported that in Communist-controlled areas, "Plain peasants said they wanted the old Chinese script for their children and for themselves. If they were to learn reading and writing it must be in the script in which the officials, the landlords and merchants read and wrote and in which all the books are printed" (p. 248). To put it slightly differently, one may ask, Did the famous Lu Hsün ever write any prose in the Sin Wenz? Did Mao Tse-tung ever write anything in it? Did or can Hsu T'e-li or Wu Yu-chang or any of the Communist advocates of Sin Wenz ever write anything in it? Even the people in the Communist-controlled areas will not learn a script in which a Mao Tse-tung or a Liu Shao-ch'i is unable or unwilling to write his own speeches or articles. And Mao Tse-tung and Liu Shao ch'i will not write their speeches or articles in the new phonetic script because they know very well that, if they do, nobody will be able to read them. So they continue to write their speeches and articles in *paihua* (the living spoken language written in characters) which they had learned through stealthily reading and loving the great *pai-*

hua novels in their boyhood days, and which has been made respectable by the Literary Revolution.

In his historical chapters (pp. 3–135), the author traces the history of the various attempts to write Chinese in a phonetic system, beginning with the first phonetic transcription by the earliest Jesuit missionaries in the last years of the sixteenth century, and coming down to the phonetic systems of recent years. In this historical treatment, the *paihua* movement—which in the last thirty-five years has successfully brought about the adoption of the living spoken tongue (*paihua*) as the language of school education and as the language of a living literature—barely receives mention, and then only as an impediment and "a defeat" of language reform as Mr. De Francis conceives it. "To a certain extent," he says (p. 13), "the victory of the *paihua* reformers represents a defeat for those who before and after the Literary Revolution have sought to write an even more vernacular style in an even simpler script."

In this Mr. De Francis was merely echoing the views expressed by such Chinese Communists as Ch'ü Ch'iu-pai and Hsiao San, and such pro-Communist writers as Hu Yü-chih. "To his mind," says De Francis in summarizing the views of Hsiao San, the Communist poet, "the previous attempts at reform of the script in China had not gone far enough. The Hu Shih movement was viewed as merely a literary reform and not really a 'literary revolution' since it said nothing about destroying the ideographs. All earlier efforts to alphabetize the language were dismissed as inadequate. But Chu Ch'iu-pai's system of Latinization was approved in every aspect" (pp. 95–96). That is almost exactly the position of Mr. De Francis' book.

But our author's political enthusiasm has literally "blinded" his researches. He has made Hu Shih himself appear to discredit his own movement! On page 12, he says: "In 1940 Hu Shih himself expressed the judgment that 'The *paihua* movement has merely been of help to a few intellectuals.'" Again, on page 225, he says: "Even the Literary Renaissance was viewed as inadequate, and by no less a person than Hu Shih himself, who stated that 'The *paihua* movement has merely been of help to a few intellectuals.'"

On January 22, 1951, I wrote to the author and requested him to furnish me with the Chinese text of the above quotation. In a very courteous letter dated January 25, 1951, he replied that my letter had led to "the mortifying discovery" that "the remark was made not by Hu Shih-chih (Hu Shih), but by Hu Yü chih." It was in the same letter that he told me that further checking of his references had revealed that similar wrong identification was made in three other places (pp. 112, 120, 123).

In short, this book is a discussion of a linguistic and historical problem by a man who is prejudiced in his political science and ignorant of history, especially of the history of Chinese literature. So biased and ignorant is he that he actually seriously believes that the language reform movement has been "tied in closely" with the nationalist movement in China (pp. viii and 219–220), and he actually seriously identifies the Chinese Communists as a part of the nationalist movement. He seems to be completely unaware of the undeniable fact that all language reform in China, whether in the form of the *paihua* movement or in the form of advocating any of the phonetic systems of alphabetization, has invariably been led by internationalists (including the Anarchist and Communist movements) and has invariably been opposed by the nationalists (including the Kuomintang or the Nationalist party, against which my open complaint has always been that the *paihua* movement has received no more than nominal recognition during the two decades of its political power). Even Dr. Sun Yat-sen, the leader of the revolution and founder of the Chinese Republic, actually wrote that the classical language was superior to, and far more beautiful than, the vernacular *paihua*.

CHAPTER 16

How to Understand a Decade of Rapidly Deteriorated Sino-American Relations[1]

At an informal gathering during the October Meeting of the American Philosophical Society, Dr. Waldo Leland made the suggestion that at the April Meeting Dr. A. W. Hummel might be asked to speak on how to understand China, and I to speak on how to understand America.

Dr. Hummel has presented his paper on "Some Basic Principles in Chinese Culture." There is no man better qualified than he to point out those fundamental principles which will not only help our American friends to appreciate China, but may also help the Chinese people to understand the American way of life.

What I undertake to do tonight is less ambitious, less basic, but I believe more urgent. I do not propose to speak on the general theme, how to understand America and the American culture. I want to talk on only one particular phase of that general problem—that particular phase which must have mystified and pained you no less than it has mystified and pained me. I refer to the strange and unfortunate phenomenon of a rapid deterioration of relationship between China and the United States during the last eight or nine years. How am I to explain it? Can I explain it to my own satisfaction?

I left my ambassadorship in Washington in September 1942. At that time China was still at the height of popularity in the mind and heart of the American people; and there was no doubt that the United States Government was sincerely and earnestly trying to build up China as a powerful ally in the com-

---

1. Originally a dinner address delivered on April 20, 1951, this paper was later published in the *Proceedings of American Philosophical Society* 95, no. 4 (August 1951): 457–459. Hu Shih was described as the "Curator of the Gest Oriental Library at Princeton University."

mon fight against aggression: China had no more sincere friends than President Franklin Delano Roosevelt, Cordell Hull and Henry L. Stimson.

Yet, in the course of only a few years, the relationship between the two governments began to become more and more difficult. This worsening of Sino-American relationship reached its first crisis in the Affair of General Stilwell and finally culminated in the secret Yalta Agreement on the Far East which, in the light of history, must be regarded as the abandonment of China to the mercy of Stalinist Russia.

This process of deterioration of relationship has continued throughout the last few years. When I returned to this country exactly two years ago tomorrow, I was surprised and greatly saddened to find a completely changed atmosphere. Wherever I went, China had become a very unpopular country! In August 1949 the Department of State found it necessary to issue a "White Paper" of a thousand pages to tell the world that the United States Government had done its best to help China but that China was beyond redemption.

All this was a mystery, an intellectual puzzle, to me. As a philosopher and historian, I could not accept such over-simplified explanations as that "the Department of State was controlled by Communists and their fellow travelers," which is just as naïve as the view that "Mao Tse-tung and his Red Army merely marched out of their caves, and the Chinese Government Armies just melted away."

No, I was not satisfied with these and other explanations. I wanted to understand what had actually happened—in particular, what had happened in the minds of the great American leaders—to bring about this estrangement of relations and this at least temporary abandonment of China by her friend of a hundred years' standing.

In a new book soon to be published on "The Collision of East and West," my Quaker friend, Herrymon Maurer, has summed up this deterioration of Sino-American relations in these words:

> For some years, the U.S. had been fond of China to the point of sentimentality. . . . Yet almost as soon as the United States and the Chinese Governments became allies, the United States began to dislike the Chinese Government as emotionally as it once used to applaud it.

What had happened to cause this emotional shift? I want to understand this phenomenon and I want to help my friends, Chinese and American, to understand it too.

I venture to suggest a theory which may help to explain this psychological or emotional change from fondness to dislike. It is a little theory or hypothesis based on psychology and common sense.

My theory is that what led to this shift was the historical event of the "promotion" of China from a friend to an ally. That promotion (or shall I say "demotion?") was the cause of China's downfall in the mind and heart of her old friend, the United States.

For nearly a century, China and the United States were merely friends, separated by the greatest ocean between them and with no aggressive designs toward each other. It was possible for the United States to cherish a truly disinterested friendship and even fondness for the China "of blue porcelain bowls and exquisite silk scrolls," for the China of Laotse and Confucius, of Li Po, Tu Fu, and Po Chu-i, of Wu Tao-tse and Li Lung-mien. This genuine and disinterested friendship was fully appreciated and requited by China, which was sending every year hundreds and even thousands of her select young men and women to American universities and graduate schools in a sincere desire to understand this great nation which had tremendous strength but was so disciplined that she would not use it for aggression.

As a beneficiary of this friendship, I can tell you that it was wonderful. It often made me think of those beautiful words of your poet-philosopher, Emerson, who said: "The essence of friendship is entireness, a total magnanimity and trust. . . . It treats its object as a god, that it may deify both." As I travelled up and down the country and walked through your many museums where hundreds and thousands of Americans looked at and enjoyed those silent yet eloquent representatives of China—the Chinese bronzes, Chinese porcelains and Chinese paintings—I could not but recall those words of Emerson and bless the nation that was so sincerely glorifying China.

But China's woe began on that memorable day in January 1942, when she was invited by the United States Government to sign the Declaration of the United Nations together with the United Kingdom, the United States, and the U.S.S.R. The other nations were invited to sign the next day according to alphabetical order. By that act of well-intentioned courtesy, China was made an ally of the three greatest powers fighting German and Japanese aggression. She became one of the Big Four! From that time on, China's relations with her Anglo-Saxon allies became more and more difficult.

As a "poor relation" of the mighty three, China could be forgiven for having acquired certain grand airs not unusual among those who are equals of the gods. She now aspired to play the role of the leader of Asia; she remembered the solemn pledge of Dr. Sun Yat-sen and his Party to give aid to every Asiatic people seeking to achieve freedom from the yoke of imperialism; and Chiang Kai-shek even dared to lecture Great Britain on India and Burma. Indeed, he even dared to say no to some of the plans proposed by General Stilwell or by President Roosevelt.

China's greatest difficulty was her failure to live up to her American ally's great expectations of her. As a great ally still claiming control over a population of 200 million, China was expected not only to hold her own in the China theatre, but rapidly to train her manpower in preparation for effective participation in the great allied offensive to come. She would have been able to fulfill these reasonable minimum expectations if she could have received even a small fraction of the material aid that Soviet Russia was then receiving from Britain and America. But Japan saw the threat of a Free China being adequately aided and armed by her allies. Japanese strategy on the Asiatic mainland—the rapid conquering of French Indo-China, Siam and Burma, the disabling of the Burma Road, the increasing effectiveness of the almost absolute economic blockade against Free China—was clearly directed toward preventing China from receiving adequate military and material aid from the outside. It was the one phase of Japanese strategy which the Allied Powers failed to break up.

And there were other expectations, probably equally natural and reasonable from the standpoint of China's great allies. Nationalist China was asked to patch up its political differences with the Chinese Communists, to consent to American proposals to arm the Chinese Red Armies, to give the Chinese Communists a greater share in the Central Government, and so on. In discussing Chiang Kai-shek's refusal to accept General Stilwell's plan to arm the Chinese Red Army, President Roosevelt said to Chiang: "When the enemy is pressing us toward possible disaster, it appears unsound to reject the aid of anyone who will kill Japanese." At a time when Great Britain and the United States were giving every possible military aid to Soviet Russia, thereby making her the greatest military power in European history, it did seem so "unsound" and so unreasonable for Chiang Kai-shek to persist in his refusal to arm and supply the Chinese Communists. Could the Chinese Red Army possibly be more dangerous than the mighty Red Army of the U.S.S.R.?

In short, it was China the new ally, the weakest member of the "Grand Alliance," that had to be somehow reconstructed and reformed so that she might be better fitted to play her part in the American war strategy, and later in the American idealistic plan for peace which was to be based on the central theme of Russian-American cooperation. And when China sometimes failed to comply with any particular line or plan in that "reconstruction," she came to be more and more disliked by her fond friend of an earlier period.

Such is the little theory I submit to you for the explanation and understanding of the sad and unfortunate deterioration of the relationship between our two countries. The United States and China were loyal friends for many decades. But China's elevation from a friend to an ally was the real cause of the worsening of Sino-American relations.

I would like to conclude and reinforce my little theory by a wise principle of human relations as propounded by the democratic philosopher of ancient China, Mencius. Mencius once said: "Between father and son, there should be no reproving admonitions as to what is good and right. Such reproving admonitions lead to alienation, and there is nothing more inauspicious than alienation (between father and son)." And Mencius told us on a different occasion that, for the same reason, the men of ancient times would not teach their own sons, but taught each other's sons, so that they might be spared the danger of frequent reproving admonitions which lead to the alienation of affection between father and son.

What Mencius did not wish to see existing between father and son, was actually practiced with vehement pressure by the government of one great power on the government of a weak ally. The inevitable result was dislike, recrimination, and cataclysmic disaster.

May not this wise Chinese warning of over twenty-three centuries ago help us all to understand the historical lesson of the past decade, and to prepare to guard against its recurrence in future relations between nations!

CHAPTER 17

Communism, Democracy, and Culture Pattern[1]

Nearly forty years ago, G. Lowes Dickinson visited Asia for the first time and made the discovery that Asia was not one, but many basically different countries and peoples. He singled out three major countries and tried to sum up their distinctive cultural patterns by three words: in India, everything is religion; in Japan, everything is government; and in China, everything is humanity.

I cite this to illustrate my own predicament when I was asked and actually undertook to prepare a short paper on the huge subject "Communism, Democracy and Culture Pattern in Asia." I soon realized that it was impossible for me to cover the whole of Asia. I have had to limit myself to the one area in Asia which I know best, namely, China.

My best excuse in thus greatly narrowing my scope is that "Communism and Democracy in China" has become the burning question in the minds of all who are interested in political theories. China has had over twenty-five years' experience of fierce struggle with World Communism. In the course of those twenty-five years, considerable parts of the populations have had to live under some form of Communist system of political and economic organization, sometimes for only brief periods of time, sometimes for several years. And in the last few years, nearly the whole of continental China has come under Communist conquest and control.

In September 1949, a constitution under the name of "a Common Program" has been proclaimed. A Central People's Government of the People's Republic of China has been established since October I, 1949. Article I of this constitution says: "The People's Republic of China is a state of the New

---

1. An incomplete, typewritten text with several handwritten pages at the end. It was probably written in the early 1950s.

Democracy, that is, a state of the People's Democracy." All that, I am sure, is quite clear to this learned assembly. The same article also says: "This state is to carry out the People's Democratic Dictatorship."

What is this political system that is called "the People's Democratic Dictatorship?"

"That is," says my former student Mao Tse-tung, "the reactionaries must be deprived of the rights to voice their opinion, and only the People are allowed to have the right to voice their opinion."

Who are the People? At the present stage in China, the People are the working class, the peasants, the petty bourgeoisie, and the national bourgeoisie. Under the leadership of the working class and the Communist Party, these classes unite together to form their own state and elect their own government to carry out dictatorship over the "running dogs" on imperialism—the landlords, the bureaucratic class, the Kuomintang reactionaries and their henchmen—these classes shall oppress them and only allow them to behave properly, and not allow them to talk and act wildly. If they talk and act wildly, they shall be curbed and punished immediately.

The democratic system is to be carried out within the ranks of the people only, giving them freedom of speech, assembly and association. The right to vote is given only to the people, and not to the reactionaries.

These two aspects, namely, democracy among the people, and dictatorship over the reactionaries, combine to form the People's Democratic Dictatorship.

Why should it be done this way? It is obvious that if it is not done, the revolution will fail, the people will suffer, and the state will perish.

The Army, the Police, the People's Court—these machineries of the State are instruments for classes to oppress classes. To the hostile classes, the state apparatus is an instrument of oppression. It is violent, and not benevolent.

These arrogant words are taken from Mao's article on "The People's Democratic Dictatorship," which was broadcast by the official organ of propaganda on July 1, 1949, in commemoration of the twenty-eighth anniversary of the founding of the Chinese Communist Party. This article formed the theoretical and textual basis for the making of the "Constitution" in September, and is now a required reading in all "political science" classes which teachers and students in all grades of school—from the primary schools to the university—must attend.

Article V of the "Constitution" stipulates the People shall have eleven kinds of freedom. But Article VII says:

> With regard to all reactionaries, feudalistic landlords, bureaucratic capital-ists, after they are disarmed and their special influences are liquidated, they must be deprived of their political rights, but at the same time given some means of livelihood and forced to reconstruct themselves to become "new men" through hard labor.

Here we find the institution of forced slave labor for the political opposi-tion is already dignified into a constitutional provision!
[MISSING PAGE]

... shout) the question at him: "Where are the farming implements?" We all help to get out the tools and vessels and place them before us. After listing them, we load them on the landowners' big wagon and carry them back to the Sub-agency.

Of course, under the present circumstances, the landowner cannot possi-bly offer any resistance. Yet to carry guns on a mission to confiscate his farm-ing implements is more symbolic than necessary. What it symbolizes is that the proletarian Communist Party, by arming the peasants, had not dealt a death blow to the feudalistic land system which has existed more than two thousand years.

Our philosopher confesses that he was sometimes moved by a sense of pity for the landowners. At the confiscation of implements in a house near the Marco Polo Bridge, he saw the father of the landowner, about seventy years old, who was running to and fro aimlessly. "I thought," says Professor Fung, "those things must have taken the old man many years to acquire. I therefore felt sorry for him. Then I caught myself: I was drifting to the stand-point of the landowner! Why should I not rejoice with those peasants who now acquire the tools instead of pitying those who lose them?"

Was our philosopher condemning the whole thing which is misnamed "Land Reform?" Or was he really sincere when he said that his experience in participating in the confiscation and redistribution of land and implements had made him realize that he was actually taking part in the Revolution?

We are now tempted to ask a question.

Is there anything in the native pattern of Chinese thought and culture which can offer some antitoxin or some power of resistance to such Communist buncombe as the People's Democratic Dictatorship or such Communist tragico-farce as the so-called "Land Reform"? What is there in Chinese thought and culture which a temporary Communist conquest and domination cannot kill or destroy, and which may ultimately prepare the Chinese people to overthrow this essentially "un-Chinese" dictatorship of unreason and violence?

As a lifelong student of the history of Chinese thought and culture, I am inclined to suggest that there [are] at least a few significant traits in the Chinese culture-pattern which may be able to offer some lasting and effective resistance to Communist ideology and practice. I suggest these three traits:

1. An almost anarchistic aversion for all government interference.
2. A long tradition of love for freedom and fight for freedom—especially for intellectual freedom and religious freedom, but also for the freedom of political criticism.
3. A traditional exaltation of the individual's right to doubt and question things—even the most sacred things.

One of the patterns peculiarly Chinese is the "no government" mentality of the Chinese people which undoubtedly came from centuries of deliberate practice of a laissez-faire political philosophy. Twenty-five centuries ago, Lao-tzu taught the political theory of *wu wei*, which means "do nothing" or "nonactivity" as a method of government. "Learn from Nature," said Lao-tzu. "Nature does nothing, yet it accomplishes everything." Therefore, according to this political philosophy, "The best government is one whose existence is barely noticed by its people." This theory of *wu wei*, just as its modern counterpart of laissez-faire, was a radical political protest against undue and incompetent interference by government. It was so attractive as a philosophical concept that Confucius several times spoke of it with apparent approval.

When China became a unified empire, the first empire-builders attempted to govern it with centralized authoritarian control. After the failure of the First Empire, some wise rulers of the Han empire realized that it was no easy task to govern such a vast country without a large standing army and without effective means of transportation and communication. These wise rulers decided to try out the political theory of *wu wei* as a method of empire-government.

These wise statesmen, notably the third emperor of the dynasty and his very wise wife, consciously practiced the laissez-faire policy and suppressed all schemes of military expansion and meddlesome internal construction. Under nearly half a century of governmental nonactivity and noninterference, the people learned to appreciate the full benefits of a unified empire. There was long internal peace and great economic prosperity. This period of conscious laissez-faire (180–130 B.C.) laid the solid foundation of the Han Empire and set the pattern for all future dynasties under the unified empire. The central government only controlled a few important tools of administration but left the villages and the country to govern themselves. There was very little government in the country. And people took pride in the fact that they never [had the] occasion to be inside a court or government building.

More than twenty centuries of *wu wei* policy has been best expressed in a most popular proverb which says:

Heaven is high, and the Emperor far-away.

This mentality of no government—this anarchistic tradition—is just the opposite of the political ideas and practices of modern totalitarianism.

The Communist agent goes to every village and invades the privacy of every home. He controls the food supply of the community, and is therefore able to regulate the life and conduct of every man and woman at the village level.

The villager has avoided government, but government now comes to every villager. But I cannot believe this inveterate individualistic and anarchistic mentality inculcated by conscious philosophy and especially by twenty centuries of unconscious living could be liquidated by a few months or even a few years of all-pervading totalitarian rule.

Another tradition of Chinese thought has been its long tradition of freedom—freedom of thought and expression, and the freedom to criticize and censure the action and policy of rulers and governments. This was a most valuable heritage from the classical age, which was an age of independent and warring states when thinkers and critics persecuted in one state could often find asylum and welcome in another. Frequent and devastating wars, heavy taxation, and misrule had imposed upon the intelligentsia the moral responsibility to speak out in the interest of the people.

One of the great disciples of Confucius said: "The scholar must be stout-hearted and courageous, for his burden is heavy and his journey is long.

Humanity is the burden he imposes upon his own shoulders: is that not a heavy burden? And only death ends his toils: is that not a long journey?" Mencius often spoke of "the individual shouldering the grave burden of the world." And every Chinese schoolboy remembers the famous saying of a seventeenth-century patriot, that "the humble individual, however humble, has a share in the responsibility for the prosperity or the downfall of the empire."

It was this sense of social responsibility which has led many a Chinese thinker to maintain the great tradition of free and frank criticism of government action even in the centuries under the unified empire when the monarchical rule was becoming more and more absolute. Many great men suffered persecution, banishment, physical torture, and even martyrdom. But the fight for outspoken political censure was carried on throughout the ages. A statesman of the sixteenth century, Lu Kuen, recorded this observation on the historical fight of intellectual and political leaders for the freedom of thought and criticism: "There are only two things supreme in this world: Authority and Reason. Of the two, Reason is the more supreme. For in the history of the struggle of courageous scholars against powerful governments, Reason always triumphs in the end. Therefore, I say that Reason is more supreme than political authority."

Again I cannot believe that this traditional love of freedom and fight for freedom can be easily blotted out by any barbarian system of totalitarian rule.

And lastly, there is the truly valuable tradition of stressing the importance of courageous doubt in all thinking. Both Confucius and Mencius were noted for their encouragement to free questioning by their students. Mencius was almost iconoclastic when he laid the dictum that "to believe in the authenticity of all historical records, is worse than having no history at all." [Here Hu has added in Chinese: "If you just learn and do not think, it means confusion. If you just think and do not learn, it means death."]

Throughout the medieval ages, it was this weapon of courageous doubt that started intellectual revolutions and overthrew powerful dogmas and even powerful religions. The best doubters of the medieval age were Wang Ch'ung of the first century and Fan Chen of about 500 A.D. [and] Han Yu in the early ninth century.

It was the ability to doubt that produced the Chinese Zenism. The great Zen masters were all advocates of fearless questioning and doubting. [The] method of Zen: never tell all, but always let the student find out for himself.

And the Chinese leaders of the philosophical revival in the eleventh and twelfth centuries too paid unreserved tribute to the signal effectiveness of courageous and creative doubt. Said Chang Tsai: "If you can doubt where other people feel no impulse to doubt, then you are making progress." Chu Hsi: "A scholar must learn to doubt. He must be able to doubt where he had found no ground for doubting. And he must be able to dispel his doubt satisfactorily."

It is unnecessary for me to remind you that all these basic traits (the anti-government individualism, the anarchistic aversion to government interference, the fight for freedom, and the right to doubt everything) are the essential elements in the democratic tradition of the modern Western world.

It is therefore no mere accident that China was the first neutral nation, the first non-European country to overthrow the monarchy and establish a republic nearly forty years ago. It is again no mere accident that after three years of close collaboration with the Communist International and the Chinese Communist Party, the Kuomintang, the party of Sun Yat-sen and Chiang Kai-shek, broke completely with the Communists in 1927 and has been fighting almost continuously ever since.

In a remarkable collection of autobiographical essays by six ex-Communists published under the title *The God That Failed*, Ignazio Silone, one of the six, said to his former Communist colleague Togliatti, "The final struggle will be between the Communists and the ex-Communists" (p. 13). Arthur Koestler, also one of the six, said to the editor Richard Grossman: "When all is said, we as ex-Communists are the only people on your side who know what it's all about." Commenting on these remarks, Mr. Grossman said: "No one who has wrestled with Communism as a philosophy, and Communists as political opponents, can really understand the values of Western democracy."

I want to conclude my brief paper by introducing to this learned assembly a few wise remarks on Communism and Democracy made by a Chinese ex-Communist, my friend Ch'en Tu-hsiu, who was the founder and leader of the CCP but who was expelled from the Party in 1928 as a Trotskyite. He died in 1942 at the age of sixty-three. Four years before his death, when he was still regarded as a Trotskyite Communist, he wrote to his Trotskyite friends: "I am only interested in my own independent thoughts, never compromise my own views to [unclear] those of any other man. What I have here expressed are only the views of myself as an individual, and do not represent any other man. I no longer belong to any party, nor do I take orders from anyone. I take my own hand and bear my own responsibility. Who will be my friends in the future, I have not the slightest inkling. I have absolutely no fear of standing alone."

Thus spoke Ch'en Tu-hsiu, the Chinese individual and rebel after shedding his mantle as the founder and leader of the Chinese Communist Party!

In the fateful years of 1939–40—the years of the Stalin-Hitler Pact—he opposed the Communist Party line and wrote to his friends that he wanted to see a victory of Democracies. He said: "If victory is won by the side of Britain, France, and the U.S.A., then [the so-called] democracy of the bourgeoisie is preserved which alone can serve as the road leading to democracy of the masses."

This seemingly harmless sentence was explosive and counterrevolutionary even in the eyes of his Trotskyite friends.

CHAPTER 18

China Seven Years after Yalta[1]

Today is February 4, 1952. Next Monday, February 11, will be the seventh anniversary of the secret Yalta Agreement signed by President Roosevelt, Prime Minister Churchill, and Marshal Stalin on February 11, 1945.

That secret agreement stipulated the conditions on which the Soviet Union would enter the war against Japan. It stated the price with which the great Anglo-American leaders were to buy Russia's entry into the Pacific War. Japan and China and Korea were to pay the price.

The fatal price China was to pay included these grave items:

1) The loss of Outer Mongolia, which has an area seventy-seven times larger than the state of New Jersey or twelve times larger than the state of New York.
2) The lease of Port Arthur as a naval base of the Soviet Union.
3) Russian control of the port of Dairen.
4) Russian control of the railway system in Manchuria.

The combination of the last-named three items, of course, meant the real and effectual control of the whole of Manchuria, which, by that time, was undoubtedly the most highly industrialized area in all Asia.

Korea was never mentioned in the Yalta secret agreement. But Korea, as the world knows, has been paying an equally heavy price as China throughout these so-called "postwar" years.

The terms of the Yalta Agreement were kept secret from the Chinese government until June 14, 1945, four months after the Yalta Conference.

The first atomic bomb was dropped on Hiroshima on August 6. Soviet

---

1. This is an address delivered at the Seton Hall University on February 4, 1952.

Russia declared war on Japan on August 8. By August 9, the Soviet armies began to move into Manchuria and Korea.

Japan surrendered on August 14. The USSR was in the Pacific War exactly five days and won the control of Eastern Asia and the domination of the whole of Asia through Stalin's masterly play of the strategy of deceit at Yalta.

In North Korea, the Russian army and the Russian-trained and Russian-equipped Korean Red Army set up the Communist regime in 1948, which two years later invaded the Republic of Korea and started the Korean War.

In Manchuria, the Russian army was in occupation for fully nine months—from August 1945 till the end of April 1946. When the Russian troops were withdrawn, the naval base of Port Arthur, the great port of Dairen, and the entire railway system in Manchuria were already under powerful Russian control; and the vast country areas of Manchuria were in the hands of Chinese Communist armies which had raced to the northeastern provinces, where they were quickly and fully armed and quipped from the huge military stocks left over by the surrendered Japanese Kwantung Army.

Manchuria and North Korea had now become the contiguous base for the new military strength of Chinese Communism, behind which lay the unlimited support of Soviet Russia, which, because of what General of the Army George C. Marshall called the "tumultuous demobilization" of the USA, was now the mightiest military power in the whole world.

Out of Manchuria, Communist armies, newly equipped and reconditioned, poured into Shantung across the sea, and into North China by land. By September 1948, Shantung was lost. By November, the whole of Manchuria was lost. By early 1949, North China was lost. Before the end of 1949, nearly the whole of continental China, except for the guerrilla areas, came under the conquest of World Communism.

By the spring of 1950, the mainland of China had completely fallen a captive of Communism. It was then that World Communism decided to strike in Korea, to clear the Korean peninsula of any free and non-Communist or anti-Communist force or influence.

That was the meaning of the invasion of free Korea by Communist Korea in June 1950.

And when that invasion failed because of United States and United Nations intervention, it was but natural that Communist China was promptly ordered to enter the war in full force.

So by today the United States has been fighting in Korea for 580 days—already two days longer than she fought in the First World War.

And today, a week before the seventh anniversary of the Yalta secret agreement, I must declare that the tragedy of Korea, as well as the tragedy of China, stems from that secret agreement which has directly and indirectly resulted in making half of Korea captive and all continental China captive.

Surely you will agree with me that it is absolutely impossible to imagine a free China and a free Korea fighting the GIs of the United States and the forces of the United Nations. It is Captive China and Captive Korea that are fighting the United States and the UN in Korea.

If proof is needed to support this statement, let me cite the stories that have come from the UN camps of Chinese prisoners of war in recent months. Of the seventeen thousand Chinese prisoners confirmed on the island of Koje off the Korean coast, twelve thousand have signed petitions in their own blood stating that they would prefer death to being sent back to Communist China. Last month, it was further reported that three thousand of these Chinese prisoners of war had actually tattooed themselves with Chinese slogans, "Fan kung" (anti-Communism) and "K'ang o" (resist Russia), thereby deliberately condemning themselves to sure death if they were ever to be returned to Communist China.

What better evidence can I offer you to show that it is not free China, but China captive, that has been fighting your troops in Korea?

It saddens my heart to describe to you the dictatorial and oppressive rule under which more than four hundred million of my people have been living and suffering during the last years. The first article of the "Common Program" (which has been hailed as the Constitution of Communist China) declares that "the People's Republic of China is a state of the People's Democracy which carries out the People's Democratic Dictatorship."

What is "the People's Democratic Dictatorship"? My former student Mao Tse-tung has frankly and arrogantly described its general features in a lengthy article entitled "The People's Democratic Dictatorship," which was broadcast on July 1, 1949, throughout Communist China and which, in its English version, is printed in full in the State Department's "White Paper on China" (pp. 720–729). From this, I quote a few sentences:

"You are dictatorial." Yes, dear gentlemen, you are right and we are dictatorial. The reactionaries must be deprived of the right to voice their opinion, and only the People are allowed to have the right to voice their opinion.

Who are the People? At the present stage, they are the workers, the peasants, the petty bourgeoisie, and the national bourgeoisie. Under the leadership of the working class and the Communist Party, these classes unite together to form their own state and elect their own government to carry out dictatorship over the running dogs of imperialism—the landlords, the bureaucratic class, the Kuomintang reactionaries and their henchmen. These Classes shall oppress them and only allow them to behave properly, and not allow them to talk and act wildly. If they talk and act wildly, they shall be curbed and punished immediately. . . .

The Army, the Police, the People's Court—these machineries of the state are instruments for classes to oppress classes. To the hostile classes, the state apparatus is an instrument of oppression. It is violent, and not benevolent.

These are no mere empty words of threat. They are insolent statements of what is now actually happening every day and every night in Communist China. Not only the smuggled letters from the suffering people in the mainland have confirmed these statements. Not only the reports of Catholic and Protestant missionaries in all parts of Communist China have verified them. Indeed the Communist governments have often deliberately reported their persecutions, mob trials, and mass executions through their own official radio stations.

To this academic assembly, I may cite three actual cases involving the life of Chinese teachers and students, who have been deprived, not only of their freedom of speech, but also of their freedom of silence.

In the spring of 1949, my friend and fellow academician Mr. Ch'en Yuan, chancellor of the Catholic Fu Jen University in Peiping, was made to publish an open letter to me in which he said emphatically that there was no real freedom anywhere except in the areas liberated and controlled by the Communists. Did my friend really say that? Did he have the freedom not to say it?

In September 1950, all newspapers in Communist China published what purported to be a written confession of my younger son, in which he denounced me as "an enemy of the people" and therefore his own enemy. Did my son actually say that? Was he free not to say it?

And during the last three months, there has been going on in Communist China a great movement of "Thought Reconstruction" in which I and my writings were made the main target of persecution and attack. Many of my students and friends were made to stand up in public and confess their past errors in being misled by the poisonous ideas of Hu Shih which they now solemnly condemned. This public persecution of the thoughts and ideas of Hu Shih began in my own university, the National Peking University in Peiping on November 14, 1951; it was formally launched in Shanghai on December 2; and it was started by the Communist authorities in Canton and South China on December 23.

On December 2, 1951, Professor Ku Chieh-kang, one of the best-known critical historians, whose autobiographical preface to his monumental work *Ku shih pien* has been translated into English by Dr. A.W. Hummel and published in book form under the title *Autobiography of a Chinese Historian*, was "invited" to speak at the "Conference to Criticize and Refute the Thoughts of Hu Shih" in Shanghai. Two weeks later, Professor Ku's speech was published in Shanghai; and on Christmas Eve, it was republished in all Communist papers in South China. The major portion of his speech was devoted to a confession of his lifelong error of being influenced by the historical methods as preached and practiced by his teacher Hu Shih. But these are his concluding sentences:

> I am now aware that I ought to make a sharp and strict distinction between friend and foe. Therefore I definitely acknowledge that Hu Shih is not only my enemy politically but also my enemy intellectually; and that I cannot discharge my own duty until I have thoroughly eradicated all the poisonous elements sown and spread by him. How glorious we all are, to be guided by Chairman Mao Tse-tung and march on to the right path of thought.

Now, did my friend say all that? And did he have the freedom not to say all that?

I think I have said enough to prove my point that my people are captive and not free, and that it is this captive China which has been fighting your sons and brothers in Korea.

Before concluding, I want to make my last point: that there is still a free China which exists as a reality, and which is always your friend, ever ready to work with you and fight shoulder to shoulder with you. By "free China," I do not mean merely the six hundred thousand trained soldiers and the seven million population on the island bastion of Formosa. Nor do I mean merely the vast numbers of Chinese guerrilla units now fighting on in many parts of China against the Communists. By free China I mean the vast majority of the Chinese people who are mentally and emotionally anti-Communist even though they are physically compelled to live and suffer under the iron yoke of Communist rule.

Free China exists as a reality because, of all the peoples conquered by

World Communism, my people are the most civilized and have long lived under a civilization noted for its individualism and centuries-long fights for intellectual, religious, and political freedom. If history and civilization mean anything at all, there will always be a free China.

And the sad experience of living and suffering under Communist rule during the last few years has enabled my people to better understand what Communism and Communist rule are. And they are determined to oppose it as soon as they can oppose it.

My friends, let me assure you: free China exists as a reality. Free China needs the sympathy and the understanding of the Free World; and the Free World cannot long survive if it does not try to win the support of a free China.

When the Free World gives the word, free China will surely respond.

CHAPTER 19

The Suffering Chinese Intellectuals behind the Iron Curtain[1]

As a Chinese intellectual leader of over thirty years standing, I want most sincerely to thank Dr. Walter Judd and his colleagues for having the great heart and making the great effort to give aid to the hundreds and thousands of Chinese intellectuals who have had the courage to flee Communist China and who have had the even much greater courage to live and suffer a sub-subsistence life in exile in preference to the life of political and intellectual slavery under the Red Slaves of Stalin. These brave men and women truly deserve your help. May your effort be blessed with the success it deserves!

I have come here to make a short speech. I have decided to talk about the abject suffering of Chinese intellectuals in Red China. When we fully understand how unbearable that suffering is, we shall all the more sympathize with those whose foresight and good luck and physical and moral courage have made it possible for them to escape it.

It is an undeniable fact, and an understatement, that in the long history of my people, there has never been a period in which the intellectuals are subjected to so great moral and spiritual torture as they are today in Communist China.

Not even in the long centuries of the unified empire under the unlimited powers of the absolute monarchy was there such universal and inescapable oppression of intellectuals as is daily and everywhere practiced in the Red-controlled mainland today.

It is true that in the days of the vast unified Chinese empire, there was no place of political asylum or refuge for the persecuted nonconformist, rebel-

---

1. A speech delivered for Aid Refugee Chinese Intellectuals, Inc. on April 29, 1952.

lious thinker or revolutionary. As the old saying goes, "Between Heaven above and Earth below, there is no escape from the tie between the ruler and the subject."

But there were in fact many wide loopholes in those days. There were no large standing armies, no secret police, no thought police, no spies and informers in every village, every school, and every home. And there was at least the freedom of conscience protected by the freedom of silence—which is even more necessary than the freedom of speech. So long as there was freedom of silence, a man could refrain from overt act of political opposition or open publication of his thoughts and beliefs, and yet remain free to think his own thoughts and worship his own God or gods without being molested or persecuted.

Not so today. The Communist regime in China claims to have five million men in the Red Army, fifteen million in the so-called "People's Militia," and ten million of Party and public functionaries. And all sons and daughters are instructed and required to inform the local Party and police of the doings and sayings of their parents at home. And every student is required to inform against his or her teachers; and every employee in the shops and factories is ordered to bring accusations against their employer. This last-named policy is what you read in the daily reports as the "Five Anti" Movement, which has already caused more than one million arrests and has forced thousands of owners and managers of shops, banks, and factories to commit suicide as the preferable way to escape worse tortures. Many of those owners and managers of private banks and factories are "intellectuals" in the proper sense of the word.

Only last week the Associated Press reported that on a single day, April 14, 1952, in the city of Canton alone there were seventeen merchants and managers who died by their own hands. Two of them jumped from a rooftop after shouting to watching crowds through megaphones these words of hatred: "No matter how innocent you may be, the Communists will ruin you. Death is less painful than Red persecution" (*New York World Telegram and Sun*, April 21). ·

In the Analects of Confucius (XIII, 18), there is this interesting conversation:

The Duke of Sheh said to Confucius: "In my place, there is a self-righteous man. His father stole a sheep, and he, the son, bore witness to the theft."

Confucius replied: "In our place, the righteous man acts differently. The father will conceal the misconduct of the son; and the son will conceal the misconduct of the father. There is righteousness in this."

When I read this passage in my boyhood, I used to think that the story told by the Duke was an improbable yarn.

But I was wrong. In the ideal and perfect democracy of Soviet Russia, this act of a son bearing witness against his father is celebrated and worshipped as the Model Act of Pavlik Morozov. At the height of collectivization, Pavlik's father had hidden away a few poods[2] of wheat at his farm—to save his family from starvation. The son Pavlik was a member of the Pioneer Club and felt it was his duty to tell the inspection police against his father and his neighbors and lead the police to where the wheat had been hidden. A few days after the confiscation of the hidden food, the boy disappeared. His dead body was found in a nearby forest. As a result of investigation, Pavlik's father and grandfather and a score of villagers were executed. Monuments were erected everywhere in honor of Pavlik Morozov's exemplary conduct, and streets and schools have been named after him.

So the sons and daughters of my people are now instructed to emulate Pavlik Morozov and to watch and inform against their fathers and mothers. A tragic story is told of a friend of mine who is a great man of science, and well known to many a medical man in this assembly. One day his son and daughter came home and asked their father who was the discoverer of penicillin. My friend told them the story of Sir Alexander Fleming and his fellow workers who discovered that wonder drug. "Father," said the daughter, "you are all wrong. The Russians discovered penicillin. You are a pro-imperialist reactionary and counterrevolutionary. We shall have to report you." So my friend was locked up in a closet while the dutiful children sent for the police.

And of course, you have heard or read about my own son's confession in which he denounced his father as an enemy of the people and therefore his own enemy. But the greatest tragedy of the Chinese intellectuals in the mainland stems from the fact that they are completely denied the freedom of silence. They must make public confessions of their life history, their education, and the intellectual influences they have received, their past and present attitude toward those influences, and their own innermost thoughts and beliefs. This is called *t'an pai*, "making yourself plain." There must be no concealment or falsification.

---

2. A pood is about thirty-six pounds.

And concealment and falsification are made impossible by the further and more perfect processes known as "self-criticism" and "criticism of self-criticism." Both are done in public meetings attended by your own students and colleagues as well as the well-trained questioners and interrogators of the Communist Party. These meetings can best be described as psychoanalysis in public. A meeting may last five, six, or ten or twelve hours. And if one meeting is not enough, you will be granted time to think over and revise your self-criticism and be prepared for the next meeting or meetings until your self-criticism is finally accepted by the crowd and the Party as satisfactory—that is, until you have sufficiently and completely humiliated and debased yourself morally, intellectually, and spiritually in the eyes of your own students and colleagues.

Many of the most self-debasing and self-humiliating confessions published under the signatures of some of the best-known and most respected intellectuals are undoubtedly the result, the inevitable result of such fierce and terribly searching "criticism of self-criticism."

Many of these self-destroying confessions have been published by the Communist regime and are accessible to us through Hong Kong. I shall cite a few sentences from the latest confession of an old friend and honored colleague at the Peking University. He said:

> I had been unconscious of my many defects until the last days of my actual participation in the Land Reform work when I began to realize those defects as a result of the method of "criticism of self-criticism." When I realized the sharpness and effectiveness of this weapon of "criticism of self-criticism," I deeply regretted that I had not learned earlier to use it.

So he went on to confess all his moral and intellectual defects, at the end of which he had to add this for good measure:

> Besides declaring Hu Shih's thoughts as the thoughts of an enemy, we at the Peking University must go a step further and refute the ideas of Tsai Yuan-pei, former chancellor of the University.

Now, what are the dangerous ideas of my former chief Tsai Yuan-pei which my good friend "volunteered" to refute? They are two in particular: freedom of thought and freedom of learning in a university. And my friend had to declare publicly that there ought to be freedom only for the thoughts and learning "of the People," that is, for the thought and learning sanctioned by the Communist Party, but for nothing else, certainly not for any ideas and thoughts of the capitalist countries. So this well-known son of Harvard University publicly declared that Tsai Yuan-pei's twin doctrine of freedom of thinking and learning in a university must be swept out and condemned in the Peking University! What greater humiliation and self-debasement could there be than to make this self-respecting and even arrogant son of Harvard publicly father the condemnation of freedom of thought and learning!

I cannot go on quoting from the many similar documents supposedly written and published by Chinese intellectuals who are captive and suffering in their captivity. But I think I have said enough to justify my conclusion that the whole pattern of intellectual life in Red China throughout the last two and a half years has been a determined policy to deny truth and the objectivity of truth, to regiment all thinking and learning, to suppress all freedom and independence of thought and expression, to deny even the freedom of silence, to crush the spirit of man and transform him into a slogan-mouthing automaton. It is intellectual slavery, abject slavery pure and simple—nay, it is moral and spiritual torture—under which the thousands upon thousands of Chinese intellectuals have been living and suffering these years.

What can you do to help them?

The greatest thing you and your great nation and the Free World in general can do is to help Free China to liberate Captive China from the crushing yoke of world Communism. That's a big order, but every civilized man and woman in the Free World cannot shirk the moral responsibility of at least thinking over it. The Free World, by its acts of commission and omission, has unwittingly contributed to the conquest and enslavement of my country and my people. It has a moral responsibility to help retrieve it.

And the least you can do is to give support to Dr. Judd and his colleagues in this great effort to aid refugee Chinese intellectuals who want to be free and deserve to be free.

CHAPTER 20

China in Distress[1]

I do not have to develop the thesis that China is in great distress. At one time China was expected to play the role of one of the four or five great powers. Where is she now? In a little over a year and a half she has fallen from that high pedestal to the miserable position of one of the satellite countries of Soviet Russia—one of the captive nations of World Communism. With the exception of a few centers of continuing guerrilla activities, China's mainland is now almost entirely controlled by the armed forces of the Chinese Communists. The central government of China is making its capital in the recently restored province of Taiwan or Formosa, but its control extends little beyond the ring of islands along the eastern and southern coast. Over four hundred million Chinese are now living under the totalitarian rule of Communism, and the Iron Curtain is fast falling over the whole of continental China.

How are the Chinese people faring behind the Iron Curtain? One of the university professors in Peiping publicly said last August that "even in her initial steps, the new China has already surpassed the degree of democracy now enjoyed by the people of the United States." How wonderful, if it were true! The *Christian Science Monitor* published on February 9, 1950, a long dispatch written and smuggled out of Communist China by its anonymous correspondent, from which I quote a few sentences: "As in all totalitarian communities, the informer system is in full swing in Communist China to prevent any unfavorable comment on the doings of the administration. In Peiping, for instance, each street has its 'warden,' a specially chosen political worker, to keep a watchful eye on the sayings and doings of his neighbors." So there is not much democracy after all.

---

1. An unpublished piece written in the early 1950s. Hu Shih expresses his concerns about China's Communist regime and offers advice on how the United States can aid Free China.

It may be pertinent for me to quote a few sentences from Mao Tse-tung himself, who has the rather rare quality of sometimes talking quite frankly. In an article entitled "The People's Democratic Dictatorship" which he proclaimed in May 1949, and which is printed in full in the Department of State's White Paper on China, Mao frankly admits that the rule of the Chinese Communists is and will be a democratic dictatorship. "The experiences of several decades tell the Chinese people to carry out the people's democratic dictatorship, that is, the reactionaries must be deprived of the right to voice their opinions; and only the people are allowed to have the right of voicing their opinions. . . . The democratic system is to be carried out within the ranks of the people, giving them freedom of speech, assembly, and association. The right to vote is given only to people and not to the reactionaries. These two aspects, namely, democracy among the people and dictatorship over the reactionaries, combine to form the people's democratic dictatorship." And he goes on to declare: "The Army, the Police, the People's Court, are instruments for classes to oppress classes. To the hostile classes, the state apparatus is the instrument of oppression. It is violent and not benevolent."

Such is the system that is now ruling over hundreds of millions of my people. It is therefore no overstatement to say that China is in distress.

What is the real explanation of China's downfall?

Some have suggested corruption as the cause. Others have offered the explanation that China owes its collapse to the lack of democratic government. Others are inclined to think that China's downfall was due to an ideological conquest.

As a student of history I am inclined to believe that what has happened in China during the last two years has been primarily a military collapse— just as the collapse of France in 1940 was primarily a military collapse.

I want to call your attention to one historical fact which differentiates the Chinese Communist movement from the Communist movement in any other country outside of Russia. This fact is rarely ever mentioned by your journalistic and professorial authorities on Chinese affairs. It is a fact which is most important to an understanding of what is happening in China.

What is this fact of such historical significance? It is that the Chinese Communist Party has had a separate and independent army of formidable force almost from the very beginning of the Party. The Chinese Communist Party was founded in 1921. It began to have an independent Red Army in August 1927. On August 1, 1949, Communist China had a tremendous celebration of the twenty-second anniversary of the founding of the Red Army.

As a matter of fact, the Chinese Communist Party, even before 1927, had considerable influence and control over a part of the National Revolution Army in those early days when the great Russian soldier General Blucher was helping Chiang Kai-shek's army-training and the famous Communist Borodin was indoctrinating its political commissars. It was only after the "split" between the Kuomintang and the Chinese Communists in the spring of 1927 that a member of the Communist-influenced army leaders left the Nationalist ranks and started the separate Red Army.

So the Chinese Communist Party has had its separate army for more than twenty-two years. That fact alone differentiates the Chinese Communist movement from the Communist parties in Germany, France, Italy, Britain, the United States, or any other country. It is this fact which justified Mr. Manuilsky in saying as early as 1935 that the Communist Party in China was the most important of all Communist parties outside of Soviet Russia.

This Chinese Red Army in its early years achieved the strength of several hundreds of thousands. But after seven years' hard fighting, the Nationalist armies under Chiang Kai-shek succeeded in defeating the Red armies many times and reducing their strength to "only a few tens of thousands," in the reluctant words of Mao Tse-tung.

The Communist military strength was at its lowest in 1936. That was the time when Chinese Communists and their friends talked most loudly about a United Front against Japan. And when the Chinese Government took up the fight with Japan in 1937, the Communist armies were incorporated as a part of the national army and were financed and equipped at the quota of 45,000 men and officers.

Throughout the eight years of China's war against Japan, this Communist army of 45,000 grew so rapidly that on April 24, 1945, Mao Tse-tung was able to say in his political report to the Communist Party Congress: "As I am writing this report, the army of the party has reached 910,000 men in arms, plus 2,200,000 men in the People's Militia."

That is twenty times growth in eight years, not counting the so-called people's militia. And this growth took place before the Red Army came into direct contact with Russian troops. Less than a year later, when Chinese Communist armies were receiving direct aid in the form of Japanese-surrendered arms and munitions, the Red Army soon claimed to have attained the numerical strength of over 1,700,000. And on last August 1 the Communist leaders proudly announced to the world that their own regular army strength was 4,000,000.

It is this tremendous strength of the Chinese Communist Party that has brought about the almost miraculous victory and conquest over Chiang Kai-shek's tired, ill-fed, and disheartened armies during the last few years. And, permit me to remind you, it is this same rapidly growing military strength that has doomed to failure all the well-intentioned American proposals for peaceful settlement and political coalition with the Nationalist Government. What the Chinese Communists wanted was the military conquest of China. The withdrawal of American troops from China and the stoppage of American military aid to China only accelerate the Communist conquest. As General Wedemeyer said as early as September 1947, "Removal of American assistance, without removal of Soviet assistance, would certainly lay the country open to eventual Communist domination."

Your great general George C. Marshall, who was in Nanking throughout the fifty days of the National Assembly which framed China's new constitution, openly admitted on January 7, 1947, that "the National Assembly has adopted a democratic Constitution which in all major respects is in accordance with the principles laid down by the All-Party Political Consultative Conference of last January." General Marshall went on to say, "It is unfortunate that the Communists did not see fit to participate in the Assembly since the Constitution that has been adopted seemed to include every major point that they wanted." But what use would the Communist leaders have for "a democratic constitution?" And what could "a democratic constitution" accomplish in the face of an armed rebellion led by the Moscow-trained masters of war and sabotage and supported by the unlimited strength of World Communism? The constitution was finished on Christmas Day 1946, and the first presidential and vice-presidential elections under the constitution were not completed until the last days of April 1948. Four months later the great military collapse began in Manchuria and North China. Can we charge the collapse to the failure of a constitutional regime which, though quite democratic and honest, had only a few months' trial?

My friends, I hope you will forgive me for indulging in so lengthy a historical explanation of what has happened in China. As an anti-Communist Chinese liberal, I am more interested in the future of China than in the past events. I am sure that you too are interested in the future of my country and my people.

What then of the future?

China is down but not out. She is still fighting. Indeed she is the only country in the world today which is still fighting Communism.

Let us not be too easily disheartened by the immediate difficulties which China must face today in her hope for the liberation of the whole mainland from Communist domination. An American friend who is one of your recognized Sinologues has written me a letter which contains these words of encouragement: "I have often thought of you during these months of bewildering happenings in China, and earnestly hoped that you would not let yourself get discouraged by the momentary bleak outlook. My historical sense convinces me—as I hope it does you—that the native skepticism and common sense of the Chinese people will reassert itself, as it so often has in other periods of their long history. I am convinced that this will happen much earlier than our gloomy political seers like to make us believe."

I fully share in the historical optimism of my scholarly friend. I am particularly pleased by his special emphasis on "the native skepticism and common sense" of my people. By skepticism and common sense he means the common habit of the Chinese people to doubt everything until they are convinced of some reasonable ground for believing. That is the best protection against all forms of highly schematized and unintelligible bunk. Add to this the equally important trait of Chinese individualism—the inveterate ability to work hard under all conditions and in all climates always with the clear objective of achieving a free and independent livelihood for oneself and one's children—and you have the best makeup for the Chinese rebel against the Communist tyranny.

Please do not dismiss these words as mere wishful thinking. Even in the last few months, reliable reports are reaching us from behind the Chinese Iron Curtain to the effect that the masses in China are already displaying silent apathy toward their new conquerors. The *Christian Science Monitor* correspondent, whom I quoted above, says, "It is safe to say that the wealthiest and poorest Chinese are the severest critics of the Chinese Communists, while the great mass in between these maintain for the most part a passive discontent. The only Chinese really contented under the new regime would appear to be the Communist leaders, the party hacks, most of whom now have important jobs, and the Army."

It is surprising that this correspondent should refer to the poorest Chinese as the severest critics of the regime. He goes on to say, "The coolies are feeling the pinch and making little effort to disguise their feelings. . . . Referring to the talk in the newspapers and over the radio about everything belonging to the people and everything being done for the good of the people, these grumblers comment: 'We are not the people. The Liberation Army are the people.'"

Here you have the beginning of the process of debunking by Chinese common sense and skepticism. It is true that a police state can very well take care of such forms of apathy or even undisguised opposition. But it is safe to view these grumblings of the poor people of China as a part of the shape of things to come.

You would probably like to have me say a word about a question that I know you are all itching to ask me before I sit down.

What can the USA best do to help China now?

I think there is one thing that the American people can do which will be most helpful to the cause of non-Communist and anti-Communist China. It is to take the China question out of partisan politics and place it together with the Marshall Plan and the Atlantic Pact, in a bipartisan and nonpartisan basis. It is then, but not until then, that there can be worked out a China policy which will be the result of impartial and dispassionate thinking and deliberation.

I belong to no political party in China and I represent no Chinese group or clique. But I know my people and I can say now that the Chinese people—the people in Free China and the vast millions living and suffering in Communist China—pray and hope that the China question may soon be restored by all our American friends to a nonpartisan or bipartisan level.

As a very humble but very earnest suggestion of the beginnings of a nonpartisan China policy, I offer these three least controversial items:

1. Nonrecognition of the Communist regime in China. This once was a controversial issue. But it should no longer be so after January 14, when the US Government formally ordered the withdrawal of all American consular personnel from Communist China.

2. The acceptance of President Truman's January 5 statement on Formosa—to the effect that China is fully entitled to exercise authority and sovereignty over Formosa by right of the joint Cairo declaration of December 1943, and by right of the Potsdam declaration of July 1945, the provisions of which were accepted by Japan at the time of its surrender in September 1945.

3. The continuance of economic assistance to Free China as President Truman has said in his January 5 statement, and as the Congress has recently authorized in its bill to aid Korea and China.

With this moral and economic support from America, I believe Free China can maintain itself on its island bastions as the symbol and nerve center of Chinese resistance to the aggression and domination of World Communism.

CHAPTER 21

The Three Stages of the Campaign for Thought Reform in Communist China[1]

According to Mr. Edward Hunter, the new terms "brainwashing" and "brain-changing" were coined by the plain people of China. Those plain folks in my country who invented these succinct and picturesque terms most probably had in mind some such old Chinese tales like the one told by P'u Sung-ling [*sic*] and translated by Herbert A. Giles in his "Strange Stories from a Chinese Studio" (pp. 56–65). The story tells of a Mr. Chu who was "an egregious dunce" and could not even pass the first examination for civil service. But, by a strange accident, he became an intimate friend and companion of the Infernal Judge in the Courts of Purgatory, who frequently visited him at night and drank with him vast quantities of wine. One night Mr. Chu got tipsy and fell asleep, leaving the judge drinking by himself. In his drunken sleep, Mr. Chu seemed to feel a pain in his stomach, and waking up he saw that the Judge had cut open his body and was carefully arranging his insides.

"Don't be afraid," said the Judge, laughing, "I am only providing you with a more intelligent heart . . . Your heart (the seat of the intellect) wasn't at all good at writing compositions, the proper orifice being stuffed up. I have now provided you with a better one which I procured from Hades." The Judge of Purgatory then quietly put back his friend's viscera and closed up the opening, securing it with a bandage tied tightly round his waist. He took the old heart and left him.

"From that moment," so the story goes, "Chu became an apt scholar," composed fine essays, and "passed first on the list for the bachelor's degree."

---

1. This is a revised version of a paper delivered at the Fifth Annual Meeting of the Far Eastern Association on April 1, 1953. On the cover sheet to this version, Hu Shih has recorded a quotation from Mao Zedong, "The re-molding of an intellectual is a long and painful process."

His old comrades who had been accustomed to make a laughingstock of him were now astonished to find him a full-blown *chu-jen* (MA).

Some such folktales probably furnished the background out of which have come the apt terms of brainwashing and brain-changing, which the plain folk of China naively conceive as some kind of almost painless surgical operation by the magic hand of an Infernal Judge of the Courts of Purgatory.

But what the Chinese Communists call the "Thought Reform" is a much more complicated and difficult affair. Indeed it is a tremendous undertaking involving thousands and tens of thousands of people and requiring long months and even long years of concentrated effort, political pressure and mass pressure, endless self-criticism and criticism of self-criticism, and endless confessions of error and self-debasement.

Mao Tse-tung, in his "The People's Democratic Dictatorship," published July 1, 1949, made this statement on the policy of Thought Reform:

> The People's State protects the people. Only when there is the People's State will it be possible for the people to use democratic methods on a Nation-wide and all-comprehensive scale to educate and reform themselves, to free themselves from the influence of reactionaries at home and abroad (which influence is at present still very great, and will continue to exist for a long time, and cannot be eliminated quickly), to reform the bad habits and bad ideas acquired from the old society, not to allow themselves to fall on the erroneous ways led by the reactionaries, and to continue to advance and develop toward a Socialist and a Communist society. The methods we use in this work will be the democratic methods of persuasion, not the methods of coercion.

This brief paragraph summed the objectives and the methods of the Communist campaign for Thought Reform. The objective is to "protect the people," to protect them from going wrong: it is to educate and "remold" (*kai tsao*) the people, to free them from the influence of reactionaries at home and abroad, and to reform (*kai tsao*) their bad habits and bad thoughts acquired from the old society. The methods are to be "the democratic methods of persuasion," that is, the methods of "criticism and self-criticism."

Even as Mao was proclaiming "the People's Democratic Dictatorship" (July 1, 1949), a program of Thought Reform had already been rigorously carried out in Manchuria and North China. The North China University of the People's Revolution was only one of the better-known large centers of

Thought Reform, to which many thousands of young and old men and women were sent for indoctrination and reform. The students there who had, or were suspected to have had, ties with the Old Regime, numbering at all times from eight to ten thousand, once included two former mayors of Peiping as well as my own younger son. The "Thought Conclusions" of my son, in which he denounced his father as an enemy of the People and his own enemy, was published in Red China in September 1950, after he had been there for nearly a year. Many older people were kept there for much longer time.

Beginning with fall opening of the schools in 1949, there was established in every school, from the primary grade to the university, what was called "the Big Course" of "Political Science" taught by trained Communist teachers, which all teachers as well as all students were required to attend. Small study groups were formed to discuss and analyze the contents of the Big Course, and to apply them to the personal and professional thinking and conduct of every member of each group.

Many university professors of national and international reputation, such as Feng Yu-lan and Ch'ien Tuan-sheng, were sent to the interior rural areas to participate in "land reform." This was a part of the Thought Reform program, and its purpose, as Feng Yu-lan has vividly described in his report, was to make those intellectuals go through the actual practices and the mental and emotional experiences of confiscation, by force, of land and farming implements from the small landlords and of their redistribution to the landless. When they were participating in these "reforms" in the interior, they had also to undergo the new experience of being subjected to the questioning and criticism of self-criticism by the local party agents and the masses. Professor Ch'ien Tuan-sheng testifies that this questioning and criticism in the rural areas was the most effective method he had ever experienced in his own ideological re-education. This relatively long period from early 1949 to the fall of 1951 was the First Stage of Thought Reform.

The Communist Party and Government had by this time secured control over all institutions of higher learning, including the Catholic and Protestant universities and the Rockefeller-founded Peiping Union Medical College. Party organizations were formed in all colleges and universities, of which there were twenty-four in the Peiping and Tientsin area alone. Representatives of the Party sat in the administrative committees of all these institutions.

But the few older universities—notably Peita and Tsing Hua—were internally still more or less intact, and because of their academic standing and

national prestige and because of their long tradition of political independence, were still capable of putting up a measure of resistance to the interference and control of the Party representatives in their institutions. They were
twice successful in actually resisting the Communist Government's program
for a thorough reorganization and regrouping of the universities and a thorough revision of the university curriculum in the direction of lowering standards and shortening the years of study.

Under the government program of university reorganization, there were
only two types of university: (1) the comprehensive university which is to be
confined to the Humanities, the physical sciences, and the social sciences
including law; and 2) the technical university, either of Technology or of
Medicine, or of Agriculture. Peking University, for example, was to merge
with Yenching University and form a comprehensive university by giving up
its colleges of Medicine and Engineering; and Tsing Hua was to give up its
colleges of Letters and Social Science and become a University of Technology. Opposition from the two universities was so strong that the Communist
vice-minister of education had to make a verbal promise that those two universities were not to be included in the scheme of reorganization, and the
whole program was postponed for many months. (See the published 1952
confessions of Dean Chou P'ei-yuan and other professors of Tsing Hua, and
of Professor Shen Shih-hua of Peita's College of Engineering.)

But the really important issue at stake was the universities' resistance to
Party control. I quote this revealing paragraph from Dean Chou P'ei-yuan's
confession published in the *Kuangming jihpao* on April 8, 1952, when the
struggle was all over:

> My understanding of the (Communist) Party organization inside the univer-
> sity was also quite wrong. I have been using the "professional standards" of
> the bourgeois class to judge the Party comrades, whom I regarded as too
> young and professionally beneath my standards. I have therefore subjectively
> and erroneously concluded that they were not to play an important role in
> matters concerning university teaching and administration. During all these
> past three years, I have ignored the importance of all ideological leadership of
> the Party in the university, and never consulted the Party organization in all
> important questions of university administration.

This resistance to Party control was to intolerable and must be crushed at
all cost. The leading universities, and Peita and Tsing Hua in particular,

therefore, must be beaten, humiliated, and forced to surrender whatever spirit of independence was left in them. This, as all the 1952 confessions undoubtedly indicate, was the real motive and the real cause for the launching of the big-scale campaign of Thought Reform which began in the last week of September 1951.

This Second Stage of Thought Reform was called "the Study Movement of the Teachers of all Schools of Higher Learning in the Peking and Tientsin Area." It included all the twenty-four universities and colleges and all the scientific research institutes in that area. Three thousand teachers took part in the beginning, and the number grew to 6,188 in November, and to 6,523 in early December.

The press frankly reported that "this study movement for ideological reform was not only to lay the foundation for a systematic and long-term study of Marxism-Leninism and Mao Tse-tung thought, but also to serve as the primary condition for the reform of higher education." The heads of the universities were ordered to set the example of self-criticism by making frank and self-debasing confessions. The students in these institutions were mobilized to bring pressure on the teachers by cheering and welcoming them in their "voluntary" effort to study and reform.

The study meetings were soon directed to concentrate on one big question: Whom do we serve? And against whom do we fight? The answer was: Of course we serve the people and fight our enemy. Who are our enemies? Our enemies are the imperialistic USA and all those reactionaries who have been poisoning the people with thoughts and ideas of American or Western origin.

So the teachers who had had the misfortune of an American education had to make solemn confession of their past errors of worship of America and love for America, and solemnly pledge henceforth to despise and hate America. The sole exception was Professor P'an Kuang-tan of Tsing Hua, who confessed that, while [he] had never been guilty of worshiping America, he could not yet have the heart to hate America.

And the professors of Peking University had to hold many meetings to accuse and repudiate Hu Shih; those of Tsing Hua University, to accuse and repudiate Mei Yi-ch'i (Y. C. Mei); and those of Nankai University, to accuse and repudiate Chang Foling. But the arch-reactionary of them all was Hu Shih, who is said to have spread the poisonous thoughts of individualism, liberalism, and reformism (that is, meliorism as opposed to revolutionism) for over thirty years and whose evil influence is said to be still deep-rooted in the country. So the campaign to "accuse Hu Shih and criticize ourselves" was extended to Shanghai in early December 1951, and to South China in the last days of the year.

But all this was not enough. Loud professions of complete ideological reform, of hating and despising America, of declaring Hu Shih's thoughts as "enemy thoughts"—all this was not enough to bring about a complete breakdown of the spirit of independence in the leading universities, and to secure a complete political control of those institutions by the Party.

Therefore, there had to be a Third Stage in the campaign for Thought Reform—which came in the first months of 1952 in the form of the "3-anti" campaign and its speedy application to the universities.

The "3-anti" campaign was anticorruption, antiwaste, and antibureaucratism. All were declared criminal [and] charged under the Communist regime.

The students and the junior staff of the universities were quickly mobilized to expose all forms of corruption, waste, and bureaucratic practices in all the universities and colleges. Very little evidence of corruption was unearthed. Of bureaucratism, there was plenty: every sign of political independence, every word or gesture of intellectual arrogance toward the Party representative, every move of resistance to government policy of university reorganization or curriculum revision, was bureaucratism.

But the most spectacular exposures came under the charge of waste—waste of the People's money in the over-stockpiling of scientific laboratory equipment and materials, in the willful purchase of expensive foreign (especially American) equipment and materials when cheaper but equally serviceable homemade goods could have been substituted, and in the wasteful loss and destruction of these materials through faulty storage and careless handling. Of all these forms of waste, there was a vast amount of alleged evidence.

There was speedily organized a gigantic "Exhibition of the Anti-waste Campaign in the Peking Schools of Higher Learning," which was open to the public. The press reported that "on the basis of incomplete estimates made in ten leading universities alone (including Peita, Tsing Hua, Yenching University, the Normal University, the Catholic Fu Jen University, and the Peiping Union Medical College), the wasteful accumulation and careless destruction of equipment and materials has resulted in a total loss of money amounting to JMP $50,800,000,000! This sum of money is enough to buy 34 jet fighter planes! It is also enough to pay for the livelihood of the 1002 university professors in the whole area of Peking for four years and five months!" All these are great crimes against the People.

So the Party comrades got the goods on the professors and the administrators of the universities. The universities were loudly criticized and publicly condemned. A *Kuangming jihpao* reporter thus described the plight at Tsing Hua University:

> During the "3-anti" war, after the entire student body had enthusiastically assisted their teachers in exposing the ugly faces of their bourgeois class ideologies, the vast majority of the professors were now able to see clearly the dirt and the poison in themselves, and have now begun to acknowledge the real danger of the whole ugly situation. In their meetings of criticism and self-criticism, very many professors were saying in tears, "My body is full of poisonous germs, and I only now wake up—as if from a dream!"

These humiliating and terrorizing reports of [the] official press (which, of course, no one dared to contradict or deny) give us ample hints of the enormity of the political pressure and the awful pressure of "the masses" as represented by the incited student body.

This third and political stage of Thought Reform by means of the "3-anti" campaign at last succeeded in crushing the spirit of political independence in the universities. "Not until the '3-anti Campaign' did I discover my real errors. . . . I now profoundly realize that my bureaucratism has made me a criminal against the People," so confessed Professor Liang Ssu-ch'eng, son of the great Liang Ch'i-ch'ao and head of the Architecture School at Tsing Hua, who had been one of the strongest opponents to the Communist Government's plan of university reorganization and revision curriculum. And Dean Chou P'ei-yuan of Tsing Hua, another leader in the opposition to the reorganization plan, was made to say, "The '3-anti Campaign' led by Chairman Mao has at last awakened me from a terrible nightmare. I now acknowledge that the Party is the leader in all our work, and that it is our most faithful and most loving friend. . . . Henceforth I shall resolutely obey the leadership of the Party, and shall closely rely upon the Party in carrying on my work." "I thank the Party, and I thank Chairman Mao. The Party has educated me and enabled me to see the light."

Thus was finally achieved the main and real objective of the entire campaign for the ideological reform of the intellectuals. The spirit of independence and resistance was apparently crushed not by Thought Reform—not by the "democratic methods of persuasion"—but by force and intimidation. At least all overt manifestations of that spirit disappeared. The Communist

Government's policy of university reorganization and curriculum revision was carried out last summer in all Red China. It met no opposition from any quarter.

• • •

How far has the Communist Party and Government succeeded in washing or changing the brains of the Chinese intellectuals?

Some intellectuals were apparently capable of achieving an easy and quick success in thought reform. Such was the case of Professor P'ei Wen-chung, the geologist and paleontologist who attained world fame as the first discoverer of the Peking Man. In an eloquent confession published three years ago, he proudly proclaimed that he had readily completed his thought reform in being able to successfully apply Marxism-Leninism to all three sciences in which he was a worker, namely geology, paleontology, and archaeology. His confession was prominently given the first place in a volume of earliest confessions published in 1950. He had attained [sic].

Other stubborn intellectuals, however, seemed to make very slow progress in this business. One of the outstanding examples of this type is Professor Chin Yueh-lin, the logician and philosopher of Tsing Hua University. In his most recent confession published on April 17, 1952, he tells us that he had been "studying" for thought reform ever since March and April 1949—exactly four years ago. By 1951, he still had made no great progress. So he was ordered to study Mao Tse-tung's essay "On Practice." "Then, by the spring of 1951," he tells us, "my thinking came near to a sudden change. . . . Two years of piecemeal understanding, culminating in the study of the Essay 'On Practice,' has made me recognize that dialectic materialism was in essence quite different from the old philosophies. The old philosophies are meta-physical and basically anti-scientific, whereas dialectic materialism is scientific philosophy: it emphatically is the truth."

And he goes on to confess, "In the 1951 discussions on the revision of university curriculum, I further recognized that the duty and function of the department of philosophy in a university was to train propaganda workers for Marxism-Leninism."

All these confessions of a "sudden change" or sudden awakening from a most rugged individualist should be considered successful "brainwashing" and even "brain-changing." Yet his Red Masters apparently were not satisfied. For he was made to go on "studying" long after his "sudden change" in the spring of 1951, and was still publishing more self-debasing criticisms during the "3-anti campaign" of 1952. And a report reached me last November that he was among the six intellectuals "purged" in that month.

Perhaps real brainwashing and real brain-changing are after all impossible tasks—miracles which could only be performed by some Infernal Judge of the Courts of Purgatory. Perhaps my former student Mao Tse-tung showed some real wisdom when in July 1949 he remarked parenthetically that "the influence of reactionaries at home and abroad . . . will continue to exist for a long time, and cannot be eliminated quickly."

CHAPTER 22

Introduction to Liu Shaw-tong's Out of Red China[1]

In the academic year of 1948–1949, Mr. Liu Shaw-tong, author of this book, was a fourth-year student at the National Peking University and working as a part-time clerk in one of the administrative offices of the university. When the Communists came in early 1949, he found himself without a job. "In order to live," he joined the Southbound Working Group (南下工作團). After a period of "study and learning," he was swept into the Red Army as a member of its vast propaganda machine—the New China News Agency. He marched with the southbound armies to the Wuhan cities (Wuchang, Han-kow, and Han-yang), where he was a member of the secretarial staff of the Political Training Department of the Fourth Field Army. After working under the Red regime for more than a year, he managed successfully to escape to Hong Kong in 1950.

After his own "liberation,"—Mr. Liu published his story in a series of sixty-one short articles, which were collected and republished in 1951 in a book under the title, *A Rebel of Red China*. The book was well received in Free China and in Hong Kong and has gone through several editions.

My young friend Mr. Jack Chia, of Fordham University, in co-operation with Mr. Henry Walter, has now made a free translation of the major portion of the book. He has edited and rearranged the original articles into twenty chapters grouped under four main sections. Some of the episodes have been somewhat freely embellished in the translation. Mr. Chia's rearranging and free translation has made Mr. Liu's book more readable. But, on the whole,

---

1. *Out of Red China* (New York: Duell, Sloan and Pearce; Boston: Little, Brown, 1953) was translated from Liu Shaw-tong's 劉紹唐 *Hongse Zhongguo de pantu* 紅色中國的叛徒 (A rebel of Red China) (Taipei: Zhongyang wenwu gongying she, 1951).

this English version is a fair and faithful presentation of this interesting and informative book to the outside world.

Mr. Liu is a young man who calls himself "a liberal with years of liberal education." His book is essentially a story of his personal experiences under, and mental reactions against, a totalitarian politico-military machine. Some of the episodes told in the book—such as the story of the independent editor Hsiao Chün, and the dramatic story of the regiment commander who rode back home, without official leave, to pay a surprise visit to his family, only to witness his aged father being publicly tried and put to death by a mob—were not events of his own experience or observation. But they were stories widely publicized by the Party.

It seems to me that the most interesting and valuable parts of the book are the numerous small details which the author has set down about the methods of "study and learning," about the People's newspapers and the People's correspondents, about the many "long-time comrades" being softened and corrupted by the life in the big cities, about the strife and intrigue in "paradise," about the crudity, the paucity and the utter emptiness of the People's propaganda, and about the gradual and widespread disillusionment of the youthful recruits in the "Revolution."

The reader should bear in mind that Mr. Liu was writing about the years 1949–1950—a time usually described as the Honeymoon Period when the Chinese Communists were completing their military conquest of mainland China. The disillusionment of the younger generation had already begun. Our author told us how his decision to escape was strengthened by what he saw in the girl Yangyang, whom persecution and cruel punishment had driven into insanity, but whose thoughts during her six months of "reform through labor" had completely failed to change.

As one of the characters in the early part of the book has remarked, "To reform an educated person is a lifetime job." Our young author saw what was coming. He saw that the Red net was tightening around him, and he escaped before the beginning of the nation-wide Movement of Thought Reconstruction, of "brain-washing," and long before the truly terroristic "3-anti" and "5-anti" persecutions of 1952.

Let us see what has been achieved in "brain-washing" in Communist China, in the last two years, since the escape of our author.

Out of the four volumes of *Selected Papers of Thought Reconstruction* (*Ssu-hsiang kai-tsao wen-hsüan*) published by Communist China, I want to quote a part of a paragraph from Professor Chin Yo-lin's latest confession (originally printed in the *Kuang-ming Daily* of Peking, April 17, 1952):

> What I have gained through two years of Study and Learning, was now converging in the result of my study of the *Essay on Practical Conduct* [by Mao Tse-tung]. It has made me realize that . . . dialectic materialism is scientific philosophy: it is actually the truth. . . . And . . . I have come to recognize that the duty of a Department of Philosophy in a university is essentially to train the propaganda workers for Marxism-Leninism.

Have Mao Tse-tung and his regime now succeeded in achieving the impossible task of successfully washing the brain of this most rugged individualistic Chinese philosopher? Or shall we pray to the gods that such a self-humiliating confession of faith may spare our professor from attending more meetings of Study and Learning?

CHAPTER 23

Introduction to John Leighton Stuart's
Fifty Years in China[1]

John Leighton Stuart, who was born and brought up in Hang-chow, China, where both his father and mother were leading missionaries, tells us that in his boyhood he always had "an aversion for missionary life." Even after his graduation from Hampden-Sydney College, he still confessed his "lack of enthusiasm for missionary service."

> It is difficult to exaggerate the aversion I had developed against going to China as a missionary, . . . haranguing crowds of idle, curious people in street chapels or temple fairs, selling tracts for almost nothing, being regarded with amused or angry contempt by the native population, physical discomforts or hardships, etc., no chance for intellectual or studious interests, a sort of living death or modem equivalent for retirement from the world.

But, after prolonged inner struggle, Dr. Stuart finally decided "to put my religious belief to what was for me then the ultimate test." He became a missionary to China and, as such, lived and worked in China for nearly half a century!

It was his good fortune that he did not have to remain an evangelistic missionary for more than two years. He was called to teach in the newly founded Theological Seminary at Nanking, where he soon distinguished himself as a teacher of the New Testament and of New Testament Greek. After eleven years in Nanking, he was invited to Peking to undertake the

---

1. The introduction to John Leighton Stuart's *Fifty Years in China* (New York: Random House, 1954), xi–xx.

great work of organizing a group of "little missionary colleges"—the Huei Wen University, the North China Union College, and later the North China Union Women's College—into a great union university.

Thus for nearly forty years he worked as a successful "educational missionary." And he confesses to us: "Whether or not I could have spent my life happily and successfully as a typical evangelistic missionary is a question about which I have more than once whimsically speculated."

In these memoirs he pays a hearty tribute to "the earnestness, high purpose, untiring efforts and unselfish devotion . . . of missionaries as a class." But, as a Chinese reader, I do hope that Dr. Stuart's frank records of his early impressions of the evangelistic missionary, of his long years of strong aversion against such life and work, of his mature judgment of the crude methods of the evangelistic missions in seeking, however unconsciously, numerical increase of converts and church membership—these records, I do hope, will not be lightly ignored by future leaders of Christian churches and mission boards when they have occasion to rethink the question of foreign missions.

Historically, the influence of the educational missionary—whether he be an astronomer or mathematician from the Society of Jesus in the sixteenth or seventeenth century, or a learned scientist, scholar or physician from a Protestant Mission in the nineteenth century—has always been greater and more lasting and far-reaching than that of the evangelistic missionary of whatever church or denomination. It was said of Robert Morrison, the first Protestant missionary in China, that after twenty-seven years in the East he had baptized only ten Chinese converts. But what a lasting influence Morrison's scholarly work—his Chinese translation of the Bible, his Chinese dictionary, and his first Chinese printing press with modern metal movable type—left on the entire Protestant missionary world in the East! Indeed, Robert Morrison inaugurated in China that one great century of illustrious Protestant missionary educators—the century of Alexander Wylie, Joseph Edkins, Alexander Williamson, S. Wells Williams, Young J. Allen, Calvin W. Mateer, W. A. P. Martin, John Fryer, Timothy Richard and a host of others equally deserving to be remembered. It was that galaxy of scholarly missionaries who, overcoming tremendous difficulties of language and culture, translated into Chinese the best works of contemporary Western science, technology, law and international law, and the geography and history of the modern world, as well as the religious literature of the Christian faith; and who, by preaching against such native customs as foot-binding and neglect of women's education, by advocating social, educational, and even political reforms, and by founding new schools and colleges, did so much in bringing about a gradual awakening in China.

Dr. Stuart will undoubtedly be remembered as one of the great representatives of that historic line of educational missionaries in China.

He came back to China in 1904, six years after the Reform Movement of 1898 and eight years before the founding of the Chinese Republic. China was at long last being aroused from her medieval slumbers. When he was called to Peking in 1919, it was already the eve of the Chinese intellectual renaissance and nationalistic revolution. The National Peking University was becoming, in the words of Dr. Stuart, "the intellectual dynamo of the nation." The Tsing Hua College, next-door neighbor to the future Yenching University, was soon to develop into one of the best and most influential national universities. The Peking Union Medical College was already being planned by the Rockefeller Foundation and was soon to rise up in that ancient capital as the most modern and best-equipped medical school and hospital in the entire Orient.

It was, therefore, not easy for the Christian missionary groups relying solely on the limited financial support of their home boards to hope to build up a real university at that late date and in Peking, the intellectual center of the nation.

Dr. Stuart's great achievement as the founder and builder of Yenching University must be judged against that background. "Dreams cost money," as he tells us. And his vivid descriptions of the successes and failures of the fund-raising campaign which he and Dr. Henry Winters Luce carried on for many years throughout the United States not only are valuable records but also often make the most interesting and most thrilling reading in this autobiography.

At last Yenching University became a dream that came true. As a friend and neighbor of Yenching who watched its growth with keen interest, I would like to say that Dr. Stuart's great success as a university builder lay chiefly in two directions. First, he and his colleagues planned and built up, literally from *scratch*, a full-sized university—the greatest of all the thirteen Christian colleges in China—with one of the most beautiful university campuses in the world. And, secondly, this university of his dreams became in the course of time more and more a Chinese university, which, with the help of the Harvard-Yenching Institute of Chinese Studies, was the first of all the Protestant missionary colleges to develop an excellent department of Chinese studies.

"Among many other advantages to Yenching," says Dr. Stuart, "the Harvard-Yenching Institute of Chinese Studies has enabled us—and through us several other Christian colleges in China—to develop Chinese studies fully up to the best standards of any purely Chinese institution."

I would like to pay a tribute to the Chinese scholars of Yenching, notably to Dr. William Hung (Hung Yeh), who deserves special credit for building up a very good Chinese library at Yenching, for editing and publishing the excellent *Yenching Journal* of *Chinese Studies* and that most useful series—the *Harvard-Yenching Sinological Index Series*.

Dr. Stuart's seventieth birthday was celebrated on June 24, 1946. Ten days later, he was urged by General George C. Marshall, Special Representative of President Truman in China, to serve as the American Ambassador to the Republic of China and to assist him in the work of the Marshall Mission. On July 10, President Truman sent his name to the United States Senate, where it was unanimously approved. Dr. Stuart's ambassadorship lasted six and a half years (July, 1946–December, 1952). In August, 1949, three months after the fall of Nanking to the Communists, he returned to the United States. In December, be had a severe stroke, and on December 11, 1952, President Truman accepted his resignation.

Dr. Stuart's memoirs of these years occupy nearly one half of the book and fall into two main parts: part one (Chapters 9–12) records the political and military events of the years 1946–49 and his own impressions and comments about those events; part two (Chapters 13–15) contains the thoughts and reflections on the Department of State's "White Paper" on *United States Relations with China*, on the tragedy of the loss of the Chinese mainland to World Communism, on his own life and life ideals, and finally on "what policy the United States should pursue in regard to China."

I must confess that I have found the chapters of part one (Chapters 9–12) rather oversimplified and often difficult to follow as a summary report of the enormously complex events from the early months of General Marshall's Mission to China down to the fall of the Nanking-Shanghai area to the Communists. For instance, here is what he says about the early months of the work of the Marshall Mission:

> I shall attempt in the light of subsequent events to reconstruct what happened in Chungking during and following the Political Consultative Conference called by the Chinese Government after General Marshall's arrival early in January. His personality and prestige and the lofty yet reasonable ideals

which had brought the delegates together created an atmosphere of good feeling and high endeavor which made possible the five resolutions which, if put into effect, would have ended the controversy, formed a coalition government on a democratic basis and led to a reorganization and training of troops on both sides under American advice . . .

What was the nature and object of the Marshall Mission? What was the Political Consultative Conference? What were the "five resolutions?" What was the "controversy" that would have ended if those resolutions had been put into effect? What was the form of the proposed "coalition government on a democratic basis?"

What was the proposed "reorganization and training of the troops on both sides under American advice?"

Dr. Stuart has given no full explanation for any one of these questions in the body of the text. However, to make the record more understandable for the reader, there is a selection of documents in the Appendix. These include:

The Directives of the Marshall Mission (December, 1945).
The Five Resolutions of the Political Consultative Conference (January 31, 1946).
The Statement by President Truman on U.S. Policy (December, 1946).
General Marshall's Personal Statement (January 7, 1947).

With the help of these documents, we can hope to understand the objectives of the Marshall Mission and, at least in part, of the ambassadorship of Dr. Stuart. In the light of subsequent events, we can also understand how difficult, and how inherently impossible, those objectives were. Such an understanding is necessary to a sympathetic appreciation of Dr. Stuart's personal reporting of the earnest endeavors and the heart-rending failures of the Marshall Mission and his own ambassadorship.

The objectives of the Marshall Mission were summed up in these directives as "the unification of China by peaceful, democratic methods . . . as soon as possible." Specifically, they were twofold:

First, "the United States is cognizant that the present National Government of China is a 'one-party government' and believes that peace, unity and democratic reform in China will be furthered if the basis of this Government is broadened to include other political elements in the country. Hence, the

United States strongly advocates that the national conference of representatives of major political elements in the country agree upon arrangements which will give those elements a fair and effective representation in the Chinese National Government."

And secondly, "the existence of autonomous armies such as that of the Communist army is inconsistent with, and actually makes impossible, political unity in China. With the institution of a broadly representative government, autonomous armies should be eliminated as such and all armed forces in China integrated effectively into the Chinese National Army."

The first objective was to cause the Chinese to form a coalition government with the Chinese Communists fairly and effectively represented; the second was to cause them to "eliminate" the autonomous armies of the Chinese Communist Party and "integrate" them into the National Army.

As Secretary of State Byrnes states in one of the directives:

This problem is not an easy one . . . *It will not be solved by the Chinese themselves.* To the extent that our influence is a factor, success will depend upon our capacity to exercise that influence in the light of shifting conditions in such a way as to encourage concessions by the Central Government, by the so-called Communists, and by the other factions. The President has asked General Marshall to go to China as his Special Representative for the purpose of bringing to bear in an appropriate and practicable manner the influence of the United States for the achievement of the ends set forth above. (*Italics mine.*)

Such was the inherently impossible dual task of the Marshall Mission. The Chinese Communists wanted to get into a coalition government: that was the Yalta formula deviously devised by Stalin for Poland and for all "Liberated Europe"; that was what Mao Tse-tung openly demanded on April 24, 1945, in his fifty-thousand-word report to the Seventh Congress of the Chinese Communist Party held in Yenan—a report entitled "On Coalition Government." But they had absolutely no intention of having their autonomous armies "eliminated" or "integrated" into the National Army: on the contrary, the Communist Army, which Mao Tse-tung on April 24, 1945, claimed to number 910,000 men in regular units and 2,200,000 men in the "people's militia force," was expanding during the first six months of General Marshall's stay in China into 1,200,000 men in its regular formations.

And what were to be the ways and means by which the Marshall Mission was to "bring to bear the influence of the United States for the achievement of the ends set forth above"? President Truman directed General Marshall:

> In your conversations with Chiang Kai-shek and other Chinese leaders you are authorized to speak with the utmost frankness. Particularly, you may state, in connection with the Chinese desire for credits, technical assistance in the economic field, and military assistance, . . . that a China disunited and torn by civil strife could not be considered realistically as a proper place for American assistance.

In plain language, the weapon was to be not military pressure or intervention, but the withholding of American aid to China.

But this weapon could only checkmate the Chinese Government and had no effect whatever on the Chinese Communists, whose armies had been racing by land and by sea to Manchuria where they could obtain unlimited aid from the Soviet Occupation Forces and from the Soviet Union, now the contiguous, strongest base of revolution for the Chinese Communists. So, during the entire period of the Marshall Mission, the Chinese Communist delegation was constantly and successfully pressing General Marshall to stop or suspend American aid to China! And General Marshall and the United States Government did many times stop and suspend all American aid to China because of the loud protests of the Chinese Communists.

So the Marshall Mission failed because of its inherently impossible objectives, which neither Secretary Byrnes, nor President Truman, nor General Marshall, nor Mr. John Carter Vincent (who more than anyone else was largely responsible for drafting the Marshall directives) ever fully understood.

And the ambassadorship of Dr. Stuart failed too, because, in his own words, he was "a tyro in diplomacy"; and because, again in his own words:

> General Marshall had originally brought me into his efforts to form a coalition government because of my reputation as a liberal American, friendly to the Chinese people as a whole, and with no pronounced sympathy for any one faction or school of thought. This included the Communists, several of whose leaders I had known fairly well.

All these seemingly harsh words I have said without the slightest intention of ridiculing the naiveté of those idealistic statesmen of an idealistic age. In fact I, too, was just as naive a tyro in national and international politics in those days of expansive idealism. So naive, indeed, was I that shortly after V-J Day I sent a lengthy radiogram to Chungking to be forwarded to my former student Mao Tse-tung, solemnly and earnestly pleading with him that, now that Japan had surrendered, there was no more justification for the Chinese Communists to continue to maintain a huge private army, and that his Party should now emulate the good example of the British Labor Party which, without a single soldier of its own, had just won an overwhelming victory at the recent election and acquired undisputed political power for the next five years. On August 28, 1945, Mao Tse-tung arrived at Chungking accompanied by the American Ambassador, General Patrick Hurley, another tyro in diplomacy, and my Chungking friend radioed me that my message had been duly forwarded to Mr. Mao in person. Of course, to this day I have never received a reply.

In conclusion, I want sincerely to voice my hearty agreement with the reflections of my old friend Dr. Stuart on the China "White Paper" and on what policy his great country should pursue in regard to China. And, since this is an introduction written by an unreconstructed, heathen Chinese to a book of memoirs by a great Christian leader, I would like to conclude with a quotation from his beloved New Testament. When in 1949 I read Secretary Dean Acheson's Letter of Transmittal of the China "White Paper" and came to these sentences: ". . . the ominous result of the civil war in China was beyond the control of the government of the United States. Nothing that this country did or could have done within the reasonable limits of its capabilities could have changed that result; nothing that was left undone by this country has contributed to it"—when I read those sentences, I wrote on the margin: "Matthew 27:24." This is the text:

> When Pilate saw that he could prevail nothing, but that a tumult was made, he took water, and washed his hands before the multitude, saying, I am innocent of the blood of this just man: see ye to it.

Because of the betrayal of China at Yalta, because of its withholding of effective aid to China at crucial times, and, above all, because of its great power and undisputed world leadership, the United States was not "innocent of the blood" of fallen China.

And I agree with Dr. Stuart that the least the United States can do to redeem itself is to continue in its refusal to recognize the Communist Government and continue to oppose admission of that government to China's place in the United Nations. That is at least in line with the great tradition of the historic Doctrine of Non-recognition upheld by Henry L. Stimson and Herbert Hoover and written into the Atlantic Charter by President Roosevelt and Prime Minister Churchill.

HU SHIH

HU SHIH, professor of Chinese philosophy and later of Chinese literature at the National Peking University, 1917-37; Dean of College of Letters at the same University, 1931-37; President of the same University, 1946-49. Chinese Ambassador to the United States, 1938-42. He is usually known as the founder of the Chinese literary renaissance which has brought about the recognition and general adoption of the living spoken tongue (*pai hua*) as the tool of literature and education in place of the dead classical Chinese.[2]

---

2. This author bio was included in the original document.

CHAPTER 24

Communist Propaganda and the Fall of China[1]

Analysis of the role of communist propaganda in the defeat of the Republic of China on the mainland may be made in terms of three general questions:

(1) What were the measures, if any, taken by the Chinese Government to restrain the spread of communist propaganda and agitation?
(2) Were the measures taken inadequate or ineffective? If so, why?
(3) Was the victory of the Chinese communists materially assisted by failure of these measures to restrain the spread of communist ideas and propaganda?

I

In general, the answer to the first question is that for 14 of its 26 years of conflict with the communists the Chinese Government under the Kuomintang (The Nationalist Party) did not take measures to restrain communist ideas and propaganda. Indeed, it could not possibly take such measures in these years, for it was cooperating with the Chinese communists—first during the period of Nationalist-Communist "Collaboration" (1923–1927), and ten years later during the period of the so-called "United Front" against Japan (1937–1947). It was only during the years when the Government was actively fighting the communists that measures could be and were taken to restrain and suppress the spread of communist agitation and propaganda.

---

1. *Columbia Law Review* 54, no. 5 (May 1954): 780–786. Hu Shih was introduced as "President-in-Exile, The Peking University" in the original document.

The Chinese Communist Party was founded in 1921, four years after the Bolshevik Revolution in Russia, at a time when many forward-looking people throughout the world cherished great hopes for the revolutionary regime in Russia. Dr. Sun Yat-sen, founder of the Chinese Revolution and father of the Chinese Republic, was especially impressed by the Russian success in reorganizing the army and re-unifying that vast country so quickly after the Revolution. In his desire to reform his own political party, the Kuomintang, into a "revolutionary party," and to build up a "revolutionary army" to overthrow the northern war-lords who had betrayed the original purposes of the Chinese Revolution of 1911–1912, Dr. Sun voluntarily invited the assistance and cooperation of the Communist International and of the Soviet Union. The trusting Sun Yat-sen made his party admit Chinese communists and even communists of other countries, supposedly on an *individual* basis, to membership in Kuomintang. Thus was begun in 1923 the four-year period of Nationalist-Communist "Collaboration," during which the Soviet Union in the name of the Comintern sent to Nationalist China all-out aid, not only in military materials, but, more significantly, in the form of political advisers like the astute Mikhail Borodin and military advisers like General Galen.

Stalin was directing the Comintern's China adventure throughout those years of collaboration, and there is no doubt that he was determined to make full use of this most extraordinary opportunity to carry out his strategy of world revolution in one of the most important strategic areas of the world—China.

The Chinese Communist Party rapidly increased its membership, captured one-third of the seats on the Central Committee of the Kuomintang, and by 1926 gained control of all the important government departments. Many communists became the Kuomintang party representatives in the army. The training centers in Moscow were sending back well-trained young organizers and propagandists to work in the party, the government and the army.

In short, the years 1923 to 1927 were the heyday of communist propaganda and agitation, sometimes very thinly disguised under Dr. Sun's "Three Principles"—Nationalism, Democracy and the People's Livelihood—but more often without any disguise at all. The Communist International was making serious efforts to convert the Chinese Nationalist Revolution into a communist revolution. This great conspiracy, called the "great Chinese Revolution" in most communist literature, might have succeeded if Chiang Kai-shek and the elder statesmen of the Kuomintang had not thwarted and destroyed it in April and May of 1927 by purging the Nationalist Party of the communists.

After 1927, the Chinese Communist Party was outlawed for nearly ten years during which time the National Government nearly unified China, gaining complete supremacy except for the armed rebellion of the communists and the Japanese invasion of Manchuria (1931), Jehol (1933), and North China (1935–1937).

When in 1937 China was forced to take up the desperate war against Japan, there began the period of the "United Front" (1937–1947), during which the Red Army was nominally incorporated into the National Army and leading communists sat as members of the People's Political Council or served in the National Government. The basis of the "United Front" was supposed to be found in the "Manifesto on Unity" issued by the Central Committee of the Chinese Communist Party on September 22, 1937. In this manifesto, five principles were "solemnly declared," the third of which reads:

> The policy of resurrection which aims at the overthrow of the Kuomintang political power, the policy of land-confiscation, *and the policy of Communist propaganda*, shall be discontinued by the Chinese Communist Party. (Emphasis supplied.)

As a matter of historical fact, under the protection of the "United Front" the Chinese communists were carrying on a powerful propaganda offensive in China and abroad. Their party was once more an open and legal party with its official representative stationed in the war capital of Nationalist China. A number of communist leaders made full use of the forum of the People's Political Council to voice the grievances of the Party and to glorify the military and territorial expansion of the Party's communist armies. Chou En-lai, the official liaison officer between the Government and the Communist Party, was made Vice-Minister of the Political Training Board of the National Military Council. The Communist Party freely published its daily newspaper, *Hsin Hua Jih Pao* (New China Daily), in Chungking throughout the war years. Chinese communists moved freely among their Chinese and foreign friends, in and out of the foreign embassies and special missions, and among the foreign journalists and VIP's.

It was in those years of the "United Front" that the communists succeeded in creating abroad the myth that they were not communists at all, but mere "agrarian reformers," and that Nationalist China was "feudal

China" and communist China was to be more accurately described as "democratic China."

In short, this period of the "United Front" was another heyday for communist propaganda. By carefully playing on the gullibility of their foreign, and especially American, friends, they successfully planted in the minds of policy-making leaders of China's wartime allies what may now be termed the Yalta doctrine for all "liberated" countries: coalition government with full representation for the Communist Party. That was the Yalta formula for liberated Europe. That was the demand put forward by Mao Tse-tung at Yenan in April, 1945. That was the formula of the Presidential Directive for the Marshall Mission to China in December, 1945.

Such were the peculiar historical situations which gave the Chinese Communist Party the unique opportunity to carry on its propaganda freely and in the open for fully fourteen years. The Chinese Government could do little to restrain the propaganda work of an open and legal party with which it was at one time "collaborating" in a great revolution, and at a later time co-operating in a "United Front" against a common enemy.

II

During the years 1927–1937 and 1947–1949, however, the Chinese Government did promulgate measures for the curbing of communist propaganda. In most cases these measures were inadequate, partly because of circumstances peculiar to China and partly because of the conspiratorial nature of communist propaganda itself.

Chief among the circumstances impeding effective repression of communist propaganda was the existence of zones of immunity along the Chinese coast—the British colony of Hong Kong and the foreign concessions and settlements over which the Chinese Government had no control. Hong Kong and the foreign concessions in Shanghai, Canton, Amoy, Hankow, Tientsin and other "treaty ports" were the birthplaces of the free press in China. They were also the places where the Chinese rebel and political exile first found refuge and asylum. It was in those cities that the first anti-Manchu and anti-monarchy revolutionary periodicals and newspapers were edited and published and circulated into the interior provinces. It was in Shanghai that the Chinese Communist Party was organized and held its first Party Congress in 1921, and that the first communist papers were published. Dur-

ing the years when the Chinese Communist Party was outlawed in Nationalist China and when the foreign settlements and concessions were either partially restored to Chinese juridical control or, later, completely abolished,
there was still the British colony of Hong Kong where the British tradition of
the free press was maintained and where literature of the Chinese communists and their front organizations continued to be freely published.

It has been said that without Hong Kong and the foreign concessions
and settlements in the treaty ports the Chinese Revolution of 1911–1912
could not have succeeded so soon and so easily. It may be said with equal
justice that without these foreign zones of immunity the communists probably could not have had so easy a success in their early organization and in
the spread of their propaganda literature.

The second circumstance making it impossible for the Chinese Government to deal effectively with communist propaganda in many parts of China
was the fact that the Chinese Communist Party, ever since 1927, has had a
formidable army of its own. Before 1937, the Red Army of the Chinese Communist Party was many times defeated and nearly broken up and destroyed
by Chiang Kai-shek's forces. But even in those early years the Red Army over-
ran several provinces and often occupied mountainous areas for months and
sometimes years. The occupied areas were, of course, subject to communist
control and indoctrination.

After 1937, when the Red Armies were made a part of the National Army,
they were thereby given unlimited opportunity for numerical growth and
territorial expansion. In April, 1945, Mao Tse-tung claimed that the area "liberated" by communist armies "now extends from Inner Mongolia in the
north to the Hainan Island in the south, penetrating into 19 provinces and
containing 95,500,000 people." These figures may not reflect the actual
state of affairs, but the fact remains that in all regions where the communist
guerrilla forces penetrated with their propaganda and agitation, the laws
and regulations of the wartime National Government could no longer be
enforced.

These two factors—the existence on the China coast of Hong Kong and
the various foreign concessions and settlements, and the 22 years (1927–
1949) of Red Army activity—should help to explain the tremendous difficulties which the Chinese Government had to encounter in its attempts to
restrain the spread of communist propaganda.

But the fundamental difficulty in dealing with communist propaganda
lay in the clandestine and conspiratorial nature of the whole communist

movement. As stated in Thesis 13 of the Second World Congress of the Communist International, 1921:

> The Communist parties must create a new type of periodical press for extensive circulation among the workmen:
>
> 1) Legal publications, in which the Communists without calling themselves such and without mentioning their connection with the party, would learn to utilize the slightest possibility allowed by the laws as the Bolsheviki did at the time of the Tzar, after 1905.
> 2) Illegal sheets, although of the smallest dimensions and irregularly published, but reproduced in most of the printing offices by workmen (in secret . . .), and giving the proletariat undiluted revolutionary information and the revolutionary slogans.

What is contemplated, of course, is the publication of propaganda in the name of all kinds of front organizations formed "under the most diverse circumstances and, in case of need, frequently changing names"[2]—written and published by "Communists without calling themselves such and without mentioning their connection with the party." Against this kind of masked activity no measure of restraint, in China or in any other country, has ever been adequate or effective. In a country like the United States, of course, the Constitution prohibits restraints on the freedom of any publication issued in the name of freedom, peace, justice, humanity, democracy, race equality, and so forth. And even in a country like the Republic of China, where the Government had been fighting the communist armed rebellion for years, there were no adequate means to curb or suppress the mushroom growth of publications that sprang up "under the most diverse circumstances," under such names as the "New Learning," the "New Social Science" or the "New Sociology," and, more often, espousing the cause of patriotism or anti-imperialism.[3]

---

2. Second World Congress of the Communist International (1921), Thesis 12.

3. An example of the type of "legal publication" emanating from the front groups was a huge two-volume work, containing about seven hundred thousand Chinese words, entitled *A Critique of Hu Shih* (*Hu Shih P'i-p'an*), which appeared in 1933 and 1934. No government censor had the patience to wade through this supposedly academic discussion and none took the trouble to check the many quotations from certain foreign authors referred to merely as "K.M." and "F.E." These "authorities" were, of course, Marx and Engels, and the volumes were about 15 percent a critique of Hu Shih

III

We now reach the third question: was the victory of the communists assisted materially by insufficient restraint on the free exchange of ideas? Was that victory materially aided by the failure of the Chinese Government to curb the spread of communist propaganda and agitation?

Naturally communists and in particular the Chinese communists like to think that their successful conquest of continental China was a triumph of communist ideology. And I am afraid that there are at least a few politicians and military men in Free China today who believe that the failure to stop or to restrain the spread of communist and pro-communist propaganda did materially aid the communist victory on the mainland. But I have studied and thought over the question and have come to a different conclusion.

I believe that the communist conquest of China, like the communist conquest of the Eastern European states and Hitler's conquest of many free European nations 14 years ago, was primarily a military conquest, a conquest greatly assisted in this case by the cold war situation and aided materially by Soviet Russia, the consolidated base for world revolution and world conquest. It is now generally understood that the Russian strategy for world revolution and world conquest presupposes three necessary conditions: (1) a strong Communist Party in every country, preferably one armed with an army of its own; (2) a fully consolidated Soviet Russia as the base for the support and assistance of the revolution; and (3) a war situation, preferably a world war situation. In the case of the conquest of the Baltic states and the states in Eastern Europe, it was not even necessary to have all three conditions. There was no strong Communist Party in any of those states. All that was necessary was the overwhelming power of the Soviet Union coupled with the war situation which gave Russia the opportunity to use her power for conquest and for military occupation.

In China, all three conditions were required before she was defeated. To begin with, the Chinese Communist Party was fully armed for 22 years before the Chinese mainland was completely conquered. Even then, communism might never have succeeded in subjugating China if Japan's aggressive war and later the greatest war in human history had not intervened. Finally, World War II made Soviet Russia the greatest military power in Europe, and then in Asia. The secret Yalta agreement of early 1945 invited and bribed Russia to enter the

---

and about 85 percent a Marxist interpretation of Chinese history.

Pacific war, and Russia returned to the Far East as the greatest military power in the entire Asiatic continent. Yalta gave Russia the right to occupy Manchuria and North Korea, thereby supplying her with a contiguous base for supporting and assisting the Chinese communists.

In conclusion, then, the victory of the Chinese communists on the mainland was not the result of, nor materially assisted by, the failure of the Chinese Government to restrain the free flow and exchange of ideas. No. It was the military collapse of a nation worn out by eight long years of fighting a desperate war against one of the greatest military and naval powers in the world, and finally hopelessly defeated by a peculiar combination of all of the three fateful conditions necessary for the military victory of communism over a major power.

CHAPTER 25

How Free Is Formosa?[1]

One of China's most respected scholars declares that, contrary to the charges of Dr. K. C. Wu, freedoms have been gradually expanded on Chiang's island bastion.

Dr. Hu Shih, generally known as the founder of the Chinese literary renaissance, has devoted most of his life to research in the history of Chinese thought. Nevertheless, he was also "drafted" to serve as China's Ambassador to the United States from 1938 to 1942. Dr. Hu had been Professor of Chinese Philosophy and later of Chinese Literature at the National Peking University; after the war, he was named president of the university. A Chinese delegate to the San Francisco Conference and the London UNESCO Conference in 1945, he has always been one of China's most respected non-partisan spokesmen. He visited Formosa in 1952 and has recently returned from another extended visit.

RECENTLY, within a single month, there appeared two contradictory estimates of the state of freedom in Formosa. In the May 17 issue of the *Freeman*, we read these statements by Rodney Gilbert, who had just returned from three-and-a-half years' residence in Formosa:

> An inspection of Formosa today reveals that the eight or nine million Chinese now on the island are getting the best government that any part of China has had for many generations—the freest, most efficient and, yes, most honest. . . .
>
> As for common ordinary freedom of speech—unthinkable in any Communist country—nobody on Taiwan [Formosa] who has a critical word to say

---

1. This is an interview conducted by the *New Leader*, a political magazine issued in New York from 1924 to 2006. See *New Leader* 37, no. 33 (August 1954): 16–20.

about this or that Government person or policy ever has to give a thought to possible eavesdroppers. . . .

There is no censorship of news, incoming or outgoing. . . . Correspondents of all nationalities come and go without let or hindrance, and the resident correspondents of the Associated Press, United Press, Reuters, and the French Press Agency send out exactly what they please. . . .

Other freedoms . . . which are taken for granted in Free China are those of freedom of movement and freedom of choice of employment. It is no longer easy to get into Taiwan. . . . But once a person is legally on Taiwan and has a police card showing that he resides there, he can ride the railroads, the buses, the planes, or wander about by car, pedicab or on foot, as freely as though he were in Vermont, Kansas or Oregon. What is more, he can work at any job he can find, or just sit on a rock, looking out to sea, reciting poetry and reveling in *dolce far niente*.

Within four weeks, the newsstands were selling the June 29 issue of *Look*, which contained an article by Dr. K. C. Wu, Governor of Formosa from December 1949 to May 1953. The article was entitled "Your Money Has Built a Police State in Formosa," and had this to say:

Formosa has been perverted into a police state, not unlike that of Red China. . . .

The dictatorial moves [of General Chiang Ching-kuo, son of President Chiang Kai-shek] to establish a secret police and control of the Army, to rig elections and corrupt legal processes were only a start. Today, a program is under way to control the minds and souls of youth and suppress freedom of speech and of the press. . . .

He [Chiang Ching-kuo] is fast building a regime that in many ways follows exactly the pattern of a Communist government; he has even organized a Youth Corps modeled after the Hitler Youth and the Communist Youth. . . .

There is no such thing as freedom of speech any more. Freedom of the press has become a farce. . . . Newspapers that annoy or offend Formosa's rulers are forced to suspend publication, and reporters and writers have often been jailed. Formosa's newspapers now print only the party line.

Which of these two sets of judgments on Formosa are we to accept? My own answer is that Mr. Gilbert and Dr. Wu were referring to two different groups of phenomena. Mr. Gilbert was painting a general picture of the life and freedom of the "eight or nine million Chinese now on the island" of Formosa. He honestly admitted that there were important exceptions to this general description. For instance, he wrote: "You can talk yourself hoarse about the shortcomings of the municipal, provincial or national authorities and there will be no comeback. But start preaching Communism—and look out."

On the other hand, it was exactly those exceptions—those particular cases of criminal offenses which under the National Emergency Law were placed under the jurisdiction of military courts—which Dr. Wu utilized to build up his sweeping generalization about Formosa as a police state. This logical fallacy of generalizing from particular and exceptional cases assumes a more serious form of misstatement when he makes this categorical assertion:

> As Formosa had been declared under a state of siege, *all cases of any nature were sent to the military courts for trial.* (Italics mine.)

This statement is baseless and untrue. *At no time* since the Communist conquest of the mainland have the military courts of Formosa had jurisdiction over "all cases of any nature."

When Formosa was declared in early 1950 to be "a region adjacent to a battle zone," ten categories of crimes were placed under the jurisdiction of the military courts of the Taiwan Peace Preservation Force. These were: offenses against the internal security of the state; offenses against the external security of the state; offenses against public order; offenses against public safety; counterfeiting of currency and negotiable securities, and forging of official documents and seals; homicide; offenses against personal liberty; robbery and piracy; kidnaping for ransom; damage and destruction of property. All other criminal offenses were under the jurisdiction of civil courts.

In April 1951, when the "New Taiwan Currency," which had replaced the old currency in the summer of 1949, was threatened by inflation, the Government issued a series of Emergency Regulations on Currency Stabilization which gave authority to the military police and military courts of the Taiwan Peace Preservation Force to deal severely with three types of violation of the currency laws: illegal transmission of money abroad, illegal traffic in gold or foreign exchange, and high-interest money-lending through "underground banking."

These are all the categories of criminal offenses that were *ever* placed under the jurisdiction of the military courts of the Taiwan Peace Preservation Force, of which Governor Wu himself was Chief Commander and General Peng Meng-chi was Deputy Commander. Military courts of the Army, Navy and Air Force and other military establishments had no jurisdiction over crimes committed by persons not in active military service.

As a result of public dissatisfaction and criticism of the incompetence and inefficiency of the military courts, and of known abuses of power by the military police, the Central Government, under the leadership of Premier Chen Cheng, moved toward reducing the jurisdiction of the military courts. A decree of the Executive Yuan on October 20, 1951 restored four of the original ten categories of offenses to the jurisdiction of the civil courts. A second decree on June 1, 1952 ordered that the jurisdiction of the military courts be henceforth limited to:

1. Offenses by military personnel.
2. Offenses under the Act on Communist Agents and the Law on Insurrection and Treason.
3. Offenses under the Law on Banditry.
4. Civilians conspiring with military personnel in smuggling.
5. Grave offenses (subsequently defined by the Ministry of Justice in minute detail) against public order and public safety.

Since June 1, 1951, "offenses against currency stabilization" had been removed from the jurisdiction of the military police and military courts.

These successive reform measures represented partial success for the movement "for the separation of the jurisdiction of the military and civil courts," a movement in which many Chinese leaders, both inside and outside the Government, have taken an active part. It is a part of the fight for civil liberties and constitutional government in Free China.

The success has been only partial, and the fight is still going on. Last month, the new Premier, O. K. Yui, was severely questioned in Parliament (the Legislative Yuan) about the constitutional guarantees in times of national emergency, especially the right of *habeas corpus* under Article 8, and Article 9 which says that "No person, except those in active military service, may be subject to trial by a military court." At the end of the session, Premier Yui declared:

270 POWER OF FREEDOM

The new Cabinet will see to it that the constitutional guarantees of freedom of person under Article 8 and civil-court trials of non-military personnel under Article 9 are upheld.

In discussing this question of the jurisdiction of military courts, I have gone into some detail, not only to refute the irresponsible generalization of Dr. Wu that "all cases of any nature were sent to the military courts for trial," but also to correct the impression created by many of his statements—the impression that Formosa was "actually" achieving "the rule of law and democracy . . . *at one time in the past*," but only recently "has been perverted into a police state," especially since Dr. Wu's resignation from the Governorship.

The fact is that Formosa was far from the rule of law and democracy in those early years of 1949–1951, at the height of the fear of Communist invasion and infiltration and of the dangers of currency inflation, and only in the last three years, and notably since June 1952, has there been a far greater measure of civil liberties and the rule of law than at any time in the past.

Let me cite an example of the present state of freedom of the press on Formosa a year after Governor Wu's resignation. The April 1 issue of the fortnightly magazine *Free China* editorially questioned President Chiang Kai-shek's power of reviewing the decisions of the military courts and, in some cases, ordering an increase in the severity of the sentence.

"The Constitution," says the editorial, "under Article 40 gives the President only the power of 'granting amnesties, pardons, remission of sentences, and restitution of civil rights.' But the Constitution nowhere gives him power to increase the sentence of any court. What the President has done on a number of occasions is clearly a violation of the Constitution. One of our best wishes on his re-election is that no unconstitutional act of this kind will ever happen again during his second Presidential term of six years."

No such open criticism of President Chiang was published at any time in the past. I may add that the same question, among others, was earnestly discussed early last April at the home of Vice President-elect Chen Cheng in three evening sessions participated in by six invited members of the National Assembly and about 20 leaders of the Government and the Kuomintang, including General Chiang Ching-kuo. I am happy to report that President Chiang Kai-shek has now given written instructions to his new Secretary-General, Chang Chun, that in the future, when the military tribunal requests him as Commander-in-Chief of the armed forces to review the graver sentences of the military courts, he will never again order any increase in the sentences.

Dr. Wu will probably retort that the freedom of *Free China* magazine has always been an "exception." He has said in his *Look* article:

> There is no such thing as freedom of speech any more. Freedom of the press has become a farce. There may be an exception in the case of a weekly [*sic*]{ sponsored by Dr. Hu Shih, the philosopher and diplomat, with his special eminence and international reputation.

The "weekly" he referred to is the fortnightly *Free China*, edited and published by a score of my liberal friends (including a few independent members of the Kuomintang), who, because I wrote the Principles of Faith of the *Free China* Association, honored me by making me its "publisher" from 1949 to 1953.

I want to say, in the first place, that *Free China* is not an exception, and that this freedom of speech and the press is now shared by all who have the moral courage to speak out. The best proof of this is found in the numerous critical articles on the May elections published in many independent newspapers both before and after the elections.

Secondly, I would like to ask: How and why did the "weekly sponsored by Dr. Hu Shih" come to enjoy what to Dr. Wu was an "exceptional" freedom of the press in the "police state" of Formosa? Has he ever known of a "police state" that permitted "exceptional" freedom of speech and the press to any individual or publication?

Free China magazine certainly did not enjoy any such "exceptional" freedom in the summer of 1951, when it got into serious trouble with the Taiwan Peace Preservation Force by publishing an editorial entitled "The Government Must Not Entrap the People to Commit Crimes." The editorial had pointed out the inherent danger of the Government policy of offering heavy monetary rewards—30 per cent of the confiscated property of the convicted offender to the "informer" and 35 per cent to the prosecuting agency—in offenses under the Emergency Regulations on Currency Stabilization. It cited a recent case of high-interest money-lending in which $1.1 million of local currency was involved and more than twenty money-lenders were arrested by the Peace Preservation police and sent to military courts for trial. The editorial asked:

Why were only the lenders, and not the borrowers, named in the prosecution? Could it not be that the borrowers were themselves the informers who enticed and entrapped the innocent victims into criminal offenses? . . . Could it not be that the Government, by its offer of over-attractive monetary rewards, was guilty of entrapping the people to commit crimes?

This editorial so greatly enraged Governor Wu's Deputy Commander of the Taiwan Peace Preservation Force that he threatened to arrest the editor of *Free China*. After mediation by mutual friends in the Government, the editor was forced to print an editorial in its June 16 issue, stating that the previous editorial had implied no intentional insult to the moral integrity of the Government agencies prosecuting the case discussed.

Apparently, in June 1951 neither Dr. Wu, the "democratic" Governor and Commander of the Taiwan Peace Preservation Force, nor the "special eminence and international reputation" of the absentee publisher of *Free China* afforded any protection to that magazine.

Three months later, *Free China* got into more trouble. On September 1, 1951, it published on its editorial page a letter written by myself from New York, requesting that the words "Publisher: Hu Shih" be dropped from its back cover. I said in part:

I was led to ponder: If *Free China* could not enjoy freedom of speech and publication, if it were denied the right of responsible criticism of Government policy, that would be the greatest disgrace in the political life of Taiwan.

I formally resign from the titular honor of being the publisher of *Free China* magazine, partly because I want to express my 100-per-cent approval of the editorial entitled "The Government Must Not Entrap the People to Commit Crimes," and partly because I want to voice my protest against such interference with the freedom of the press by any military organ.

Again, neither "democratic" Governor Wu nor the "special eminence" of Dr. Hu Shih could afford any protection to the magazine. The Taiwan Peace Preservation head-quarters took the unusual action of buying up all the available copies of *Free China* at the newsstands, and ordered the Northwest Airlines not to carry the issue out of the island.

Then Premier Chen Cheng intervened. In a letter which he wrote me on September 14 and sent to *Free China* magazine to be published in its September 15 issue, the Premier thanked me for my outspoken words, which "we accept with gladness." While defending the urgent need for drastic measures to protect the new currency, he admitted unintentional mistakes in their enforcement. His letter concluded with an assurance that there would always be freedom of the press on Formosa, which, he said, was evidenced by the publication of my letter in *Free China* magazine.

Thus, if the "weekly sponsored by Dr. Hu Shih" has in any sense enjoyed some exceptional freedom in Formosa, it has earned it by fighting five long years and winning it—winning it not only for itself, but for all Formosa papers and for all the non-Communist and anti-Communist papers of Hong Kong which come into Taiwan every day by air transport. Its existence and its influence eloquently refute K. C. Wu's charge that Formosa is a police state. The battle for freedom and democracy has never been fought and won by craven, selfish politicians who remain silent while they enjoy political power, and then, when out of power and safely out of the country, smear their own country and government, for whose every mistake or misdeed they themselves cannot escape a just measure of moral responsibility.

I cannot conclude this discussion without answering a few questions I have been asked ever since Dr. Wu started his smear-Formosa campaign.

HOW ABOUT THE FREE ELECTIONS WHICH GOVERNOR WU
CLAIMS TO HAVE INITIATED IN FORMOSA AND WHICH HE SAYS
ARE NO LONGER FREE?

In December 1952, I watched the local elections in the eastern coastal and partially aboriginal district of Taitung, and I was greatly impressed by the extraordinarily high percentage of voters of both sexes who came to the polls. It was to be expected that the Kuomintang, the powerful Government party, had great advantages over the minor parties and those candidates with no party affiliations. But, because of the very high literacy of the Taiwan population and because the secret ballot is always the most effective weapon of democratic control, the elections have been and still are quite free.

In the recent May 2 elections, the Kuomintang candidate for Mayor in the capital city of Taipei, on whose election the party had staked all its great power and influence, was overwhelmingly defeated by a non-party candidate. The same was true of the central-west district of Chia-yi, where the Kuomintang candidate for magistrate was badly defeated by a candidate with no affiliation to any political party. After the elections, many newspapers, including the *New York Times* and the *Hong Kong Times*, editorially commented on the defeat of the Kuomintang candidates at Taipei and Chia-yi as the best evidence that elections in Formosa are free.

WHAT DO YOU THINK OF GENERAL CHIANG CHING-KUO, SON OF PRESIDENT CHIANG, WHOM DR. WU REGARDS AS THE "HEIR AND SUCCESSOR" OF THE GIMO?

I have known Chiang Ching-kuo for many years. He is a very hard-working man, conscientious and courteous, patriotic and intensely anti-Communist. His intellectual outlook is rather limited, largely because of his long years in the Soviet Union. Like his father, he is free from corruption and therefore not free from self-righteousness (again not unlike his father). He honestly believes that the most effective way in dealing with the Communists is to be as ruthless with them as they are with anyone opposing them.

While I strongly disagree with Chiang Ching-kuo's methods in dealing with Communists and suspected Communists (and I said so publicly on the first day of my arrival on Formosa in 1952), I have grave doubts about the mental state of anyone who says: "Who can guarantee that, in the event of the Gimo's death and an attractive offer from Peking, he [Chiang Ching-kuo] may not turn Formosa into a rich province of Red China?" In any case, there is no possibility of his being "the heir and successor" of President Chiang. Politically, he has no place in the Government and plays no important role. His exact position is that of a faithful factotum to his father. He is not popular with the armed forces, and there is absolutely no constitutional or organizational channel through which he can become his father's heir and successor.

HOW ABOUT THE YOUTH CORPS WHICH YOUNG CHIANG HAS ORGANIZED IN FORMOSA AND WHICH, ACCORDING TO DR. WU, IS "MODELED AFTER THE HITLER YOUTH AND THE COMMUNIST YOUTH"?

Here is a perfect example of Dr. Wu's methods. Listen to his own description of the Youth Corps: "Then Ching-kuo organized his Youth Corps. He ordered all superintendents, professors and teachers to become officers and all students enrolled as members. We now have a Red version of the *Hitler Jugend*."

Have you ever known a Hitler or a Stalin so stupid as to enroll *all* students in his youth corps, and to order *all* superintendents, professors and teachers to become their officers? Was K. C. Wu really so ignorant? Or was he trying to deceive the public?

When the so-called "Young Men's Corps of Anti-Communism and National Salvation" was first organized in 1952 (apparently with the loud approval of Governor Wu), one of the wisest educators in Taipei remarked to me:

> When they take in *all* students as members and *all* teachers as their officers, it means there is no secret organization, and no secret training and indoctrination will be possible. They are merely wasting more money and more of the students' precious time to have another parading and slogan-shouting organization to be added to the New Year's Day parade!

That is what Dr. Wu calls "a Red version of the *Hitler Jugend*" on Formosa.

May I conclude by quoting the wise observation of Rodney Gilbert: "The very fact that there is public objection, and chance of change, is part of Formosa's pattern of freedom."

CHAPTER 26

The Right to Doubt in Ancient Chinese Thought[1]

The late Professor Carl Becker of Cornell University once told me that he had on the door of his office this quotation from the Confucian *Analects* (論語): "Hui gives me no assistance. There is nothing that I say which does not please him."

Hui was Yen Hui (顏回), the most gifted student of Confucius. The Master on many occasions had no hesitation in regarding Yen Hui as his best student. Yet, he had this one grievance against him: Yen Hui was pleased with everything the Master said—and never questioned or doubted what he said. Therefore, said Confucius, "Hui gives me no assistance." Becker was so impressed by this passage that he had it posted on the door of his office for all his students to read.

What Confucius expected of his favorite students was the exercise of the right to doubt, to question, and not to be pleased or satisfied with whatever a great master or authority might say. Confucius himself fully exemplified this right to doubt in his teaching. On several occasions, he expressed satisfaction that his students were able to "come back" at him and to "stir me up."

One of the burning questions of the time was the religious question as to whether dead people had knowledge and feelings. The basic idea underlying the ancient rites of burying expensive utensils and even living human beings with the dead was the belief that a man might retain knowledge and feelings after death. Confucius and his school were quite definite in advocating the use of "token utensils" (*ming ch'i* 明器), such as "clay carriages and straw effigies," for burial. "What a pity," said Confucius, "that the dead should be expected to use the real objects intended for the living! Would that not be

---

1. This paper was delivered at the Sixth Annual Meeting of the Far Eastern Association in 1954. It was later published in *Philosophy East and West* 12, no. 4 (January 1963): 295–300.

tantamount to killing human beings to be buried with the dead? It is inhuman even to make 'burial puppets' which are lifelike, for would that not be too close to using real human beings to accompany the dead?"

This question was fully discussed in the "Book of T'ankung" (檀弓), which is linguistically contemporaneous with the *Analects*. In the *Analects*, Confucius took an explicitly humanistic and agnostic stand on the question. When a student asked how to serve the gods and the spirits, Confucius said: "We have not yet learned how to serve man; how can we serve the ghosts?" The same student then asked, "What is death?" The Master said: "We do not know life; how do we know death?"

On another occasion, he said to the same student: "Yu (由), shall I teach you what it is to know? To say that you know when you do know, and that do not know when you do not know—that is knowledge."

This Confucian skepticism was no denial of the possibility of all knowledge, but a frank admission that there are things which we do not or cannot know. It was an assertion of the right to doubt—to maintain an attitude of courageous doubt even in matters traditionally regarded as sacred or sacrosanct.

This seemingly harmless agnosticism was probably more revolutionary than we can now realize. Probably it was meant to be an intellectual veil or shield for a denial of human intelligence after death, and a denial of the existence or reality of all gods, spirits, and ghosts. And probably it was a shield for the more radical naturalistic conception of the universe, as already taught by Lao Tzu (老子) and apparently accepted by Confucius—a conception of the universe in which Nature (*t'ien* 天) does nothing and yet leaves nothing undone and in which the gods and the spirits play no role and exert no influence.

In the *Book of Mo Tzu* (墨子), it was definitely recorded that a follower of the school of Confucius actually maintained that there were no gods or spirits. And Confucius himself not only actually used the phrase "government by doing nothing," but also said, "What does Heaven (*t'ien* 天) say? All seasons go on and all things grow. What does Heaven say?" And it must be remembered that the naturalistic conception of the universe was eloquently propounded by such an influential Confucian thinker as Hsün Tzu (荀子) in the third century B.C., who said: "The course of Nature (*t'ien*) is constant. It does not exist for a benevolent ruler like Yao, nor does it cease to work for a despotic ruler like Chieh."

In short, it was the spirit of doubt—of what Goethe called "creative doubt"—which initiated, inaugurated, and animated the classical age of Chinese thought, the age of Lao Tzu and Confucius, down to Mencius (孟子), Chuang Tzu (莊子), Hsün Tzu, and Han-fei (韓非).

Lao Tzu doubted almost everything: he doubted the benevolence of Heaven and postulated a naturalistic universe; he doubted the efficacy of war and resistance to evil and taught five centuries before Jesus of Nazareth the doctrine that he who resists not is irresistible; he doubted the usefulness of too many laws and too much government, and taught a political philosophy of *wu-wei* (無為), of doing nothing, of non-interference, of *laissez faire*; he doubted the utility of all the artificiality and over-refinement of civilization and advocated a return to the simplicity of the state of Nature, in which human inventions "that multiplied the power of man by ten times or a hundred times" shall not be used and man will discard all writing and restore the use of the knotted cords.

Confucius doubted the survival of human intelligence after death and taught man to be intellectually honest and to be contented with services to man. He also doubted the validity of class distinctions and taught a democratic philosophy of education, that men are near to each other by nature, that only practice sets them apart, and that "with education there will be no classes."

Of the great founders of Chinese classical thought, Mo Tzu was the exception that proved the rule. Mo Tzu doubted the doubters, and wanted to restore faith and belief in the traditional religion of the people—the religion of gods and spirits. He believed that all evil came from doubt, from freedom of thought and belief, especially from diversity in standards of right and wrong. Therefore, Mo Tzu taught the authoritarian doctrine of "Upward Unification" or "Upward Conformity" (*shang t'ung* 尚同) of right and wrong— that "what those above believe to be right must be accepted as right by all those below and that what those above regarded as wrong must be regarded by all those below as wrong." And the people, hearing of any wrong notion or conduct, must not fail to report it to the authority above. This was called the doctrine of "Upward Unification," which sounds alarmingly similar to what is now more eulogistically termed "democratic centralism."

Mo Tzu's religion of Upward Unification did not exterminate all doubters. The age of Yang Chu (楊朱), Mencius, Hui Shih (惠施), Chuang Tzu, and Hsün Tzu testified that the torch of creative doubt was carried on undimmed and undiminished throughout the fourth and third centuries B.C. To quote two of these great doubters, Mencius and Chuang Tzu: Mencius, the democratic philosopher who believed in the goodness of the nature of man, said: "The great man is he who cannot be corrupted by wealth and honors, cannot be budged by poverty and lowliness, and cannot be bent by power and authority." And Chuang Tzu, the greatest skeptic of all skeptics, declared: "Even though the entire world sings my praise, I am not a bit more persuaded. Even though the entire world condemns me, I am not a bit more dissuaded."

It was this spirit of courageous doubt which survived the military conquest, the totalitarian regime, the book-burning, and the great persecution of private teaching under the Ch'in Empire in the last decades of the third century B.C., and which survived and blossomed in the post-classical age of Han (漢) thought—most notably in the critical philosophy of the great Wang Ch'ung (王充) (A.D. 27–100).

Wang Ch'ung was probably the greatest doubter in the entire history of Chinese thought. He, like Lao Tzu, doubted almost everything, including Confucius, Mencius, and the fundamental beliefs of the State-patronized religion of Han Confucianism. He left some 84 essays, which he called *Lun-heng* (論衡), literally meaning "Essays of Weighing and Measuring," that is, "Essays in Criticism." He says of these essays, "These scores of essays can be summed up in one sentence: *I hate untruth*."

This ends my brief paper on "The Right to Doubt in Ancient Chinese Thought." In conclusion, I would like to cite a challenging passage from Professor Kenneth Scott Latourette, who, in reviewing Dr. Wing-tsit Chan's (陳榮捷) *Religious Trends in Modern China*, has raised this challenging question:

> Why is it that, of the advanced cultures upon which the West has impinged in the past four hundred and fifty years, that of China has suffered the greatest disintegration? Of the high civilizations, namely, those of the Muslim world, of India, of the smaller Buddhist countries, Ceylon, Burma, Thailand, . . . and Outer Mongolia, of Japan and of China, that of China has undergone the most profound and sweeping changes. Where are the causes to be found? Are they in the older civilization of China? Can it be that the responsibility must be laid at the door of Confucianism and the manner in which it was inculcated and perpetuated, especially after the T'ang [618–907] or must the reason be sought elsewhere?

I shall attempt to offer an answer to Latourette's question as the conclusion to this paper.

I presume that by "the most profound and sweeping changes" Latourette did not mean what has been going on in continental China during the past few years, which certainly are not voluntary changes, but temporary barbarization brought about by military conquest.

If by those changes he meant the voluntary changes which have come about, first very slowly and only in the last half-century very rapidly, throughout the four hundred years since the first coming of the Portuguese trader and missionary—then my answer is: The causes are to be sought and found in the thought and civilization of China, and in particular in what I have here discussed as the spirit of doubt, which has ingrained itself in the Chinese mentality ever since the days of Lao Tzu and Confucius. This spirit of doubt has always manifested itself in every age in a critical examination of our own civilization and its ideas and institutions. Such self-critical examination of one's own civilization is the prerequisite without which no "profound and sweeping" cultural changes are ever possible in any country with an old civilization. All such great and fundamental changes in the history of China—whether they be the result of China's own reformers or the natural outcome of China's coming into long contact with a foreign culture—have always been brought about by a critical examination of the older civilization and a profound dissatisfaction with its institutions.

Let us remember how sweepingly Lao Tzu and Chuang Tzu criticized and condemned the civilization of their own times. Let us remember how zealously Confucius and almost all the Confucians upheld the utopian social and political ideas of the Golden Age in remote antiquity as the criteria by which to compare and criticize their own age.

And, leaving out the great founders of Chinese Buddhism in the third and fourth centuries A.D., let us remember how the early Chinese Christians like Hsü Kuang-ch'i (徐光啓) and his friends thought that their small Christian community in seventeenth-century China was comparable to the best society of the great Three Dynasties. And let us remember the early admirers of the West—from Wang T'ao (王韜) down to K'ang Yu-wei (康有為)—they, too, were thinking that the modern civilization of the West, in the words of Wang T'ao, "embodied the best ideals of our classical antiquity."

And, needless to add, the leaders of the intellectual and cultural renaissance of the last sixty years have been men who knew their own cultural heritage intimately but also critically, and who had the moral and intellectual courage to criticize and condemn its weaknesses and shortcomings.

It is therefore the Chinese spirit of doubt and self-criticism which has made possible those voluntary though often "profound and sweeping" cultural changes in China. And I may add that it is the very absence of this tradition of doubt and self-criticism which has made such changes impossible in practically all those other Asian countries mentioned by Latourette in his review.

CHAPTER 27

The Importance of a Free China[1]

Last Tuesday night (March 8, 1955), your Secretary of State, Mr. John Foster Dulles, made a great speech reporting to the nation on his recent trip to the Far East. In that speech, he made this reference to Free China:

> My last stop was at Formosa. . . . I exchanged there the instruments of ratification which officially brought into force our mutual defense treaty covering Formosa and the Pescadores. The ceremony was cheered by those who crowded into the room to see it, and by many thousands who lined the streets as I drove by. They saw in the treaty a significance—also seen by overseas Chinese I met—that so far as the United States can assure it, there will always be a free China.

That last sentence—"there will always be a free China"—will go down in history as a great prophetic sentence, comparable to the saying, "There will always be an England." It will not only be long remembered by the nine million Chinese on Formosa and the twelve and half million overseas Chinese, but will soon be grapevined to the Chinese mainland and whispered there from person to person among the hundreds of millions of Chinese who have been living and suffering for the last five years under Communist tyranny. Those hundreds of millions of my people in Captive China will be greatly heartened by those cheering words uttered by a Christian statesman— "There will always be a free China."

When one speaks of "Free China" today, one usually means the Republic of China now in exile on Formosa and the nearby islands. But when a patri-

---

1. A speech delivered at the Sweet Briar College Forum "Understanding Asia" on March 11, 1955, and again at the Council on World Affairs in Charlottesville on March 14, 1955.

otic Chinese thinks or dreams of "a Free China," he naturally has in mind the whole of the Chinese mainland, which he cannot help envisaging as liberated from Communist control and once more independent and free. The former is Free China in a narrow and immediate sense; the latter is Free China in a broader and idealistic sense.

Let us first have a look at Free China as represented in Formosa. Formosa has an area of about 13,800 square miles and a population of about nine million. Its area is roughly the size of the state of New Jersey plus Connecticut and Rhode Island. Its population is about the population of New Jersey plus Massachusetts. It has the size of the Netherlands and a population about the same as that of the Netherlands. The population is more than 98 percent Chinese, of whom the bulk are descended from early settlers from Southern Fukien and Eastern Kuangtung and speak the Amoy and Hakka dialects of those regions. Nine years of an educational campaign to learn the "National Language" has actually achieved the miraculous result of having the "Mandarin" dialect universally understood and spoken throughout the island, especially among the young people who have gone to school in the last decade. I cite this as one of the best evidences of the nationalistic sense of the people.

Formosa and the Pescadores were ceded to Japan as a part of the price China had to pay after her crushing defeat in the first Sino-Japanese War of 1894–95. It must be acknowledged that Japan, during her fifty years of rule over Formosa, had built up a fairly good foundation for the modernization of the education, agriculture, and industry in the area. That good foundation has been kept up and in many cases been improved upon by the Chinese government after taking over the islands in 1945. For instance, ten years ago, 71 percent of school-age children were in school; and when I was there last year, I found that an average of 81 percent of school-age children were in school and the school buildings were everywhere overcrowded. Ten years ago, only a few hundred students of Chinese origin were admitted to institutions of higher learning; today, nearly ten thousand students are enrolled in one National University, three provincial colleges, and other institutions of collegiate training.

The war-damaged industries have been repaired and are achieving productivity exceeding their prewar level. Two stages of agrarian reform have been carried out on the island under the wise guidance of the Sino-American "Joint Commission on Rural Reconstruction" (JCRR). Agriculture is producing enough food to feed a rapidly increasing population, with a surplus to export.

American aid, both economic and military, has played a very important role in enabling Free China to carry on agricultural and industrial modernization as well as to equip and train a large modern army, a small navy and a small air force. The three services total about six hundred thousand men.

On December 2, 1954, the United States and the Republic of China signed in Washington a mutual defense treaty, which was ratified by the Chinese Legislative Yuan (Parliament) and by the US Senate in February, 1955. In the Preamble, the parties to the treaty express their desire "to declare publicly and formally their sense of unity and their common determination to defend themselves against external armed attack, so that no potential aggressor could be under the illusion that either of them stands alone in the West Pacific area." Article V of the treaty says: "Each party recognizes that an armed attack in the West Pacific area directed against the territories of either of the parties would be dangerous to its own peace and safety and declares that it would act to meet the common danger in accordance with its constitutional processes." All this means that the treaty is intended to be a clear and unmistakable warning to any potential aggressor in the West Pacific area.

Article VI defines the terms "territories" and "territorial" to mean, in respect of the Republic of China, "Taiwan and the Pescadores"; but it adds: "The provisions of Articles II and V will be applicable to such other territories as may be determined by mutual agreement."

A resolution was introduced in Congress on January 24, 1955, and was passed by both the House and the Senate with virtual unanimity. In essence, this Joint Resolution recognizes that "the secure possession by friendly government of the western Pacific island chain, of which Formosa is a part, is essential to the vital interests of the United States and all friendly nations in or bordering on the Pacific Ocean;" and it authorizes the President of the United States "to employ the armed forces of the United States as he deems necessary for the specific purpose of securing and protecting Formosa and the Pescadores against armed attack, this authority to include the securing and protection of such related positions and territories of that area now in friendly hands and the taking of such other measures as he judges to be required or appropriate in assuring the defense of Formosa and the Pescadores."

It was in eulogy of the Joint Resolution of Congress that Secretary Dulles said last Tuesday: "That non partisan action, taken with virtual unanimity, did more than any other recent act to inspire our Asian friends with confidence in us."

And it was in this mutual defense treaty that Mr. Dulles said the Chinese people in Formosa and overseas saw a significance "that so far as the United States can assure it, there will always be a free China."

The Sino-American mutual defense treaty and the joint resolution of Congress plainly and eloquently recognize the international importance of a Free China as it exists on Formosa. In brief, the western Pacific island chain of which Formosa forms a part is vital to the interests of the United States and all friendly nations in or bordering on the Pacific Ocean, and must not be permitted to fall into the hands of unfriendly and aggressive governments.

Historically, the same logic can be applied with equal force and cogency to the whole of continental China, to Korea, and to Vietnam. It is now more and more generally recognized that the fall of China to the domination of world Communism has been and will long continue to be the principal cause of all the disturbances and troubles in the West Pacific and all parts of Asia. Certainly the war in Korea and Communist China's intervention in the war in Korea and its military and financial support of the Communist war in Indo-China have been the direct fruits of the Communist conquest of China. A free and democratic China would never have carried on a three-year war in Korea or a seven-year war in Indo-China; nor could it have become a constant threat to the peace and security of her other neighbors.

But no logic nor historical lesson will ever be sufficient ground for democratic and peace-loving nations to undertake a war for the sake of liberating a captive nation and redressing an historical wrong. When Denmark, Norway, France, and the other free states of Europe were conquered by Hitler in 1940, nothing could be done to save them. And when, in the years 1947–48, another group of free nations in Eastern and Central Europe were conquered one after another by world Communism, again nothing could be done to save them or to liberate them.

In this modern world, wars are only forced upon nations of the free world by the aggressor-states which always retain the initiative and start wars at a time of their own choosing. It was only when great wars had been fought and the aggressor states had been defeated that long-conquered states were liberated and even new states created as a part of war strategy or as a part of peace policy. Thus after the First World War were Belgium and Serbia liberated and many new states created from the Baltic to the Balkans and were the ancient states of Poland and Czechoslovakia resurrected from long oblivion. And thus were the many conquered states of Europe and Asia liberated after the Second World War.

You may recall that when the United States was forced into the last World War, President Franklin D. Roosevelt asked the American public to suggest a suitable name for the war. I was among the thousands of people who sent in suggestions to the President. Being a tyro in diplomacy and a pacifist of twenty-five years' standing, I foolishly suggested to President Roosevelt that the war be called "The Last War!" I understood that an overwhelming majority wanted to name it "the War of Liberation." But the President publicly announced that he preferred to call it "the War for Survival."

So even the most idealistic President Roosevelt did not wish to sponsor "a war of liberation."

There will be no war for the liberation of the conquered and enslaved nations of Eastern and Central Europe or of Asia, or for the liberation of Captive China, or for the liberation of a Russia held captive for thirty-eight years.

The liberation of China will always be the hope and the dream of my people—of all the freedom-loving Chinese now in Formosa and overseas, and, in particular, of those hundreds of millions of my people now living and suffering under the Communist knot.

Will that hope, that dream of a Free China ever come true? That dream will come true as surely as day follows night. When? and How? To the question of When, my answer has always been in the form of a Chinese fortune-teller's favorite rhyme:

It may be as far away as the skies,
But it may be as near as under your own eyes.

As a man of faith, I am inclined to accept the last line.

But how? How will Captive China be made free and independent again?

History has taught us the lesson that the liberation of conquered countries or areas has come only when that liberation was clearly recognized as a necessary and vital part of the grand strategy of a war forced upon the free and peace-loving peoples. As a dreamer of a Free China, this historical lesson leads me to foresee a day when such a war will be forced upon the free world, and in the course of such a war, China, because of its great strategic importance, will ultimately be liberated from the control of world Communism.

What has happened in the Formosa Strait area since last September, what has led to concluding of the Sino-American mutual defense treaty and the passage of Joint Congressional Resolution last January—all point to a dangerous contingency that the Communist regime in China, with the threatening backing of Moscow, may be seriously contemplating starting such a war by attacking the offshore islands and invading Formosa. At the present moment, it seems that no amount of neutralism or appeasement or even further surrender is likely to avert such a contingency.

Secretary Dulles was apparently worried when he said last Tuesday that "the Chinese Communists seem determined to make such a challenge."

But you will ask, how could the Chinese Communists be so foolish as to risk a major war by attacking these islands and invading Formosa?

The answer to this question lies in the great political and psychological importance which Red China sees in the existence of a Free China. *Life* magazine said the other week: "Alongside Red China, Formosa looks like small potatoes." But those small potatoes are decidedly deadly thorns in the eyes of Mao Tse-tung and his fellow slaves of world Communism. Formosa stands as a symbol of Free China—as a bastion, a refuge, and a beacon light of hope for freedom. So long as Formosa stands free and unconquered, it will continue to inspire the hope and dream for freedom in those hundreds of millions of Chinese people now patiently suffering under the most unbearable physical and mental torture ever known in human history.

All talk about the possible coexistence of "Two Chinas" is silly, simply because Communist China is in mortal fear of a Free China, however small and harmless—and however solemnly "leashed" by a powerful but peace-loving ally.

No, Communist China can never permit the existence anywhere of a Free China, and is determined to "liberate" it, that is, to liquidate it by force at no matter what cost.

That, in sum, is the political, psychological, and moral importance of Free China.

That explains the first part of my ventured prediction, namely, that a war may be forced upon the free and peace-loving peoples by the Chinese Communists by a military attack on the offshore islands and Formosa.

Now, the second part of my remark stated that "in the course of such a war, China, because of its great strategic importance, will ultimately be liberated from Communist control." You may ask, what is the great strategic importance of continental China?

China's great strategic importance lies in its huge population—its tremendous manpower. In modern warfare, especially in the strategy and tactics as practiced by the Communists both in Europe and in China, Korea, and Indo-China, manpower constitutes one of the most important elements of war strength. Marshall Zukov once described to General Eisenhower how the Russian armies used human beings to overcome a mined field. And the Communist war for the conquest of the Chinese mainland first made famous the new term of "the strategy of human waves" or "human ocean," which means the ruthless use of waves after waves of unlimited manpower to absorb and exhaust the superior firing power of the opposing forces. And what happened during the three years of the Korean War shows that the most modern mechanical weapons of war and the most powerful firing power can be bogged down by the ruthless use of unlimited supply of human beings as cannon fodder.

World Communism's propaganda apparatus has, in its psychological warfare against the free world, made full use of this factor of its great superiority in manpower as a basic weapon, knowing very well that the free world sets a high value on human life and is numerically inferior in manpower.

As long ago as November 7, 1949, when continental China was fast falling to the Chinese Communists, Mr. Malenkov, making the principal speech on the thirty-second anniversary of the Bolshevik Revolution, proudly warned the world: "We now have 800,000,000 friendly people on our side."

But the most wonderful feat of Communist psychological warfare on this score took place on November 1, 1954. On that day, the Peking Communist radio broadcast to the world the startling news that, as a result of an accurate "direct census" taken at midnight, June 30, 1953, it was now ascertained that the total population of China numbered 601,938,035! This, said a later broadcast, "is 1.7 times the population of India, 3 times that of the Soviet Union, and four times that of the United States, and 12 times that of the United Kingdom," and constitutes more than a quarter of the whole world's population.

Now, we know that China cannot possibly have that many people, and could not possibly have made any great increase of population during these recent years of war, devastation, and mass liquidation of millions of people. One of the greatest authorities of population statistics who has made a special study of Chinese population estimates is my old teacher, Professor W. F. Willcox of Cornell University, who holds that the Chinese population in 1930 was about 342 million. I am one of those few Chinese scholars who offer evidence to support the Willcox estimate.

The interesting fact is that the Chinese Communists chose last November to make that fantastic announcement. The "Numbers Game" was highly successful. The up-to-date *World Almanac* duly revised the figure for Chinese population in accordance with the Communist figure. And in that one speech of last Tuesday; Mr. Dulles not only used the words "600,000,000 Communist dominated Chinese," but also in another place referred to "its almost unlimited manpower."

Even 342 millions is a tremendous supply of manpower. The vital question, therefore, is: Will that huge population be left to be drawn upon, indoctrinated, drilled, and trained for war by the enemies of civilization? Or will civilization, at a time of struggle for survival, fight to win back that vast store of human strength and worth? That is the great strategic importance of a Free China.

CHAPTER 28

Intellectual China Still Resistant to Communist Dictatorship

The Suffering Intellectuals in Red China[1]

I

During the past twelve months, a comic-tragic drama of vast scale has been going on inside Red China. The theme of the drama is thought control and thought reform in the entire field of the Humanities, that is, literature, philosophy, and history. The drama is in three acts. Act I opens on a comical scene of the persecution of a most harmless scholar, Professor Yü P'ing-po, for his historical and textual studies of an eighteenth-century novel, *Hung Lou Meng* (The Dream of the Red Chamber). Act II is a long and tedious comedy of a nationwide chase and exorcism of the Ghost of Hu Shih, who is said to have dominated the fields of literature, history, and philosophy for more than thirty years and whose Ghost (*yu-ling*) is found still to have been haunting those fields "long after the Liberation." Failing to exorcise the said Ghost, the Red hunters and hounds finally lay hold of a living man and devour him together with scores of his friends. So the comedy of Ghost-chasing ends in the third act in a brutal tragedy of the persecution, arrest, and disappearance of Hu Feng, a prominent left-wing writer, who has been accused of the hei-

---

1. The content of this essay is similar to Hu Shih's "Sishi nianlai zhongguo wenyi fuxing yundong liuxia de kangbao xiaodu liliang—zhongguo gongchandang xiaosuan Hu Shih sixiang de lishi yiyi" 四十年來中國文藝復興運動留下的抗暴消毒力量—中國共產黨消算胡適思想的歷史意義, which was written in 1955. See *Hu Shih shougao* 胡適手稿 (Hu Shih manuscript) (Taipei: Hu Shih jinianguan, 1970). If this is an English translation of the 1955 article, it might not be translated by Hu Shih himself since the English of this piece is below his standard.

nous crime of secretly forming a clique to "oppose the Party, the people, and the Revolution."

A vast output of condemnatory literature, including a good amount of documentary material, has come out of the Chinese mainland. The total output has been estimated to exceed four million words, about a third of which has reached me. Out of this mass of material, the story of this great purge can now be told in a fairly intelligible form.

II

In September 1954, a Shantung University (Tsingtao) magazine published an article by two young men, Li Hsi-fan and Lan Ling, who had only recently graduated from that institution. The article was a criticism, from the standpoint of Marxism-Leninism, of a recent study by Professor Yü P'ing-po of the eighteenth-century novel *Hung Lou Meng* (The Dream of the Red Chamber). Professor Yü, a student and friend of mine, was then a professor at the Research Institute of Classical Literature at Peking University. His important work, *A Study of the Hung Lou Meng*—a revised and enlarged version of his earlier work published in 1923—was published in 1952 and immediately had a phenomenal success, reaching its sixth printing in less than two years. The *Literary Gazette* (*Wen-i Pao*), the highest organ of literary criticism in Red China, hailed it as "a very great achievement in the study of this greatest of China's novels." A criticism of this great authority on the *Hung Lou Meng* by two unknown young authors published in a provincial university journal, therefore, attracted no attention from the general reading public.

But that article by the two young students did attract the serious attention of the Communist lead[er]ship in Peking whose duty was to watch and correct the "behavior pattern" (*tso-feng*) of all writers, and especially of those writers of bourgeois or petty bourgeois origin. According to an unusually frank article entitled "Who Directed Us onto the Road of War?" (in *China Youth*, November 1954), the young men revealed that the editors of the *People's Daily*, the official organ of the Party and the Red Government, sent for them and interviewed them several times and gave them "the greatest encouragement and most important direction." "It was the Party," said they, "that led us onto the path of war and guided us how to go on." In a later stage in the campaign to purge Hu Shih, the *People's Daily* proudly said (January 4, 1955), "While the first shots fired by the two young men were of great value, it must not be forgotten that this war was initiated by the Party and directed and supported by the Party." It is highly probable that even the "first shot" was initiated by the Party as a feeler.

The Party then suggested that the *Literary Gazette* might reprint the young men's article. Without fully realizing the intentions of the Party leadership, the editors of the *Gazette* reluctantly reprinted the article with an editorial note saying that "the article is by two young authors who are just beginning their studies of Chinese classical literature and who have proposed some criticism of Mr. Yü P'ing-po's recent writings on the *Hung Lou Meng*—from a scientific standpoint," and that "while certain points in the article have not been thought out with sufficient care and are therefore not sufficiently comprehensive, their approach is basically correct." The editors never realized—until it was too late—that those lukewarm and patronizing comments were soon to cause their own downfall and purge.

Shortly after, another feeler in the form of a critical article on Yü P'ing-po's *Study of the Hung Lou Meng* itself, also written by the same two young men, was published in the literary supplement of the *Kuang-ming Daily* (October 10). In this new article, it was pointed out, for the first time, that Yü's study was "merely a repetition of the fallacies propounded years ago by Hu Shih."

Then, on October 23, 1954, the *People's Daily* issued the official call to war in a leader under the caption "We Ought to Pay Attention to the Criticism-Refutation (*p'i-p'an*) of the Erroneous Views in the Study of the *Hung Lou Meng*." It says, "The so-called New School of *Hung Lou Meng* study whose representative is Hu Shih has occupied the commanding position for more than thirty years, and even today we can see in the writings of Mr. Yü P'ing-po the continuation of the viewpoint and methodology of the bourgeois and reactionary school of Hu Shih."

The article gave praise to the two essays by the two young comrades, which were described as "the first shots in more than thirty years—the first shots of the counteroffensive against the bourgeois standpoint, viewpoint, and methodology of the Hu Shih school in the study of classical literature—the valuable first shots!" "Why are these first shots valuable? Precisely because our literary circles—before and even after those first shots—have paid no attention whatsoever to that one dangerous fact, namely, that the school of Hu Shih has still retained its dominating rule in the entire field of the study of classical literature."

The *People's Daily* leader ends in this solemn declaration of war: "This question, viewed from its ideological content, is another serious war of the workers' class against the bourgeoisie on the battlefront of thought. The objective of this war ought to be the clear demarcation of right and wrong, black and white—the eradication of all idealistic and subjective standpoint, viewpoint and methodology of the bourgeois class, and the correct learning of how to apply the standpoint, viewpoint and methodology of Marxism."

On the next day (October 24), the *People's Daily* published a third essay by Li Hsi-fan and Lan Ling under the title, "Which Road to Take?" The only road is of course that of Marxism. But, the young authors pointed out, "the entire line (road) of Hu Shih's academic work has been aiming at the prevention of the spread of Marxism among China's youth." As proof, they quoted this passage which Hu Shih wrote in November 1930, in introducing his three studies of the novel *Hung Lou Meng* to be included in an anthology of his selected essays for school use:

> My young friends, do not regard these critical studies of a novel as my attempts to teach you how to read a novel. They are only a few illustrations of a method of thinking and studying. Through these illustrations I want my readers to acquire a little of the scientific spirit, a little of the scientific attitude, and a little of the scientific method.
>
> The scientific spirit lies in the search for facts and for truths. The scientific attitude consists of a willingness to recognize facts and follow evidence wherever it may lead you—without regard to preconceived ideas or personal feelings. The scientific method is only "a boldness in forming hypotheses combined with a meticulous care in seeking verification." When evidence is lacking, we can only suspend our judgment. When evidence is insufficient, we can only suggest a hypothesis, but should not arbitrarily arrive at a conclusion. A hypothesis is regarded as true only when it is verified.
>
> I only wish to teach a method by means of which a man may not be deceived by others. It may not be quite edifying for a man to be led by the nose by Confucius or Chu Hsi, nor is it heroic for one to be led by the nose by Marx, Lenin, or Stalin. I myself have no desire to lead anyone by the nose. I only hope to contribute what little I have, to teach my young friends to acquire a capability to take care of themselves so that they may not be easily beguiled by others. (underlining added by the author)

On the same day, an urgent meeting of the Writers' Union was called to "unfold the war." It was presided by Cheng Chen-to, a vice-minister of culture, and was summed up at the end by Chou Yang, another vice-minister of culture and one of the real bosses in the Party's control of literature and art. The chairman declared, "All those whose standpoint and viewpoint are not in conformity with Marxism—that is, all those who still retain the standpoint of Hu Shih's Pragmatic studies of the *Hung Lou Meng*—must thoroughly and seriously criticize themselves."

Professor Yü P'ing-po duly criticized himself, but was apparently let off lightly. "In criticizing the mistaken views of Mr. Yü," said Chou Yang, "we do not mean to strike him down as a man." The campaign was now to be concentrated on the eradication of the reactionary thoughts of Hu Shih.

On November 5, the *People's Daily* published a leading article under the title, "Thoroughly Eradicate the Poison of Hu Shih's Reactionary Philosophy!" It opens with the question, "Why do we say that the criticism-refutation of the erroneous views prevalent in the study of the novel *Hung Lou Meng* is 'another war of the workers' class against the bourgeoisie on the ideological front'?" The answer is, "The gravity of the situation lies in the fact that that battleground . . . has for more than thirty years been occupied by Hu Shih, the representative of bourgeois idealism, and even long after the Liberation, . . . the influence of Hu Shih's school in the realm of the study of classical literature has never received its well-deserved purge." "Now that the first shots have been fired from the front line, the firing power of the war must now be directed against Hu Shih, the headman of bourgeois idealism, the deadly enemy of Marxism."

The article, after a lengthy attack on the philosophy of Pragmatism (which Hu Shih had helped to popularize during Dr. John Dewey's visit to China in 1919–21), concludes in these words, "With the passing of the old China, Hu Shih's political ideas have become bankrupt. But the so-called 'scholarship and thought' of Hu Shih and his Pragmatism are still exerting their influence on the academic world. His ghost (*yu-ling*) is still embodied in the person of Mr. Yü P'ing-po and others who form a part of the cultural circle. Clearly recognize the reactionary nature of the Hu Shih thinking and completely eradicate its influence—that is the present duty of the cultural world!"

Such were the orders of the Party. But as the campaign of criticism and refutation progressed, it was soon discovered that the poisonous influence was not confined to the field of classical literature. As Chou Yang said on December 8, "Hu Shih, . . . the earliest, the most determined, and the most uncompromising enemy of Marxism-Leninism in China, . . . the most important and most concentrated representative of bourgeois ideology in China, . . . has covered many fields, including literature, philosophy, history, and language. And the idealistic philosophy of Pragmatism which he has imported from the American bourgeoisie and made the foundation of his own thought, is still occupying a big space in the brains of the Chinese people and the Chinese intellectuals. Therefore, an all-out and from-the-roots exposure and refutation of the bourgeois idealism of the Hu Shih school is the most important combat duty of the present-day Marxist."

So the question of the scope of anti–Hu Shih campaign was referred to a joint meeting of the Council of the Academy of Science and the Presidium of the Writers' Association Union, which was held on December 2, and which was announced ten days later that the Academy of Science and the Writers' Association Union were jointly to organize "Discussion Meetings" for the criticism-refutation of Hu Shih's thoughts, and that the discussions were to be concentrated on these nine main topics:

1. Criticism of Hu Shih's philosophical thoughts.
2. Criticism of Hu Shih's political thoughts.
3. Criticism of Hu Shih's historical viewpoints.
4. Criticism of Hu Shih's thoughts on literature.
5. Criticism of Hu Shih's viewpoints on the history of philosophy.
6. Criticism of Hu Shih's viewpoints on the history of literature.
7. The place of research (*k'ao-chu*, investigation by evidence) in the study of history and of classical literature.
8. The common-man nature (*jen-min hsin*) and artistic achievement of the novel *Hung Lou Meng*.
9. Criticism of all past studies of the *Hung Lou Meng*.

So the war now became a war against Hu Shih on nine fronts. According to a speech by Mao Tun, Communist Minister of Culture, the discussion meetings were to last for about six months. A year has passed, [yet] the criticism of the poisonous influence of Hu Shih's thoughts is still seen in the recent publications, especially in the academic journals, of Red China.

Note: The published articles on the erroneous views of Hu Shih and Yü P'ing-po's studies of the *Hung Lou Meng* must have numbered in the hundreds. For a convenient and good summary, see "The Dream of the Red Chamber Case" (Current Background, no. 315, March 4, 1955, published by the External Research section, American Consulate General, Hong Kong), which contains full translations of eight of the earlier articles in this controversy.

The literature on the purge of Hu shih's thought is even more extensive. These Chinese works have come out of Red China:

Selected Papers in Criticism-Refutation of Hu Shih's Thoughts. Vols. 1, 2, 3. Total pp. 974. January–April, 1955. Peking.

Li Ta, *Criticism-Refutation of Hu Shih's Reactionary Thoughts.* 1st ed. January 1955. 2nd ed. March 1955. Hankow.

Yao P'eng-tzu, *Criticism-Refutation of Hu Shih's Reactionary and Anti-scientific Philosophy of Pragmatism.* March 1955. Shanghai.

Chang Ju-hsin, *Criticism-Refutation of Hu Shih's Pragmatic Philosophy.* June 1955. Peking.

III

Where did Hu Feng come into the great purge? And who is he? I shall answer the last question first.

Hu Feng is a pen name, meaning "the Barbarian's winds or fashions." His real name was Chang Kuang-jen. He was born in 1902 in a small village in Ch'i-ch'un hsien, in eastern Hupei. In one of his autobiographical sketches, he tells that his interest in the new literature began in his middle-school days when he first read Hu Shih's *A Book of Experiments in Poetry*, and the periodicals *The Guide* (a Communist weekly edited by Ch'en Tu-hsiu) and *The Endeavor* (a liberal weekly edited by Hu Shih and his friends). In college in Nanking and Peking, he was swept into revolutionary activities in the years 1926–27. He was in Japan between 1930 and 1933, when he studied literature and moved among the liberal and radical writers of Japan. After 1934, he was an active member of the "Left-Wing Writers' League" in Shanghai, and was considered a favorite friend and follower of Lu Hsun (1881–1936, a pen name of Chou Shu-jen), the famous author and the acknowledged leader of the Left-Wing Writers. After the death of Lu Hsun in 1936, Hu Feng has often been regarded as his faithful disciple and successor.

Lu Hsun was one the original group of Peking University Liberals, which included Ch'en Tu-hsiu, Hu Shih, Chou Tso-jen (Lu Hsun's younger brother), and others, and which edited the monthly *Hsin Ch'ing Nien* (The New Youth), the earliest organ of what has been called "'the Chinese Rena[i]ssance Movement." Lu Hsun's first short stories and "impressions" were printed in that magazine. After 1925, he left Peking and gradually drifted into the pro-Communist group of left-wing writers. Many of his later writings were in support of the Communist movement. He even undertook to study and translate some of Communist works on literary criticism.

But Lu Hsun was a rebel, and a liberal at heart. He was, at least in his last years, not happy in the leftist group, which was often subject to the underground control and discipline of Communist agents, one of whom was Chou Ch'i-ying (Chou Yang), the future literary dictator of the Red China. In a letter to his young friend Hu Feng, dated September 12,1935, Lu Hsun said:

> With regard to San Lang [三郎],[2] I can express my opinion almost without thinking. My opinion is: he should not join (the Party) at present. In recent years, I find it is from among those who remain outside (of the Party) that there have arisen a few new writers who have produced some works of freshness. Once inside (the Party), one is pickled in all kinds of nonsensical friction, and is heard no more.
>
> In my own case, I always feel being chained to an iron chain and having the foreman whipping me from behind my back—whipping me however hard and vigorously I worked.
>
> (Letters of Lu Hsun, pp. 946–47)

So Lu Hsun, whom the Chinese Communists have canonized as "the Maxim Gorki of New China," was in 1935 revolting against Communist control of writers and of literature. In that sense, Hu Feng has been a faithful disciple of Lu Hsun.

Hu Feng founded and edited several short-lived literary periodicals—*July, Hope, Clay,* and others. He published three volumes of his collected poems, and a number of collected prose works of sketches and literary criticism. Throughout the war years, he never went to Yenan. He has not been a member of the Communist Party. He was essentially a liberal, an individualist, a lover of freedom and of humanity. He has thought out his own individualistic and humanistic theory of literature, which holds that "the basic spirit of the new literature stems from the author's self-effacing sincerity and love, from his true knowledge and flaming vision of the realities of life, not blemished by the slightest degree of dishonesty. That we call Realism." It was only

---

2. Xiao Jun 蕭軍 (1907–1988), one of Lu Xun's disciples and a famous left-wing writer.

natural that his writings and his theory of literary criticism should constantly come into sharp conflict with the leadership [of] the Communist Party.

As early as May 1942, Mao Tse-tung gave his "Talks at the Yenan Round Table discussion on Literature and Art," in which he was laying down the principles of Communist Party control of literature, namely, that "literature is to be made into an effective war weapon for the people's revolution—a weapon for unifying and educating the people and for attacking and destroying the enemy"; that "literature is subordinate to politics" and "political criteria should be placed above artistic criteria"; that "writers and artists must study Marxism-Leninism," which is "the science every revolutionary must learn," and "writers and artists are no exception."

These "Talks" soon became the sacrosanct edicts to all good and correct writers in areas under Communist control. After the Communist conquest of the mainland, they became universal laws of literary theory and literary criticism which formed the required readings in every campaign for "the rectification of the behavior-pattern of all writers and artists in Red China."

But Hu Feng had no use for Mao Tse-tung's "Talks," which he privately described to a friend as "that pamphlet which has been made into a totem." He and his friends continued to defy all forms of Party control of literature, and to resist all orders for ideological re-education. He used to say, "Where there are people, there is history. Where there is life, there is struggle. Wherever life and struggle are found, there ought to be poetry." "Look at Balzac. Did he have a proletarian standpoint or a Marxist worldview? He was a Royalist. And yet he was praised by Engels as the greatest triumph of Realism."

In the years after the Communist conquest of continental China, he clearly saw that Chinese literature had become formalistic and lifeless. Rigid control and frequent purges had smothered and killed the vitality of literature. He and his friends were being constantly criticized, refuted, [and] suppressed. Yet Hu Feng the idealist still hoped for a "breakthrough," for a better day, and for a more vital literature. In January 1951, he wrote from Peking to a friend, "This altar of literature ruled by petrified corpses! ... But I am sharpening my dagger, and watching which way the wind blows. When I can see and aim correctly, I'll be willing to cut off my own head and throw it out—to smash that rotten-smelling iron wall to bits!"

This is Hu Feng the man, and the rebel.

IV

Where and when did Hu Feng come into the fray and get caught in the great purge? He came in at a time when he had already "cut off his own head and thrown it at the iron wall of Communism." He came in at the exact time when his enemies were eagerly waiting for him to jump into the battle.

Early in 1954, Hu Feng had decided to take a desperate counteroffensive by presenting directly to the highest powers of the Party a very frank and honest statement of his grievances, his observations of the dying literature in the whole of the mainland, and his proposals for a drastic reform. He had prepared a lengthy memorandum during the months of April and May, and called it "Explanatory Materials concerning Several Theoretical Questions (in Literature)." It is not known at what time he presented the memorandum to the Central Committee of the Communist Party. But it is certain that he had presented it sometime before the criticism of Yü P'ing-po and Hu Shih was actually begun.

This memorandum is said to contain about three hundred thousand words. It was later ordered to be printed by the *Literary Gazette* as a Supplement to its January (1955) issues. But, probably because of its damaging criticism and exposure of Communist policy of control over literature and the arts, this Supplement has never been permitted to reach the outside world. The Hong Kong subscribers to the *Gazette* have not yet received it.

From the numerous though fragmentary quotations in the Communist press, we may try to give a brief of Hu Feng's remarkable document. It is divided into two main parts. Part I seems to consist of a very outspoken presentation of the despotic but stupid control of writers and artists by the Party, together with a vivid description of the stifled and lifeless state of literature which has resulted from that policy of control. Part II is said to be "concrete recommendations concerning the literary activities of the future."

The most interesting part in Part I of the memorandum appears to be what Hu Feng described as the "five swords" which the Party leadership as represented by Comrades Lin Mo-han and Ho Ch'i-fang had been dangling over the heads of all writers. The five swords are:

Sword number 1: "That a writer, before he can do creative work, must first acquire a complete and thorough Communist worldview."

Sword number 2: "That only the life of the worker, the peasant, and the soldier can be considered as real life (for the writer to study), and that the ordinary life of the ordinary man and woman is no life at all."

Sword number 3: "That only the writer whose thoughts have been remolded can produce creative work." "As to those who have gone through remolding but who have not been directly remolded by Comrade Lin Mo-han and his colleagues, they are either not granted suitable conditions for work, or not permitted to do their creative work, but are required to devote their whole time to the task of further remolding. If such writers should dare to produce anything, it will not be allowed to be published; and, if published, it must [be] vehemently attacked, such attacks are called 'criticism' or 'readers' opinion.'"

Sword number 4: "That only the accepted literary forms of the past are to be considered as 'national literary forms,' and that only the 'continuation' and 'glorification' of the excellent tradition of the past can help to overcome the defects of the new literature." "If anyone should advocate the acceptance of the revolutionary and realistic literature of other nations, that would be 'surrendering to the literature of the bourgeoisie'!"

Sword number 5: "That, in literature, there are subject matter of importance and subject matter of no importance, and that the importance of subject matter determines the value of a literary work." "And what is subject matter of importance? It is said that it must be things of light—of the bright side—because the Revolution has succeeded and there cannot be any more strife between the old and the new, there cannot be any more people dying, even though the dying and the strife may have taken place before the Revolution. And now that the Revolution has succeeded, there cannot be any more backwardness and darkness, even though it be backwardness and darkness to be overcome by struggle. . . . All this makes it impossible for an author to write anything at all. What he now writes, of course, is all sweetness and light, but it is also all falsehood and fraud."

Here seems to be Hu Feng's summing up of his indictment, "Subjectivism in theory and sectarianism in manner of action have attained the position of absolute power since the Liberation, and have therefore, in the brief course of a few years, achieved this result: the little vitality which the New Literature has taken over thirty years of struggle to build up has all been withered by stifling."

Hu Feng's Part II—some concrete recommendations for the future—has never been adequately reported. From a few very fragmentary quotations, we understand that his central theme is complete freedom for all creative workers in literature. He proposes that all the present literary periodicals, central or local, such as the *Literary Gazette, People's Literature, Learning in Literature*, etc. should be suspended. In their place, there should be founded some seven or eight literary magazines of national scope, each to be under the chief editorship of an author whose influence has been recognized as having the character of leadership. The chief editor should have complete editorial power and freedom, including the freedom to collect around him twenty or thirty authors to form a "work cooperative unit." Each magazine may have on it authors who are members of the Communist Party or its Youth Corps, but their number should be limited to about one-third of the total staff, and their Party cell should not be permitted to exert supervising power over the paper.

The "differences or even basic divergences" which exist among these leading periodicals in their understanding of problems of literary creative work, or in their attitudes toward those problems, should be and can be resolved by the free competition among these free and independent organs themselves.

These recommendations from a courageous and honest man who apparently had some following, should enable us to see that the author of the memorandum was undoubtedly a very naive idealist had who never understood either the nature of Communism or the character of his Communist oppressors. His judgment may have been unduly influenced by some of his leading associates who were members of the Communist Party but who nevertheless shared his libertarian and individualistic views.

That was the remarkable document which Hu Feng had presented directly to the highest leadership of the Communist regime with a request that it be seriously considered and be given an opportunity for public discussion. He and his closest friends were anxiously waiting for any clue of the kind of response or reaction to his memorandum when the air was suddenly filled with war cries against the bourgeois idealistic thoughts of Yü P'ing-po and Hu Shih. In the midst of the campaign, one new development gave Hu Feng a ray of hope. That was the sudden attack on the *Literary Gazette* by the *People's Daily* (October 28, 1954) on the ground that the editors of the *Gazette*

had failed to notice the danger of the long domination of the field of classical literature by the school of Hu Shih, and had further failed to encourage
such "newborn forces" in literature as the two young men who had fired the
first shots at Yü P'ing-po and Hu Shih. This last point was of special interest
to Hu Feng, whose many young friends had often been "smothered" by the
Party critics and censors. And the entire internal warfare between the two
powerful groups—the official organ of the Party and Government and the
highest literary organ in the country, misled him to think (as he actually
wrote on that day and a few days later) that "here the situation is one of a
great shake-up," and that "the breakthrough is here."

On the same day (November 28), he wrote, "I even heard that that document of over two hundred thousand words may soon be published. If that be
true, it may mean that the highest powers have decided to give some thorough consideration to the question."

So Hu Feng spoke on November 7 and again on November 11 at two of the
many joint meetings of the Presidiums of the Federation of Literary and Art
Circles and the Writers' Union. One of his friends by the name of Lu Ling
also made a long speech. Both Hu Feng and Lu Ling attacked not only the
Literary Gazette, but also the *People's Daily* and a host of other leading Communists for having been equally guilty of long years of deliberate suppression and oppression of "newborn forces" in the literary world. And they
openly criticized the Party's policy of control and suppression, which they
held to have been responsible for the dearth and dying of good literature
under the new regime.

It apparently took nearly a full month for the Communist leadership to
come to a decision as to how to deal with Hu Feng and his many friends. A
drastic and brutal decision had undoubtedly been made when Chou Yang
rose to reply to Hu Feng on December 8. Chou's long and defiant speech
ended in this dictatorial tone: "I say no. We are all in the right. You are all
wrong." Hu Feng had lost the war.

V

Hu Feng was soon ordered to write his self-criticism. He wrote on December
13 to a friend, "I was misled by an over-optimistic estimate, and advanced
foolishly. . . . The responsibility chiefly is mine. . . . Ashamed in facing my
fellow fighters."

His lengthy self-criticism was finished on January 11, 1955. A note of self-examination on his memorandum was finished on January 15. Both were ordered to be revised. The revised versions are dated February 5. An additional note of further confession of error is dated March 26. These three confessions were not published until May 13.

In the meantime, the public was mobilized to demand drastic measures in dealing with Hu Feng and his clique. And the Party was searching for evidence to convict them of the gravest political crimes of counterrevolution.

Hu Feng's three confessions were at last published in the *People's Daily* on May 13, 1955, together with extracts from thirty-four letters which Hu Feng had written to his onetime associate Shu Wu in 1943–50. These extracts were printed under the caption: "Some Materials Related to the Hu Feng Counterrevolutionary Clique." Shu Wu had deserted his group in 1952 and was now asked to surrender these old letters.

These "materials" were published as proof to show that Hu Feng's self-criticism and confessions were all falsehoods and "ought to be stripped off." In particular, they were to substantiate these charges against him: (1) that he had for over ten years persistently opposed and resisted the Party's ideological and organizational leadership in the literature movement; (2) that he had opposed and resisted the rank and file of revolutionary writers led by the Party; and (3) that, because of such opposition and resistance, he had for years carried on a series of cliquish activities.

The editorial preface to these documents contains this threatening command: "Possibly there are others of the clique who, like Shu Wu, have been deceived by Hu Feng and are now unwilling to follow him any longer. They ought to offer to the Party more materials for the further exposure of Hu Feng. Concealment cannot long last. Nor can a strategic retreat (that is, a self-criticism) deceive any one. . . . Now, Lu Ling must have received more secret letters from Hu Feng. We hope he will surrender them. And all others who have received secret letters from him ought to surrender them. Surrendering the letters is better than keeping them or destroying them."

More extracts from sixty-nine letters written by Hu Feng to Lu Ling and others in 1949–55 were published on May 24, and labeled "The Second Series of Materials." These extracts were to prove (1) that he had blasphemously reviled and attacked the Communist Party, its leadership, and the talks of Comrade Mao at the Yenan Round Table on literature; (2) how he had expanded his reactionary cliquish organization, establishing "beachheads" and ordering his accomplices to infiltrate into the Party for the counterrevolutionary purpose of stealing documents and information; and (3) how he had given orders to his accomplices to start concerted attacks on the literary line under the leadership of the Party, and how he, after his own setback, had planned to retreat and wait for future opportunities.

Some of these letters have been quoted in my biographical sketch of Hu Feng. I would like to quote one more dated February 8, 1955:

> Do not be sorrowful. Must remain calm. There are still many things we have to endure, and rebirth can only be sought through forbearance. All is for the work—for a more remote and greater future!

On May 25, the day after the publication of the "Second Series of Materials," the Federation of Literary and Art Circles and the Writers' Association Union held a Joint "enlarged" meeting attended by seven hundred writers. The meeting passed several drastic resolutions against Hu Feng, including a proposal to the Supreme Prosecutor's Office that necessary action be taken to prosecute the counterrevolutionary crimes of Hu Feng.

On June 10, a "Third Series of Materials" was published, consisting of extracts from sixty-seven letters, of which three were from Hu Feng, fifty were letters to him, four to his wife from his friends, and ten were letters exchanged among his friends. The *People Daily* said editorially that these new evidences showed that "those who constitute the central core of the Hu Feng Clique" were "Special Secret Police agents of (American) Imperialism and Chiang Kai-shek's Kuomintang, reactionary army officers, Trotskyites, and turncoats of the Revolution."

The only "proof" of Hu Feng's connection with Chiang Kai-shek's secret police consist of the three letters from Hu Feng in which he, in 1947, requested a friend to seek the assistance of an ex-chief of Peiping Police for locating and freeing two friends who they thought might have been arrested for suspected connection with the Communists.

The arrest of Hu Feng was reported in the *New York Times* on July 18, 1955, quoting from a Communist radio announcement from Peiping. But the arrest was probably made long before that date, most probably on May 24 or 25. We will never know for certain. Nor will we ever know what has become of him, of his wife and his many friend—a group of brave souls who have put up a desperate and impossible fight for a free and vital literature in Communist China!

CHAPTER 29

The Communist Regime in China Is Unstable and Shaky[1]

MR. PRESIDENT, I wish to join your numerous friends in expressing to you the hearty congratulations of my delegation on your election to the Presidency of the Twelfth Session of the General Assembly, an honor which you and your nation so well deserve. My delegation pledges to you our full and wholehearted support.

One of the very recent good tidings from Asia is the independence of the Federation of Malaya. My delegation in the Security Council and in the General Assembly has expressed its satisfaction in connection with the admission of Malaya to membership in the United Nations. The independence of Malaya is important in itself. It is also important as a part of that general movement which has, since the end of the Second World War, conferred freedom and independence upon many nations in Asia and Africa which are now sitting in our midst as our fellow Members.

Unfortunately, in the contemporary world, in contrast to this movement of national liberation, there has been the opposite movement of national enslavement. Many countries in Europe and Asia have been deprived of their human freedoms and national rights. We in the United Nations can never forget the fate of these enslaved peoples.

In the resumed Eleventh Session of the General Assembly, we discussed the report of the Special Committee on the Problem of Hungary. My delegation is moderately satisfied with the resolution which the resumed Eleventh Session passed by an overwhelming majority. I wish we could have done more.

---

1. Hu Shih's address to a Plenary Meeting of the Twelfth Regular Session of the General Assembly of the United Nations on September 26, 1957.

306 POWER OF FREEDOM

Today, I wish to pay a tribute to the freedom fighters of Hungary in the form of a report on the great repercussions which the Hungarian uprising has produced on my people on the Chinese mainland.

The Chinese people on the mainland seemed to have learned a great deal about the Hungarian uprising, and were greatly excited by it.

Even in the official communist press, the Chinese people could find a number of important documents published in full. One of those published documents was the Soviet declaration of October 30, 1956, which gave great joy to the Chinese people who sympathized with the cause of Hungarian freedom. For, as we all recall, in that declaration the Soviet Union was telling Hungary and the entire world that the Soviet Government has ordered its military command to withdraw the Soviet units from Budapest and that the Soviet Government was prepared to begin negotiations with the Hungarian Government on the question of Soviet troops on Hungarian territory.

What was most exciting to the imagination of my people living under communist tyranny was the clear and indelible impression that the powerful and ruthless communist dictatorship in Hungary, after ten years of absolute political control and ideological remolding, was suddenly swept away by the spontaneous uprising of ill-armed students and factory workers. That regime suddenly found itself deserted by the people, by its own army, and by its own police force, and was restored only by the intervention of Soviet troops.

Moreover, the Hungarian revolution appeared to look beyond communism and aspire to a democratic revolution, abolishing the secret security police, discarding the one-party system, restoring a free press and a free radio, and pledging to hold free elections in the near future. It was these anti-communists and democratic manifestations that made the Hungarian uprising more exciting to my people on the mainland.

Even Mao Tse-tung himself admitted in his speech on 27 February 1957:

Certain people in our country were excited when the Hungarian events took place. They hoped that something similar would happen in China, that thousands upon thousands of people would demonstrate in the streets and oppose the People's Government.

The events in Hungary have given rise to two important anti-communist movements on the Chinese mainland during the last few months. One of these has been a nationwide outbreak of anti-communist movement among the students in the universities, colleges, and middle schools. The other has been one full month of outspoken criticism and attack on the Communist Party by many Chinese intellectuals in the universities and in the so-called "democratic parties."

There are about five million boys and girls in the middle schools, colleges, and universities. These millions of Chinese youths come from all walks of life and know the real conditions of the people. The most acute suffering of the vast farming population, the universal impoverishment of the Chinese nation through the so-called socialist construction, and the large-scale enslavement of the people in all forms of economic and political regimentation—all these cannot but be most deeply felt by every sensitive young student daily witnessing the hardships of his or her own family life.

It is absolutely untrue that the communist regime in China has won over the minds and the hearts of the young. What happened in Hungary last October has proven beyond doubt that the young students and workers of Hungary have not been captivated by fully ten years of communist rule and indoctrination. The recent student revolt in China furnishes us the best proof that, after eight years of absolute rule and ideological molding, the students in China are almost unanimously in opposition to the communist regime.

The recent student revolt began in the Peking University on May 4, a date made memorable thirty-eight years ago by the historic "May 4" student movement of 1919, which was also started by the students of Peking University.

On that evening of May 4, 1957, eight thousand students gathered at commemoration meeting, at which nineteen student leaders made fiery speeches openly attacking the communist regime for suppressing freedom and democracy in the schools and in the country. From that evening on, the wall-newspapers of the Peking University became the open forum of the free opinion of the students.

The Peking University student leaders edited and printed a periodical entitled "The Relay Cudgel of Democracy," which they mailed to all colleges and schools throughout China as a clarion call to all students to join the common fight for freedom and democracy. They also sent their representatives to contact the students in the thirty-odd universities and colleges in the Peking and Tientsin area.

As one of the student leaders put it:

The call is for the mobilization of an army of one million youths to fight communism, to oppose the so-called revolution, and to overthrow the real enemies of the people. We must fight for democracy, for freedom, and for the rights of man.

The response was unanimous from all student bodies in every part of China—from Mukden in the north to Canton in the south, from Shanghai and Nanking in the east to Chongqing and Chengdu in the west.

By the first week of June, the student movement threatened to break out into a popular uprising of the Hungarian type. On the evening of June 6, a few university professors and "democratic" politicians met and talked over the situation, and their general impression was that the students in Peking and Shanghai—the two most important and largest centers of student population—were on the verge of declaring a strike and going into the streets to demonstrate against the communist regime. One of the professors said: "This situation resembles the eve of the Hungarian revolution."

But the communist regime, realizing the gravity of the situation, took repressive measures in all the large centers of student population to isolate the student groups, arrest the ringleaders, and prevent all street demonstrations.

The most serious case of student rioting took place in the industrial city of Hanyang in Central China. Nearly a thousand students of the First Middle School of Hanyang went on strike on June 12, 1957, and demonstrated in the streets, shouting anti-communist slogans and hoisting anti-communist banners. The student procession marched on to the county headquarters of the Communist Party and beat up the party officers there. In the evening, the students broke into the local military conscription center, apparently with the intention of obtaining arms. The rioting was continued the next day when security police arrived in full force and opened fire on the students. A large number of arrests were made, including the vice-principal of the school and a number of teachers who had led or participated in the demonstrations.

News of the Hanyang student riots were not made public until nearly two months later. And, just ten days before the opening of the Twelfth Session of the General Assembly of the United Nations, on September 7, Reuters reported that "three ringleaders of student riots in Hanyang last June were executed yesterday at a mass meeting of 10,000 spectators" and that "other leaders were sentenced to prison terms of from five to fifteen years."

The official communist report said—and this is interesting to us here—that the instigators of the Hanyang student riots had called them "the Hungarian uprising in miniature."

The student unrest, protest, and riot formed one of the two great manifestations of the anti-communist feelings of my people in the mainland. The other great manifestation was the one full month of outspoken and scathing criticism of the Communist Party by Chinese intellectuals. That holiday of one month of freedom began with May 8 and abruptly ended on June 7, 1957. It was a month of free speech especially granted by "instruction of the Central Committee of the Chinese Communist Party."

To have exactly one month of specially granted freedom of speech throughout eight long years of communist rule—that in itself constitutes a sufficient commentary on the barbarity of the communist regime.

Now, why was that one month of free speech granted at all? Was it granted because otherwise these noncommunist intellectuals and politicians would remain silent? No. For, under the communist tyranny, the people have no freedom of silence—which is often more important than freedom of speech. In the old days, as long as a man remained silent, he would not be molested. But, under the communist tyranny, there is no freedom to remain silent. You are called to the microphone to broadcast a speech prepared for you, or you are required to sign your name to an article written for you.

There is no freedom of silence. And, because they have no freedom of silence, the Chinese intellectuals have been compelled to speak insincerely or untruthfully, to pay compliment when compliment is undeserved, or to condemn friends or teachers whom they could not possibly have the heart to condemn. In short, the absence of the freedom of silence has forced many Chinese intellectuals to tell political lies, which is the only possible escape from this new tyranny and which, by the way, is also the only effective weapon to defeat the purposes of that tyranny.

For instance, when the communist regime, some years ago, ordered a nationwide purge of the poisonous effects of the thoughts of Hu Shih—that's me—every friend or student of mine had to speak his piece in refutation and condemnation of me, knowing very well that I would surely understand that he or she had no freedom of science.

So, in the same manner, when the communist dictators announced a year ago that, from now on, the communist regime would carry out a policy of liberalism in dealing with science, literature, and art, a policy of "Letting a hundred flowers blossom and letting a hundred schools of thought contend"—when that announcement was made, everybody smiled and applauded and said aloud: "How wonderful!"

So, in the same manner, when the dictators announced last year that the regime's new policy in dealing with the "democratic parties" was to be a policy of "Long-Term Coexistence and Mutual Supervision"—when that announcement was made, again everybody smiled and applauded and said aloud: "How wonderful! How generous of you!"

But the stirring events in Hungary last October and the great unrest among the Chinese students brought about a great change in all this. The intellectuals and politicians were now prepared to speak out, prepared to say for the first time what they really wanted to say in plain and honest language. And the communist leadership, too, was conscious of the wide and deep repercussions of the Hungarian revolution in the thought and feelings of the Chinese people. The communists also wanted to find out the real feelings of the people, the intellectuals, and the democratic politicians. The communist leadership was so confident of its own power that it thought it could afford a little freedom for the intellectuals to speak up. In his February 27 speech, Mao Tse-tung made this savage brag:

> Since those Hungarian events, some of our intellectuals did lose their balance, but they did not stir up any storm in the country. Why? One reason, it must be said, was that we had succeeded in suppressing counter-revolution quite thoroughly.

Mao Tse-tung was so confident of his thoroughness in suppressing the counterrevolution that he was now ready to invite the intellectuals and politicians of the "democratic parties" to assist the Communist Party in the coming campaign of "rectification" within the Party. The noncommunist politicians and intellectuals were invited to speak out frankly about what they had observed as the defects and mistakes of the communist regime. And, it is reported, in the original version of Mao's speech of February 27 there were explicit assurances of complete freedom of speech.

So the great experiment of free speech began in early May. For a full month, everybody was free to voice his criticism of the Party and the communist regime; the few newspapers of the "democratic parties" were temporarily freed from communist control and were able to print any news or opinion, however unfavorable to the communist regime. Even the official press of the regime was instructed to print critical opinions without adverse comment.

But the tremendous volume of outspoken criticism against the regime and the great vehemence and bitterness of it all were far beyond the complacent expectations of the communist leadership.

The Communist Party was accused openly of believing and practicing the notion that "the entire country belongs to the party as its war booty." The dictatorship of the Proletariat, for which Mao Tse-tung has coined the absurd name "the People's democratic dictatorship," and which is no more and no less than the absolute dictatorship of the Communist Party over the people, was openly attacked as the root and the source of all the mistakes and evils of the communist regime.

These critics stated openly that 90 percent of past and present cases of "suppression of counter-revolution" were the result of wrong judgment and miscarried justice. And the democratic parties proposed that a higher commission of appeal and redress be established to re-examine all cases of suppression of counterrevolution. Many phases of the so-called socialist construction were severely criticized, and some critics said frankly that bureaucracy was a far more dangerous enemy than capitalism itself.

The communist regime was attacked as a slavish imitation of the Soviet Union. The sincerity of Soviet friendship was questioned openly and the opinion was voiced that the Soviet Union should not be paid for the arms and ammunition which it had supplied to Red China in the Korean War.

And, of course, the criticism most frequently voiced was that, under the communist rule, there were no freedom, no human rights, and no free elections.

All these were anti-communist, antiregime, and even "counterrevolutionary" voices which it was difficult for the communist leadership to answer or to refute. And there was no doubt, during the whole month of outspoken criticism, that the Communist Party was greatly discredited in the eyes of the people.

So the communist leadership became very angry and regretted the whole affair as having given aid and comfort to the enemies of the socialist revolution. On June 7 the "freedom holiday" came to an abrupt end. The *People's Daily* now declared that there had been a political conspiracy on the part of the leaders of the democratic parties to extend their own spheres of influence and to overthrow the power of the Communist Party. It further declared that the wise leadership of the Communist Party had foreseen all this and had actually planned this period of one month of open airing of grievances, complaints, and criticisms as a method of sifting the fragrant flowers from the poisonous weeds. An editorial in the *People's Daily* of July 1 contained these interesting revelations:

> Carrying out the instructions of the Central Committee of the Chinese Communist Party, the *People's Daily* and all other papers of the Party published little or no opinion from the positive side during the period between May 8 and June 7. The purpose was to let all the ghosts and evil spirits "bloom and contend" to their utmost, to let the poisonous weeds grow as tall as they could. This is to say that the Communist Party, realizing that a class struggle between the bourgeoisie and the proletariat is inevitable, let the bourgeoisie and the bourgeois intellectuals initiate this battle.
>
> Some people said this was a secret trap. We say this is an open strategy. For we have told our enemies beforehand that we would hoe the poisonous weeds only after letting them grow out of the earth.

Thus, the movement of "Letting a hundred flowers blossom and letting a hundred schools of thought contend" suddenly turned into a campaign to persecute and purge the "Rightists"—a campaign which is still going on on the Chinese mainland, with a dozen leading intellectuals selected to be the targets of public interrogation, persecution, humiliation, and degradation.

To these victims of the new communist persecution, and to the hundreds and thousands of my people who dared to speak out and fight against the tyrannical rule of communism—to all these, we of the Chinese delegation wish to express our heartfelt sympathy and profound respect.

Such are the manifestations of the great repercussions which the Hungarian revolution has left in the minds and hearts of my people still living and suffering under communist tyranny.

I have made this report primarily to pay a tribute to the Hungarian fighters for freedom. But those popular manifestations which I have summarized are also clear and unmistakable evidence to prove that the Chinese communist regime, which has had eight years of military and political control of the Chinese mainland, is as unstable and as shaky as was the Hungarian regime under Rakosi and Gero.

Like the Hungarian regime of last October, the Chinese regime also found itself in 1957 deserted by the youth of the nation and opposed and condemned by the intelligentsia. And above all, it is hated by the hundreds of millions of the inarticulate but teeth-gnashing farmers and workers.

More than 80 percent of my people are farmers. The communist program of forced industrialization has imposed on the farming class a burden much bigger than they can possibly bear. Collectivization of agriculture and government monopoly of trade in all foodstuff have introduced inefficiency, bureaucratism, and corruption into the management of the main livelihood of the Chinese people. Throughout the hinterland of China millions of my people are actually dying for lack of food. This man-made famine has driven my people to desperation and actual starvation. That is why the communist regime has long been hated and detested by the vast majority of the people.

I was a representative at the founding meeting of the United Nations at San Francisco. This time I return to the United Nations after an absence of twelve years. I must confess that it pains me to see this august Assembly waste so many precious hours on the question of the so-called "Chinese representation."

In the preamble of the Charter of the United Nations, the founding nations have declared that one of the ends of the Charter is "to reaffirm faith in fundamental human rights, in the dignity and worth of the human person." To that end, nine years ago the General Assembly of the United Nations proclaimed to the world the Universal Declaration of Human Rights. But this monstrosity of communist tyranny as it is practiced in China is the very negation of the Charter and the very negation of the Universal Declaration of Human Rights.

There, in the mainland of China today, men and women who dared to be independent are being arbitrarily arrested, imprisoned, executed, or otherwise disposed of. There, many millions of farmers have been dispossessed and are being subjected to a most brutal form of human slavery. There, many millions of innocent citizens are sent to camps of slave labour—which is dubbed "reform through labor." There, in the Chinese mainland, sons and daughters are required to inform against their own parents. The home has no more privacy and the individual has no more "dignity and worth of the human person." He has none of the fundamental human rights, not even the freedom of silence.

If such a barbaric regime be worthy of membership in the United Nations, then the United Nations is not worthy of its Charter and not worthy of its Universal Declaration of Human Rights.

CHAPTER 30

A Sum-Up and a Warning[1]

Tension in the Taiwan Straits was started on August 23, 1958, just 3 months ago. I was then in New York City, beginning to pack my books and to wind up a mess of nine years' accumulation, in preparation for my return to Taiwan. I must confess that, during the first days of Communist shelling of the islands of the Quemoy group, I was a bit worried.

I realized that this concentrated and continuous shelling of the islands was a probing tactic; it was a test—a test of the strength of Free China's front line of defense, a test of her capability to supply the offshore islands, a test of her troops defending the fortified islands, and of her navy and her air force. And it was also a test of the morale of the people of Free China at a time of crisis. And above all, it was in all probability intended to be a severe test of the reliability of the Sino-American Treaty of Mutual Defense (which specifically covers Taiwan and the Penghu Islands) and the U.S. Congressional Resolution of January 1955 (which was understood to apply to the offshore islands.)

The questions then uppermost in our minds were: How effectively can Free China meet the test in the face of our obvious difficulties of distance, lack of new weapons, and lack of logistic equipment? And how ready and willing is our American ally to meet the challenge—in the face of an adverse public opinion which was then overwhelmingly on the side of appeasement and "disengagement?"

I confess I was worried in those first days of savage shelling of the islands. But my worries did not last long.

The fortifications on Quemoy stood well. The troops and the population on the islands remained calm. Their morale proved excellent.

---

1. An address delivered at the American University Club of the Republic of China on November 26, 1958. It was later published in *Tensions in the Taiwan Straits* (Taipei: Free China Review, 1959), 63–69.

And the people of Taiwan stood the test well. "No signs of panic, no hysteria, no hoarding, work goes on as usual."

And the response from the great leaders of the U.S.A. was truly heartening. Secretary of State Dulles was a rock of strength. President Eisenhower proved himself once more a great soldier and a great statesman. "A Western Pacific Munich," said Eisenhower, "would not buy peace and security. It would encourage the aggressors and dismay our friends and allies."

As Mr. R. C. Chen told you two weeks ago, "Since August 23rd, Uncle Sam has sent to Taiwan more than one billion U.S. dollars worth of the best military equipment for the joint defense of freedom."

And we were soon reading of the good news of our victories in the air. The Associated Press described the Chinese airmen as "the best fliers in the world." The "Sidewinders" were used for the first time over the Taiwan Straits. But it was said that more than "80% of the MIGs knocked down were destroyed without the use of the Sidewinders."

And our naval men and marines also did very well. "The Chinese," said Admiral Felt, "have learned in the past two months the techniques and tricks of amphibious warfare which we spent years to learn." So the Communist blockade of Quemoy was broken by the Chinese armed forces, with American arms. So the half-million-round Communist artillery barrage failed.

This, then, is my sum-up: Free China, with the timely and generous aid of American arms and equipment, has been able to meet the severe test of the last three months. Her great ally, the U.S.A., has been ready and willing to meet the challenge. All evidences point to a joint Sino-American victory over an apparently well planned Communist campaign of probing aggression. It is a victory of Chinese anti-Communist patriotism and national unity. It is also a victory of the U.S. policy of firmness and fidelity to the pledged word as enunciated by President Eisenhower and Secretary Dulles from the very beginning of the tension in the Taiwan Straits.

Bishop Ward has characterized the Communist shelling of Quemoy as a test of Sino-American solidarity. And I agree with him that the test has resulted in much strengthening of that solidarity.

But this hard-earned victory in the first round of the conflict must not make us complacent. We must be constantly on our guard.

World Communism is one, and is highly centralized in control. Its strategy of world conquest is conceived on a world scale and its tactical moves may be carried out in different parts of the earth either simultaneously or at different but always well coordinated points of time.

Earlier this year, it was the Middle East that was threatened. But, before the situation in the Middle East calmed down, war suddenly broke out in the Far East by the savage shelling of Quemoy. And now, while the Chinese Communist guns are still shelling our offshore island every day or every other day, the city of Berlin has already been threatened by new dangers of a long blockade or a war.

On November 10, Premier Nikita S. Khrushchev of the Soviet Union made a speech in Moscow, in which he demanded the termination of the Four Power occupation of Berlin. He said that the Soviet Union was ready to hand over its occupation functions to the puppet Communist regime of East Germany.

I quote a few sentences of the Khrushchev speech:

The time has evidently come for the powers which signed the Potsdam agreement to give up the remnants of the occupation regime in Berlin. The Soviet Union, for its part, will hand over those functions in Berlin which are still with Soviet organs to the sovereign German Democratic Republic. I think that this would be the right thing to do.

Let the United States, France and Britain form their own relations. with the German Democratic Republic and come to an agreement with it if they are interested in certain questions connected with Berlin.

Should any aggressive forces attack the German Democratic Republic . . . then we will consider it as an attack on the Soviet Union, on all the parties to the Warsaw Treaty. We shall rise then to the defense of the German Democratic Republic, and this will mean the defense of the root interests of the security of the Soviet Union, of the entire Socialist camp and of the cause of peace all over the world. . . .

On November 16, the *Pravda*, the official organ of the Communist Party, published an article under the title, "There Can Only Be One Solution to the Berlin Question." The article quoted the key sentences from Khrushchev's speech of November 10th, and remarked that this is "a decision of the Soviet Government," and that "the Soviet Government is inflexible in its decision to implement the long matured measures."

To this enlightened assembly, I need not go into the details of the story of the divided and occupied city of Berlin which is an "island" surrounded on all sides by East Germany. Nor is it necessary to describe the very serious predicament in which the other three occupation powers, the United States,

Great Britain and France, will be placed if and when the Soviet Union will unilaterally terminate the agreement of occupation signed on June 5, 1945, by the military commanders of the four powers and confirmed by the Potsdam agreement.

In brief, the occupation troops of those three powers will be forced to deal with the East German regime which they have refused to recognize. And the many millions of freedom-loving German people in the Western section of Berlin will be forced to submit to Communist rule which they hate. Or they will have to face a second Berlin Blockade in which the troops and the vast population can only be supplied by an airlift to be organized on an unprecedented scale.

And, of course, there is always the danger of a great war breaking out in such a highly explosive situation.

In the last two weeks, the Western Powers have, on several occasions, declared their determination not to be ousted from Berlin, and to hold the Soviet Union responsible for maintaining the status quo in Berlin. Sixteen days have passed since the Khrushchev speech of November 10th, and the Soviet Union has not yet carried out its threat to end its occupation of Berlin and to transfer its functions to the East German regime.

The initiative is in the hands of the gangsters. And experts on world affairs hesitate to foretell what the outcome of the new Berlin crisis may be like.

But I for one would like to sound a serious warning to all of us who are immediately concerned with the fate of a free China and a free Asia. My warning is: Whatever may happen in Berlin and in Europe, there will be no lessening of tension in the Taiwan Straits. On the contrary, it can be safely predicted that, while the attention of the entire western world is focused on the Berlin crisis, world communism will start its sudden and aggressive moves in Asia—surely in the Taiwan Straits, and most likely also in Korea, or in Vietnam—and possibly also in Iran, which was specifically mentioned in Khrushchev's speech on November 10th.

For, let us never forget, World Communism is one, and its machinations and manipulations are calculated and well co-ordinated.

And let us never forget what happened ten years ago in China during the long months of the first Berlin Blockade.

The first Berlin Blockade began in July 1948, lasted ten months and a half, and was not ended until May 1949. It was during those ten and a half months that the fate of China was sealed.

When the entire western world was watching and admiring the thousands of dramatic airlifting planes flying into and out of Berlin, Shantung was lost, the whole of Manchuria was lost, North China was lost, and the Communist troops crossed the Yangtse River and occupied the evacuated capital of Nanking in April 1949. The city of Shanghai fell in May. And when the Berlin blockade was at last ended in May, the main part of China had been lost to the armed conquest of world Communism.

There is a Chinese proverbial expression for this kind of tactics. It is called the method of "attacking the west while making a big howl in the east."

Let us all remember the tragic lesson of the first Berlin Blockade of 1948–1949. Let us warn ourselves and our friends never to lessen our daily and hourly vigilance.

CHAPTER 31

John Dewey in China[1]

John Dewey was born October 20, 1859, and died in 1952, in his ninety-third year. This coming October there will be a celebration of the Centennial of his birth in many parts of the free world.

Forty years ago, early in 1919, Professor Dewey and his wife, Alice, left the United States for a trip to the Far East. The trip was to be solely for pleasure. But, before their departure from San Francisco, Dewey was invited by cable to give a series of lectures at the Imperial University of Tokyo and later at other centers of higher learning in Japan.

While in Japan, he received a joint invitation from five educational bodies in China to lecture in Peking, Nanking, Shanghai, and other cities. He accepted the invitation, and the Deweys arrived in Shanghai on May 1, 1919—just three days before the outburst of the Student Movement on May 4th in Peking. That was the Student Movement which is often referred to as "The May Fourth Movement."

It was the Student Movement and its successes and failures that so much intrigued the Deweys that they changed their original plan to return to America after the summer months and decided to spend a full year in China. Dewey applied to Columbia University for a year's leave of absence, which was granted, and which was subsequently extended to two years. So, he spent a total of two years and two months in China, from May, 1919, to July, 1921.

When Miss Evelyn Dewey wrote in her Preface to the volume of Dr. and Mrs. Dewey's letters that "the fascination of the struggle going on in China

---

1. This is a public lecture delivered at the Third East-West Philosophers' Conference held at the University of Hawaii in July 1959. It was later published in Charles A. Moore's *Philosophy and Culture—East and West* (Honolulu: University of Hawaii Press, 1962), 762–769. It was also translated into Chinese by Hsia Tao-p'ing and published in *Hu Shih Yanjiang Ji* 胡適演講集 (Taipei: Hu Shih jinian guan, 1970), 2:315–335.

for a unified and independent democracy caused them to alter their plan to return to the United States in the summer of 1919," she was referring to their keen interest in the Student Movement. It is in order, therefore, to give a brief sketch of the May Fourth Movement and its nationwide influence as a background of this talk on John Dewey in China.

World War I had ended only a few months before, and the Peace Conference in Paris was drafting the final terms of the peace treaty. The Chinese people had hoped that, with Woodrow Wilson's idealistic "Fourteen Points" still echoing throughout the world, China might have some of her grievances redressed at the Peace Conference. But in the first days of May, 1919, authentic reports began to reach China that President Wilson had failed to render his moral support to China's demand that the former German possessions and concessions in Shantung be restored to China: and that the Peace Conference had decided to leave the Shantung question to Japan to settle with China. The Chinese delegation was helpless, the Chinese government was powerless. The people were disappointed and disheartened, but helpless.

On Sunday, May 4th, the students in Peking called a mass meeting of all colleges and secondary schools to protest against the Paris decision and to call on the government to instruct the Chinese delegation in Paris to refuse to accept it. The whole thing was a spontaneous and unpremeditated outburst of youthful patriotism. The communists' claim that "the May Fourth Movement" was a part of the World Revolution and was planned and led by Chinese communists is sheerly a big lie. There was no communist in China in 1919.

After the speeches and resolutions, the mass meeting decided on a demonstration parade which ended in forcing the closed gates of the house of the Minister of Foreign Affairs, who has been notorious for his pro-Japanese policies. The marching students went into the house and beat up one of the luncheon guests, who happened to be the Chinese Minister to Tokyo, recalled for consultation. In the turmoil, the house was set on fire—probably to frighten away the demonstrators. A number of students were arrested on their way back to their schools.

That was what happened on the fourth of May, forty years ago.

The Deweys were still in Shanghai when the news of the Peking student movement was first published and was immediately arousing sympathetic responses from students and the general public all over the country.

When the Deweys arrived in Peking, they saw the student movement at its highest moments during the first days of June. Hundreds of students were making speeches in the streets, preaching to the people that China could regain her lost rights by boycotting Japanese goods. On June 5, the Deweys wrote to their daughters at home: "This is Thursday morning, and last night we heard that about a thousand students were arrested the day before. They had filled the building of Law [of the National Peking University, used as a temporary 'prison'], and have begun on the Science building."

Later, on the same day, they reported the most astonishing news: "In the evening, a telephone call came that the tents [of the soldiers] around the university buildings where the students were imprisoned had been struck and the soldiers were leaving. Then the student inside held a meeting and passed a resolution asking the government whether they were guaranteed freedom of speech, because if they were not, they would not leave the building merely to be arrested again, as they planned to go on speaking. So they embarrassed the government by remaining in 'jail' all night."

The Deweys later explained that the government's ignominious surrender was due to the fact that the merchants in Shanghai had called a strike the day before as a protest against the arrest of the thousand students. And they remarked: "This is a strange country. The so-called republic is a joke . . . But in some ways there is more democracy than we have. Leaving out the women, there is complete social equality. And while the legislature is a perfect farce, public opinion, when it does express itself, as at the present time, has remarkable influence."

On June 16, the Deweys wrote home that the three pro-Japanese high officials (including the Minister of Foreign Affairs) had resigned from the government, and the students' strike had been called off.

On July 2, they wrote home: "The anxiety here is tense. The report is that the [Chinese] Delegates did not sign [the Peace Treaty]." Two days later, they wrote: "You can't imagine what it means here for China not to have signed [the Peace Treaty]. The entire government had been for it. The President up to ten days before the signing said it was necessary [to sign]. It was a victory for public opinion, and all set going by these little schoolboys and girls."

I have quoted these letters to show a part of the first impressions Dr. and Mrs. Dewey had during their first two or three months in Peking. Somehow, this "strange country" had a strange appeal to them. They decided to stay on, for a year at first, and finally for two years and two months. They visited 11 of the 22 provinces—4 provinces in the North, 5 in Central China, from Shanghai to Changsha, and 2 in the South.

A word may be said about the preparations made for the reception of Dewey's lectures. A month before his arrival in China. I was asked by the sponsoring organizations to give a series of four lectures on the Pragmatic Movement, beginning with Charles S. Peirce and William James, but with special emphasis on Dewey. A series of articles on Dewey's educational philosophy was published in Shanghai under the editorship of Dr. Chiang Monlin, one of his students in Teachers' College at Columbia.

A number of Dewey's students were asked to interpret his lectures in the Chinese language. For example, I was his translator and interpreter for all his lectures in Peking and in the provinces of Shantung and Shansi. For his several major series of lectures, we also selected competent recorders for reporting every lecture in full for the daily newspapers and periodicals. What came to be known as "Dewey's Five Major Series of Lectures" in Peking, totaling 58 lectures, were recorded and reported in full and later published in book form, going through ten large reprintings before Dewey left China in 1921, and continuing to be reprinted for three decades until the communists put a stop to them.

The topic of the Five Series will give some idea of the scope and content of Dewey's lectures:

    I. 3 lectures on Modern Tendencies in Education
    II. 16 lectures on Social and Political Philosophy
    III. 16 lectures on Philosophy of Education
    IV. 15 lectures on Ethics
    V. 8 lectures on Types of Thinking

His lectures in Peking included two other series:

    VI. 3 lectures on Democratic Developments in America
    VII. 3 lectures on Three Philosophers of the Modern Period (William James, Henri Bergson, Bertrand Russell—these lectures were given at special request as an introduction to Russell before the latter's arrival in China in 1920 to deliver a number of lectures.)

Dewey's lectures in Nanking included these series:

    1) 10 lectures on the Philosophy of Education
    2) 10 lectures on the History of Philosophy
    3) 3 lectures on Experimental Logic

Typing on his own typewriter, Dewey always wrote out his brief notes for every lecture, a copy of which would be given to his interpreter so that he could study them and think out the suitable Chinese words and phrases before the lecture and its translation. After each lecture in Peking, the Dewey notes were given to the selected recorders, so that they could check their reports before publication. I have recently re-read most of his lectures in Chinese translation after a lapse of 40 years, and I could still feel the freshness and earnestness of the great thinker and teacher who always measured every word and every sentence in the classroom or before a large lecture audience.

After one year of public lectures in many cities, Dewey was persuaded by his Chinese friends to spend another year in China, primarily as a Visiting Professor at the National Peking University, lecturing and discussing with advanced students without the aid of an interpreter, and devoting a part of his time to lectures at the Teachers' College in Peking and in Nanking. He was interested in the few "experimental schools" which had been established by his former students in various educational centers, such as Peking, Nanking, Soochow, and Shanghai. Some of the schools, such as the one at the Teachers' College in Nanking, were named Dewey schools.

The Deweys left China in 1921. In October, 1922, the National Educational Association met in Tsinan to discuss a thorough revision of the national school system and curriculum. Article 4 of the New Educational System of 1922 reads: "The child is the center of education. Special attention should be paid to the individual characteristics and aptitudes of the child in organizing the school system. Henceforth, the elective system should be adopted for secondary and higher education, and the principle of flexibility should be adopted in the arrangement and promotion of classes in all elementary schools." In the new school curriculum of 1923 and the revised curriculum of 1929, the emphasis was placed on the idea that the child was the center of the school. The influence of Dewey's educational philosophy is easily seen in these revisions.

Dewey went to China in May, 1919—forty years ago. Can we now give a rough estimate of his influence in China after the passing of forty years?

Such an estimate has not been easy, because these forty years have been mostly years of great disturbance, of civil wars, revolutions, and foreign wars—including the years of the Nationalist Revolution, the eight years of the Japanese War and the Second World War, the years of the communist wars, and the communist conquest of the Chinese mainland. It is exceedingly difficult to say how much influence any thinker or any school of thought has had on a people that has suffered so much from the tribulations of war, revolution, exile, mass migration, and general insecurity and deprivation.

In our present case, however, the Chinese communist regime has given us unexpected assistance in the form of nationwide critical condemnation and purging of the Pragmatic philosophy of Dewey and of his Chinese followers. This great purge began as early as 1950 in a number of inspired but rather mild articles criticizing Dewey's educational theories, and citing American critics such as Kandel, Bode, Rugg, and Hook in support of their criticism. But the purge became truly violent in 1954 and 1955, when the Chinese communist regime ordered a concerted condemnation and purge of the evil and poisonous thoughts of Hu Shih in many aspects of Chinese intellectual activity—in philosophy, in history, in the history of philosophy, in political thought, in literature, and in histories of Chinese literature. In those two years of 1954 and 1955, more than three million words were published for the purging and exorcising of the "ghost of Hu Shih." And in almost every violent attack on me, Dewey was inevitably dragged in as a source and as the fountainhead of the heinous poison.

And in most of the articles of this vast purge literature, there was a frank recognition of the evil influence of Dewey, Dewey's philosophy and method, and the application of that philosophy and method by that "rotten and smelly" Chinese Deweyan, Hu Shih, and his slavish followers. May we not accept such confessions from the communist-controlled world as fairly reliable, though probably slightly exaggerated, estimates of the "poisonous" influence left by Dewey and his friends in China?

I quote only a few of these confessions from Red China:

1) "If we want to criticize the old theories of education, we must begin with Dewey. The educational ideas of Dewey have dominated and controlled Chinese education for thirty years, and his social philosophy and his general philosophy have also influenced a part of the Chinese people" (*The People's Education*, October, 1950).

2) "How was Dewey's poisonous Pragmatic educational philosophy spread over China? It was spread primarily through his lectures in China preaching his Pragmatic philosophy and his reactionary educational ideas, and through that center of Dewey's reactionary thinking, namely, Columbia University, from which thousands of Chinese students, for over thirty years, have brought back all the reactionary, subjective-idealistic, Pragmatic educational ideas of Dewey. . . . As one who has been most deeply

poisoned by his reactionary educational ideas, as one who has worked hardest and longest to help spread his educational ideas, I now publicly accuse that great fraud and deceiver in the modern history of education, John Dewey!" (By Ch'en Ho-ch'in, one of the great educators of the Dewey school, who was responsible for the modernization of the Shanghai schools, who was ordered to make this public accusation in February, 1955. It was published in the *Wenhui Pao*, February 28, 1955.)

3) "The battlefield of the study of Chinese literature has, for over thirty years, been occupied by the representative of bourgeois idealism [that is, Pragmatism], namely, Hu Shih, and his school. Even years after the 'Liberation' when the intellectual circles have supposedly acknowledged the leadership position of Marxism, the evil influence of that school has not yet received the purge it rightly deserves" (*The People's Daily*, the official organ of the Chinese Communist Party and Government, Nov. 5, 1954).

4) "The poison of the philosophical ideas of Pragmatism [as represented by Hu Shih] has not only infiltrated the field of the study of Chinese literature, but has also penetrated deep into the fields of history, education, linguistics, and even the realm of natural science—of course, the greatest evil effect has been in the field of philosophy" (*Kuang-ming Daily*, of Peking, Dec. 15, 1954).

These confessions should be sufficient to give us an idea of the extent of the evil influence of Dewey and his followers and friends in China. According to these confessions, the Pragmatic philosophy and method of Dewey and his Chinese friends have dominated Chinese education for thirty years, and have infiltrated and dominated for over thirty years the fields of the study of Chinese literature, linguistics, history, philosophy, and even the realm of natural science!

What is this Deweyan brand of Pragmatism or Experimentalism that is so much feared in communist China as to deserve three million words of purge and condemnation?

As I examine this vast purge literature. I cannot help laughing heartily at all this fuss and fury. After wading through literally millions of words of abuse, I find that what those Red masters and slaves dread most and want to purge is only a philosophical theory of thinking which Dewey had expounded in many of his logical studies and which he had made popular in his little book, *How We Think*. According to this theory, thinking is not passive and slavish deduction from unquestioned absolute truths, but an effective tool and method for resolving doubt and overcoming difficulties in our daily life, in our active dealings with Nature and man. Thinking, says Dewey, always begins with a situation of doubt and perplexity; it proceeds with a search for facts and for possible suggestions or hypotheses for the resolution of the initial difficulty, and it terminates in proving, testing, or verifying the selected hypothesis by successfully and satisfactorily resolving the perplexing situation which had challenged the mind to think. That's the Deweyan theory of thinking, which I have in the last forty years tried to popularize by pointing out that that was an adequate analysis of the method of science as well as an adequate analysis of the method of "evidential investigation" (*k'ao-chü, k'ao-cheng*), which the great Chinese classical scholars of the last three centuries had been using so efficaciously and fruitfully. That is the method of the disciplined common sense of mankind: it is the essence of the method of science, consisting mainly in a boldness in suggesting hypotheses, coupled with meticulous care in seeking verification by evidence or by experimentation.

Two corollaries from this conception of thinking stand out preeminently. First, the progress of man and of society depends upon the patient and successful solution of real and concrete problems by means of the active use of the intelligence of man. "Progress," says Dewey, "is piecemeal. It is always a retail job, never wholesale." That is anathema to all communists, who believe in total and cataclysmic revolution, which will bring about wholesale progress overnight.

The second corollary is equally anathema to the communists, namely, that, in this natural and orderly process of rational thinking, all doctrines and all theories are to be regarded, not as absolute truths, but only as tentative and suggestive hypotheses to be tested in use—only as tools and materials for aiding human intelligence, but never as unquestioned and unquestionable dogmas to stifle or stop thinking. Dewey said in his Peking lecture on moral education: "Always cultivate an open mind. Always cultivate the habit of intellectual honesty. And always learn to be responsible for your own thinking." That was enough to scare the Commies out of their wits, and enough to start years of violent attack and abuse on Dewey and Pragmatism and the "ghost of Hu Shih."

And the most amusing fact was that all those years of violent attack and all those millions of words of condemnation began in 1954 with a communist discussion of a popular Chinese novel of the eighteenth century entitled

The Dream of the Red Chamber. Why? Because nearly forty years ago I was tempted to apply the method of scientific research to a study of the authorship, the remarkable family background of the author, and the history of the evolution of the text of the novel. In the course of subsequent years, numerous hitherto-unknown materials were discovered and published by me, all of which have verified and strengthened my first researches. That was a conscious application of the Dewey theory of thinking to a subject-matter which was well known to every man and woman who could read at all. I have applied the same theory and method of thinking to several other Chinese novels, as well as to many difficult and forbidding problems of research in the fields of the history of Chinese thought and belief, including the history of Ch'an or Zen Buddhism.

But the best-known example or material with which I illustrated and popularized the Deweyan theory of thinking was the great novel *The Dream of the Red Chamber.* Nearly thirty years ago (November, 1930), at the request of my publisher, I made an anthology of my Essays, in which I included three pieces on *The Dream of the Red Chamber.* I wrote a preface to this anthology intended for younger readers. In my wicked moments, I wrote these words in introducing my three studies of that novel:

> My young friends, do not regard these pieces on *The Dream of the Red Chamber* as my efforts to teach you how to read a novel. These essays are only a few examples or illustrations of a method of how to think and study. Through these simple essays, I want to convey to you a little bit of the scientific spirit, the scientific attitude of mind, and the scientific method. The scientific spirit lies in the search for facts and for truth. The scientific attitude of mind is a willingness to put aside our feelings and prejudices, a willingness to face facts and to follow evidence wherever it may lead us. And the scientific method is only "a boldness to suggest hypotheses coupled with a meticulous care in seeking proof and verification." When evidence is lacking or insufficient, there must be a willingness to suspend judgment. A conclusion is valid only when it is verified. Some Ch'an (Zen) monk of centuries ago said that Bodhidharma came all the way to China in search of a man who would not be deceived by man. In these essays, I, too, wish to present a method of how not to be deceived by men. To be led by the nose by a Confucius or a Chu Hsi is not highly commendable. But to be led by the nose by a Marx, a Lenin, or a Stalin is also not quite becoming a man. I have no desire to lead anybody by

the nose: I only wish to convey to my young friends my humble hope that they may learn a little intellectual skill for their own self-protection and endeavor to be men who cannot be deceived by others.

These words. I said then, were penned with infinite love and infinite hope. For these words, I have brought upon my head and the head of my beloved teacher and friend, John Dewey, years of violent attack and millions of words of abuse and condemnation. But, ladies and gentlemen, these same millions of words of abuse and condemnation have given me a feeling of comfort and encouragement—a feeling that Dewey's two years and two months in China were not entirely in vain, that my forty years of humble effort in my own country have not been entirely in vain, and that Dewey and his students have left in China plenty of "poison," plenty of antiseptic and antitoxin, to plague the Marxist-Leninist slaves for many, many years to come.

CHAPTER 32

China's Lesson for Freedom[1]

On October 3, 1952, General Eisenhower made a great speech in Milwaukee, eighty-five miles north of Chicago. In that speech, he said:

> Let not our memories be too short. Only a few years have passed since many moved among us who argued cunningly against this plain truth [that "communism and freedom are opposed as danger is to safety, as sickness is to health, . . . as darkness to light"].
>
> Their speech was persuasive, and their vocabulary clever. Remember? It went like this, "After all, while we stand for political democracy, they [the Communists] stand for economic democracy. Fundamentally these are but two slightly different roads to the same goal. We both believe in freedom."

General Eisenhower went on to say:

> We must all remember that sophisticated lie. We will never forget it. For it partly poisoned two whole decades of our national life. It insinuated itself into our schools, our public forums, some of our news channels, some of our labor unions and—most terrifyingly—into our government itself. . . .
>
> These years have, indeed, been a harrowing time in our history. It has been a time of both honest illusion and dishonest betrayal—both terribly costly. It has been a time which should have taught us, with cold finality, the truth about freedom and communism.

When I was asked to talk on "China's Lesson for Freedom," I took it for granted that I was asked to tell the story of how China lost her freedom, of how the Chinese people lost their freedom—as a case study, as a concrete

---

1. An unpublished manuscript, a speech delivered in the 1950s.

illustration of the historic lesson that communism is directly opposed to freedom and must result in the destruction of freedom.

China's lesson for freedom can be most aptly summed up in the Eisenhower formula—"honest illusion and dishonest betrayal." The words best describe the historical relationship between the Chinese Nationalists and the Chinese Communists, between Chinese nationalism and world communism, throughout the last three decades. Parenthetically, I may add that these words of Eisenhower's most aptly sum up all the great tragedies that have befallen many once free and independent nations during the last fifteen or ten years. But I shall confine myself to China's historic lesson.

The struggle between Chinese nationalism and communism lasted twenty-six years before the fall of the mainland to Communist conquest. Fourteen out of the twenty-six years were periods in which the Chinese Communist Party was supposedly cooperating with the Nationalists. The first period, from 1923 to 1927, was known as the period of "Nationalist-Communist Collaboration." That collaboration was based on a joint declaration signed in January 1923, by Dr. Sun Yat-sen and Adolph Joffe, a representative of the Soviet Union and the Comintern. In that declaration, it was stated that Joffe entirely agreed with Dr. Sun that "there do not exist here [in China] the conditions for the successful establishment of either Communism or Sovietism," and China "can count on the support of Russia" in her effort "to achieve national unification and attain full national independence." Under this explicit understanding, the trusting Dr. Sun made his party (the Kuomintang) admit to its full membership Chinese Communists and even Communists of other countries, all supposedly on an individual basis and not as members of Communist parties.

This great trust was soon betrayed by the Communists, who at one time were able to capture one-third of the seats on the Central Committee of the Kuomintang and gain control of all the strategically important departments in the government. As the Nationalist Revolution began to be successful in its military expedition against the Northern warlords, the Communist International was making serious efforts to convert it into a Communist revolution. That great conspiracy, called "the great Chinese Revolution" in all Communist literature, might have succeeded if Chiang Kai-shek and the elder statesmen of the Kuomintang had not thwarted and destroyed it in April and May 1927 by purging the party of the Communists.

That was the first case-history of "honest illusion and dishonest betrayal." After ten years of separatist growth and armed insurrection and after years of defeats and long fights, the Chinese Communist Party once more declared its willingness to cooperate with the National Government in the war against the common enemy, Japan. Thus was begun the second period of Nationalist-Communist cooperation, the ten years of the "United Front" (1937–47). The basis of the "United Front" was supposed to be found in the "Manifesto of Unity" issued by the Central Committee of the Chinese Communist Party on September 22, 1937. Of the five solemnly declared principles in the manifesto, one pledged that the former Red Army "shall be under the control of the National Military Council," and another that "the policy of insurrection which aims at the overthrow of Kuomintang political power, the policy of land confiscation, and the policy of communist propaganda shall be discontinued."

As a matter of historical record, none of these pledges was ever carried out, and the Chinese Communists were making full use of the "United Front" for the unlimited growth and expansion of its Red Army, which, according to public statements by Communist representatives at the war capital of Chungking and Mao Tse-tung's declaration in April 1945, was able to expand from a small force of about 25,000 men in 1937 to the size of 910,000 men in 1945—an increase of 3,640 percent in eight years! This army was never under the control of the National Military Council: it was moving in every direction, and Mao declared in April 1945 that the territory "liberated" and occupied by the Communist armies extended into nineteen provinces and contained over ninety-five million people.

After the Soviet Union entered the Pacific War and occupied Manchuria, the Red armies were racing northeastward to reach Manchuria to be reequipped and supplied by the Russians and take over the most highly industrialized area in the whole of Asia. It was these armies that after 1947 conquered the whole of Manchuria and North China and later the entire mainland.

That was the second and more serious case-history of "honest illusion and dishonest betrayal."

It is a historical fact that the Communist Party and movement in all countries without exception were started by discontented and idealistic intellectuals. It may be worthwhile and indeed necessary to inquire wherein lies communism's magic power of appeal to radical and liberal men and women of so many countries. In other words, what is the source of "honest illusion" on the part of so many well-meaning though misguided intellectuals?

Speaking primarily from my observation and reflection on the history of the Communist movement in China, I am inclined to think that the magic power of appeal of communism of the Marxist-Leninist brand is mainly threefold: (1) the idealistic appeal of a hitherto unrealized Utopia, (2) the emotional appeal of the power of a radical revolution to right all wrongs and redress all injustices, and (3) last, but not least, the magic power of big and undefined words.

The first appeal—the powerful attraction of a utopian ideal—needs no elaboration in detail. A classless society of free and voluntary labor, wherein society takes from every man according to his ability, and gives to every man according to his needs: the universal appeal of such an ideal can never be denied.

The second appeal—that of the revolution as the most effective means to realize the quick and radical changes in society—is most powerful to impatient souls who find specific remedial reforms too slow and too inadequate and superficial to satisfy their idealistic dreams. I know many young and even middle-aged idealists who despaired of the processes of evolution and reform and turned to work for "the day" when the dictatorial powers of a successful revolutionary regime might overnight achieve what the *Communist Manifesto* envisaged as "the forcible overthrow of the whole extant social order." Little did they realize that a violent revolution, as Lenin openly declared, is the most totalitarian affair. All despotism, the oppression of all freedom, the repressive measures against all opposition—all these were justified by the cause of the Revolution.

Many of these impatient souls have died in the process. Many others live to see "the Revolution"—only to learn from their own leaders that even a revolutionary government cannot work miracles and that "the Revolution must go on and on."

These impatient spirits may never live long enough to grasp the meaning of the democratic philosophy as expressed by John Dewey that "progress is always made piecemeal," and that "progress is not a wholesale matter, but a retail job, to be contracted for and executed in sections."

It is easy for us to laugh at and belittle the third appeal of communism—the magic power of big words. But it is no laughing matter. The Communists have been masterful manipulators of big and undefined words, words with which to eulogize and glorify, words with which to condemn, and words with which to snare and to enslave the minds of millions. Democracy, Democracy of the Masses, Democracy of the Proletariat, the People's democracy, the People's Republic, the People's Government, the people's state apparatus, the

People's Army and Police, and my former student, Mao Tse-tung, has even invented the term "the People's Democratic Dictatorship"! And there are big words with which to convict and condemn people eternally, and without redress. In Red China today, I am called a bourgeois reactionary, and my thoughts are called "Hu Shih's bourgeois reactionary idealistic thoughts"— that [is] enough to condemn me and my ideas forever and ever.

General Eisenhower has singled out the magic word "economic democracy." Just before the fall of continental China, one of the "liberal" papers in Tientsin wrote an elaborate editorial on "economic democracy vs. political democracy," in which the editor said, "The American democracy gives the citizen a ballot; but the Soviet democracy gives him a loaf of bread." And an impoverished populace is supposed to know which to choose.

I shall conclude by telling a real story of an old friend of mine to illustrate how strangely the magic power of words could work on an intellectual of no mean standing. I refer to the late Ch'en Tu-hsiu, the founder and editor of the famous monthly magazine *Hsin-ch'ing-nien*, who later became a founder and the first leader of the Chinese Communist Party. He was overthrown in 1927, and later expelled from the Party as a Trotskyite. In his last years, he lived and died an independent liberal.

In his early days, he used to say that he worshipped only two deities, Democracy and Science. When he founded the Communist Party, he thought he had at last found his twin gods, Democracy and Science, in one. He found Science because he had come to regard Marxism as scientific. And he found democracy because he had come to believe that the Communist ideal of "proletarian democracy" or "democracy of the masses" was more democratic than the "bourgeois democracy" of the capitalistic countries of the Western world. In his last years, he confessed that it took him many years of hard thinking and bitter experience to arrive at the firm conviction that "democracy" is a way of life and has a definite content which is no other than the rights and liberties long enjoyed by the peoples of the Western democracies: the freedom of thought and belief, the freedom of speech, of the press, the right of due process of law, the right of labor to strike, etc. And he came to the startling discovery that there is no such thing as "democracy of the proletariat," which becomes an empty word if all the democratic rights and liberties of the Western democracies are to be condemned and excluded from the connotation of the word "democracy," as they are condemned and excluded by Marxist-Leninist-Stalinist communism. Democracy of the proletariat minus all these rights and liberties, especially the freedom of opposition, is no democracy at all, but despotism and totalitarianism of the worst possible type.

It has actually taken Ch'en Tu-hsiu a whole life to be freed from the magic power of the magic words, "democracy of the proletariat" and "democracy of the masses."

China's lesson for freedom is, therefore, threefold:

1. That blind worship of an untried or unchallenged "end" or "ideal" without due consideration of the necessary means of achieving it inevitably leads to the immoral philosophy of the end justifying the means.
2. Impatience in social and political thinking invariably leads to theoretical or ideological justification of violence and violent revolution, which tends necessarily toward dictatorship, despotism, and the destruction of freedom.
3. Do not belittle the magic power of big words, which are the most important stock-in-trade in the hands of modern tyrants and despots. The only antitoxin is a little measure of doubt, a few ounces of incredulity, and a little rigid, merited discipline to make ideas clear.

Even I myself was at one time greatly attracted by this utopian ideal. And I know many of my own friends have never consciously or seriously questioned the soundness of socialism as a social, economic, and political ideal. This very general acceptance of an untried utopian ideal of society is all the more dangerous because it is blindly applauded and accepted without serious thinking.[2]

The Machiavellian makers of the Bolshevik Revolution have fully capitalized on this unthinking and unquestioning attraction of the ideal—on the part not only of the general public, but also of the majority of intellectuals.

Out of this blind worship of an ideal, there has come the terrible and immoral political philosophy of "the end justifies the means." If the end is so generally desired, then all means, all methods, however brutal and inhuman, however ruthless and murderous, are justified. Against this unreasoning zeal for an idolized ultimate ideal, it is useless to quote the Chinese sage who said that the wise ruler would not kill one innocent man nor commit

---

2. Next to the first and second sentences of this paragraph Hu has written, "declaring publicly that socialism was a logical consequence of the democratic movement!" It is unclear whether Hu is referring to himself or to his friends.

one unjust act in order to gain an empire. Nor is it of any avail to preach the pragmatist philosophy of William James and John Dewey that the most important thing is not the end, but the means of securing it. So millions and tens of millions have been murdered, and hundreds of millions have been enslaved, and a "living hell" has been created in my beloved China—all in the name of an unknown god—the blindly worshipped ideal of a utopian society!

CHAPTER 33

The Conflict between Man's Right to Knowledge and the Security of the Community

Some Reflections on China's Failure to Restrain the Spread of Communist Agitation and Propaganda[1]

Professor John Hazard, in his letter of invitation to me to join this Conference, formulated his inquiry in these words:

> The Republic of China has fought a losing battle to maintain power on the mainland. It would seem important to any consideration of the subject to know what measures were taken to restrain the free exchange of ideas during that conflict and whether those measures were inadequate. In the light of the subsequent victory of the Communists, it would be helpful to have your thoughts on whether the victory was assisted materially by insufficient restraint on the free exchange of ideas.

I would like to reformulate Professor Hazard's inquiry in plainer language as follows:

1. Did the Chinese Government take measures to restrain the spread of Communist agitation and propaganda?
2. Why were those measures inadequate and ineffective?
3. Was the victory of the Chinese Communists assisted materially by the inadequacy or the failure of those attempts to restrain the spread of Communist propaganda?

---

1. An incomplete speech transcript written in the 1950s.

To simplify the inquiry, I shall answer the first and last questions very briefly at the outset, leaving the second and the most important question to be discussed in the main body of my paper. Of course the Chinese Government made serious attempts to restrain the free spread of Communist ideas and Communist propaganda. There were measures against the counterrevolution in the early years of the Nationalist Government, the Press Law of 1930, the revised Press Law of 1937, and the July 1947 Proclamation of General Mobilization Against the Communist Armed Rebellion. It is the wherefore of the failure of all these measures that may be of interest to this Conference.

As to the question, was the victory of the Chinese Communists aided materially by the failure to restrain the free spread of Communist ideas and propaganda? [T]he shortest and the best answer is the last sentence of Thesis 13 adopted by the Second World Congress of the Communist International in July–August 1920, which reads:

> Without involving the masses in the revolutionary struggle for a free Communist press, the preparation for the dictatorship of the proletariat is impossible.

A free Communist press—the free and legal press for the Communist Party and its front organizations and fellow travelers, has materially assisted the victory of the Communists, not only in China, but in every other country in the world, and is justifiably regarded as the necessary material condition without which "the preparation for the dictatorship of the proletariat is impossible."

I

What is the real meaning of "a free Communist press" which is so necessary to the preparation for the dictatorship of the proletariat in all countries of the world? It is my belief that a clear understanding of what is fully implied in this term is absolutely necessary to our discussion of why it has been so difficult for China, or for any other non-Communist or anti-Communist country, to restrain the free spread of Communist ideology and propaganda.

At the Second World Congress of the Comintern held in 1920, twenty-one Conditions were laid down for the admission of Communist Parties to the Third International. The very first Condition deals with propaganda and agitation. It stipulates:

> The entire party press should be edited by reliable Communists who have proved their loyalty to the cause of the proletarian revolution. All periodical and other publications, as well as all party publications and editions, are subject to the control of the presidium of the party, independently of whether the party is legal or illegal.

The third Condition deals with "the illegal apparatus" and the necessity of "a combination of legal and illegal work."

> The class struggle in almost every country of Europe and America is entering the phase of civil war. Under such conditions, the Communists can have no confidence in bourgeois laws. They should create everywhere a parallel illegal apparatus, which at the decisive moment should be of assistance to the party to do its duty toward the revolution.
>
> In every country where, in consequence of martial law or of other exceptional laws, the Communists are unable to carry on their work legally, combination of legal and illegal work is absolutely necessary.

This necessity is more fully explained in Thesis 12 adopted by the same Second Congress:

> For all countries, even for the most "free," "legal" and "peaceful" ones in the sense of a lesser acuteness in the class struggle, the period has arrived when it has become absolutely necessary for every Communist party to combine systematically all legal and illegal work, legal and illegal organization. . . . It is especially necessary to carry on illegal work in the army, navy and police.

It is easy for us to understand what is meant by "illegal work" or "illegal organization," which simply means secret and underground work, and for which the fundamental principle of organization has been clearly defined, namely, "the creation of Communist nuclei everywhere . . . in every trade and industrial union, co-operative association, factory, tenants' union, in every government institution—everywhere, even though there may be only three people sympathizing with Communism, a Communist nucleus must be immediately organized" (Paragraph 18 of The Role of the Communist Party in the Proletarian Revolution, adopted by the same Congress).

But Thesis 12 goes on to say:

On the other hand, it is also necessary in all cases without exception not to limit oneself to illegal work, but to carry on also legal work overcoming all difficulties, founding a legal press and legal organizations under the most diverse circumstances, and in case of need, frequently changing names.

Surely here the term "legal organizations" could not mean the open Communist parties, nor the term "legal press" mean the official organs of those parties such as the *Daily Worker* of New York or the *Hsin-hua jih-pao* of the Chinese Communist Party.

Let me quote the next thesis (Thesis 13):

. . . On the whole, by means of deceit, the pressure of capital and the bourgeois government, the bourgeoisie deprives the revolutionary proletariat of its press.

For the struggle against this state of things, the Communist parties must create a new type of periodical press for extensive circulation among the workmen:

1) Legal publications, in which the Communists without calling themselves such and without mentioning their connection with the party, would learn to utilize the slightest possibility allowed by the laws as the Bolshevik[s] did at the time of the Tzar, after 1905.

2) Illegal sheets, although of the smallest dimensions and irregularly published, but reproduced in most of the printing offices by workmen (in secret . . .), and giving the proletariat undiluted revolutionary information and the revolutionary slogans.

Thesis 13 concludes with these words I have already quoted:

Without involving the masses in the revolutionary struggle for a free Communist press, the preparation for the dictatorship of the proletariat is impossible.

So we can now understand what world Communism means by "a legal press," "legal publications," and "a free Communist press." These terms mean one and the same thing, namely, the various kinds of publications of front organizations formed "under the most diverse circumstances and frequently changing names," and publications written and published by "Communists without calling themselves such and without mentioning their connection with the party."

Against this kind of "legal work" and "legal press" or "free Communist press," no measure of restraint, in China or in any other country, has ever been effective or adequate.

In a country like the United States of America, whose Constitution expressly says that "Congress must make no law abridging the freedom of speech or of the press," there is of course no adequate legal means to restrain the freedom of any writing or publication issued in the name of Freedom, Democracy, Peace, Justice, Humanity, Racial Equality, Anti-fascism, Anti-war, Anti-militarism, Anti-aggression, etc.

Even in a country like China where the Communist Party was outlawed for a number of years and where the Government forces fought the Red Armies for many years, there was no adequate means of curbing or guarding against the mushroom growth of publications that sprang up "under the most diverse circumstances," most often in the name of "the New Learning," "the New Science," "the New Method of Knowledge and Reasoning," "the New Sociology," "the New Democracy," and equally frequently in the name of Patriotism, of National Salvation, of Anti-imperialism, of a United Front against Japan, etc.

All the measures for the regulation and control of books and periodicals were inadequate in dealing with the cunning and subtle methods of the "free Communist press." The Press Law of 1930, for example, stipulated that publications "must not contain items with the intent of undermining the Kuomintang, or of undermining Dr. Sun Yat-sen's Three Principles of Nationalism, Democracy and the People's Livelihood," or "items with the intent of overthrowing the National Government, or of injuring the interests of the Republic of China." But what could the Government do to those publications which never mentioned the Kuomintang party or Dr. Sun's three principles, but which were ostensibly discussing and reinterpreting the economic background of the Taiping Rebellion of the middle of the last century, or the Peasants' Uprisings at the end of the Ming Dynasty, or the Boxers' War of 1900—from the point of view of the New Science of History? And what could the Ministry of Education do to a book on A System of Logic which teaches everything about historical materialism and dialectic materialism without ever mentioning Karl Marx or ever using those terms?

In the years 1953-54, there was published in Shanghai a huge work in two volumes, totaling about 700,000 words, under the title of *A Critique of Hu Shih* (*Hu Shih p'i-p'an*). No government censor had the patience to wade through these supposedly academic discussions in seven hundred thousand words, or took the trouble to check the many quotations from such foreign authors referred to in the footnotes merely as "K.M." and "F.E." (Karl Marx and Friedrich Engels) or from some foreign document referred to merely as "Manifeste du . . ." And certainly I myself was not going to inform the government that this work was about 15 percent a critique of Hu Shih but 85 percent a rewriting of the history of Chinese philosophy and of much of Chinese history in general—entirely from the Marxist standpoint.

A few quotations from the author's general introduction will make clear the real propaganda value of such a cleverly camouflaged work. "Why," said the author,

> do we undertake this series of Critiques? Because we recognize that the development of culture, like the development of society, proceeds in accordance with the law of progress as laid down by Hegel. From the era of 1898 [that is, the era of Liang Chi-chao and his friends] to the era of May Fourth, 1919 [that is, the era generally known as the Chinese intellectual renaissance], that was the first Negation. From May Fourth to "1927" [that is, the Communist Revolution in China], that was the second Negation, which was the Negation of Negation. Therefore we want to subject to a critical examination all the modern European culture that has been introduced into China since May Fourth, 1919. The reason is obvious. In the past, the fight was against the medieval civilization of China, and everything that came from the West was accepted as new and good. . . . Actually that European civilization was already crumbling to pieces at the time of the Imperialist War of 1914–18; and a newer and higher civilization of the future was already at the stage of rapid and vigorous growth. Under such circumstances, if we want to make the history of Chinese civilization go forward, it is necessary for us to take up the task of bidding farewell to the old and welcoming the new. Only when the old are [*sic*] gone can the new come in and stay. A critical examination of the old is therefore of unusual importance.

So a critique of Hu Shih was in reality a dialectic movement negation— the negation of negation, which became a movement to prepare China for the "newer and higher civilization of the future." And the author in his preface to the first volume (which purports to be a critique of Hu Shih's *History of*

Ancient Chinese Philosophy) tells us a secret: "I want to call the readers' attention to the fact that this volume actually contains a book of mine own: a *History of Ancient Chinese Philosophy*, which at the same time contains within it another and briefer book: the *Economic History of Ancient China*."

I cited this example to show the subtle and devious way in which the free and legal publications of Communist propaganda were usually camouflaged, and against which no censorship, no measures of restraint in China or elsewhere could be adequate.

I have seen hundreds of such free and legal publications in China; and I have no doubt that all of us must have seen hundreds of such cleverly camouflaged publications in other countries. And in the light of recent history, I can recall at least a score of such free and perfectly legal publications in the English language which may be said to have materially assisted the victory of the Communists, not only in the mainland of China, but in many, many other countries of the world. But they do not teach the overthrow of the constituted government by force and violence, nor do they create "a clear and present danger" to the nation. There are no measures adequate to cope with such free and legal publications of Communist and pro-Communist propaganda, without which, said the Comintern thirty-four years ago, the preparation for the dictatorship of the proletariat is impossible.

II

So much with regard to what may be ascribed to the intrinsic nature and method of Communist propaganda and agitation which defies all measures of restraint in any country with a civilization and with some respect for public opinion.

I now wish to point out three undeniable and peculiar historical facts or situations which have further complicated the problem of Communist propaganda and agitation in China and have made it all the more impossible for the Chinese Government to deal with them. These three historical facts are:

1. that most of the Communist propaganda literature was printed and published in the foreign settlements and concessions of Shanghai and other treaty ports, and in the British colony of Hong Kong, over which the Chinese Government either had only very limited juridical and political control or had no control at all.

2. that out of the whole period of twenty-six years of China's struggle with world Communism, the Chinese Communist Party was legal for at least fourteen years, from 1923 to 1927, and again from 1937 to 1947.
3. that, for fully twenty-two years out of the twenty-six years, the Chinese Communist Party maintained a Red Army of considerable force which from time to time occupied large areas of territory where autonomous administrations were set up.

All these three historical situations must be taken into consideration before one can really understand what an impossible task it was for the Chinese Government to attempt to restrain or suppress the free flow of Communist propaganda.

It is a historical fact that Hong Kong and the foreign settlements and concessions in the "treaty ports" of China—the symbols of Western imperialism in the Far East—were the first cradles of the free press on the China coast. The first Chinese newspapers and periodicals were published there, and the first modern printing press with machine-made metal type was started in Hong Kong and Shanghai. For a century, Shanghai was the center of Chinese book printing and publishing. It was in Hong Kong and Shanghai and the other foreign settlements with extraterritorial jurisdiction that the first anti-Manchu and antimonarchy periodicals and papers were printed and circulated into the interior provinces. It was in those cities that the Chinese rebels and political exiles, as well as the outlaws of the hinterland, first found asylum. The Chinese Government, whether under the Manchu dynasty or in the early decades of the Republic, was powerless to suppress or stop the spread of radical or revolutionary ideas freely propagated and broadcast from inside those foreign-controlled cities. And it was in Shanghai that the Chinese Communist Party was organized and held its first party congress in 1921. It was in Shanghai that the first Communist papers were edited and published. It was in Shanghai that the representative of the Communist International and of Soviet Russia, A. Joffe, met Dr. Sun Yat-sen and discussed the questions of collaboration between the Comintern and the Kuomintang, Dr. Sun's party. After the end of the Second World War, when all foreign settlements and concessions—with the only exceptions of Port Arthur and Dairen—were restored to Chinese sovereignty, Hong Kong became the most important center for the printing and publication of Communist books and periodicals. A checking of the Communist publications on my own shelf shows that at least ten of Mao Tse-tung's books and pamphlets were published in Hong Kong between 1947 and 1949, when Communist publications were banned in all parts of China under the control of the Central Government.

It has been said that the Chinese Revolution of 1911 which overthrew the Manchu dynasty and founded the Chinese Republic could not have succeeded so soon and so easily if there had not been the freedom of the press in Hong Kong and in the foreign settlements and concessions at the treaty ports. It may be said with equal justice that, had there not been Hong Kong and the remaining foreign settlements and concessions on the China coast, the Communists probably could not have so easy a success in their early organization and in the spread of their propaganda literature.

The second important historical fact was that the Chinese Communist Party was a legal and open party during two very critical periods of Chinese history: first, from 1923 to 1927, when the Comintern and the Chinese Communist Party were collaborating with the Nationalist Party; and ten years later, from 1937 to 1947, when the Communist armies were nominally incorporated as regular units of the National Army in the war against the common enemy, Japan, and leading Communists took part in the People's Political Council, an advisory body representing all political parties and nonpartisan groups of the nation.

During the first period of four years, Chinese Communists were admitted as regular members of the Kuomintang and many of them held important positions in the Nationalist Party, in the Government, and even in the new Nationalist Revolutionary Army, which was being trained with the aid of Soviet military advisers and indoctrinated by political commissars with Communist training. At the first party congress of the Kuomintang, held in 1924, the newly elected Central Committee of the newly reorganized party included many leading Communists. Under the leadership of the Soviet adviser, Borodin, the Chinese Communists were soon in control of many organs of propaganda and agitation. By 1926, Mao Tse-tung was acting chairman of the Department of Kuomintang Propaganda, and other leaders of the Communists were heading the departments of Party Organization and of Peasant Organization. Communists were serving as Kuomintang party representatives in many units of the Nationalist Army.

In those brief years of Nationalist reorganization and of General Chiang Kai-shek's military expedition against the northern warlords, the Communist control of revolutionary agitation and propaganda was so powerful that the whole movement nominally incorporated as regular units of the Nationalists in the war against the common enemy, Japan, and leading Communists took part in the People's Political Council, an advisory body representing all political parties and nonpartisan groups of the nation.

[Missing pages]

CHAPTER 34

The Chinese Tradition and the Future[1]

On behalf of the Chinese members of the Conference, I wish to say that we all want to voice our warm and sincere appreciation to the University of Washington for its initiative and active leadership in calling and organizing this Sino-American Conference on Intellectual Cooperation. The inspiration originally came from George Taylor, but without the hearty support of President Odegaard of the University of Washington and President Chien Shih-liang of the National University of Taiwan, the Conference would have been impossible. Let us all hope that the results of our five-day Conference may not fail to justify the idealistic expectations of the founders and the co-sponsors of this bold experiment in international intellectual cooperation.

I deeply appreciate the great honor of being asked to make one of the opening speeches of this Conference. But I must say that the subject assigned to me is a very difficult one: "The Chinese Tradition and the Future." What is the Chinese Tradition? And what of its Future? Either one of the two questions will be a sufficient challenge to our thinking. And here I am asked to answer both questions in a brief ceremonial opening speech! I am certain of my failure. I can only hope that my failure may provoke the best minds of the Conference to do further and more thorough thinking on this important question.

---

1. An opening speech for the Sino-American Conference on Intellectual Cooperation held at the University of Washington, July 10-15, 1960. It was later published in the *Sino-American Conference on Intellectual Cooperation: Reports and Proceedings* (Seattle: University of Washington, Department of Publications and Printing, 1962), 13–22. For a Chinese translation, see Hsü Kao-juan 徐高阮, trans., "Zhongguo chuantong yu jianglai" 中國傳統與將來, *Central Daily News*, July 21-23, 1960. Also see *Hu Shih yanjiang ji* 胡適演講集 (Taipei: Hu Shih jijian guan 1970), 1: 220–247.

THE CHINESE TRADITION

I propose today to view the Chinese tradition, not as something ready made and static, but as the culminating product of a long series of important historical changes or evolutions. This historical approach may turn out to be a fruitful way to achieve a better understanding of the Chinese tradition, of its nature, its merits and defects, all in the light of the historical changes that have made it what it is.

The Chinese cultural tradition, it seems to me, is the end-product of these significant periods of historical evolution:

(1) The Sinitic Age of antiquity, which, as archeological evidences have abundantly shown, had already developed in the Yin-Shang period a highly advanced civilization with its fully developed stone sculpture and bone carving, its beautiful workmanship in the bronze vessels, its well-advanced picto-ideographic language as shown in the many thousands of oracular bone inscriptions, and its extravagant state religion of ancestral worship which apparently included human sacrifice on a fairly big scale. Later, in the great Chou period, civilization continued to develop in all directions. Many feudal principalities grew into great nations, and the co-existence and rivalry of powerful independent states tended to promote the flowering of the arts of war and of peace. Statecraft flourished and talents were encouraged. *The Book of Three Hundred Poems* was becoming the common textbook of language education. The age of poetry was leading to the age of philosophy.

(2) The Classical Age of indigenous philosophical thought, which was the age of Lao-tzu, Confucius and Mo Ti, and their disciples. This age left to posterity the great heritage of Lao-tzu's naturalistic conception of the universe and his political philosophy of non-interference or *laissez-faire*; the heritage of Confucius humanism, his conception of the dignity and worth of man, his teaching of the love of knowledge and the importance of intellectual honesty, and his educational philosophy that "with education, there will be no classes"; and the heritage of the great religious leader Mo Ti, who opposed all wars and preached peace, and who defended and elevated the popular religion by preaching the Will of God, which he conceived to be the love of all men without distinction.

There is no doubt that the ancient civilization of China underwent a fundamental transformation through those centuries (600–220 B.C.) which constituted the Classical Age of Chinese Thought. The basic characteristics of the Chinese cultural tradition were more or less shaped and formed by the major philosophical teachings of the Classical Age. In subsequent periods, whenever China had sunk deep into irrationality. superstition and other worldliness, as she actually did several times in her long history, it was always the humanism of Confucius, or the naturalism of Lao-tzu and the philosophical Taoists, or a combination of both naturalism and humanism, that would rise up and try to rescue her out of her sluggish slumbers.

(3) The third important historical evolution was the unification of the warring nations by the militaristic state of Ch'in in 221 B.C., the founding of the second or the Han Empire in 206 B.C., and the subsequent more than twenty centuries of Chinese life and experience under a huge unified empire, with no neighboring countries having any civilization comparable to the Chinese. This long and rather unique political experience of an isolated empire life, removed from the lively rivalry and competition of the independent and contending nations which had produced the Classical Age of Chinese Thought, was another important formative factor in the make-up of the Chinese tradition.

A few resulting features may be cited here. (a) China never succeeded in solving the problem of the unlimited power of the hereditary monarch in a huge unified empire. (b) A redeeming feature was the conscious adoption of the political theory of *Wu-wei* (non-interference) in the early decades of the Han Empire (200 B.C.–220 A.D.), thus establishing the political tradition of leaving much *laissez-faire*, freedom, and local self-government in the administration of an immense empire without a huge standing army and without benefit of a huge police force. (c) Another redeeming feature was the gradual development of a system of open and competitive examinations for the selection of men for the civil service, thus inaugurating the first civil service examination system in the world. (d) A uniform code of law was worked out in the Han Empire, and that code was revised from time to time throughout the later dynasties. The Chinese legal system, however, was defective in its failure to permit public pleading and to develop the profession of lawyers. (e) Another important feature of empire life was the long continued use of the dead classical language as the language of the civil service examinations, and as the common written medium of communication within the large unified empire. For over two thousand years, the dead classical language of ancient China was maintained as the recognized tool of education and as the respectable medium for all poetry and prose.

(4) The fourth important historical evolution actually amounted to a revolution in the form of a mass conversion of the Chinese people to the

alien religion of Buddhism. The indigenous religion of ancient China, which had neither the conception of Heaven in the sense of Paradise, nor that of Hell as the place of Last Day Judgment, was easily overwhelmed and conquered by the great religion of the Buddha with all its rich imagery, its beautiful ritualism, and its bold cosmology and metaphysics. Buddhism gave to China not only one Paradise, but tens of paradises; not only one Hell, but many hells, each varying in severity and horror from the others. The old simple idea of retribution, of good and evil, was soon replaced by the idea of transmigration of the soul and the iron law of *Karma* which runs through all past, present, and future existences. The ideas of the world as unreal, of life as painful and empty, of sex as unclean, of the family as an impediment to spiritual attainment, of celibacy and mendicancy as necessary to the Buddhist life, of alms-giving as a supreme form of merit, of love extended to all sentient beings, of vegetarianism, of the most severe forms of asceticism, of words and spells as having miraculous power; these and many other items of un-Chinese beliefs and practices poured from India by land and by sea into China and were soon accepted and made into parts of the cultural life of the Chinese people.

It was a real revolution. The Confucianist *Book of Filial Piety*, for instance, had taught that the human body is inherited from the parents, and must not be annihilated or degraded. And ancient Chinese thinkers had said that life is of the highest value. Now Buddhism taught that life is an illusion, and that to live is pain. Such doctrines led to practices which were definitely opposed to the Chinese tradition. It soon became a form of "merit" for a Buddhist monk to burn his own thumb, or his own finger or fingers, or even his whole arm, as a sacrifice to one of the Buddhist deities! And sometimes, a monk would publicly announce the date of his self-destruction, and, on that day, would light his own faggot pyre with a torch in his own hand, and would go on mumbling the sacred names of the Buddhas until he was completely overpowered by the flames.

China was being Indianized, and was going mad in one of her strange periods of religious fanaticism.

(5) The next important historical evolution may be described as a series of China's revolts against Buddhism. One of these revolts took the form of the founding and the spread of the medieval religion of Taoism. Religious Taoism was originally a consolidated form of the native beliefs and practices, freshly inspired by a nationalistic desire to supersede and kill the foreign religion of Buddhism by imitating every feature of it. The Taoists accepted the

heavens and hells from Buddhism, gave them Chinese names, and invented Chinese gods to preside over them! A Taoist canon was consciously forged after the model of the Buddhist sutras. Many Buddhist ideas, such as the transmigration of the soul and the causal chain running through past and future lives, were bodily appropriated as their own. Orders of priests and priestesses were established after the fashion of the Buddhist Brotherhoods of monks and nuns. In short, Taoism was a nationalistic movement to boycott Buddhism by manufacturing an imitation product to take over its market. Its real motive was to kill this invading religion, and it was well known that Taoist influence played an important part in all the governmental persecutions of Buddhism, notably in those of 446 and 845.

Other Chinese revolts against Buddhism took place within Buddhism itself. A common feature in all such revolts was the discarding of what the Chinese people could not swallow and digest in Buddhism. As early as the fourth century A.D., Chinese Buddhists had begun to realize that the essence of Buddhism lies in Meditation and Insight, both of which are combined in *dhyana* or *ch'an* (*zen* in Japanese pronunciation), which means meditation but which also relies on philosophical insight. From A.D. 400 to 700, the various Chinese schools of Buddhism (such as the Lanka School founded by Bodhidharma and the T'ien-t'ai School) were mostly schools of Ch'an (Zen).

What came to be known as the "Southern School" of Ch'an (Zen)—which after the eighth century has come to monopolize the name Ch'an (Zen) to itself—went even farther and declared, as did the monk Shen-hui [670–762] (who, according to my researches, was the real founder of this school), that insight alone was enough, and meditation could be discarded.

The entire movement of the so-called "Southern School" was founded on a series of successful lies and forgeries. Its story of Bodhidharma was a lie; its story of the 28 Indian patriarchs was a forgery; its story of the apostolic succession through the transmission of an apostolic robe was a fraud; its life-story of the "Sixth (Chinese) Patriarch" was largely pure fiction. But the greatest of all its fabrications was the story of the origin of Ch'an (Zen), which runs as follows: The Buddha was preaching on the Mount of the Holy Vulture. He simply lifted a flower before the assembly, and said nothing. Nobody understood him. But the wise Mahakasyapa understood him, and smiled a smile at the Master. That was supposed to be the origin and the beginning of Zen!

The historical significance of this Zen movement lies in the war cry that "It relies on no words, spoken or written, but points direct to the heart." It has no use for the voluminous and never-ending scriptures, which, by the eighth century, must have amounted to 50 million words in preserved Chinese translations (not counting the tens of millions of words in the Chinese commentaries). What a wonderful revolution! Blessed be those wonderful liars and forgers whose ingenious lies and forgeries could achieve a revolution that discarded a sacred canon in 50 million words!

(6) The next great historical evolution in the Chinese tradition may be described as "The Age of Chinese Renaissance," or "The Age of Chinese Renaissances." For there was more than one renaissance or rebirth.

First, there was the Renaissance in Chinese literature which began in earnest in the eighth and ninth centuries, and which has been continued to our own times. The great poets of the T'ang Dynasty—Li Po and Tu Fu in the eighth century, and Po Chü-i in the ninth—opened up a new age of Chinese poetry. Han Yü (d. 824) succeeded in revitalizing the "classical prose" (ku-wen) and made it a useful and fairly effective tool for prose literature for the next 800 years.

It was the Zen monks of the eighth and ninth centuries who first made use of the living spoken tongue in their recorded discourses and discussions. This use of living prose was continued by the great Zen masters of the eleventh century and was taken up by the Neo-Confucianist philosophers of the twelfth century, whose conversations were often recorded as they were actually spoken.

The common man and woman always sang their songs and told their tales in the only language they knew, namely, their own spoken tongue. With the development of the art of block-printing in the ninth century and of printing with movable type in the eleventh century, it became possible to have the popular or "vulgar" tales, stories, dramas, and songs printed for a wider audience. Some of the popular tales and great novels of the sixteenth and seventeenth centuries became best sellers for centuries. These novels and tales became the standardizers of the written form of the living spoken tongue. They have been the teachers and the popularizers of the vulgar tongue, the *pai hua*. Without those great tales and novels, it would have been impossible for the modern movement for a literary renaissance to succeed in the brief space of a few years.

Second, there was the Renaissance in Chinese philosophy which attained its maturity in the eleventh and twelfth centuries and which gave rise to the various schools and movements of Neo-Confucianism. Neo-Confucianism was a conscious movement for the revival of the pre-Buddhist culture of indigenous China to take the place of the medieval religions of Buddhism and Taoism. Its main object was to restore and re-interpret the moral and political philosophy of Confucius and Mencius as a substitute for the selfish, anti-social and other-worldly philosophy of the Buddhist religion. Some Zen monks had remarked that the teachings of the school of Confucius were too simple and insipid to attract the best minds. The task of the Neo-Confucianists, therefore, was to make the secular thought of a pre-Buddhist China as interesting and attractive as Buddhism or Zen. And those Chinese philosophers did succeed in working out a secular and rational philosophy of Neo-Confucianism with a cosmology, a theory, or theories, of the nature and method of knowledge, and a moral and political philosophy.

Various schools grew up largely because of the different viewpoints about the nature and method of knowledge. All that made matters more interesting and exciting. In the course of time, the schools of Neo-Confucian philosophy were able to attract to themselves the best minds of the nation, which no longer flocked to the Zen masters in the Buddhist monasteries. And, when the best minds ceased to be interested in Buddhism, that once great religion gradually faded into nonentity and died an almost unmourned death.

And third, there was the third phase of the Chinese Renaissance which can be characterized as "The Revival of Learning" under the impetus of a scientific method—the method of "evidential investigation."

"No belief without evidence" (*wu cheng tse pu hsin*) is a well-known quotation from an early post-Confucian work. And Confucius himself emphatically said: "To say that you know a thing when you know it, and to say that you do not know when you do not know it: that is knowledge." But such injunctions on veracity and evidence seemed to have been easily swept away by the powerful tides of religious fanaticism and pious credulity which overwhelmed medieval China. The method and habit of thinking in terms of evidences, which barely survived in the wisest judges of the law courts, were fortunately kept up in some of the best schools of classical scholarship. With the spread of the printed book, it became easy for the Chinese scholar to compare references, collate texts, and collect and evaluate evidences. Within the first two or three centuries of book-printing, the spirit and method of evidential thinking and evidential investigation could already be discerned in the founding of Chinese archeology, in the writing of a great history on the basis of carefully compared and evaluated sources and evidences, and in the rise of a new classical scholarship which was courageous enough to apply that spirit and methodology to the examination of a few of the sacred books of the Confucianist Canon. One of the founders of this new classical scholarship was Chu Hsi (1130–1200), the greatest of the Neo-Confucian philosophers.

The method of evidential investigation (*k'co-cheng* or *k'ao-chü*) was consciously developed in the seventeenth century, when one scholar would cite 160 evidences to establish the ancient pronunciation of a single word, and another would devote decades of his life to collecting evidences to prove that almost half of a major classic of the Confucian Canon was a fairly late forgery. The method proved to be so efficacious and fruitful that it became the intellectual fashion of the scholars of the eighteenth and nineteenth centuries. The whole era of 300 years (1600–1900) has often been labeled the age of evidential investigation.

THE GREAT CONFRONTATION AND THE FUTURE

The above historical account brings the Chinese traditional culture to the eve of the last period of historical change the era of confrontation and conflict of the Chinese and Western civilizations. The West's first contacts with China and the Chinese civilization had already begun in the sixteenth century. But the era of real confrontation and conflict did not begin until the nineteenth century. In this one century and a half, the Chinese tradition has undergone a real test of strength, indeed, the most severe test of strength and survival in her entire cultural history.

From our historical sketch, we have seen that the indigenous civilization of ancient China, having been richly nourished and properly inoculated by the Classical Age, was sufficiently competent to meet the cultural crisis brought about by the invading religion of Buddhism. Because of the extreme simplicity of the native religion, however, the Chinese people were for a time overwhelmed and conquered by the highly complicated and attractive religion of Buddhism. And, for nearly a thousand years, China accepted almost everything that came from India, and her cultural life in general became "Indianized." But China soon came to her senses and began to rebel against Buddhism. Buddhism was persecuted, boycotted, and serious attempts were made to domesticate it. And, with the rise of Ch'an (Zen) Buddhism, an internal revolution was achieved by openly discarding the entire canon of Buddhist scripture of over 50 million words. So, in the end, China was able to achieve her own cultural survival and rebirth by a series of literary, philosophical, and intellectual renaissances. So, although she was never able entirely to free herself from the 2,000 years of Buddhist Conversion and Indianization, China did succeed in working out her own cultural problems and continuing to build up a secular and essentially Chinese culture.

As early as the last years of the sixteenth century and the early decades of the seventeenth, a strange but highly advanced culture was knocking on the gates of the Chinese Empire. The first Jesuit missionaries to China were carefully selected and prepared for the first introduction of the European civilization and the Christian religion to the most civilized nation of the age outside of Europe. The first encounters were friendly and successful. In the course of time, those great missionaries were able to offer to the best minds of China, not only the best and latest achievements of European mathematical and astronomical science, but also the Christian religion as best exemplified in the saintly lives of those men.

The period of forceful confrontation and conflict between China and the West began about 150 years ago. To this learned assembly, pre-eminently learned in modern history, I need not retell the story of China's tragic humiliations resulting from her ignorance, arrogance, and self-complacency. Nor do I need to recount the long tale of China's numerous failures in her clumsy and always too late efforts to bring about reforms in the various aspects of her national life. Nor do I have to tell the more recent story of China's serious endeavors, especially in the republican period, to critically study her own civilization and to propose reforms in the more basic aspects of her cultural tradition such as the language, literature, thought, and education. You and I have all been eyewitnesses of such recent efforts and events, and most of the senior members of the Chinese delegation have been participants in those activities.

My task today is to call your attention to a few considerations directly or indirectly connected to our question as to the future of the Chinese tradition. Before we can speculate about its future, should we not first take an inventory of the present status of that tradition after 150 years of confrontation with the West? Should we not first make a general estimate of how much of the Chinese tradition has been definitely destroyed or dropped as a result of this contact with the West; how much of the Western culture has been definitely accepted by the Chinese people; and, lastly, how much is still left of the Chinese tradition? How much of the Chinese tradition has survived the great confrontation?

Many years ago, I said publicly that China had made truly earnest efforts to rid herself of many of the worst features of her cultural tradition: "In the brief space of a few decades, the Chinese people have abolished bodily torture in the courts, which must have been in practice for thousands of years; they have abolished foot-binding, which has existed over a thousand years; they have abolished the so-called 'eight-legged' balanced prose composition which had been required in all stages of civil service examinations throughout the last five hundred years. . . ." And we must remember that the Chinese people were the first non-European people to abolish the institution of hereditary monarchy, which must have existed in China for more than five thousand years. The mere fact that "even the emperor must go" must have had tremendous psychological effect upon the vast majority of the people.

These and hundreds of other items of quick collapse or slow disintegration have been the natural casualties of this period of cultural impact and collision.

No tear needs be shed on these cultural casualties. Their abolition or disintegration should be considered as a part of China's emancipation from the shackles of her old and isolated civilization. For thousands of years, Chinese political thinkers could not solve the problem of how to check the unlimited power of the hereditary monarch in a huge unified empire. But a few decades of contact with the democratic countries of the West were enough to give the solution: "Get rid of the monarch and abolish the hereditary monarchy altogether." The same is true of many of the other voluntary abolitions. Eight centuries of Neo-Confucianist philosophy had failed to voice a protest against the inhumanity and barbarity of foot-binding, but a few missionaries with a fresh point of view were enough to awaken the moral sense of the Chinese people, and abolish foot-binding forever.

How much has China voluntarily accepted or adopted from the Western civilization? The inventory list will never be complete. For there must have been literally many thousands of items which have been voluntarily accepted by the Chinese people either because they never had them or their counterparts before, or because they were superior or more useful than their Chinese counterparts. Quinine, corn, peanuts, tobacco, the lenses for eyeglasses, and thousands of other things were accepted because the Chinese never had such things before and they wanted to have them. The mechanical clock was early accepted and in no time completely replaced the Chinese water-clock. That is the best example of one superior gadget replacing its inferior counterpart. From the mechanical clock to the airplane and the radio, thousands of products of the scientific and technological civilization of the West can be listed in our inventory. In the intellectual and artistic world, the inventory list will have to begin with Euclid and end with our contemporary scientists, musicians, and movie stars. The list will be endless.

Now the question: After all the discardings and erosions from the old civilization, and after the many thousands of voluntary adoptions from the modern Western civilization, how much is left of the Chinese tradition?

More than a quarter of a century ago, in 1933, I was speaking on the different types of cultural response in Japan and China. I pointed out that the modernization in Japan might be called the type of "centralized control," while China, because of the absence of a ruling class, was becoming modernized through a different kind of cultural response which might be described as "cultural change through long exposure and slow permeation." I went on to say:

> In this way practically all of our ideas and beliefs and institutions have been freely allowed to come under the slow contact, contagion, and influence of the Western civilization and undergo sometimes gradual modifications and sometimes fairly rapid and radical changes. . . . We have not concealed anything, nor have we dogmatically withheld anything from this contact and change. . . .

Years later, I again spoke more or less in the same vein:

> All westernization in China has come as a result of gradual diffusion and permeation of ideas, usually initiating from a few individuals, gradually winning a following, and finally achieving significant changes when a sufficient number of people is convinced of their superior convenience or efficacy. From the footwear to the literary revolution, from the lipstick to the overthrow of the monarchy, all has been voluntary and in a broad sense "reasoned." Nothing in China is too sacred to be protected from this exposure and contact; and no man, nor any class, was powerful enough to protect any institution from the contagious and disintegrating influence of the invading culture.

What I was saying in those bygone days amounts to this: I had considered the numerous slow but voluntary changes as constituting a rather democratic and rather likable type of cultural change through long exposure and voluntary acceptance. I meant to imply that neither the voluntary discardings, nor the numerous acceptances, would tend to destroy the character and worth of the recipient civilization. On the contrary, the discarding of the undesirable elements should have the effect of a great liberation; and the new cultural elements accepted should only enrich and vitalize the older culture. I was never afraid that the recipient Chinese civilization might disintegrate and disappear after so much is thrown away and so much is taken in. I actually said:

> Slowly, quietly, but unmistakably, the Chinese Renaissance is becoming a reality. The product of this rebirth looks suspiciously occidental. But scratch its surface and you will find that the stuff of which it is made is essentially the Chinese bedrock which much weathering and corrosion only made stand out more clearly—the humanistic and rationalistic China resurrected by the touch of the scientific and democratic civilization of the new world.

This I said in 1933. Was I over-optimistic then? Have I been disproved by the events of the intervening decades?

And what of the future? What has become of the "Chinese bedrock—the humanistic and rationalistic China"? And what will become of it now that the whole of the Chinese mainland has been under the totalitarian control of the Chinese Communists for the last eleven years? And will "the humanistic and rationalistic China" be strong enough to survive the long years of "Iron Curtain" rule which permits no contact with, no contagion of, and certainly no "long exposure" to the poisonous influence of the Free World?

Prediction of the future is always hazardous. I have in recent years read over four million words of "purge literature" published in Communist China. Every piece of "purge literature" tells us what the Chinese Communist Party and Government are afraid of and what they are anxious to uproot and destroy. Judging from this vast amount of "purge literature," I believe I am justified to conclude that the men now in control of the Chinese mainland are still afraid of the spirit of freedom, the spirit of in dependent thinking, the courage to doubt, and the spirit and method of evidential thinking and evidential investigation. The writer Hu Feng was condemned because he and his followers had shown the spirit of freedom and of independent thinking and had dared to oppose Party control of literature and the arts. My friend and former colleague Liang Shu-ming had to be purged because he had exemplified the dangerous spirit of doubt. And "the ghost of Hu Shih" has deserved three million words of condemnation because Hu Shih had been largely responsible for the popularization of the traditional classical scholar's spirit and method of evidential investigation, and because Hu Shih had the unpardonable audacity to describe that spirit and method as the essence of the method of science!

Judging from these purge documents, I am inclined to believe that what I had glorified as "the humanistic and rationalistic China" still survives on the Chinese mainland, and that the same spirit of courageous doubt and independent thinking and questioning which played important roles in the Chinese revolts against the great medieval religions and in their final over-throw may yet live long and spread even under the most impossible condi-tions of totalitarian control and suppression. In short, I believe the tradition of "the humanistic and rationalistic China" has not been destroyed and in all probability cannot be destroyed.

Index

Moscow Treaty. *See* Treaty of Friendship and Alliance
Mount Pilatus, Switzerland, 69
Mount Taishan, 81
Mukden (Shenyang), China, 70–72
Mukden Incident, 7–8, 67, 70–72, 94, 123
Mussolini, Benito, 11, 108
mutual respect, 31–32

Nanchang, China, 131
Nanchang Uprising, 134
Nanjing, China. *See* Nanking (Nanjing), China
Nankai School of Economics, 22
Nankai University, 22, 241
Nanking (Nanjing), China, 95, 122, 131–134, 143–145, 154, 178, 184, 252, 318
Nanking Incident, 131–133, 184–185
Nanning, China, 77
National Army, 144–146, 148, 172, 184–187, 232, 254, 260–262, 331, 344–345
National Assembly, 233
National Education Association, 323
National Emergency Law, 268
National Financial and Economic Affairs Committee, 25
National Government, 67, 95, 122, 133, 135–136, 138–142, 147, 185–186. *See also* government
National Institute of Social Sciences, 179–180
National Language Romanization (Gwoyeu Romatzyh, or G.R.), 202
National Salvation Societies, 140–141, 143
National Socialist (Nazi) Party, 37, 105–108
National University of Taiwan, 346
nationalism, 99, 105–106, 111–112, 122, 130, 202–205, 330, 349–350
Nationalism and Language Reform in China (De Francis), 202–205
Nationalist China, 13–14, 20, 122
Nationalist Party (Kuomintang): Chiang Kai-Shek and, 142, 174; Chinese Communist Party and, 35–39, 129–135, 139, 153, 157–158, 165, 182–185, 209, 217, 232–233, 262, 330; communism and, 124–125; Communist collaboration and, 259–261; communist propaganda and, 258, 262, 337, 340; guerilla activity of, 176; Hu Shih and, 53; Japan and, 50; language reform and, 205; Nanking and,

178; in Taiwan, 273; United Front and, 260–261, 331
Nationalist-Communist collaboration, 129–133, 183–184, 217, 258–260, 330, 343–344
naturalistic philosophy, 3, 40–45, 277–278, 347–348, 357–358
Naval Disarmament Treaties, 71
"Nazi-Soviet Relations, 1939-1941," 126–127
Nelson, Donald, 151, 186
Neo-Confucianism, 351–353, 355
neutrality, 10–12, 20–21, 39
New China Daily (*Hsin Hua Jih Pao*), 260, 339
New China News Agency, 246
New Culture Movement, 50
New Democracy, 155–157, 163–164
"New Democracy, The" (Mao), 155, 163–164
"New Disorder in East Asia and the World at Large, The" (Hu Shih), 9
New dynasty, 85
New Educational System, 323
new world order, 17, 66, 70–72, 76, 95, 113–114
New York Evening Post, 6
New York Times, 67–68
New Youth, 29n4
Nine-Grade Impartial Judgment, 87
Nine-Power Treaty, 65–67, 71, 74
nongovernmental organizations (NGOs), 25
noninterference, 41, 214–217, 278, 347–348
North Atlantic Pact, 175, 235
North China, 89, 95, 131, 149, 188, 220, 238
North China Union College, 250
North China Union Women's College, 250
North China University of the People's Revolution, 238–239
North Korea, 150, 158–160, 166–167, 170–175, 177, 187–189, 265. *See also* Korea
North Korean Communist Army. *See* Red Army (Korea)
Northeast Army, 142
Northern Shensi (Shaanxi), China, 80
Northward Expedition, 131
Northwest Army, 142
Nuli Zhoubao (Effort Weekly), 23–24